KETOFY EVERYTHING BUT THE KITCHEN SINK!

Scott Swenson
Tyo Presetyo

DEDICATION

I WOULD LIKE TO DEDICATE THIS COOKBOOK TO ALL THE SPECIAL MEMBERS OF THE KETO GROUPS ON FACEBOOK – ESPECIALLY THOSE IN KETO PLUS AND KETOGENIC DIET OPEN DISCUSSION FOR ALL YOUR SUPPORT AND ENTHUSIASM – FOLLOWERS OF THE BLOG HTTP://SHECALLSMEHOBBIT.COM, AND OUR FAMILIES. THE HOBBIT WOULD LIKE TO THANK KAREN FOR HER SUPPORT, GUIDANCE, PATIENCE, AND INSPIRATION EVERY DAY. A SPECIAL THANKS TO THE WONDERFUL ADMINS AND MODERATORS THAT I CALL FRIENDS: BEN MCDONALD, KAREN OGILVIE, ANU VUPPALA, LARISSA L. CHMIELEWSKI, NANCY MASON, STEVE ANGEL, DEBBIE JONES, KATY LEE GIRRES, CATHY TURNER, SANDRA WATSON, MONICA LEWIS POTACZALA, KIMMIE CREAN, FADALIA GRAY, RACHEL STRANDT, RETHA HARRISON, AND MALYNDIA HIGGINS

KETOERS WORLD-WIDE. WALK PROUD, EAT WELL, AND KCKO!

A special thank you to Michela Schwartz for the cover photo. She posted it on Keto Plus with the comment "The book said I could eat the whole tray, sorry Santa!" (LOL!) and I fell in love with it. She's graciously allowed us to use it here.

TABLE OF CONTENTS

SHE CALLS ME HOBBIT

TO KETOFY OR NOT KETOFY, THAT IS THE QUESTION. WHY WE DO WHAT WE DO.

"Ketofied Foods = Foods Adventures on Keto = Permanent Keto Lifestyle. Who wants to be bored to death with limited foods options on Keto? While we live in a food-based society, with many carbed and modified foods, KETOFYING is a must hobby for every ketoers. Otherwise, it will just be another on and off diet with many excuses"
~Tyo Prasetyo

This perfectly sums up part of the reason we do what we do when it comes to this blog and the FB groups we belong to. Ketofying food for us is taking a temporary change in diet and making it a lifestyle change that is sustainable. While we respect the opinions of those who say 'just be strong' and 'you are going to regret ketofying "normal" foods,' we strongly disagree. It doesn't always work that way. Tyo sums up the first one clearly. Since the beginning of civilization, our cultures in one way or another have a strong link to food. Historically, feasts have been a method of celebration, giving thanks, offering up respect to a deity, and an important part of our social interaction. Don't think so? Chew on this for a minute.

- Passover
- Valentine's Day
- Easter
- Thanksgiving
- Cookouts
- Dinner on dates
- Celebration banquets
- Business lunches
- School functions

Outside of these 'special occasions,' for many families and couples, dinner table is a place to gather without the distractions of a TV\computer\phone\work\school to reconnect emotionally over the day, talk about the future, and just enjoy each other's company. We meet and connect over food. It's what we do as social creatures. While the food part isn't the focus of these gatherings, it is an important part of it. Ketofying foods allows everyone to be on the same playing field. Have you ever been out with someone and have them look at the bland salad you're having while they are chowing down on a burger and say 'I feel bad for you eating that' or 'come on, you can give it a break this once?' By ketofying food, we REMOVE that social barrier of discomfort by having something that is attractive, tasty, and healthy all at the same time and removes that isolation.

Those of you with families, how much work is it to make 2 different meals? A lot. What if you could make one meal that tastes good and everyone can enjoy? What about those special occasions? Should you be an outcast because you 'can't have any of the good stuff?' HELL NO. In the process, you are giving those you care about healthy food that tastes good. That, my friends is a win-win. There is absolute NO reason we cannot have the best of both worlds. None.

There's a second part to this and it specifically applies to people with atypical neurology – depressions, anxiety, ADD, other mood disorders. People who do not fit into the 'perfect world' or 'think like everyone else' can find ANY diet or change of lifestyle difficult if not crippling. We resist change, it throws off our balance, and can take what would be a simple uncertainty to overcome for some and thrust us into a funk that is hard to recover from. There's another part of this and it has to deal with 'cheating.' When people like us 'cheat,' we feel horrible afterwards not just physically, but emotionally. While others can shake it off as a misstep, for many it is a failure. Those who don't understand this cannot grasp the difference to us, a 'failure' becomes '**we are a failure**.' The darkness comes soon after that, and we give up because since we are failures at what others seem to do effortlessly, we are not able to continue or 'get back on the horse.' There's something wrong with us. We will never succeed. We are destined to be less than them.

We are not.
We are valuable.
We are not failures.
We are different.
We need different approaches.
We CAN succeed.

Ketofying foods gives us that option. When a moment of indecision stretches to an overwhelming desire to stuff something sweet or 'naughty' in our mouths, while others have three options, we only have two – eat whatever we can find at the local convenience store, or eat something we have already here that will give us that hit we need while keeping us on track. We don't have the 'just say no' option. There's an additional benefit to this – imagine the pride and emotional response you get when you realize you just ate BROWNIES...

...and the next day you are down a pound. GO YOU!!!

Some call these 'trigger foods' that makes you want carbs. I don't quite get that logic, if you have something that satisfies you right at your fingertips, what is there to trigger you towards? Eating the whole tray? Fine. Do it. You will be fine. What many don't tell you is it takes 3500 ADDITIONAL CALORIES above and beyond what you will burn in a day to put on ONE POUND OF FAT.

Yes.
3500.
That's 10 Snickers bars.
30 of my brownies I linked above.
PLUS a Big Macs.
At once.
PLUS whatever you've eaten already for the day.

Fine. Let it be a trigger food. If all we have is frigging delicious keto food, we're good with that. I'll puke before I can eat 10 pans of brownies.

Keep Calm, Keto On.
LCHF doesn't have to me Lousy Cooking, Horrible Flavor.

You've got this.
I've got this.
WE'VE got this.

~The Hobbit

MY BODY AS HOUSE? I THOUGHT IT WAS A TEMPLE? KETOLOW CARB IN BASIC TERMS

What is 'keto' and how the hell does it differ from other diets? What the hell are 'ketones' anyway? How do you get them? How much do they cost? Why is this 'keto' thing something I should do or should I? As I mentioned in my 'You may ask yourself, well, how did I get here?' post, I wasn't on board with this thing at all. I didn't get it. It was against conventional wisdom and everything I've heard\learned\been taught my entire life. "FAT IS BAD!!! You should eat WHOLE GRAINS AND LOTS OF CORN AND RICE! MARGARINE, NOT BUTTER!!! GET CANOLA OIL, IT'S GOOD FOR YOU!!" and "You don't need to change the way you eat, just eat less!" I'm sure you've heard all this before too. The last part does work, the issue is once you get done eating less, you most likely will eventually go back to eating more. Maybe not a lot more, but enough. And guess what happens then? FAT COMES! HOW DID THAT HAPPEN?? I STOPPED EATING FAT???

This is where some science and understanding of how the body works with nutrition as well as understanding the difference between body fat and dietary fat. There are many different studies, research docs, links, companies, health clinics, etc that will tell you pretty much what you want to hear if you look hard enough. How does someone get a handle on this stuff? It's hard. And I resisted HARD when the lady brought all this up. I couldn't wrap my head around it and was determined she was going to ruin the little progress I had doing it my way. Oops. Nope. I was wrong. She was right.

First, we need to get some terms and misconceptions right out of the way. The diet (you know, that stuff we eat and not something that we buy as a weight-loss plan) consists of MACRO and MICRO nutrients. Macro – being big because that is what 'macro' means – are the main items in our diet. Micro are the supplementary (yet still important) items in our diet. I'm not going to get into micro-nutrients in this post but those are the vitamins and minerals we also need to survive. Nope, let's talk about the big boys:

Macro nutrients:

Carbohydrates
Dietary fat
Protein.

Now, the collective wisdom sometime in the 70s decided that dietary fat was bad for us and that carbs were the thing we needed to stock up on. Why or how this came about isn't important but you should know that for the first several millions of years that the human species has existed, carbohydrates were not part of our diet. Not until about 10,000 years ago when agriculture became a business did we start eating any significant amount of carbs. What does that tell us? The human body not only survives quite well with low to no carbs, it prefers it. Yes. IT PREFERS IT!! Carbs only have one purpose in the body – quick fuel. Protein is the building blocks of the body (and can be used for fuel in the absence of fat or carbs). Fat is fuel and essential for healthy hair, skin, nails, etc. So, what does this mean in simple terms? Each gram of carbs or fat equals one calorie of glycogen, which is the fuel your body uses to run. Now, carbs have 4 calories per gram, fat has 9. So, first off, fat is more dense which means it is more fuel efficient than carbs. It also takes longer for your body to process which means fat makes you feel full longer. Second, any extra 'energy' that you take in that you can't use, well, that gets stored as body fat. Yeh. That crap that hangs over the belt and makes it so the jeans you bought last year don't fit any more. Not cool.

YOU DON'T NEED CARBS.

But you're probably saying 'hey Hobbit, so what if I don't need them, they're not hurting me and they are fuel, right?' (and if you said that out loud and got a strange look from the dog, cat or significant other, then that makes me smile). They can hurt you in the form of body fat. Since carbs only have one purpose in the body, any 'extra' fuel that you are not using must be stored, and it is stored as fat. As an additional thing to note, each part of that storage also includes 4 parts water. So, each extra carb you store, you store 4 parts water too. OUCH.

Let's look at it like your body is a house. This house has both a generator and regular electric system. Carbs are the generator, fat is the electric system, protein is wood. Now, to keep your house warm you can do a couple of different things – run off the generator, run off electric, or run off wood that you scavenge from the structure of the house. Let's look at 3 scenarios:

- You run mostly off the generator, but since the generator puts out more energy than you can use in one day, you need to add some batteries to store it. And then those batteries get full, so you add more batteries. And more. And more. And more. Now you need to add more rooms to the house to hold all those batteries. All the while this is happening, you are running out frequently to get more gas (calories) to keep the generator running. This is your body on carbs. Those batteries? FAT.

- You decide to not fill up the generator any more. Eventually, after a few days, the generator runs out of gas. But, since you have all those batteries taking up space in the house, it starts running off the batteries instead. As each battery dies, you get to throw it away. Eventually, all the batteries run out. Now, depending on what you chose to do, a couple of different things happen. If you get more gas (carbs), you start the cycle all over again and start filling the batteries back up. If you let the batteries run out, the electrical system kicks in and since you only pay for what you use and electricity from the power company is much cheaper over a month than gasoline, you save money (aka be more calorie efficient). In addition to this, since the electricity is not only more efficient, it is stable. You are always 'full.'

- You don't get gas. The batteries run out. The electric doesn't kick in. You start taking pieces of wood from the house to make heat. At first, you take a little here, a little there, but eventually you've ruined the structure of the house.

Situation number 1 is your body on the typical Western Diet. We constantly are 'recharging' our system by feeding ourselves way more carbs than we need, which leads to fat storage in the body.

Situation number 2 is your body on ketosis. After a few days of dropping your carb intake down below 30g a day, the body starts running off stored fat in the form of ketones. Since you are running off stored fat as well as a constant and efficient supply of dietary fat, you are 'sparing' the structure of your body – the protein. And since you are no longer spending money constantly on gas (carb calories), you now have money to build onto the house (add protein which is used for muscle growth). The added benefit to this is the more you add to your house, the more energy you burn at an efficient rate.

Situation number 3 is starvation. This is when you don't get enough fat and have eliminated carbs. Your body will start converting muscle to glycogen to keep the system running. Eventually, you will destroy your house. Don't do this:)

I hope this helps explain why many of us have chosen to take the low-carb, high fat, moderate protein route.

YOU MAY ASK YOURSELF, WELL, HOW DID I GET HERE?

So, what exactly prompted me to start up this blog? We must go back a few years to 2010. QUICK, MARTY! TO THE DELOREAN! YOUR HEALTH IS IN TROUBLE!! I never took care of myself once I hit adulthood. I wanted to but life seemed to get in the way, working multiple jobs to make ends meet, having a family, buying a house, etc. Stress my friends, is a killer, but you don't need me to tell you that. I was married to a woman that loved her junk food and was also one of those people that pissed you off as she could eat whatever she wanted and never seemed to gain a pound. Me on the other hand, in my mouth and straight to FAT, but I'm getting a little ahead of myself.

Growing up, we ate well for the time. Not a lot of processed foods or sugar cereals. We had a large garden (oh, how I hated working in it!) and our parents had a freezer plan for meats. We ate the typical diet of the time – lean meats (chicken, fish, some beef, leaner cuts of pork), a lot of veggies, and the usual starches of bread, oatmeal, potatoes, etc. We always had a good breakfast before school, a lunch, and dinner. Desserts were a treat and not something in the usual diet. I seem to remember we only had desserts around the holidays. The same went for candy. Junk food was rare, our dad might get a bag of chips and a 2-liter bottle of soda once a month to have while watching the Celtics play on a weekend, otherwise, it wasn't in the house. I played sports all through school and all seasons – soccer or cross-country running in the fall, cross-country skiing in the winter, and baseball in the spring through the summer. We were typical 70s kids, if it was light out, we were outside playing. I had a paper route in primary school and rode my bike all over town. As I got older, I worked with my dad doing landscaping. In other words, typically active for the time. Yet, I was always 'chubby' no matter how active I was. It was frustrating but I believed that was 'just the way I was built.'

Getting into adulthood, nothing changed except I got less active. Bicycle gave away to a car and motorcycle. Sports gave away to running the kids around, shopping, office-type jobs, and sitting in front of the TV. See where this is going? Yeh, right to my belly and ass. A LOT. As I think back, there are very few pictures of me once I hit my 20s. I used to tell myself that was because I was always the one taking the pics but in reality, nope, it was because I was embarrassed about how frigging fat I became and how I looked. The real kicker hit when I quit smoking around 2000 or so, if you ever smoked and then quit, you probably did like me and replaced that addiction with something else and that something else usually is FOOD. Oh, wonderful, glorious FOOD (I'll cover my thoughts on this addiction in a later post)!! I got fat. No. No I didn't. I got morbidly obese. After a year or two of pigging out on everything I could get my hands on, it slowed a little. I lost a little. Life wasn't that bad. Life has a way of screwing you up just when you say 'life isn't that bad.' It got bad. A series of bad decisions, life tragedies, and other events tossed a wrench into things. It was time for a change before it was time to push up daisies.

I'm 5'2". Yep, I'm a short guy. I've always been 'stocky' which I learned means 'fat and short.' I remember having to get my pants in the section of the store for kids like me and most of them were Toughskins. Remember those??? I dreamed of wearing Levis like all the cool kids, but not one cut or pair could get over my thighs or ass and still fit around the waist. I hit my epic size around 2008-10, hitting a staggering 252lbs. It wasn't until I realized that not only could I not tie my shoes without getting out of breath, I couldn't even reach them to tie at all! Of course, in typical American fashion, did I think about maybe losing weight? Nope. I bought slip-ons instead. Yeh.

Lazy won. To be honest, I'm not sure what motivated me to change, I think it was a New Year's resolution, you know, those things we make and then break January 3rd? In 2010, I made one. I was going to hit the gym, lose weight, and get in shape. This was me about that time:

I read a lot about 'dieting' and tried everything I could find on the market. I tried that Alie stuff – a series of rather pricey pills that when you take them, it flushes 'fat' out of you. They worked. Kinda. What they do is flush all the DIETARY fat out of your meals. Quickly. VERY QUICKLY. You could tell when you had something fatty to eat when on Alie, your rectum leaked. Constantly. Following the conventional wisdom of the time, that told me I was fat because I was eating too much fat. Fat is the devil all the medical professions said. Don't eat FAT and you won't get FAT. So, I cut fat out of my diet, started doing cardio every night, and became obsessive with reading labels. Guess what? I started to drop some weight. Then more. And more. THIS WORKS!!! Well, it does and doesn't. What I know now is when you are morbidly obese and you put yourself in a massive calorie deficit, you could eat nothing but Snickers bars and still lose weight. My diet at the time was very low fat, low protein and high carbs, but, when you are only taking in about 750 cals a day, the macros don't mean much. I was constantly

hungry so I ate a lot of small meals. I ate a lot of high carb snacks that I thought were healthy because that is what the packages said. I lost a LOT of weight in a short period and I got rather lean. How much of a change? When I started in January of 2010, I was 252lbs. By June, I was 145. Yup, over 100lbs in 6 months. This was me the day I went out to get new clothes because nothing fit me anymore. I was proud of myself. 145 dropped to 130. I had never been this size my entire adult life. I was stoked. What I missed at first though, was that as much weight as I had lost and now 'working out' for 2-3 hours a night, my strength hadn't changed. I had muscle tone but no real increase in strength. I was still constantly hungry as well. I didn't sleep well. I had constant anxiety and 'brain fog.' I would struggle concentrating. This pretty much sucked and I didn't know what to do to change it. Again, I fell into that frame of mind that 'that's just the way I'm built.' Interesting to think how the mind will tell you what you want to hear, huh? The other side of this was, since I finally hit a goal, I started eating more so I would stop losing weight. I need to make a clear point – I didn't start pigging out, I just increased my calorie intake to moderate or what should be 'maintenance' levels while still eating the same type of foods – low fat, high carb, low-to-

moderate protein. Following the advice of doctors and 'health experts,' I didn't see a thing wrong with this. I would be one of those success stories, I lost all the weight and I WOULD KEEP IT OFF!!!

Guess what.
Nope.
I was wrong.
THEY were wrong.

Long, sorry, but no one has ever accused me of being brief. I had no real strength, and not surprisingly, when I upped my calorie intake…I upped my weight and it wasn't lean mass. I got depressed. I was a failure. I put a chunk of that fat back on in a year – about half of what I had lost. I stayed that way for several years, dabbling here in and there with the same method. I figured that I just wasn't the same as everyone else, that's why I didn't see great gains in strength. I did know how to lose the fat if I wanted to.

2014 comes along, time for that annual physical that I had avoided for several years. I had a full battery of blood work done. No surprise, being over-weight, I found out I was pre-diabetic and had high cholesterol. Right around this time, my girlfriend hit a mid-life crisis. She wasn't technically overweight, but she felt she had 'old woman's body.' The ribs to the hips was one line, a little paunch in the belly, and the butt was starting to droop. I thought she still looked good, but it wasn't about what I thought, it was what she thought. She's one of those people who will research something to death before making a move. I didn't know what she was planning on doing. She got a few training corsets to try to shape her mid-section. Not long after that, I started hearing about 'wheat belly,' 'ketones,' 'ketogenic,' and 'gluten-free.' She would send me articles, I'd breeze through them, only paying half attention. I had lost a lot of fat a few years prior, I knew what to do. Why couldn't she see this?

Why? Because she had an open mind, and I did not.

The monthly shopping run came and our grocery list had changed. The breads, rice, beans, all the grains were gone. This pissed me off a little, but I had absorbed some of what she had been telling me and could see that grains and gluten could be an issue. So, thinking I knew better, I went shopping, filling the cart up with 'gluten-free' products without even glancing at the labels. Yeh, that didn't go over well when I got home. I had completely ignored the idea of keeping carbohydrates low, because I didn't pay attention. No, wrong, I didn't WANT to pay attention. I was stuck in the idea that I knew everything I needed to do. We had a few spats over this, ultimately we decided that I would do it my way and she would do it hers. It took a few weeks of me making a meal that she wouldn't eat to get that I still wasn't paying attention. In those few weeks, she started seeing changes for the better. I saw NOTHING. Yet, I was still determined to do it my way. It took a few consecutive days of her sending me information, telling me about this thing called 'keto,' where your body returns to a primal state, using naturally occurring ketones instead of glucose from sugars to power itself. Still sounded like crap to me, fat was what was making me fat, and not eating it was making me starving constantly, but no pain, no gain, right? After another week of her having success and listening to me get frustrated because I wasn't, she asked me one more time if I wanted to do it her way. At this point, I was pissed off. I agreed to try her way, knowing full well it would fail and all this fat she was going to have me eat would make me fat. I started following her with the intention of proving she was wrong and I would fail. The first week, she had me eating so much dense foods, I was forcing myself to eat. There was butter on everything, coconut oil in my coffees, meat, meat, and more meat. I KNEW I was going to blimp up!

Crap. Nope. End of week 1, I was down 7lbs. Some of this was water weight, but some of it wasn't. My mind shifted. This could work. I still wasn't 100% convince this wasn't just a blip on the screen. I decided to quiet my inner voice and give this a real shot. The next week, more losses. I started reading, actually reading all the things she had sent me prior. Ketogenic diets are not a fad, the science points back millions of years. It was developed officially in 1921 as a natural way to help children control seizures. I didn't realize the importance of this point until later. I felt better. I had more energy. My clothes were getting looser, my constant hunger a thing of the past. She's the cook of the house, I've always been the baker. I used to make breads almost daily, as well as cakes, cookies, brownies, etc. Since wheat was no longer in our diet, suddenly, these things were gone. She started trying to create different meals for us to eat with recipes that would replace the high carb foods we loved with ones that would fit this way of eating, seeing if we could take what started as a diet and do like so many who do keto, make it a sustainable lifestyle. Diets end, and with that usually comes returning to your old habits and the return of the weight. We both realized this shouldn't happen. Since I was the baker, I started to dabble in a few things that she told me about from her research, mainly baked goods she didn't want to try because of the complexity and number of ingredients. I gave a few a shot, expecting the worst. Seriously, how could some ground up nuts, MOZARELLA CHEESE, and an egg make a Danish??

Actually, pretty well. I decided that we should keep around the recipes for what works for us, so we would print them out and stuff them in a drawer. The drawer started filling up. As I started to bake again, I started modifying a few of the recipes – some out of necessity because we didn't have all the ingredients, some because I wanted to see if I could do things a little simpler. When you eliminate wheat flour, you lose a bunch of different properties in just one ingredient. I started researching alternate ingredients (almond, flax, coconut flours, protein powders) as well as using traditional ones in different ways to get the results I wanted. Over the course of a few weeks, I had 3-4 things that I felt I did well that were my own creations. My girlfriend started with 'you should...' or 'I wonder if you could make this but keto-friendly?' More often than not, I could.

I'm highly ADD, disorganized, forgetful, inattentive. She's very pragmatic, organized, calm, and remembers EVERYTHING. She also suffers from chronic anxiety. Remember me mentioning keto helped seizures? It also helps other neurological disorders – like ADD and anxiety. We've both noticed a marked improvement. I hate writing longhand – and can never read what I wrote a few weeks later – so needed to come up with a better solution for me. The simple answer – online. I grabbed a free blog account, not knowing much more than how to make a post, which was fine as my original plan was just to use this for us to keep track of a handful of new creations. Plans have a way of changing. While all of this was going on, she started telling me I should get a hobby. I was spending more and more of my 'free' time working, staying busy and trying to keep boredom at bay.

She started digging into the fitness side of this way of living, I started to look at the science to get a better understanding it, as well as now getting mildly obsessed with cooking and baking. I was enjoying it. Social media is such a huge part of our lives now, I started looking for groups on Facebook that were targeted at keto. I found a bunch and joined. In the beginning, I just read what was posted and tried to learn. I started noticing a trend – people would post pictures of their meals and recipes. Many of them were, in my opinion, not that great of a compromise when it came to taste and texture vs staying in the lifestyle. I started reading blogs focused on the foods – there are several. I noticed few patterns: they were primarily run by women, targeted to women, the photography is lovely (food porn), the comments heavily biased towards 'it doesn't look like the picture, what did I do wrong,' overwhelmingly heavy on eggs (a 'cake' made with just eggs and flavorings tastes a lot like a puffy, flavored egg), and the recipes horribly complex. Primarily driven by curiosity and ego, I tried a few of them. I had similar results as many of the comments, as well as significant frustration of having to separate 12 eggs, whip to stiff peaks, gently fold dozens of ingredients in, and keep your fingers cross that it didn't fall apart and end up in the trash. Oh, and there were never any suggestions on what to use with all those egg yolks J. I decided there had to be a better, simpler way to do many of these things, especially when I would see in a recipe 4 different ingredients that fundamentally do the same thing. WHY? Money. The one other thing I noticed in these blogs was the insistence if you didn't use the exact ingredients they used, it would fail miserably. Out of convenience, these blogs also happen to either sell these ingredients, or were paid to advertise them. Lightbulb moment. It wasn't about the ingredients as much as it was making the blogger money. I started to get a little tickle in the back of my head that I couldn't identify. I began trying to create my own versions of some of these commonly-requested dishes for the challenge of it and for our own use. I had more successes than failures. I was starting to get how all these ingredients work together and how to look at a 'regular' recipes and have a basic plan on what needed to change to make it healthy for us and people like us. I started taking pictures of my creations and sharing them in the FB groups. People wanted to know my recipes, after being asked a bunch of times if there was a way they could save and print them, I remembered the blog I started. I entered in some of my better dishes and shared the links. I clearly remember being excited when I had 5 people look at it in one day :).

Most of the groups I was a part of were primarily focused on the lifestyle and less on the foods. For me, separating them was impossible. Food is such a part of the fabric of our day-to-day lives, the only way to make it a sustainable lifestyle is to make sure the critical component – food – could both fit and be enjoyable. A few like-minded people started a new group that would just focus on the foods and recipes, there were very few of those on Facebook that weren't run by a major blogger (which means 'which weren't all one person's recipes'). I got invited to the group as member number 12. I posted up all my recipes. The group gained several hundred members the first day, within 3 days I was asked if I wanted to help administer the group. I said yes. I realized the two founders were not invested in either the lifestyle or the group, I think it was started on a whim as within a week, I was the only administrator actively watching the group. I took advantage of this to start building membership and group philosophy to what I thought was needed. We would stay focused on the food. We would encourage people to not limit their food choices. We would be supportive of each other above everything else. The group started to grow. People started asking me for recipes and ideas. I started to ramp up my baking and posting on my blog, naming it She Calls Me Hobbit – my nickname from my girlfriend since I remind her of Tolken's iconic characters. I discovered a niche – common foods people were missing from their prior way of eating in an easy-to-duplicate way that didn't taste like eggs, with a little humor tossed in, from a man, targeted at both sexes. It started to work. A sister group was started by Steve Angel, and I started helping him run that one as well. This drew me into the science and health. I started soaking it up, taking it apart, and then figuring out how to present it to others in a way that wasn't so intimidating as well as battle some of the half-truths and clear misconceptions floating around.

Right about this same time, I befriended Tyo Prasetyo, who was very popular in the groups, creating foods like myself in a more scientific approach. I noticed he was getting similar questions as myself – how can I save these, print these, when are you going to publish a cookbook? An idea started. I took a chance and moved my blog over to a paid-hosting company. This gave me much more freedom in design. I reached out to my new friend and pitched an idea to him – why don't we combine our efforts, I'll go through all his recipes as well as any new ones, post them on the blog as his, and let people know that we had joined forces. He loved the idea. So did the people in the groups. Traffic doubled that next week.

After getting all his recipes up-to-date, I realized between the two of us, we had enough recipes to fill about a 200-page cookbook. Was there any serious interest? How much would it cost upfront? Was it worth the effort? Initial response from the groups was a resounding 'yes.' I researched self-publishing, comparing several different options and saw there were many drawbacks to most of the approaches. We would lose creative freedom. We would have to be like all the others and stage photographs to look 'just perfect,' which is the opposite of my core feelings the pictures had to look just like the finished product, as that is a big part of the feedback I was getting, 'I made this and it came out just like the pictures!' The approval could be months away and distribution limited, with much of the promotion and fees being my responsibility. Finally, there was no guarantee it would even be publish. I settled on one that gave us everything we wanted. I took the chance and put together the first cut. I had to learn publishing quickly – there's a lot of rules and guidelines for printing. My format was approved a week prior to Christmas 2015, and released within 24 hours. We decided the best thing we could do with any money we earned, which we didn't expect to be a lot, was to donate to charity. I honestly expected this to be at best $1-200 a month, tops. 6 months later we've made over $8000 in donations (between sales and matching funds from my better half, myself, and my sister). While nothing compared to The Food Network or the 'big bloggers', not too bad for a couple of amateur 'keto' cooks with absolutely no experience and minimal exposure.

This, along with the community that has been built in these two Facebook groups and those of you who visit me here, drive me to continue to better my life and possibly help others along the way. When it comes down to it, I have The Lady to thank for giving me my life. She is the reason I am what I am today. I cannot state strong enough how her support, inspiration, research, and love for me has changed my life...and indirectly, changed the lives of others that happen to wander into my little sphere of hobbitness. Every success story I read give me that energy to keep up the good fight and stay strong. While I get comments thanking me, it is each and every single one of you – from The Lady to my sister (who has supported me and encouraged me from day one) to the newest follower or member – that I need to thank. You all are my lifeblood.

Thank you.

INDUCTION-DUCTION, WHAT'S YOUR FUNCTION...WITH APOLOGIES TO SCHOOLHOUSE ROCK :)

So, you've been hearing about this 'keto' and 'LCHF' stuff, but what the hell does it really mean in simple terms...and more importantly, how can you get you sum' of dat? Yes. Let's talk BASICS:

– What is keto?
– How is it different from LCHF?
– How does it work?
– Is it safe?
– How do I get started?
– What is induction?

There's a lot of confusion out there for people trying to improve their health. Not only are they getting conflicting advice from their doctors, nurses, the media, the USDA, the AMA, the ADA, but they are bombarded with widely varied information from armchair experts on the internet as well. As one of those armchair people, let's get some stuff sorted out, clarified, and then we can get you rolling on being a better YOU. Sound like a plan?

What is Keto?

Keto is short for 'ketogenic.' Great. Thanks, Hobbit for clearing that up... :(. HA! I'm not gonna leave you hanging :). Ketogenic is a medical term that means your body stops using glucose as its primary fuel. Instead, it uses things called 'ketones.' I can get into the whole chemical composition of them but eh, I did say 'simple' so let's skip that part. Your body has three potential fuel sources – glucose, fatty acids, and ketones. Fatty acids are the unique ones of the batch as they have more than one purpose in the body as well as more than one way of being used as fuel. Ketones are interesting in they are also multi-use. Glucose...not so much. Ketogenic occurs when your intake of glucose-rich foods (carbohydrates) is reduced low enough that there isn't sufficient intake of them to match the body's needs to use them as fuel. Since the body wants to survive, it has other options, the preferred one being ketones. The body makes ketones for fuel in the liver, yeh, the same place it makes glucose. In the simplest explanation, when your carb intake is low, low, low, the body takes fatty acids and converts them to ketones primarily, and glucose for those few organs that cannot use ketones. The liver is also able to convert ketones in the bloodstream into glucose as well. See? The body knows what it wants to do (which is live) and how to get the job done. Your body doesn't NEED carbs because of this. Yes, it still does need glucose for those functions where ketones aren't going to work (as well as it being part of glycogen which fuels the muscles) but it can make it on demand.

Right.

That means carbs are not an essential nutrient IN THE PRESENCE of fat (dietary and\or body fat).

As a side note, fatty acids are also used in other needs of the body without being converted to ketones or glucose. I won't get into them for this article but thought I should include it.

Ketogenic was first coined as a term between 1919 and 1921. Yeh. Almost 100 years ago. So, those who call this a fad diet?

HA.

100 years isn't a fad.

What about millions of years? Is that a fad?

MILLIONS.

Early man, the hunter-gatherers didn't have Wonder Bread, Tyson Nuggets, or Oreos. They had whatever they could find, WHEN they could find it.

Right.

Early man (and woman, sorry)?

Ketogenic.

So, what is so important about the early 20th century that it got a name?

Epilepsy – specifically in children.

A few enterprising doctors discovered that by eliminating carbs from epileptic children's diets, the occurrence and severity of seizures greatly diminished or disappeared. Unfortunately, they did this with little understanding of 'proper' nutrition. The children were given diets without fats and the primary source of protein was gelatin – which is mostly non-essential amino acids. Yeh. The kids were malnourished. A few years later, another group of doctors refined this plan, adding in fats for fuel and proper proteins for health.

The important thing to note here is this was succeeded with PROPER PROTEIN, NO CARBS, and SUFFICIENT FAT. The key there is 'PROPER' and 'SUFFICIENT' which are different than 'EAT ALL THE FAT!' Too much fat isn't good. Too much of anything isn't good. Keep that in mind.

So, this diet plan? It worked. Quite well, but no one recognized the other potentials until the last 50 years or so. Recently, it has become a powerful tool for weight loss (you've heard of the Atkin's Diet I assume), controlling and repairing metabolic damage, hormonal imbalances, and even has shown success with many neurological disorders and even cancer!

WOOT!

GO HUMANS!!!

The beauty of keto?

You can get healthy without feeding big pharm since you have this power, this 'medicine,' RIGHT IN YOUR BODY!!

Ok, so what is the difference between 'keto' and 'LCHF,' if any?
There is a difference. Some call them the same thing, but they are not. Technically, keto is VLCHF (Very Low Carb High Fat) instead of Low Carb High Fat. Low Carb is less than 100g. Keto is less than 30g. High Fat means more of your calories come from fat than any other macro. It does not mean eat all the bacon.
Sorry.
Yeh.
I know.
That sucks :(.

Is it safe?
Definitely.
It is a natural process.
End of discussion.
It's as safe as any other balanced form of nutrition.

How do you get started?
Simple.
Eliminate carbs.
Ok. So not THAT simple.
First, you need to recognize where carbs come from:

To put it simply, any non-animal food source...and a few animal food sources as well. Meats don't have carbs. Eggs do. Veggies do (but not all carbs are equal, more on that in a second). Grains do. Beans do. Fruits do. So do berries.

So, how do we eliminate carbs?
We really don't.
We LIMIT them while getting in the right amount of protein and filling in the empty spaces with fats.
Wow, that seems like we have to give up EVERYTHING!
No.
No we don't.
Why?
Because not all carbs are equal.
Fiber.
Fiber is a carb but it TYPICALLY doesn't affect blood sugar. For some, it does. When you look at a label, you will see Total Carbs and then they will break it down into Fiber, Sugar, Other. At the most basic level, we only want to worry about the SUGAR. But, starting out, I want you to worry about ALL of them until you know if you are someone that should worry about fiber or sugar alcohols (the 'Other'). This beginning period?

Induction – aka learning now to eat this way and get into ketosis initially.

So, what do we do in this 'induction' phase?
We cut back drastically on carbs.
We make sure we eat enough protein.

We eat some fat.
We suffer a little.
Ok, some of us suffer a lot.
It hurts.
Physically while we detox off carbs (I HATE the term 'keto flu,' let's call it what it is – Carbohydrate Withdrawal and Detox).
EMOTIONALLY is where it really hurts.
No bread.
No pasta.
No rice.
No CAKE AND COOKIES!!

This isn't forever, I promise you. Only in the beginning. Why? To get you on the right path mentally and physically. Once you start LEARNING YOUR BODY, you can learn other things too, like how to make a cake that won't make you fat. How to make rice and potatoes from cauliflower. How to master Fathead for the win. How to make bread with 200000 egg whites (ok, I'm not going there...). How much fiber can you handle. How sugar alcohols affect you. So, to get started, I recommend a multi-pronged plan. What we want is you to succeed. In order to do that, this has to be something that you can reasonably do and not get all stressed out over. What are the steps?

– First, eliminate the grains. That means bread, pasta, rice, breaded foods, etc. Read the labels. Box the stuff up and take it to a food pantry or shelter. It won't get wasted and you will feel good just doing it. No matter what, get it out of the house.

– Learn to deal with those things gone for a few days.

– Get rid of the boxes of sugar, bottles of honey, maple syrup, and molasses. Yeh, that's sugar. Don't worry, the Hobbit won't let you down. When you're ready, we can help you replace those with things that are safe. WHEN YOU ARE READY.

– Get rid of the fruits and any veggies that aren't green and leafy. Yeh, that means potatoes, too :(.

– Embrace your protein sources – meats, eggs, high protein veggies, seeds (not to be confused with nuts).

– Don't be afraid of fat – butter, coconut oil, olive oil, bacon, etc., but do it in MODERATION.

– Supplement magnesium, potassium, and sodium. You will need these electrolytes as the water balance in your body changes.

– KEEP IT SIMPLE!!! Forget the fancy ketofied recipes for now. Get the basics down. Eat like you did before carbs, just without the dinner rolls, the 3 cups of rice (use more veggies), and the 3 donuts for breakfast. Yes, that means instead of a burger on a roll, fries, and a diet Coke, have the burger with a slab of cheese, maybe some bacon, wrap it up in lettuce (remember GREEN AND LEAFY), cook up some broccoli for a side, and wash it down with water\coffee\tea. Breakfast, forget the oatmeal, have eggs or an omelet (and once you get through induction, I'll point you to some wonderful keto-safe waffles and pancakes at the end of this book). Give the Hot Pockets to a coworker, bring some chicken salad instead (or tuna).

– MEASURE EVERYTHING! You will be surprised just how wrong you are on what is actually a 'serving.' HINT – it's a lot less than you think.

– Track everything. You will be shocked to find out how many carbs are hidden in things you never thought of.

– Read labels.

– READ EVERYTHING. Studies. Blogs. Groups. Learn. Learn. Learn.

– Ask questions. All of them.

We want you to succeed. To do that, you need a strong foundation. This is induction. Build that foundation. 3-4 weeks is all it takes, then you can work on building that beautiful house of YOU.

LET'S TALK ABOUT FAT

Let's talk about FAT. Not that which we are trying to get rid of, but the fat we put into our mouths. There seems to be a common misconception that being keto means you can eat ALL THE FAT.
No.
That is wishful thinking.
While many forms of the ketogenic diet are called 'low carb\high fat,' that doesn't mean you must eat as much fat as your macros say you CAN have. Fat macro is a guideline, just like carbs it is a LIMIT. You can go under your 20g of carbs. Likewise, you can go under you XXXg of fat. You have a choice when eating – either high carbs to preserve muscle mass, or high fat to preserve muscle mass. Protein is a constant (and a goal either way). If we get enough carbs or fat in our diet, then we don't break down muscle for fuel. Yeh, breaking down muscle is a bad thing. BUT, if you overdo either fat or carbs, you do have the potential of not getting the results you are looking for.
Right.
No weight loss.
There's a lot of talk out there that 'fat doesn't make you fat' and to a degree, that is true. Eating fat doesn't AUTOMATICALLY make you fat. Eating too much fat or carbs can STORE FAT.
Yes.
That means you cannot go wholesale and eat 10# of bacon slathered in butter with a side of lard and wash it down with a BPC containing 1/4 cup of heavy cream and 2tbsp coconut oil. As fun as that sounds, it doesn't work that way. Excess fat calories must go someplace. That means STORED. Yeh. Body fat. Calories do matter. No, calories in\out isn't as simple as some make us believe, but in the same breath, they cannot be discarded. I'll touch on that at the end of this post, before I do, let's talk more on fat.

So, you are probably thinking – 'Ok Hobbit-san, so what are you trying to tell us??'
Use dietary fat INTELLIGENTLY.
BALANCE.
Yes, Grasshoppah, **BALANCE.**

To preserve muscle mass (remember, muscles burn calories just by existing, fat doesn't), we need to make sure we are getting enough. How much is 'enough?'

You need 0.39g of dietary fat per pound of lean body mass to protect protein (enough energy to function without breaking down muscle). So, let's use this example. We have a 200lb, 5'5" woman. Their body fat percentage is about 50%, meaning their lean body mass (you, minus the fat) is roughly 100lbs (102lbs to be exact but we like simple math). The minimum fat they need a day to stay healthy is going to be 39g.

I'm going to guess many of you are eating a lot more than that.
That's not a bad thing… but remember **BALANCE**.

You do want to eat more than that because you want to make sure you get enough calories to go above your BRM (basal metabolic rate – the number of calories a day your body uses just to stay alive) if you haven't slowed your metabolism down too much by dropping your calories too low. See my article later in this book on why too few calories is as bad if not worse than too many. So, yes, after you've had ALL your protein, you want to make sure you have enough fat to keep your calories up to a safe level WITHOUT HAVING TOO MANY as well as keep you from chewing off your arm out of hunger. Looking at our 200lb person above, their BMR for their CURRENT size is 1533 calories, while their TDEE (total daily energy expenditure, all the calories they use in a normal day) is 1840. What that person wants to do to lose weight is to eat LESS than their TDEE but MORE than there BMR. Since they should be getting a minimum of 84g protein a day (344 calories) and they need at least 39g fat (351 calories), that gives them a minimum of (1533-695) 838 calories to have for the rest of the day between carbs and fat, since carbs should be 20 or less (20×4=80), they can eat another 84g (758 calories) of fat and LESS than 160g (maintenance calories). Typically, this means their macros they were given\calculated would have a fat gram range of 112-142g for a safe deficit. Looking at these numbers, we can now see that she doesn't need to eat ALL the fat, just eat enough to be healthy. She can occasionally go even lower – moving calories around keeps the metabolism guessing which isn't a bad thing – if she doesn't make it a constant thing (yes, this is one of the reasons that fasting and intermittent fasting works so well). She will also want to change these numbers as she sheds the fat and gets healthier. Weight loss and healthy living isn't static, things change. So, should your macros.

Another reason you should watch out for fats, many people who are overweight are leptin resistant and ghrelin sensitive. These two are ying and yang of each other and work with serotonin and dopamine to regulate hunger. Leptin tells you when to stop eating and raises serotonin to satiate you, Ghrelin does just the opposite. Ghrelin is a hormone found in the gut and THRIVES on saturated fats, so for some people, the more fats they eat, the more they want to eat. It's not an 'addiction' but a hormonal imbalance. Try lower fat, slightly more protein, and incorporating but insoluble and soluble fiber into your diet (with plenty of hydration). Doing this might help as well as allow you to tap into the 4th macro.

The 4th macro?
BODY FAT.
This is the macro you WANT to mobilize, right? If you are using everything you eat for energy, you're not using body fat.

You might notice something else, I'm talking grams and **not percentages.** There's a reason for it. I could go into a whole Hobbit discourse but Lyle McDonald put it so simply, I'm going to use his explanation:

"When someone puts protein, carb, or fat requirements in terms of percentages only for a diet setup, it doesn't necessarily have any relevance to what that person actually needs. For example, it's not uncommon to see diets for bodybuilders set up with 25-30% protein. Others take a more conservative 15% and use that across the board for athletes or general intake. But what do those percentages actually mean? Obviously nothing unless you also know how many calories that person is eating.

Let's use our 200 lb example individual above and look at his protein intake. Let's split the middle value for weight training and say he actually needs 150 g/day of protein and put him at two different caloric extremes: 1000 cal/day (a starvation diet) vs. 10,000 calories/day (Parillo style). Let's set protein at 30% which most would say is sufficient (or excessive depending on who you're talking to).

1000 cal/day at 30% yields 300 calories from protein, or 75 grams of protein. He'd need 60% protein on 1000 cal/day to get 150 grams of protein per day. 10,000 cal/day at 30% yields 3000 calories from protein, or 750 grams of protein. Although both diets are 30% protein, the first is half of what our guy actually needs (75 g/day vs. 150 g/day); the second diet has 5 times as much protein as he actually needs. Yes, these are extreme examples and deliberately chosen that way. But they point out that the percentage itself has no relevance whatsoever to what our guy's actual requirements are."

Ok, what about calories in\out?

Calories in\out isn't a myth, **it is a misunderstood, WAY over simplified, and often misquoted theory.** Calories in\out is real. What many miss are not all calories are equal. The law of thermodynamics is real. It's the **UNDERSTANDING** of it that is wrong.

If you are in negative energy balance, your body will burn some of its own energy. If you are in positive energy balance, your body will store energy. These are irrefutable conclusions that logically follow from the laws of physics, specifically the first law of thermodynamics.

Thus, being in an energy deficit equals weight loss and being in an energy surplus equals weight gain, right? Yet it's wrong to equate energy balance with weight change. Within the context of a sedentary individual on a balanced diet that only changes his or her energy intake, it is generally correct. However, as a law, which is how most people perceive it, it is false.

The logical error is that not all bodily mass corresponds with stored energy. For example, when you go on a ketogenic maintenance diet, you will almost certainly lose body mass without being in a deficit. The lost bodyweight will mostly be water as a result of the lower carbohydrate content of your diet and changes in your body's electrolyte balance. Foods that cause abdominal bloating and water retention can similarly cause weight gain without a caloric surplus. Not to mention diuretics, the menstrual cycle, drugs, changes in mineral consumption, colon cleanings, creatine, etc. There are many ways to change your weight long term without changing your body's amount of stored energy.

Moreover, you can be weight stable while being in a deficit You can gain muscle (technically lean body mass, but that's what most people mean when they say 'gain muscle') just as fast as you're losing fat and a a result your weight will remain the same. This invalidates the idea that energy balance dictates weight change, since evidently being weight stable does not mean you are in energy balance and being in a deficit does not mean you will lose weight.

If someone gained more muscle than he lost fat, he was in a caloric surplus by definition." This was the objection I received from several people when I tried to explain the above earlier. As we saw above, however, this is based on the flawed assumption that energy balance dictates weight change.

This isn't just a semantic argument where people just have different definitions. The energy balance equation is a mathematical principle.

Change in body energy = Energy intake – energy expenditure

With the metabolizable energy densities of fat and lean body mass we can precisely calculate the deficit or surplus someone was in based on that person's body composition change. Someone who gained 3 pounds of muscle and lost 1 pound of fat must have been in a net energy deficit of 1810 calories. Taking this a step further, you can lose fat in a surplus(!) Fat loss occurs during a surplus when you gain muscle fast enough to offset the energy your body receives from the fat loss.

Following the same logic, you can also gain fat in a deficit. If you lose muscle 5.2 times as fast as you get fat, you gain fat while remaining in a deficit. Unless your weight loss program really sucks though, I should hope this only ever occurs if you stop training, you have a serious medical condition or there are drugs involved.

The TL:DR summary:

Energy balance and weight change are almost wholly distinct from each other.

Your weight can change without any change in bodily energy storage due to changes in water weight and mass in your digestive tract.
You can be weight stable yet be in a deficit. So, you can gain muscle and lose fat at the same time.
If you're gaining weight, you may still be in a deficit, because you can gain muscle faster than you lose fat.
If you're losing weight, you may still be in a surplus if you lose a lot of muscle mass.
You can lose fat in a surplus if you rapidly gain muscle.
You can gain fat in a deficit if you rapidly lose muscle mass.

IT'S JUST ONE DAY, NOT YOUR WHOLE LIFE

So, how many of you are not that happy today with yourselves? Overdo it for the holiday? If so, IT'S NOT A BIG DEAL. It's one day. Really, that's all it is. Today is a new day and a chance to do something completely different than you did yesterday. So, maybe you feel like crap. Maybe you are 4-5lbs up today from water weight. Ok. It happens. What you don't need to do is something drastic. As a matter of fact, that's probably THE WORST thing you can do, but if you do, you will far from be alone as in the next 3 weeks, more people will start a diet than any other time of the year. How many more? 97% more than any other three-week period in the year – including bikini season. Oh, and guess what? 87% of them will quit before Easter. Generally, it has been determined they quit not because they succeed, but because they don't see the results they want in the period time they want and find the 'diet' too restrictive to sustain. HA! Well, we've got this, don't we? Damn straight.

We know these things already:

A properly applied ketogenic diet that fits OUR needs, physiology, and neurology works.
A properly designed LIFESTYLE that incorporates ketofied foods that we enjoy makes this more sustainable.
Being out of ketosis will add 3-6lbs of water weight.
Going into ketosis will drop 3-6lbs of water weight.
Any unproductive gains of the past are temporary if we want them to be.
We – if overindulge – did not fail, we are not failure. Nope. We tried something different and the results weren't that productive.

We know how to do something productive and can do it because we have in the past.

We've got this. We decided something yesterday and it didn't work, the beauty of it all is we get another new day to make decisions. Funny how life is like that :). And yes, we made the decision. No one forced the food into us, we did it for a variety of reasons – not wanting to insult someone, not wanting to be the outcast, not wanting to have a fight, etc. – but we DID it. We own it. We move on. I've made it well known that I didn't go into this willingly. I fought it hard. I had my 'big fail' in the parking lot of Walmart with a dozen Boston Cream donuts. I'm still here. I'm better now than I was then. If I can do this, you can too :). Some of you are frustrated with people you know and love. How can they not 'get' what they served isn't good for you (or them)? Guess what? Not too long ago, you didn't get it either. I didn't get it. We didn't get it. Have patience with them. Understand they mean well, they just don't understand. Hell, when we first started this, I went out and bought $$$ in gluten free foods, not understanding that 'gluten free' doesn't mean 'carb free.' Damn, there's a difference??

DOLLARS AND SENSE (AS IN COMMON...) - KETO DOESN'T HAVE TO PUT YOU IN THE POORHOUSE. PART ONE - VEGGIES

Keto on a budget. Is it possible? Yes, and this is coming from a man that realistically spends more for 2 than most families of 4. If I wasn't a food blogger, I could conceivably cut my costs in half. You CAN do this on a reasonable budget. I shop once a month, for the whole month. Yup. ONCE. One trip. One day. Repeat 30 days later. I've got this down to a science :).

Shop around.
Don't forget the Dollar Store.
Find out when they markdown the meats, time your trips then if possible.

Next, think about what you used to buy before going keto. Now, remove the carby foods and processed stuff.
No more pasta, rice, bags of potatoes, packages of Oreos, Cheez-its (I'm sorry....), etc.
BANG.
You just saved some money, didn't you?
Think about it.
I'm going to assume you ate meat before, right?
Well, you still are going to.
That part hasn't changed.
Take the money you aren't spending on carb stuff, use it to get your veggies. They are low calorie, low carb, high fiber = less hungry = EAT LESS = SPEND LESS!

Go frozen, they cost significantly less than 'fresh.'
Yes. Frozen.
Frozen? Hobbit, you been drinkin'??
Nope. Stone sober. Bear with me for a sec ☐
Unless you are buying your veggies at the farm, frozen are more fresh.
Wait.
What?
Yes. More fresh. Here's why:

Typical 'fresh' produce:
– harvested
– STARTS TO AGE!
– Trucked to processing plant
– sorted\washed
– packaged
– boxed
– put in shipping depot

Day 2 – produce age 2 days
– loaded on a truck 12-24 hours later
– moves about the country at 50-70mph, 8 hours a day

Day 3-4 – produce age 4 days
– Arrives at distribution center
– Sits

Day 5? Day 6? – produce age 6 days
– Ordered
– loaded on another truck
– delivered to the store (30 minutes away? 4 hours?)
– Unloaded
– Checked in
– Stocked on shelf

So, how fresh IS it by the time it sits in the produce section for 6 hours, 12 hours, 3 days? How long will it be in your home? How much will end up wasted??

Now, let's think about frozen veggies:
– harvested
– STARTS TO AGE!
– Trucked to processing plant
– sorted\washed
– packaged
– FLASH FROZEN
– AGING SUSPENDED!!
– put in shipping depot

Day 2 – produce age 1 day
– loaded on a truck 12-24 hours later
– moves about the country at 50-70mph, 8 hours a day

Day 3/4 – produce age still…1 day
– Arrives at distribution center
– Sits

Day 5-6 – produce age still…1 day
– Ordered
– loaded on another truck
– delivered to the store (30 minutes away? 4 hours?)
– Unloaded
– Checked in
– Stocked on shelf

Sits in store cooler 2, 5, 11, 14 days. Produce age? 1 day.

So, for easily half the cost of 'fresh,' you are getting fresher food that also will store longer. If you have a chest freezer, you can buy in bulk when the specials are running and stock up. Just think of the gas and time you'll save :).

Now, this doesn't mean ALL 'fresh' produce should be swapped for frozen. Some not-frozen items last quite well just the way they are, such as:

Kabocha (sooo versatile!! Read on it!)
Cabbage (Napa and bok choi too) – lasts a long time, low cost per serving, very dense so can be used for more than one meal, and excellent to be used as noodles, wraps, probiotics, etc.
Radishes – sauted, they are so close to potatoes you would struggle to know the difference, inexpensive.

Celery
Avocados – slice, brush with lemon juice, freeze
Mushroom – slice, freeze
Onions – keep dry and out of the light, they will last months.

Save your cutoffs – you know, the radish and onion tops, that last 1.5" of zucchini, that wilted celery.
Toss them in the freezer until you have a big bag.
Thaw.
Roast in the oven on a baking sheet for 30 minutes or so.
Toss in a pot of simmering water or your crock pot for a few hours.
Hey, you make bone broth, right? So, why not veggie too?

You're welcome ⏷

Next installment – What you do and DON'T NEED to buy, the Dairy Chronicals.

DOLLARS AND SENSE (AS IN COMMON…) - KETO DOESN'T HAVE TO PUT YOU IN THE POORHOUSE. PART TWO - THE DAIRY AISLE

THE DAIRY CHRONICLES

What about when we get to that other end of the store? The dairy aisle? What do we do there? How can we save money and eat keto? Typically on the Facebook groups, we see more discussion about dairy products than carbs.
Yup.
We do.
Let's break this up into two segments.

SEGMENT ONE – The downside of dairy.

Yeh, for some people, dairy isn't something that agrees with them. No, I'm not just talking about the lactose intolerant. Actually, I'm not going to talk about that at all. Why? Lactose = milk sugar <> keto. Right. That means you should already have eliminated those milk products that are higher in carbs out of your diet – 1%, 2%, skim, whole milk, regular ice cream, regular yogurt, etc. So, you might wonder … 'hey Hobbit, what the hell are you going to talk about then??'

CASEIN.
You will find casein higher percentages in you soft cheeses, yogurt, cottage cheese, cream cheese, etc. Casein is a milk protein. Ever know an infant that can't drink milk-based formula and needed to be switched to soy or goat milk-based?
Yup.
Casein.
If you cannot properly digest this protein (and it is estimated this affects about 60% of the western population), your body treats it like a foreign substance. What does your body do when it detects a foreign substance? Ramp up the immune system. Increase cortisol production. Tissue inflame. We hear people call this 'stalled.' It's not. A stall is when you hit metabolic 'zen' when calories used equals calories consumed. Dairy sensitivity is an INFLICTION, not a stall. Your body senses a threat, acts on it, and protects itself. So, if you have been doing 'all the right things' and aren't seeing success, CUT THE DAIRY.

Well, except the butter. Butter doesn't have more than trace amounts of casein. You're good there ⏷

SEGMENT TWO – what should I buy?

In a perfect world, where money is no object and selections is unlimited:

– grass-fed butter
– grass-fed, locally sourced cream and cheeses
– organic Greek yogurt from … you guessed it … grass-fed cows

Ok. But we're talking on a BUDGET and we all know that things like Kerigold ain't cheap. So, what about us more budget-conscious people? What are we to do?

Ok, here's the very necessities in the dairy aisle for ketoers:

–
–
–
–
–

Did you write that down? Added those to your list? What? There's nothing to write down? EXACTLY.

YOU ARE NOT REQUIRED TO EAT ANY DAIRY PRODUCTS TO BE KETO!

But I know some of you are thinking… 'Hobbit, where am I going to get all that fat I NEED TO EAT without my dairy?'

Meat sources.
Nuts.
Veggies.

BUT!
The common misconception for many people is that fat is a GOAL MACRO.
It isn't.
Fat isn't a goal. If you get your protein sources from say, oh I don't know, MEAT, your fats come along with it. You don't NEED to eat ALL THE FAT. You just need enough to spare protein (about 0.4g\LEAN body mass) and keep you from stuffing your face because you're hungry. Too much fat WILL MAKE YOU FAT. So will too much carbs. A 4oz skinless chicken thigh has about 10G fat (90calories) and 30g protein (120 calories). Add the skin, those numbers turn to 20g fat, 30g protein – 180 and 120 calories respectively. Heh. Do the math. 60% fat, 30% protein. Almost perfect ratios of someone not insulin resistant.

Ok, so what if you want to have some dairy and can afford it, just not the 'good stuff?'

Look for coupons and sales on non-grass-fed dairy.
Store-brand butter.
Regional dairy or store-brand (most regional chains' store brands ARE regional dairy)
Plain Greek yogurt
Get your cheeses **in bulk** and\or on sale, then freeze it
Look at your labels, usually whipping cream is less expensive by half over HEAVY whipping cream, yet the carb and fat content is almost identical.

If it fits your budget, great. If it doesn't, honestly, you don't NEED it.

Next installment – What you do and DON'T NEED to buy, GOING NUTS!

DOLLARS AND SENSE (AS IN COMMON…) - KETO DOESN'T HAVE TO PUT YOU IN THE POORHOUSE. PART THREE - GOING NUTS!

Keto on a budget. Welcome to part 3 of this series. Going NUTS!!

What about nuts? Do you HAVE to use them?
THEY ARE SOOO EXPENSIVE!!
What about my PEANUT BUTTER????

When is a nut, not a nut.

All nuts are seeds, but not all seeds are nuts. Some are just that – seeds. Others are legumes – you know…beans. Beans are a seed but not a nut. Wait. Beans? Can we have beans????
Maybe.
Depends.

Can you fit them into your macros and budget?

If so, then yes.

Specifically, peanuts and peanut butter without sugar added and cashews. Yes, those are not nuts, they are legumes. Unfortunately, cashews are pricey, so let's just skip right past them and they are high in carbs. Peanuts can be relatively affordable, but you want to shop around. Consider PBFit powder, while more expensive than a jar of Skippy, because all the liquids have been removed, you get 2-3 times the number of servings per container. Yeh. More economical.

What about NUTS that are NUTS??

Almonds.

Walnuts.

Pecans.

Brazil nuts

Macadamia nuts

Ouch. Those hurt at the cash register. The hurt even more when you add on flours and meals to the grocery list. So, do you NEED to use nuts?

NO.

NO YOU DON'T.

Nuts are a luxury, a 'nice to have' like grass-feed everything.

Nuts are good with fat.

They have good minerals.

They have some protein.

So, do a bunch of other foods that are a less expensive. Get nuts as a treat, not a staple. Whatever you do, don't get your nuts in the baking aisle. You know, those bags from Fisher Nuts or Blue Diamond? Yeh, the ones on the shelves right next to those lovely...errrr...horrible Nestle Morsels? Don't go there. Well, don't go there unless you LIKE 1) being tempted and 2) want to spend more money than you must. How much more? How about anywhere from 50-200% more! Yeh. I thought so. Ok.

So, you want nuts but if you don't get them in the baking aisle, Hobbit, what do you do??

Shake a tree?

Nope.

I'm gonna send you some place you probably don't frequent.

You know that section in the store you avoided like the plague when you had Doritos, HoHos, and bags of Oreda fries in your cart? The section since now that you are on a budget you also avoid because, hell, that crap is EXPENSIVE?? Yeh. The ORGANIC SECTION. Wait. WHAT?? THAT SECTION REQUIRES GIVING UP YOUR FIRST BORN AND TWO LIMBS JUST TO WALK DOWN!! Nope. Not all of it. You know those ugly tubes on the wall, with the stupid scoops that spill over, bags that you actually HAVE TO FILL AND PUT YOUR OWN LABEL ON??

Yeh.

Those.

Look pass the 14 types of rice, every trail mix you can think of, and granola loaded with oats. Find the nuts and seed. Those prices are less. A lot less. And you can pick how much you get...yeh...to fit your budget. I know, I know, but then you have to bag your own food, weigh it, deal with a few nuts\seeds falling out of the scoop. This is gonna add 5 minutes more to your shopping time! But, what if I told you that those 5 minutes saves you $5. That's like taking a salary of $60 an hour. Sounds better, doesn't it? Get your nuts in the organic bins. While you are there, look for something called 'Pepitas' aka pumpkin seeds. Why? They are CHEAP. In my area they are less than $5\lb, or half as much as the nuts right next to them.

Yeh, but you're thinking...pumpkin seeds? HA! If they are that cheap, they must SUCK! No. No they don't. In more ways than one. They taste pretty good. They save money. They can be ground into a flour for baking much easier (and less wear on your processor\blender than say... almonds). They are more nutrient-dense than most nuts. They have many of the minerals we need when keto.

DOLLARS AND SENSE (AS IN COMMON...) - KETO DOESN'T HAVE TO PUT YOU IN THE POORHOUSE. PART 4 - THE GREAT PROTEIN CONTROVERSY!

Ok, let's get this right out of the way: if you're thinking 'protein' spikes your BG, you've been drinking the wrong Kool-Aid. No, no it doesn't. What you are doing is using protein WRONG. So, before we get to the details of "Keto on a budget, Welcome to part, we're going to honestly and intelligently discuss the Great Protein Controversy.

I know you've seen it because I have "Protein spikes blood sugar," "too much protein is BAD," "whey protein will give you kidney issues!"
Bull.
All of the above.
BULL.

Let's hit those in order, shall we?

1) Protein spikes blood sugar: No it doesn't. Protein DOES increase insulin but less than 2% of all protein ingested IF DONE WITH THE RIGHT STUFF AND PROPERLY becomes glucose. TWO PERCENT. And that's 2% of the 56% of amino acids (proteins) that CAN be converted to glucose. So, you are asking 'why Hobbit do I see this all over the place??'

Bad interpretation of science.
Agendas.
Inability to actually READ the studies.

The most common study that gets dragged out did show a significant increase in BG after a group ingested protein in powdered form mixed with water. Now, first, I'd love to point to this study but I CAN'T FIND IT! Do you know why? Because it's CRAP. Go ahead, try it. Open up Google and search "whey protein blood sugar spikes" then come back here.
Did you do it?
Did you find that study right at the top of the search results?
Did you find endless results showing that whey protein spikes blood sugar?

NOPE.
You didn't.
You found just the opposite, didn't you.
HA!

You know why that study posted in places is wrong? No one bothered to read the entire content. Yes, it did show a significant increase in BG, that I will agree. But, what people missed was how the study was performed. I read it. Something jumped right out at me. They gave 2 different drinks to the participants: Whey protein CONCENTRATE and the other BCAAs (branch chain amino acids). Both showed a significant increase in BG.
They should, considering the screwed up way the study was done...
Screwed up??
Yeh.
Whey concentrate contains not only whey, but lactose... MILK SUGAR (it also contains casein which can cause inflammation).
Ok, so with that in mind, we might see a small bump in BG from the lactose.

Buuuuuttttt....
The part that SCREAMED at me 'THIS IS CRAP' is the BCAAs.
Why?
BCAAs CANNOT BE CONVERTED TO GLUCOSE!
It's chemically and metabolically IMPOSSIBLE.
BCAAs bypass the liver.
They are KETOGENIC aminos.

They cannot be broken down into glucose.
PERIOD.
So, why the spike?
Reading the study, BOTH DRINKS ALSO CONTAINED 50g of PURE GLUCOSE!!
So, yeh, the BG spiked but NOT FROM THE PROTEIN!!!!!!

Now, keep this thought in your head as we go down further, I'm going to discuss something later that will help you with having protein and NOT spiking BG.

2) Too much protein is BAD: Too much of ANYTHING is bad, but too much protein is not only extremely difficult to do, it's the only macro that doesn't get stored in the body in excess. That's right. Protein can't be made into FAT like fats and carbs can. You pee it out. How much protein is too much? Typically for a non-athletic individual, the proper protein amount is 0.8-1.5g per lean body mass, with little if no issues all the way up to 2.5g. For someone who is say, 200lb and has 40% body fat, that means about 120lb lean mass x 1.5 = 180g grams of protein.
Yeh.
180g
About 4 large chicken breasts.
LARGE chicken breasts.
End of discussion.
Thank you.

3) Protein causes kidney issues: Yes, if you are T1D and hit ketoacidosis, you can have kidney issues. If you ALREADY HAVE KIDNEY ISSUES, you shouldn't eat excessive protein.
If you are not one of the above?
Forget about it…

Sooooo, now that we know protein has the potential to be safe (and if you've read my posts on how to improve your body composition, you know it's also IMPORTANT), what are the things we should be doing?

1) Get your protein primarily from natural sources if possible – that means meats and nuts.
2) Get your protein primarily from animal sources – plant protein is less bioavailable than animal protein.
3) Use whey in baking and for the occasional drink
4) Embrace whey ISOLATE (NOT CONCENTRATE) as a fantastic baking ingredient. Why ISOLATE? No lactose. No casein. Just the good stuff.
4) EAT protein PROPERLY. You should eat protein at the beginning of your meal, not at the end. Protein is insulinogenic, which means it increases insulin production. Insulin isn't the devil. Insulin is what carries things into the cells like glucose and amino acids. Without insulin, that stuff would just float around and do you no good (and you'd be T1D). Insulin RESISTANCE is bad. That means your body makes insulin but the cells primarily reject it. So, the body floats that stuff around and eventually puts the glucose into fat cells. Here's the deal, the liver starts releasing glucose based off the insulin production, not the other way around. So, if you are IR and have too much insulin floating around, the liver thinks you need more glucose and provides it. Yeh. High blood sugar is the result. And since there is more glucose and now more insulin, the cells fight back even harder since they already can't take in everything that is floating around.
So, then, why is eating protein first a good idea?
It tempers the insulin release.
Protein takes longer to break down so, you eat that first.
While the faster digesting foods are being handled, the protein is still making its way through the process. The fast digesting foods start an increase in insulin, that is just starting to taper off when the aminos get their turn to do what they need to do, the insulin increase created by the amino release doesn't overload the cells, they are ready for it, and the aminos go where they need to go, your BG stays level, and everyone is happy.

So, is keto on a budget possible? We see many comments in the FB groups about items being too expensive, which can be true. Can you eat well with keto and not end up getting a second mortgage just to put food on the table???? What about whey, that crap isn't cheap!!!!
Well, you are probably doing two things:

1) Buying it in the wrong place
2) Not looking at the quantity properly

Do NOT get your protein powder from GNC or another 'healthy\fitness' box store. WAAAAYYYY over-priced (and usually crap quality).
If you have a Trader Joe's (we don't so I'm going off information from trusted others), the bulk bins there have affordable whey isolate. So most likely does your local health food store... and the beauty of bulk bins is you control how much you get so...how much you SPEND!

All else fails, get it online.
We ONLY get ours online. Sometimes Amazon (that Prime membership pays for itself fast) and other times from Z Natural Foods. Don't be afraid of the interwebs, people!!!! Look to combine other items to get free shipping.

BE SMART!!

You can get Piping Rock unflavored (nice quality) for about $12.50 a pound. Yeh, that's a small tub but this addresses number 2 – not looking at the quantity properly.
Look at my recipes.
I use whey isolate frequently.
In 1/4 cup or less measures.
Yeh.
So 1lb is about 18 recipes worth.
Try to do that for $13 with a lb of almond meal....
Or a 1/4 cup is 28g protein for less than $1.
Right. One dollar a serving.
See what I mean?

DOLLARS AND SENSE (AS IN COMMON...) - KETO DOESN'T HAVE TO PUT YOU IN THE POORHOUSE. PART 5 - YOUR GREATEST INVESTMENT FOR SUCCESS

Here's your Quick Fix, guaranteed success!!
Got your attention, huh?
We all want a quick fix.
We don't want to suffer or do extra work!

Sorry.
This isn't a quick fix.
You can't undo years in a few weeks or months.
This isn't a diet.
This isn't a fad.
This isn't 1-800-EAT-FATS
Nope.
This is bigger than that.

The first four parts of this series have been on how to shop while on keto and not going broke, I'd be a BAD HOBBIT if I didn't talk about something else before I get to sweeteners... and that is the process of making the most critical, most expensive yet inexpensive investment.

Investing in yourself.
This is your LIFE. Make it healthy. Do it RIGHT. BE INVOLVED.

If you wander around the internet keto blogs and groups, there's a lot of stuff out there that you can spend money on – promises of pills that will 'put you into ketosis in minutes,' 'keto coaches,' 'pay for meal plans,' recipes\mixes you can only get if you buy their cookbook, and '7 day cleanse' programs. Some work, some don't. NONE are required.

As I've talked about in earlier segments of the 'Dollars and Sense' series, keto doesn't have to suck you dry financially. You don't NEED anything SPECIAL to succeed.

Wait.
Yes you do.
That 'special' thing is YOU.

There is no magic pill that is going to undo years of damage. There's no supplement that is going to transform you into the best you that you can be. It isn't that easy...yet, it isn't that hard either.

Ketone Supplements:

I HATE seeing these things out there, not only because the are MLMs (Multi-Level Marketing...AMWAY anyone???) but also because they don't work and they are a waste of money. The ketone supplements out there that promise to put you into ketosis quickly are CRAP. You know what they are?
Powdered MCT oil (coconut oil with the long chain fatty acids removed) and CAFFEINE!!
Yes.
A ballistic coffee in a pill.
Seriously.
I'd much rather drink my morning happiness than choke it down.
Any respectable keto resource is going to ban anyone from promoting these.

Keto coaches:

These aren't always that bad, but you must be careful WHO your coach is. Some have only a passing friendship with science, some are dangerous to your health, and some are just in it to sell you more things. While I have absolutely no problem with people making a living, and being compensated for their time, work, and knowledge, I have a huge issue with taking advantage of people. If you feel the need to have someone hold your hand, then a coach might be for you, but on the other hand, there are many free resources that can accomplish the same thing – connect with people on Facebook and make your own relationships. If you don't want to do this, then research your coach well. Of course, if you are going to put all that work into researching a coach, maybe put that effort into improving YOUR knowledge instead?

Buying meal plans:

Why? Did you start keto and completely forget how to human? You've been eating for your whole life and I assume since you were old enough to reach the stove or microwave, you'be been feeding yourself as well. Why the need to have someone else tell you what you need to cook on Monday, Tuesday, etc? This isn't a diet plan. This is a fundamental change in how you LIVE. Did you eat food every day before? What has changed? Did a chicken breast magically become an exotic dish overnight? NOPE.
Oh, so we are dropping the carbs out. Ok. Eliminate grains, pasta, breads, Twinkies, Oreos, and sweet veggies. Replace with green leafy veggies and keto-friendly side dishes which you can find recipes for all over the internet for FREE! Don't over-think this. Seriously. It isn't rocket science, it's EATING. Start with the basics and let go of the stress (and hold onto your money).

Cookbooks:

Yes, we sell a cookbook here and we will be releasing another one this summer. Making a cookbook is significant work but we CHOSE to do that work. We also CHOSE to incur the costs of creating recipes, which can be quite substantial at times. That isn't YOUR fault. You shouldn't have to compensate us for something WE CHOOSE to do. I see no reason to 'hold back' recipes and make them cookbook-exclusive. How are you going to know if the recipes are worth PAYING FOR if you don't know what they are? All the Hobbit and Keto Iron Chef recipes in our cookbook are right here on the site. NOTHING is held back. We put out a cookbook for those who wanted one, but we also understand that buying a cookbook isn't a necessity for everyone, might not be affordable, and we want people to enjoy our recipes and succeed no matter what their circumstance is. I've made other people's recipes that look great and taste like ground up skunk feet with a side of rat poop. I'd be furious if I paid $30 for a cookbook to get a specific, exclusive recipe and it turned out like crap and wasted MY MONEY not only on the cookbook, but expensive ingredients! If the author is holding something back so you will spend money...pass.

Cleanse programs

Keto is by nature cleansing. You eliminate the processed foods and toxins from your diet just by going keto. Pass on these. Not only are they a waste of money, they can be very uncomfortable to do and potentially create more health issues than you already have. Yeh, that's worth spending money on…

So what do you do?

Would you hire someone to raise your kids 24/7? I'm not talking about a babysitter, daycare, or even a nanny, I'm talking about someone who becomes the parent of them for money, only giving you updates on their lives via email a couple of times a week, yet still expect that child to bond with you?
No you wouldn't.

Would you go clothes shopping by randomly walking into stores, asking the clerk for clothing out of the back room, not try it on, and expect it to not only fit, but look awesome and be a fantastic value?
Nope.

Would you buy an energy-saving device that unscrews the light bulbs when you leave a room, or would you save that money and use, oh, I don't know, a light switch instead?????

Would you pay to have empty trash cans emptied anyway?
Nope.

So, if none of these things get the Hobbit stamp of approval, what does?
YOU.
Invest in you.
That means EDUCATE yourself.
Learn YOUR BODY.
Read.
Read some more.
Watch videos.
Then read again.

I donated to a charity, in return I got a sleeve of address labels. I haven't mailed a letter in 10 years… If you buy our cookbook, you at least get something useful in return. We didn't make this blog to sell cookbooks. We enjoy doing it and enjoy helping people. Each of your comments, your success stories, your improving your lives are our payment.

Instead, INVEST IN YOU.

Charity begins at home.
Take that money, buy a glucose meter and strips, learn how to use it, use it to make changes to improve your health.
Take that money and buy whey isolate, almond flour, meat, whatever. Make meals with LOVE for you and your family.
Take that money and buy weights or a gym membership. Put that money into building up you from the inside out.
Take that money and buy a new outfit that YOU think YOU LOOK GREAT IN. Spend it on your self-esteem.
Not my ego.

You are your own best coach. If you want to succeed, you need to be a part of the process…and not a bystander. See something you don't recognize as a term, acronym, or just doesn't click with you?
Look.
It.
Up.
Ask questions.
You don't have to 'get' science to be alive and healthy. What you do need to do is learn what works and what doesn't for you as an individual. This requires some effort, some 'blood equity' in YOURSELF. You are your greatest investment. We have ONE life. Don't waste it.

Live.
Learn.

Love.
Laugh.

Everything we do needs to be in support of those FOUR things. That's all that matters. If you can nail those, then you can accomplish ANYTHING. Yeh, even fitting into that size 4 dress that you wore in high school (not that it's still in style but you know what I mean).

MEASURE TWICE, CUT ONCE - WHY 'LAZY KETO' MIGHT NOT BE WORKING FOR YOU

Hey, you know what I woke up to yesterday, the last week of April?

Snow.
Yeh.
WHITE STUFF.
What the hell?
You know what is still on the ground today?
Yup.
SNOW.
Have you ever tried to mow snow? Doesn't work. Yes, I've tried it. Hey, I figured it might work like a snow blower... Hobbits don't always have the smartest ideas... Ok, so what does Hobbits mowing snow have to do with keto? Measuring. How the eye-brain connection isn't your best source of measurement. Yes, I have a point :). I looked outside yesterday and relayed to my sister we got about 2in of snow (she lives in the desert and likes to make me feel like a dope for living where there's snow). Just for giggles, I measured it.
Guess what?
It wasn't 2in of snow.
It was 4.5in of snow.
125% more than I thought I saw.
Eh, but it's just snow, right?
Right.
What if that was, sayyyyy... pecans? Blueberries? A burger? What if I'm watching my weight and carbs? How would this be affected? Say I grab a handful of pecans. I'm thinking yeh, that's just a little snack. Hell, it doesn't even take the edge off. I could eat that whole bag... but I won't. That would be BAD. But a quick handful – what, maybe two tablespoons worth? How bad can that be?

Perceptions – Pecans: 2 tbsp chopped – 85 calories. NOT BAD!! My hand isn't that big, after all, I'm a Hobbit.
REALITY – Pecans: ONE CUP! 684 calories! That's 1/3 of all the food I can eat today!!!!!!

What about some blueberries, you know, they are ok to have occasionally, right? Toss a few into my protein pancakes that don't suck for variety :).

Perception – Blueberries: 2 tbsp 3g carbs. I can handle that. Wait. That's about 8 berries, that's only one per pancake. Seriously??? That can't be right, I'll add a few more.
REALITY – Blueberries: 1/2 cup (about 30 berries or 5 per pancake) 12g CARBS. HALF YOUR CARBS FOR THE DAY JUST IN BERRIES!

Ok. So, you might be thinking 'well, that's just those few things,' but it's not. I would do this all day, I bet you do too. Think about it.
It adds up.
FAST.
Next thing you know, you're waaayyyy over your calories, fats, and carbs.
Gee, why did I 'stall???'
YOU DIDN'T
You over-ate.

Today in one of our groups, we had a thread going on this very subject. I posted up this pic of ONE chicken breast I pulled from our freezer and asked people to guess how many servings it is. The first guess was one or two, upgraded to 3. It's actually 8.5 servings. 29.333 oz. 969 calories, 204g of protein. 22g fat.

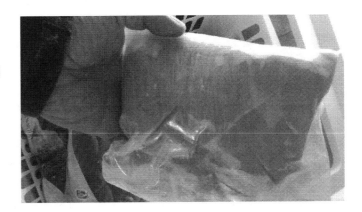

An actual serving of chicken breast is 3.5oz uncooked which comes out to about 3oz cooked if not pre-brined. I think I made my point or at least I hope so.

Soooo, what is the solution??

The opposite of what we tell people to measure their progress:

Use.

A.

Scale.

They aren't expensive, you can find a decent electronic one for under $13. We have one that we use daily, cost $11. Ok, so $11 for a scale when you can use that money for food instead? Yes. Your success and health could depend on it. Look at it this way, would it be worth it for you to spend $11 if it can help you get off medication? Feel better? Look better? Do it.

Here's another reason you should have a scale: baking.

As a foodie, I do post all my recipes in standard baking measurements because honestly, it seems that grams confuse people while the archaic cup and\or teaspoon makes perfect sense. Here's the thing... when I make my recipes for myself, I don't use the old-school measurements. I use grams. I then convert them all for you to volume measurements because that's what people want. There's a problem with that... Volume isn't accurate. If a recipe doesn't come out, I read where people say they used the same ingredients, they're fresh, and they measured exactly. Exactly... what? For example, I say '1/4 cup coconut flour.' There's MANY variables to that such has the brand, how fine it is, how packed it is, is it to the top of the cup? A little higher? A little lower? Is your cup the same exact size as mine? I'm going to bet it isn't. How do I know this? I have 4 different individual 1/4 cup measuring cups PLUS 3 multi-cup measures that have 1/4 marks.

None of Them Are EXACTLY THE SAME. Now, maybe we're only talking a 1/4 of tsp difference. Or maybe we're talking a teaspoon or more. Why is that a big deal? Say with coconut flour, for each extra teaspoon in a recipe, it needs AT LEAST an extra tablespoon of liquid. So, either you are going to be too dry, too wet, or the balance of the whole recipe just got thrown off...and that's with just one ingredient!

Or even worse, take concentrated stevia. Now, stevia is SUPER SWEET. How sweet? One pound of stevia has the same sweetness as 675 pounds of sugar or Sukrin. THAT'S REALLY SWEET.... and not in the good way if overdone.

How hard is it to overdo it?

Not hard at all.

This is one tsp of stevia concentrate, equal to 1 cup of sugar. The same measurement is equal to 1.5 cups of sugar when packed. Wild, huh?? One is 1 and a half times sweeter than the other. We just went from a tasty cake to one that will make your lips pucker.

KETO LIGHT OR DARK 'CORN' SYRUP. YUP. NO CARBS. NO CALS

You must now how frustrating it is to be getting ready to ketofy a recipe and see this:

Light Corn Syrup.

Like there isn't anything more ANTI-KETO than this. Sugar from CORN. WTH? So, it's there as a sweetener AND as a thickening\texture agent. Crap. Yeh, you could use a syrup from one of the commercial houses but 1) they are not cheap and 2) if you have a sensitivity to sugar alcohols (like we do), 3/4 cup of sweet syrup out of a bottle is going to be not so sweet 1-3 days in the bathroom. I'll pass. I am about to make a pecan pie for Thanksgiving and I want it to be as close to traditional as possible. That means...corn syrup. Or not. Nope. How about a simple recipe that will replace this sweet nectar with something that is ZERO CARBS and ZERO calories...and only costs pennies to make? Interested? Good.

Time=15mins

Ingredients (light 'corn' syrup):

- 3/4 cup water
- 1 cup (or equivalent) of your favorite sweetener
- 1/4 tsp butter extract
- 1/4 tsp vanilla extract
- 3/4 tsp Xanthan Gum

Ingredients (dark 'corn' syrup):

- 3/4 cup water
- 1 cup (or equivalent) of your favorite sweetener
- 1/4 tsp butter extract
- 1 tsp vanilla extract
- 1/2 tsp maple extract
- 3/4 tsp Xanthan Gum

The process is dead simple and the same for both. Pour the water into a bowl. Microwave on high for two minutes. Quickly whisk in your sweetener until completely dissolved. Nuke for another 30 seconds. Add extracts. Whisk. Sprinkle xanthan gum on the top while whisking until all of it is incorporated. It should start getting thick as you whisk. Let cool to room temp, it will be the right consistency for syrup as well as damn close on flavor. Use like you would corn syrup in pies and other recipes.

THE HOLY GRAIL (OK, SO THAT MIGHT BE STRETCHING IT A LITTLE) KETO SWEETENED CONDENSED MILK!

YES!! You can do all those recipes that call for this like PUMPKIN PIE, 5 LAYER BARS, or hell, just dump it in your coffee for a sweet treat.

Servings=16
Time=30mins

Ingredients:

- 1 14 oz. can of unsweetened coconut milk
- 3 tbsp. heavy cream
- 1/3 cup sweetener
- 2 tbsp. butter
- 1/2 tsp Xanthan Gum Powder

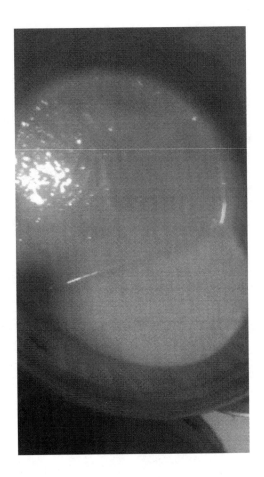

Heat the coconut milk and cream in a sauce pan on medium heat, whisking occasionally until it starts to bubble. Once bubbling, add the butter and whisk in. Once butter is combined, add the sweetener a little at a time, constantly whisking so it doesn't clump up. Continue to heat and whisk while bubbling, about 15 minutes or so until it starts to thicken and goes from white to a pale amber. Shut off heat, whisk in xanthan gum. Let sit for about 5 minutes on the burner with burner off, whisking every 30 seconds or so. Remove from stove and pour into container. Let cool completely.

Nutritional info (1/16th of total – based off my ingredients, check yours!):
Calories: 63, Fat: 5g, Protein: 5g, Carbs: 3, Fiber: 1, Net Carbs: 2

CHOCOLATE OR BUTTERSCOTCH CHIPS. OH YES

Another result of the 5-layer bars. Chocolate and butterscotch chips, good for cookies too!!

Alternatively, if you can find sugar-free, low carb chips of each, you could use those. I've had zero luck in our area so kitchen Hobbit is my solution :).

Servings=16
Time=30mins

Chocolate:

1/3 cup Coconut Oil
2 tbsp. cocoa powder
1/3 cup granulated sweetener
2 tbsp heavy cream

Melt the coconut oil in the microwave until completely liquid. Wisk in the cocoa powder until smooth. Add stevia slowly while whisking until smooth. Add heavy cream, whisk until incorporated. Let sit for a couple of minutes, then whisk again. Get out what you are going to use for a mold and pour into the mold. I use a silicon bread pan but anything will work – muffin tins, bar molds, even ice cube trays. Put the mold in the freezer.

Butterscotch chunks:

1/3 cup butter
1/4 cup Coconut Oil
1 tsp vanilla extract
1/2 tsp almond extract
1/3 cup granulated sweetener
2 tbsp. heavy cream

Melt the butter in a sauce pan over low to med-low heat. You want it to be lightly bubbling. What we want to do is brown the butter slightly but not burn it. Stir often until it darkens some, about the color of caramel. Remove from heat, whisk in the rest of the ingredients until well combined. Immediately pour into your mold, then put in freezer with the chocolate. While you're at it, if you are going to chop the chocolate and butterscotch up instead of hoping you can smash into pieces, put your knife in the freezer too. Yeh. Do it. It will keep the chunks from sticking to the knife when you prep it. You're welcome ☺.

Nutritional info chocolate chips (1/16th of a batch – based off my ingredients, check yours!): Calories: 48, Fat: 5g, Protein: 0g, Carbs: 0.1, Fiber: 0, Net Carbs: 0.1

Nutritional info butterscotch chips (1/16th of a batch – based off my ingredients, check yours!): Calories: 38, Fat: 4g, Protein: 1g, Carbs: 0, Fiber: 0, Net Carbs: 0

3 INGREDIENT, KETO CARAMEL!!

3 Ingredient salted (or not) Keto Caramel!!!

I've been struggling with this one for a while. I love some gooey, sweet and salty sauce on my baked goods and ice cream, but if you buy it, it is LOADED with sugar and carbs. I've tried countless different ideas I've found online and each one has failed in some way – most of the time I get a layer of clear fat on top of what ends up being hard candy (so not a complete failure, lol) and that just won't cut it. FINALLY, I found the solution and it's soooo easy!!

Servings=12
Time=30mins
Ingredients:

1/4 cup butter (salted if you like salted caramel, or unsalted if not)
1/4 cup heavy cream
1 cup sweetener

Melt the butter over med-low heat in a non-stick pan. On my stove, 2.5 is is med-low, you might have to adjust accordingly but I hate these recipes that give 'med-low' when all you have is numbers:(. Stir frequently so it doesn't burn, you are looking for it to get to a mid-amber color. Once this happens, remove it from the heat and pour into a bowl. Quickly whisk in the cream, while whisking, add the sweetener slowly. Whisk for about another 15 seconds, then pour back into the pan and return to the heat. Stir this constantly, making sure it doesn't burn. Wait for it to thicken some, not really thick, but thick enough that is ooooozes off whatever you stir with instead of dripping off like water. Remove from heat. Pour BACK into the bowl. Whisk vigorously for another minute or so, then either use it or pour into a glass container and refrigerate. Done!!

Makes 1/4 cup of caramel. Nutrition information based off 1 TBSP of finished product.

NUTRITION COUNT PER serving: Calories: 153, Protein: 0g, Fat: 17 g, Carbs: 1g, Fiber: 0g, NET CARBS: 1g

MAKE YOUR OWN ALMOND AND COCONUT MILK, THE EASY WAY

Ever get the urge for a recipe, something you just must have, then reach into the cupboard and realize you used your last can of coconut milk 2 days ago? Or open the fridge and find that someone has used all your almond milk to make chocolate milk? Crap! Now, you could swap in half heavy cream and half water, but what if you don't have any of that or are dairy sensitive? A trip to the store. At 9:30 at night. And it's snowing. A LOT.

There's a few ways you can go about this, typically homemade coconut milk is done by soaking shredded coconut overnight, then pounding the hell out of it in a blender or food processor, straining and squeezing it for every drop. Same with almond milk, soaking almonds overnight, rinsing, adding water again, processing, squeezing, dripping, frustrating. Plus, there's that whole 'overnight' thing. Might as well go to the store! Oh, and that stuff in the cartons? About 5% of the good stuff, the rest is water and fillers. The cans are better, but still usually have some added stuff you might not want. Plus, that stuff isn't exactly cheap. There's an easier way to do this. Much easier. And faster. How does 5 minutes sound? Or less if you have a Blendtec or Vitamix? Yeh, I thought you'd like that :). I bet you have some coconut flour or almond flour, right? And a faucet? You can do this and unlike the traditional homemade stuff, you can tell exactly what your macros are because...

NO STRAINING.
NO SQUEEZING.
NO #$!@#$ DRIPPING!!
NO GUESSING WHAT IS IN IT

Curious?

This has to be the easiest Hobbit process out there, but it's not the Hobbit's. The Lady figured this one out. Sooooo simple. So very simple. Ready?

Ingredients:

1 part coconut flour or almond flour**
3 parts water**
1 pinch xanthan or guar gum (to stabilize and prevent separation)

** For example, you need 1 cup of coconut milk, use 1/4 cup coconut flour and 3/4 cups water. Nutritional value equal to 1/4 cup coconut flour. For high-fat, creamy coconut milk, add 1 tbsp. coconut oil before blending.

Put everything into a food processor with the chopping blade or Blendtec\Vitamix blender. Crank it up on high for 30 seconds in a Blendtec\Vitamix, 5 minutes with a household processor or blender. Done. Drink or use in a recipe. Will stay good for 4-5 days in the fridge if sealed in a jar.

Nutritional information: varies

KABOCHA - THE LOW-CARB ALTERNATIVE TO SWEET POTATOES AND SQUASH. YES. REALLY! FALL HERE I COME!

Kabocha, the Japanese pumpkin, not to be confused with Kabota, the Japanese tractor company :). I happen to LOVE squash, especially now when there's a bite in the air here in New England and we are getting ready for fall and winter. Time for comfort foods...but how in the hell do we do comfort foods on low-carb? With the Kabocha, it just got a little easier!

The Kabocha is packed with micro nutrients – especially high in Vitamin A as well as C, some B vitamins, iron, and calcium. The skin is edible and packed with fiber, the 'meat' soft like a butternut but bright orange and sweet like a sweet potato. It's low water so when roasted, it doesn't get all runny and crap like traditional squashes. But, the beauty of Kabocha over its cousins is LOW CALORIE AND LOW CARB! Seriously! Now, the nutritional info on this appears to be all over the map, but consensus puts the calories at about 60 per 100g (about 1 cup) with carbs being 7, fiber being 1 for a net of 6 (not including the skin which is all fiber carbs). Compare that to butternut at 16g of carbs or sweet potato at 28, and you can see why I love this stuff.

Picking out kabocha at the store can be a little difficult if you don't know what you're looking for. You will normally find it in the same bin as butterCUP squash, they look similar but are two completely different animals. I've even seen kabocha with a 'buttercup' sticker and 'buttercup' with a kabocha sticker, so if you learn the visual cues, you can get the right one every time.

Buttercup has a traditional stem, smaller and softer. It has a raised, knobby base, sometimes multi-level 'button' on the bottom. You don't want those. Nope. You want to get the ones with this big, knarly stem at the top that looks more like tree branch than a squash stem, and the button on the bottom is small or non-existent. If the button is big, raised in a couple of levels, or not smooth at all, pass on it. That's a buttercup and not kabocha.

A 2lb kabocha will yield about 4 cups cooked meat, including skin, perfect for feeding a family of 4. Most kabochas that I find are in the 1.75-2.25lb range. If you can find ones about the size of a softball, those are PERFECT for the low-carber to have as they are about 100g (1 cup) of squash and only 6 net carbs! You cook kabocha just like you would any other squash, but because of its sweeter meat, you have more options – cinnamon and butter makes a nice, sweet side dish for roasted pork, or salt and pepper it to go with chicken or turkey. One of my favorite ways to prepare it is as a chili bowl, filling the cavity where the seeds lived with homemade, low-carb chili. You can cube and roast it, slice and roast it, or just cut it in half, flip upside down on a baking sheet, and bake for about 45-1 hour or until it is soft when pushing on the skin. Roast up one up, when it's cooled, break it up into 1/2 cup servings and freeze

Basic kabocha breakfast cereal:

1 scoop unflavored (or flavored if don't mind a few extra carbs – Dynamize Elite Whey Vanilla has 2 net carbs) protein powder
1/2 cup cooked kabocha squash
1/4 cup walnuts or pecans, chopped
1/4 cup water
Cinnamon to taste

Mix the protein powder and kabocha up roughly until combined, add water and mix until not quite smooth. Nuke in microwave until hot – 30-45 seconds. Top with cinnamon and nuts. EAT!

MUST HAVES AND NICE-TO-HAVES FOR KETO COOKING AND BAKING

I thought I'd share my 'must haves' and 'nice to haves' for cooking. I'll skip over the meats and veggies since most of that is personal preference (although I do love kabocha and I keep all my bacon grease) and focus on 'cupboard' items that I've found have helped with this WOE\WOC. Most of these are not brand-specific. I do use certain brands due to personal or financial reasons, but in general, these are available in good quality from a variety of sources so pick the ones that suit your budget and social needs.

Must haves:

coconut flour (like Nutiva if buying, but most of the time we make ours as a byproduct of making coconut milk)
almond flour (or almonds and a good blender\processor, make milk, dry the pulp for flour)
coconut oil (both refined and unrefined)
golden flax meal
xanthan or guar gum
flavored extracts
cocoa powder (unsweetened)
baker's chocolate (unsweetened)
almond milk (avoid the flavored type)
coconut milk (avoid the flavored type)
butter (salted and unsalted)
sweetener of your choice (stevia, erythritol, etc.) – I like Stevia
psyllium husks or husk powder (found in the pharmacy by the Metamucil)
whey protein isolate (not concentrate or blends)

Nice to haves:

unsweetened shredded coconut
unsweetened flaked coconut (I get regular and toasted)
pepitas (pumpkin seeds, I roast then process into flour, found in the bulk nut\granola\rice bins at the grocery store)
coconut butter
hemp seeds
chia seeds
arrowroot powder (used in low quantities)
miso paste
hemp seed oil
MCT oil
pea protein

SWEETENER, BULKING\BINDING AGENT, LIQUIDS, AND FLOUR CONVERSIONS

Sweetener, bulking\binding agent, liquids, and flour conversions

One of the most common questions we get on Facebook and the blog is: "how much of xyz should I use instead abc?" Let's hit a few of the big ones.

Sweeteners vs Sugar

- Stevia powdered concentrate – 1/32 tsp = 1 tsp sugar, ¾ tsp = 1 cup sugar
- Stevia liquid drops – 6 drops = 1 tsp sugar, 96 drops = 1 cup sugar.
- Stevia BULK – 1 tsp\cup = 1 tsp\cup sugar.
- Erythritol\Xylitol\Sucralose – 1.3 cups = 1 cup sugar

Keto Flours vs Wheat Flour

- Almond Flour\Meal – 1 cup = 1 cup white flour, 1.3 cups whole wheat flour
- Pepita Flour\Meal – 1 cup = 1 cup white flour, 1.3 cups whole wheat flour
- Coconut flour – 1 cup = 2 cups white flour, 2.6 whole wheat flour (plus increase liquid by half)
- Protein Powder = ¼ cup = 1 cup white flour, 1.3 cups whole wheat flour

Binders\Egg replacers vs Eggs

- Flax Meal – 1 tsp flax + 3 tbsp = 1 egg
- Psyllium husk\powder = 1 tsp psyllium + 3 tbsp water = 1 egg

Thickening Agents vs Corn Starch

- Xanthan Gum – ½ tsp = 3 tbsp cornstarch
- Guar Gum – 1 tsp = 3 tbsp cornstarch

Liquids vs Whole Milk

- Heavy Cream to Milk – ¼ cup HWC + ¾ water = 1 cup whole milk
- Protein Powder to Milk – 1 tbsp + 1cup water = 1 cup whole milk

INGREDIENTS WE LIKE TO USE

Below is a list of ingredients we like to use. This doesn't mean you must use these brands for best results. These are the ones we have tried and had success with, as there are many other brands out there, this is a recommended list and not all-inclusive :).

Protein Powders:

- Dymatize Flavored Whey Isolate , I use this one often
- NOW Foods Sports Whey Protein Natural Vanilla
- Isopure Whey Protein Isolate, Unflavored
- Now Foods Organic Whey Protein, Natural Unflavored
- Piping Rock Unflavored Whey Protein
- Muscle Blend Unflavored Whey Isolate (Bulk packaging)
- Now Foods Micellar Casein Powder
- Hardcore Micellar Casein
- Now Foods Pea Protein

Inulin

- Inulin Fiber (Chicory Root) – LC Foods

Eggs, replacers, binders, and thickening agents

- Dried Egg Whites
- Egg Yolk Powder
- Xanthan Gum Powder
- Psyllium Husk
- Guar Gum Powder
- Golden Flax Seeds
- Ground Flax Meal

Flours

- Organic Coconut Flour
- Almond Flour

Oils

- Refined Coconut Oil
- Virgin Coconut Oil
- Nutiva Organic Hempseed Oil
- Nutiva Red Palm Shortening

COMMON KETOFIED RECIPE INGREDIENTS EXPLAINED

1. Psyllium Husk – is a laxative, lol. In baking, it is a binding and leavening agent. It also has a 'flex' property which makes it useful in quick breads to help hold structure or in a cake that needs to bend and not crack (like a pumpkin roll). Some swear by it in bread, I swear at it. I do love it for tortillas:)
2. Micellar Casein – helps with structure as well as texture. Has a slightly sweet flavor. Can cause inflammation if sensitive to dairy products.
3. Isopure Whey Protein Isolate, Unflavored – helps with structure as well as texture, can also help with flavor, adds sweetness if a flavored one is used, adds protein.
4. Xanthan Gum Powder – thickening and binding agent, think corn starch on steroids
5. Inulin Fiber (Chicory Root) – The inulin can do what starch does which is creating a 3-dimensional structure after hydrated. It also makes a polymer with the protein powders to create a network structure that stay rigid after baking, especially with casein isolate since casein is the one that makes mozzarella extendable but can't capture gas produced by the leavening agent, such as baking powder, baking soda, or yeast on proofing (fermentation). So, the inulin will become the gas pockets and the casein will be the web that holding those gas pockets together, Then… Boom! Gluten + Starch properties. has been KETOFIED. Inulin is a resistant starch – the starches feed intestinal biomes, not you.
6. Nutritional yeast – high fiber ingredient that has a distinct 'cheese' taste.
7. Chia – high fiber, high omega-3 seed, can be used as thickening agent in baked goods, makes cereal with milk (let sit overnight in coconut or almond milk).
8. Guar Gum Powder – thickening agent, properties between xanthan and corn starch
9. Egg Yolk Powder.. is the bulk ingredients that gives melt in your mouth sensation
And Dried Egg Whites.. It does what an egg white does, but without the liquid that can make a dough or batter recipe became soggy.

Other great things to have on hand:

Refined Coconut Oil: neutral taste, not all the nutrition you will get in Virgin Coconut Oil but also no coconut taste, great for frying, ballistic coffee, and baking.

Virgin Coconut Oil – has a distinct coconut taste, but is packed with all the good stuff. Use it in fat bombs, ballistic coffee, or any recipe where the taste will complement the other ingredients.

Golden Flax Seeds High in fiber and Omega-3 fatty acids. A mild nutty taste, it works as an egg replacer when used as a binder. Also, makes good breakfast cereal addition and even sprinkled on a salad.

Pea Protein – Vegetarian replacement for whey isolate or just as an addition to it. Distinctively stronger tasting than unflavored whey – not 'pea' tasting, more of a dusky mild taste – it works excellent in baking as it is lighter than whey, binds well, and tends to be less gritty in the final product. One of my favorites to use in **Iron Giant** – specifically the **chips** and **crab rangoons**.

Coconut Butter – one of my favorite guilty pleasures. A creamy, mildly pasty, spreadable 'butter' of coconut. Can be used in many situations as a topping like peanut or almond butter, as well as on waffles and pancakes. I like to use in in **coconut cookies** to take them to the next level :).

THE IRON GIANT DOUGH - THE BASICS

Whoa. What a crazy couple of days. All this started with trying to make pasta. EPIC FAIL. The results were like trying to eat rubber bands...with less flavor. I was bummed. I was hoping I could pull it off. I had strips and strips of hand-cut 'noodle' that were useless. Or not. In steps The Lady. "Hey, you should fry those and see what happens instead of throwing them out right away. You can always throw them out later." BRILLIANT.
See, she's the brains of the operation, I'm just the hack.
Humming The Pet Shop Boys

So, I heated up some oil in a pan and figured I'd give it a shot. The results? MINDBLOWING. In one quick step I had crispy Asian wide noodles. The next thing I knew, I had crispy chow mein noodles. A few other ingredients and BANG!!

KEETOS!
Yes. Keto Cheetos.
They are a thing.
Oh yes, quite a thing.
I'll be posting up those recipes soon, I want to get the basic dough up for you because it has some rest time involved.

This post covers the basic dough needed. You can refer to it in any place in this book you see "Iron Giant Dough."

Servings=4
Time=30mins prep, 120mins rest

Ingredients:

- 1/2 cup + 1/4 cup whey (or veggie!) flavored protein powder
- 1 tsp olive or Coconut Oil (melted if coconut oil)
- 1 egg

Whisk egg and oil together until frothy. Add 1/2 cup of protein powder. Mix well to combine. You will get a sticky dough. Let rest for 15 minutes. Trust me, it will look even stickier when you come back :). Dump the additional 1/4 cup of protein on top. With a rubber spatula, mix and fold until you have a kinda dry dough with some powder still on the outside. Using your hands, knead the dough for about 5 minutes until you get a smooth, not sticky ball of dough. If the ball still sticks to your hands, put back in the bowl and roll it around until it is covered in protein again and repeat the kneading. Cover in plastic wrap, store in the fridge for at least an hour before using.

Nutritional information (based off my ingredients, double-check!): Calories: 103, Fat: 2g, Protein: 20g, Carbs: 0g, Fiber: 0g, Net Carbs

WHATCHA COOKIN', GOOD LOOKIN'?

COMFORT FOODS

SAVORY PUMPKIN (KABOCHA!!) SOUP - LOW CARB! OH, I LOVE THIS WOE!

Ingredients (makes three servings):

2 cups chicken stock (I used homemade, you can do bullion or canned\boxed, but beware, most commercial stock has carbs
1.5 cups cooked kabocha squash
2 tbsp. heavy cream
1 tsp turmeric
1.5 tsp tarragon
1 tsp salt
1/2 tsp white (or black) pepper
1 tsp garlic powder
2 tsp onion, diced

Cook up the onion quick until soft. Put in bottom of crockpot. Put everything else in a blender and blend until smooth. Dump in crockpot. Set on low. Walk away and forget about it for 8 hours.

Serve with ribs if you are me, otherwise, serve with anything that is savory.

Nutritional info for soup: Calories: 82, Fat: 7, Protein: 7, Carbs: 5, Fiber: 1, Net Carbs: 4

RIBS! I WANT MY BABY BACK, BABY BACK, BABY BACK

The Hobbit's Rib Rub:

1.5 tsp salt
1.0 tsp white (or black) pepper
1.5 tsp paprika
1.0 tsp chili powder
1.5 tsp garlic powder
1.5 tsp onion powder
0.5 tsp nutmeg

Dump all this in a bowl and whisk it up to mix well. You want to make sure all the clumps are broken up and the salt is distributed evenly. Get out your ribs. Dump the mixture evenly along the length of the glorious meat, then take your hand and rub it in well. The fats on the meat will warm from your hand and make this almost a paste. This is good. Once you have it all evenly covered, wrap the ribs up in plastic and toss in the fridge overnight. Next day, get your ribs out. Can you smell it? Doesn't it already smell AWESOME? Preheat your oven to 425F. Yes. That high. Trust me on this one. Get out a baking pan (one with a raised lip is recommended unless you like cleaning the oven. I DON'T!). Line it with parchment or silicon baking mat. Put your ribs on it. Place in your oven for 15 minutes. You should be able to hear them start to sizzle and crackle, then turn down to 325F for about an hour or more. I know, not precise but it depends on the size and cut of your ribs. When you check them at about an hour, look at the ends of the bones. Are the starting to discolor? Has the meat pulled about a half-inch up them? If so, they are ready to grill! If not, leave them in until this happens. Remove them from the oven when ready, then toss them on the grill – right side up for 5 minutes to get the fats under the bones moving and dripping. You want that fat ooooozing out and hitting the grill to add a little smokey taste to the ribs when you flip them. Now flip. Cook upside down for about 5 minutes, checking to make sure they don't burn (Note: Mine caught on fire briefly, this is why The Lady doesn't let me play with matches). Repeat this one more time – 2 minutes per side. Remove from grill and let rest for 5 minutes before cutting and serving. Enjoy them with cauli-tots, mashed cauliflower, savory Kabocha soup, or grilled veggies. Trust me on this one, you will never miss ribs plastered with BBQ sauce. Ever.

HOW ABOUT SOME OVEN-FRIED STUFF PORK CHOPS AND BROCCOLI KETO QUICHE?

For the pork chops (makes 2 servings):
Oven-fried stuffed pork chops with broccoli quiche
Servings=2
Time=30mins

2 4-5oz pork chops of your choice
2 tbsp. feta cheese
1/4 cup chopped spinach
2oz shredded cheddar cheese
1/4 cup pork rinds (ground)
1 egg, whisked

Pre-heat oven to 350F.

Slice the pork chops open to make a pocket. Mix the feta, cheddar and spinach together in a bowl, then stuff into the cavity in the chops. Take a toothpick and 'sew' the opening closed. Dredge the chops in the egg, covering all sides, press into the pork rinds, also covering all sides. Place in baking pan lined with parchment, silicon mat or lightly greased. Set aside while making the quiche.

Quiche (makes two servings):

1/4 cup broccoli (or cauliflower if you choose) cooked and diced

1/4 cup, sliced mushrooms (optional)

2 tbsp Onion

2 tbsp diced peppers

2 Tbsp pork rinds (or coconut flour)

0.25 oz Cheese – Mozzarella

2 Large Egg

1/2 tsp garlic powder

1/2 tsp onion powder

1/4 tsp red pepper flakes

Cook up the onions, peppers and mushrooms in a pan until mushrooms are soft. Remove, then stir into the broccoli. Whip the eggs up, then add the pork rinds, onion powder, garlic powder, cheese, and pepper flakes. Stir until combined. Split the veggie mix between two small spring pans (or ramekins, muffin tins or put it all in small baking dish). Pour egg mixture over veggies, then give one or two stirs to combine. Put both the chops and the quiche in the oven on the top rack. Bake for 15-20 minutes or until the chops start to brown and the quiche browns around the edges. Remove from oven and let rest for 5 minutes. Plate up and serve! Enjoy date night, I know we will

Nutrition info (1 5oz stuffed pork loin chop): Calories: 380, Fat: 23g, Protein: 42, Carbs: 2, Fiber: 1, Net Carbs: 1

Nutrition info (1 serving of quiche with rinds and mushrooms): Calories: 156, Fat: 9g, Protein: 13.1, Carbs: 3.3g, Fiber: 1g, Net carbs: 2.3g

HOBBIT SAUSAGE AND GRAVY BISCUIT CASSEROLE

Hobbit Sausage and Gravy Biscuit Casserole

Servings=6

Time=45 min

Ingredients for Filling:

1lb breakfast sausage
1/4 cup heavy cream
3 tbsp. water
2 tbsp. butter
2 tbsp. diced onion
1 tsp black pepper
1 tsp salt
1 tsp minced garlic or garlic powder
1/4 tsp xanthan gum (or 1/2 tsp guar gum)

Preheat oven to 325F

Preheat a skillet (use a cast iron if you have one for best results) on med-high heat. Melt butter, then add sausage. Brown the sausage, breaking it up into small pieces. Add spices and onion, continue to saute until onions softened. Add cream and water, mix well into sausage mixture. When liquid starts to steam, sprinkle gum over liquid and mix very thoroughly. Turn off heat, dump into a casserole or large bread pan.

Ingredients for Top:

1/4 cup almond flour
2 tbsp. Pea Protein
2 tbsp. whey isolate
4 tbsp. butter. melted
3 eggs
1/2 tsp xanthan gum
1/2 tsp salt
1 tbsp. apple cider vinegar
1/2 tbsp. baking powder
1 tsp baking soda
2 tbsp. flax meal
1/2 tsp black pepper

Dead. Simple. So simple it should be illegal. Dump everything in the blender, putting in the vinegar first, the baking powder and soda in last, Pulse until smooth. Pour\scrape on top of the sausage mixture. Using a rubber spatula or spoon, smooth out the top and then immediately place in the oven for 30 minutes or until the top is a nice brown. Remove. Let cool for a few minutes. Slice and serve.

Nutritional information for Complete slice: Calories each 453 slice, Fat 40g, Protein 20G, Carbs 5g, Fiber 2g, Net Carbs 3g

HOBBIT'S PORK PIE WITH A CRUST THAT IS ACTUALLY A CRUST!

Hobbit's Pork Pie with a crust that is actually a crust!
Servings=6
Time=60 min

Ingredients for crust:

1/2 cup almond meal
1/4 cup flax meal
1 egg (room temp)
4 tbsp. butter, melted
1/2 tsp salt
2 tbsp. Unflavored Whey Protein Isolate

Ingredients for Filling:

1lb breakfast sausage (learn to make your own here)
1/4 cup heavy cream
3 tbsp. water
2 tbsp. butter
2 tbsp. diced onion
1 tsp black pepper
1 tsp salt
1 tsp minced garlic or garlic powder
1/4 tsp xanthan gum (or 1/2 tsp guar gum)

To make the crust:

Whisk melted butter and egg until very smooth. Add the rest of the ingredients, working them in until you have a solid dough. Put in the fridge for 15 minutes while you prepare the filling. Preheat a skillet (use a cast iron if you have one for best results) on med-high heat. Melt butter, then add sausage. Brown the sausage, breaking it up into small pieces. Add spices and onion, continue to saute until onions softened. Add cream and water, mix well into sausage mixture. When liquid starts to steam, sprinkle gum over liquid and mix very thoroughly. Turn off heat, leave on burner to gently cool while finishing crust.

Preheat oven to 350F

Remove dough from fridge. Split into two balls, one slightly larger than the other. Take the larger ball and place between two silicon mats or parchment paper sheets. Roll into a rough circle to fit your pie plate, with enough to go up the sides. Remove top sheet, flip dough over into pie plate, press down to fill plate, remove other sheet. Roll out other ball to fit as top crust. Spoon all the sausage mixture into bottom crust, leveling out so it fills it completely. Place top crust on pie, crimp edges. Put a few small slices in center of top crust so steam can escape. Place in oven for 30 minutes or until top crust is a deep golden brown. Remove and let stand 5 minutes before slicing and serving.

Nutritional information for crust: Calories each 185 slice, Fat 16g, Protein 7G, Carbs 4g, Fiber 2g, Net Carbs 2g
Nutritional information for Filling: Calories each 268 slice, Fat 24g, Protein 13G, Carbs 1g, Fiber 0g, Net Carbs 1g
Nutritional information for Complete slice: Calories each 453 slice, Fat 40g, Protein 20G, Carbs 5g, Fiber 2g, Net Carbs 3g

KETO CHICKEN POT PIE? WHY, YES, THANK YOU, I THINK I WILL :)

Hobbit's Keto Chicken Pot Pie
Servings=6
Time=60mins

- My Fathead pie crust (See Pastry section in this book for recipe)
- 1 lb. cubed chicken breast
- 1 bag (16oz) of stir fry frozen veggies (or any veggies you like)
- 1 cup water
- 1 tsp salt
- 1/2 tsp Xanthan Gum Powder
- 1 tsp poultry seasoning

Preheat oven to 350F

Make the crust, if you need a video walkthrough on it, I have one on my YouTube channel which you can access from the website, so you can see how it is made, then just plop into a pie or casserole dish. Brown the chicken in a skillet. While it is browning, nuke your veggies until about half cooked – not quite soft, not frozen :). When the meat is browned, add the veggies. Stir a few times, then spoon veggies and chicken into the crust. Pour off the drippings from the skillet into a bowl, add the water and seasonings, whisk. Once combined, sprinkle the xanthan gum in while whisking. Pour the 'gravy' over the veggies and chicken, top with top crust. Bake in the oven for 30 minutes or until the top is brown. Let rest 4 minutes before slicing and serving.

Nutritional information (based off my ingredients, double-check!): Calories: 553, Fat: 41g, Protein: 39g, Carbs: 9g, Fiber: 4g, Net Carbs: 5g

PIZZA, STROMBOLI, AND PASTA, OH MY!

FATHEAD FOR THE WIN! STROMBOLI (AND BASIC FATHEAD RECIPE)

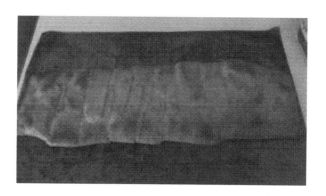

Fathead stromboli!
Servings=4
Time=30mins

1.50 Cup, 2% Milk Natural Reduced Fat Shredded Mozzarella Cheese
4.00 tbsp(s), Almond Meal
3.00 tbsp(s), Coconut flour
1.00 Large Egg
4.00 tbsp(s), Butter – Salted (melted)
2 oz pepperoni
2.00 oz(s), Cheese, provolone

First, let's make the crust. Mix all the dry ingredients in a bowl, then add one well-beaten egg and butter. Stir until well combined. Set aside. In a separate bowl, melt your mozzarella in the microwave on 30-40% (depending on power) for 2 minutes, stirring and blending after 1 minute. Stir again to make sure it is good and blended.

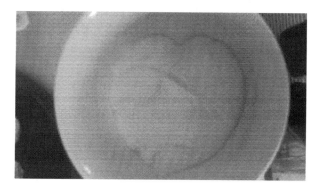

Immediately add this to the rest of the mixture and fold it over and over to incorporate as much of the cheese with the others.

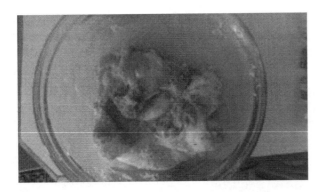

Nuke it for 10 seconds on high, then fold\knead it until you have a uniform color with no obvious 'cheesy' spots. Repeat the nuke if you if it starts getting hard to work the cheese. Once you have it uniform, roll it into a ball, then nuke one more time for 10 seconds on high. Now preheat oven to 425F, Place it between two sheets of parchment or silicon baking mats. Press down with your hand to flatten it out as much as you can, then using a rolling pin to roll out the dough in a large rectangle of uniform thickness (about the thickness of two quarters stacked). Trim if needed. Starting at one end, make slices down each side about 1/3rd of the way across. This will let you braid\wrap the dough across the top of the filling. Lay the pepperoni up the center of the dough, topping with the cheese. Fold the the dough over the top, alternating sides all the way down, sealing the ends. Place on baking sheet and pop in the oven for about 20 minutes or until the crust browns up nicely. Remove, let cool for a few minutes, then slice up and serve!!

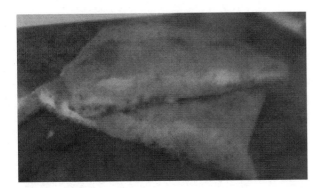

Nutritional information (based off my ingredients, double-check!): Calories: 375, Fat: 29g, Protein: 22g, Carbs: 9g, Fiber: 4g, Net Carbs: 5g

FATHEAD MADE SIMPLE (WITH CHICKEN-BACON-RANCH STROMBOLI)!

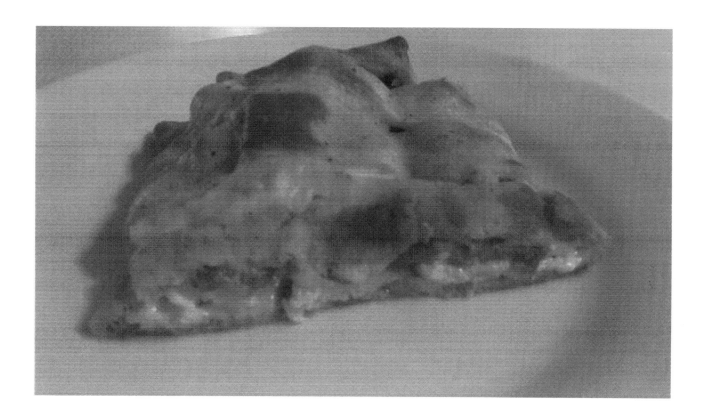

Fathead with Chicken-Bacon Ranch Filling

Servings=4

Time=30mins

Crust: Use Fathead process from *Fathead for the Win!* In this section. Replace half of the butter with bacon grease.

Filling:

10.00 oz., Chicken Thighs-Boneless and Skinless – cooked (substitute cooked breast or turkey for a lower-fat result).

12.00 strips, Bacon – Fried

2.5 tbsp. Greek yogurt

3 tbsp. mayo

2 tsp onion powder

1 tsp garlic powder

1/4 tsp dill

1/4 tsp parsley

1/4 tsp chives

1/2 cup more mozzarella for filling

Preheat oven to 425F

First, make the crust. Mix all the dry ingredients in a bowl, then add one well-beaten egg and – for this recipe something a little different – BACON GREASE. Complete rest of process as described in referenced recipe. Mix the filling (outside of the cheese and meats) together in a bowl, then spread up the center of the dough. Lay the chicken and bacon along the middle of the dough, from one end to the other, on top of the filling. Top with some more shredded mozzarella (1/2 cup). Fold the dough over the top, alternating sides all the way down, sealing the ends. Place on baking sheet and pop in the oven for about 20 minutes or until the crust browns up nicely. Remove, let cool for a few minutes, then slice up,

Nutritional information (based off my ingredients, double-check!): Calories: 553, Fat: 41g, Protein: 39g, Carbs: 9g, Fiber: 4g, Net Carbs: 5g

MY VARIATION - CHICKEN BLT FATHEAD STROMBOLI

Chicken BLT Fathead Stromboli
Servings=4
Time=30mins

Crust: Use Fathead process from *Fathead for the Win!* In this section. Replace half of the butter with bacon grease.
4.00 tbsp, Mayonnaise
12.00 strips, Bacon – Fried
1/4 cup shredded lettuce
1/2 tomato (I'm using roma)
1/2 cup more mozzarella for filling

Mix the chicken in with the mayo until completely coated. Lay the bacon along the middle of the dough, from one end to the other. Spread the chicken mixture on top of the bacon, leaving about 3/4" on either end dry. Top with some more shredded mozzarella (1/2 cup). Fold the the dough over the top, alternating sides all the way down, sealing the ends. Place on baking sheet and pop in the oven for about 20 minutes or until the crust browns up nicely. Remove, let cool for a few minutes, then slice up, top with lettuce and tomato, and serve!!

Nutritional information (based off my ingredients, double-check!): Calories: 553, Fat: 41g, Protein: 39g, Carbs: 9g, Fiber: 4g, Net Carbs: 5g

NO WHEAT 'WHOLE WHEAT' PIZZA CRUST - NON-FATHEAD!!

Hobbit's No wheat 'whole wheat' pizza crust
Servings=8
Time=60 min

Ingredients:

1 eggs
2 tbsp unflavored whey isolate plus 2 tbsp for dusting
4 tsp butter
1/2 cup almond flour or meal
1/2 cup flax meal
1/2 tsp salt

Beat the eggs until smooth, then add the melted butter and beat until completely combined. I use a hand whisk for this but a fork would work just as well. Add all the dry ingredients and mix thoroughly with a spoon or rubber spatula. You should get a slightly sticky and soft dough. DO NOT USE IT YET. Place in the fridge for 30 minutes (or longer if you are prepping for another day). Once the 30 minutes are up, you should have a much firmer dough that you can work with.

PREHEAT OVEN TO 400F

Spray down your pan with cooking spray or coat it lightly with coconut\olive oil. Put the dough in the center of your pan. Work it from the center out to form the crust at the thickness and shape you desire. We like ours a little crispy and thin on the bottom, YMMV ;). Once you have it the shape you like, place it in the oven for 10-12 minutes or until the edges start to brown. Remove.

Ingredients for buffalo sauce:

1 tbsp tomato paste (no sugar added)
1 tbsp Worcestershire sauce
2 tbsp hot red pepper sauce
1 tsp crushed garlic
1 tsp onion powder
1 tsp white vinegar
2 tbsp water

Whisk until combined. Dip your chicken in it to coat once cooked. Pour remainder on crust as sauce. Add chicken, bleu cheese, and top with cheese toppings. Return to the oven for 4-6 minutes or until the cheese is how you like it. Slice and eat!.

Nutritional information: Calories each slice CRUST ONLY 158, Fat: 14g, Protein: 8, Carbs: 8, Fiber: 7, Net carbs: 1

A STROMBOLI THAT'S NOT A STROMBOLI - HOBBIT'S BISCUIT CRUST DINNER PASTRY

Servings=4
Time=30 min
Crust Ingredients:

1 lg egg
3/4 cup Almond Flour (We LOVE Anthony's for quality and price)
1/4 cup oat fiber
1 tbsps. coconut flour

1/3 cup oil of your choice (coconut, butter, olive, avocado, bacon grease, etc.)
1 tbsps. baking powder
1/2 tsp salt
1/2 tsp garlic powder
1/2 tsp onion powder
1/4 tsp baking soda
1/4 cup water, warm (whatever is "hot" out of your tap)

Preheat oven to 375F

Beat egg well in a bowl or zip it up in a blender. Add dry ingredients and mix until gravel-like texture. Add oil, mix until well combined. Add water, mix quickly and roughly to a lumpy dough. Let sit while you get out two sheets of parchment or a couple of silipats. Wet both sheets with water or a little oil to help once you get the dough rolled out to not stick as much. Dump the dough on one sheet, cover with the other, then roll out to a rough rectangle about 12" wide and 16-18" long. Remove top sheet. Run your filling up the middle, leaving about 1/2" from the ends uncovered. Lift one side of your bottom sheet up and fold the dough over the top so it is just a little past center. Carefully peel the sheet off that side (a thin spatula or butter knife can help break the edge free to make this a little easier). Repeat on the other side so it overlaps the first side slightly. Use wet fingers to seal up the top and ends. Place in the oven for 15-20 minutes or until the top starts to brown. Remove. Let cool for 5 minutes before serving (you don't want your family to complain, right? Food safety! BURNT TONGUES HURT!). Cut into 4 servings. Serve with the side of your choice. ENJOY!!

Nutritional information per serving of crust: Calories each 207 , Fat: 18g Protein: 6g, Carbs: 6g Fiber: 3g Net: 3g

HOBBIT DID A RARE THING, ACTUALLY USED FATHEAD FOR PIZZA! (HOBBIT'S MODIFIED FATHEAD RECIPE)

Hobbit's Keto Chicken Broccoli Alfredo pizza
Servings=8
Time=30 min

Crust: Use Fathead process from *Fathead for the Win!* In this section
1/4lb chicken breast or thighs
1/2 cup cooked broccoli
2 tbsps. butter

2 oz. Monterrey cheese

1/4 cup heavy cream

1/2 cup shredded mozzarella cheese (for topping)

Instructions:

Preheat oven to 425F

Make the fathead. Roll it out into a circle on parchment or silicone mat. Put in the oven for 10 minutes. While that is baking, melt the butter and cheese in a saucepan on the stove. Add cream. Whisk until smooth. Remove crust from oven. Spread the sauce on the crust. Add chicken and broccoli. Cover with cheese. Put back in the oven for 8-10 minutes until cheese is melted and crust to desired crispness. Cut into 8 slices. Chow!

Nutritional information (based off TWO slices): Calories: 553, Fat: 41g, Protein: 39g, Carbs: 9g, Fiber: 4g, Net Carbs: 5g

FETA, SPINACH, AND PINE NUTS (???) SAVORY PASTRY. EVEN 'CARB-EATERS' WOULD LOVE THIS

Savory Spinach-feta-pine nut pastry

Ingredients:

Crust: Use Fathead process from *Fathead for the Win!* In this section

2.00 tbsp(s), Nuts, pine nuts, dried

1/4 cup Mozzarella shredded for filling

4.00 oz(s), Cheese, feta

1.50 cup, Spinach – Raw

olive oil or egg white for wash

1 tbsp poppy, fennel, caraway, or sesame seeds (optional)

Preheat oven to 350F

Prepare dough. Take the mozzarella and sprinkle it down the center of the dough, then do the same for the feta. Now lay the spinach on top, then sprinkle the pine nuts to finish up the stack. Yeh. Pine nuts. You can leave them out if you don't have any (seriously, who keeps them around but us?), but if you can use them, you should. They add a unique texture to the finished pastry and they don't taste like pine needles once cooked. I promise. Starting at one end, make slices down each side about 1/3rd of the way across. This will let you braid the dough across the top of the filling. I used a cheese knife today, just the perfect size. One you have the slices done, starting at each end, alternating until you meet in the middle, lay each strip over the top to create a braided appearance. Don't worry, you don't need to really braid it, just criss-cross them :). Then brush the top with some olive oil or egg wash, sprinkle the top with poppy, fennel, sesame, or caraway seeds for that extra effect. Let it sit for a few minutes while you pre-heat your oven to 350F. Place in the oven, toss a few ice cubes on the oven floor and quickly shut the door. The ice cubes will flash steam, giving the dough a nice crust when done. Let it back for 15-20 minutes or until the top has a nice brown crust. Cut into 4 pieces and serve!

Nutritional information per serving (based off my ingredients, double-check!): Calories: 392, Fat: 34g, Protein: 16g, Carbs: 6g, Fiber: 3g, Net Carbs: 3g

MY VARIATION - HOT PASTRAMI SANDWICH FATHEAD STROMBOLI, DATE NIGHT STAPLE

Hot Pastrami Sandwich Fathead Stromboli
Servings=4
Time=30mins

Crust: Use Fathead process from *Fathead for the Win!* In this section
4.00 oz(s), Pastrami – Turkey (I use Carolina as it has ZERO carbs)
2.00 oz(s), Cheese, provolone
2 tbsp brown mustard

Preheat oven to 425F

Prepare dough as directed. Place it between two sheets of parchment or silicon baking mats. Press down with your hand to flatten it out as much as you can, then using a rolling pin to roll out the dough in a large rectangle of uniform thickness (about the thickness of two quarters stacked. Trim if needed. Starting at one end, make sliced down each side about 1/3rd of the way across on each side. This will let you braid the dough across the top of the filling. Lay the pastrami up the center of the dough, then spread the mustard over it, topping with the cheese. Fold the dough over the top, alternating sides all the way down, sealing the ends. Place on baking sheet. Pop in the oven for about 20 minutes or until the crust browns up nicely. Remove, let cool for a few minutes, then slice up, and serve!!

Nutritional information (based off my ingredients, double-check!): Calories: 375, Fat: 29g, Protein: 22g, Carbs: 9g, Fiber: 4g, Net Carbs: 5g

HOBBIT POCKETS. WHAT? KETO. HOT. POCKETS. YES, THEY ARE A THING!

Hobbit Pockets
Servings=6
Time=30mins

Crust: Use Fathead process from *Fathead for the Win!* In this section

Filling:

10.00 oz, Chicken Thighs-Boneless and Skinless – diced and cooked (substitute cooked breast or turkey for a lower-fat result).
2 tbsp butter
2 oz cream cheese
2 oz shredded cheddar (or jack)
1/2 cup mozzarella for filling

Preheat oven to 425F

In a sauce pan, melt the butter. Once melted, add the cream cheese and stir until it is melted. Add the garlic and onion powder, whisk until dissolved. Add shredded cheddar, whisk until smooth. Remove from heat. Prepare crust as directed. Put the dough between two sheets of parchment or silicone mats. press down and shape into a rectangle about 10×16 (a little smaller than a large casserole dish). Using a knife or pizza cutter, cut down the middle longways, then cut across the other way until you have 6 equal rectangles on both sides of the center cut. On one side of the large cut, spread about a tablespoon of the cheese sauce in the middle of each square, being careful not to get too close to the edges. Now, put on one layer of chicken, topped with a layer of mozzarella. Carefully pick up the edge of the parchment on the opposite side where you put the fillings, then fold the unfilled side over the top of the filled side. Taking your fingers, gently press a few spots on the edge you can easily reach. Now, slowly peel back the parchment. If you take your time and are gentle, it should peel off nicely.

Take a fork and crimp all around the edges to seal. Place on a baking sheet. Put in the oven for 10-12 minutes if you are going to freeze for reheating, 12-14 if you are going to eat hot. Once the tops are the color you want them to be for your tastes, remove from oven and move immediately to a rack for at least 2-3 minutes. This allows the bottom to not get soggy on a plate or sheet. Eat or freeze.

Nutritional information (based off my ingredients, double-check!): Calories: 229, Fat: 21g, Protein: 19g, Carbs: 5g, Fiber: 4g, Net Carbs: 1g

WHAT IF I TOLD YOU WE COULD HAVE PASTA THAT DOESN'T SMELL OR SUCK????

The Precious' Keto Pasta that doesn't suck or smell
Servings=4
Time=30 min

UPDATED! *Consider this before purchasing glucomannan! Some have had issues with certain brands, this stuff isn't cheap so I would recommend getting what others have used. It will save you in the long run. Brands I've personally used with success: LC Foods, Now Foods.*

Ingredients:

1 lg egg
2 tbsp. glucomannan powder
4 tbsp oat fiber
1 tbsp baking powder
1/2 tsp salt
1/2 tsp garlic powder
1/2 tsp onion powder
1 tbsp coconut flour

3/4 cup water, warm (whatever is "hot" out of your tap)

Beat egg well in a bowl or zip it up in a blender. Add dry ingredients and mix until gravel-like texture. Add water, mix until well combined. Form into a log and let rest for 8-10 minutes. Break into balls about the size of an egg, run through your choice of pasta machine (extruder or roller), meat grinder, or roll out (do it between parchment\silipat and slice to form noodles). Refrigerate for at least an hour, it will keep for up to 5 days.

To prepare noodles, boil a couple cups of salted water (I used 4 cups water + 2tbsp salt). Add pasta to boiling water and reduce heat immediately to just slow boil. Leave pasta in for 3-4 minutes for thick noodles, 1-3 for spaghetti.

Drain and use with your favorite sauce or dish. Yes. You can also use these in soups 😀

Nutritional information per serving: Calories each 48 , Fat: 2g Protein: 2g, Carbs: 19g Fiber: 17g Net: 2g

ETHNIC FOODS

HOBBIT CRACKS THE CODE - TEMPURA BATTER. KETO. YES. OH YESSSS

Hobbit's Keto Tempura battered chicken

Servings=4
Time=30 min

Ingredients:

1lb chicken breast, cubed
2 eggs
1 scoop (about 1/4 cup) unflavored whey isolate plus 2 tbsp for dusting
1 tsp baking powder
1/2 tsp baking soda
1/2 tsp salt
1/2 tsp Xanthan Gum Powder
Preheat a skillet (use a cast iron if you have one for best results) on med-high heat. Brown the chicken on all sides. Remove from skillet to a paper towel.
Heat up some oil to fry in of your choice in a deep fryer or small sauce pan to about 350F.
Put the two tbsp protein powder in a bowl, set aside.
Make the batter.
Whisk the eggs. Add the dry, whisk until well combined. Take a couple of cubes of chicken, toss around in the bowl of protein powder (dry) so the batter will stick better. Drop them in the batter to coat all sides. Let excess drip off, then drop in hot oil. Keep them moving so all sides get a nice light brown. Remove to plate, repeat.

Done.
Eat them like this, make a sauce like sweet and sour, do whatever you want. LOOK HOW FLUFFY THAT IS!!!

Nutritional information: Calories each 75 (per 15 pieces of batter-covered item, not including choice of meat), Fat:4g, Protein: 10, Carbs: less than 1

HOBBIT'S SPICY KETO CRUSTED CHICKEN BREASTS WITH KETO SPANISH RICE

Hobbit's spicy keto crusted chicken breasts with keto Spanish rice
Servings=2
Time=30 min

For the chicken:

2 boneless chicken breasts
2oz cream cheese
2 tbsp mayo
1 tbsp diced jalapenos
2 tbsp flax meal
2 tbsp Parmesan cheese
2 tbsp hot pepper sauce, separated into 1tbsp ea.
1oz shredded pepper jack cheese

Instructions:

Preheat oven to 350F
With a meat hammer, or do like I do and place between two cast iron skillets, hammer the breasts until flat and about 1/4"
thick. Put the cream cheese in the microwave for 30 seconds to soften. Stir in the jalapenos and pepper sauce. Spread half of
the mixture on one side of each breast, top with shredded Jack. Roll up into a roll and secure with toothpicks. Mix the flax and
Parmesan together. Mix the other tbsp of hot sauce and mayo together. Using your hands, coat each rolled up breast with the
mayo mix, then roll in the dry mix. Place in a cast iron skillet and put in the oven for 20-30 minutes or until the coating browns
and the chicken is baked.

While the chicken is baking, make the rice.
Ingredients:

1.5 cups of riced cauliflower, water squeezed out
1 tbsp hot pepper sauce
1 tsp tomato paste
2 tbsp diced jalapenos
1 tbsp diced onions
1/2 cup water

Brown the cauliflower in a skillet on medium heat until most of it is browned. Mix the wet ingredients in a bowl. Add the onions and peppers to the cauliflower, saute for 2-3 minutes or until onions start to soften. Add liquid. Mix thoroughly, then turn down to medium low until chicken is done.
Serve up!!!

HOBBIT DOES AN AMERICAN-ASIAN FAVORITE - SWEET AND SOUR CHICKEN!

Hobbit does an American-Asian favorite – Sweet and Sour Chicken!
Servings=4
Time=45mins

1/4 cup Priya's Keto Ketchup (available at www.ketoforindia.com)
1/4 cup white vinegar
1/4 cup water
1/4 tsp lemon extract

1/4 tsp orange extract
1/8 tsp lime extract
1/3 tsp xanthan gum

Preheat oven to 350F

Put all the sauce ingredients together in a bowl, whisk well. Brown your meat lightly, just enough to cook the outside but not all the way through. While the meat is browning, pre-cook your veggies in the microwave (8 minutes on high for my bag of veggies). Spread the veggies in the bottom of a large casserole dish. Once browned, add the meat and stir to mix. Pour the sauce over the meat and veggies, then stir well to make sure everything is coated. Put in oven for 15 minutes. Remove and stir to make sure everything stays coated, then put back in for 15 more minutes.
Remove.
Serve!

HOBBIT HACKS SOUTHWEST EGGROLLS - KETOFIED

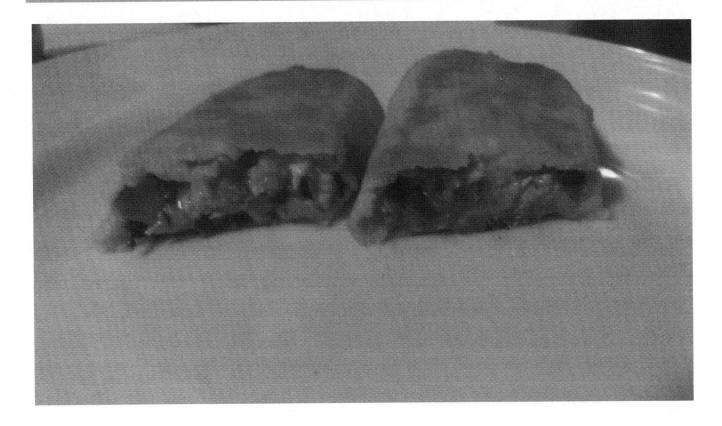

Hobbit hacks Southwest Eggrolls – ketofied
Servings=8
Time=30 min
1 batch fathead dough (see Pizza section in this book)
1/4lb chicken breast or thighs
1/4 cup chopped spinach
1 tbsp diced onion
1/4 cup pepitas
1 tbsp taco seasoning

4oz shredded pepper jack cheese

Instructions:

Preheat oven to 425F

In a skillet, cook the chicken until just cooked through (do not overcook). Remove from pan to cool. Add the spinach, onions, and pepitas to the skillet, cook until the spinach is soft. Add taco seasoning and stir until coated. Remove from heat. Once cool, dice the chicken into small pieces (about 1/2" square), then add to the spinach mixture, stirring to combine. Add cheese, stir again. At this point you should be able to grab a handful of the mixture, squeeze, and have it hold shape. Make your fathead if you haven't already. Do one last 10 second nuke, then roll it out into a rectangle about the thickness of 2 quarters stacked. Using a pizza cutter or knife, cut down the middle long ways, then make three cuts across the width so you have 8 squares\rectangles of about the same size. Grab some of the chicken mixture, place on one end of each square, distributing until all the squares have equal amounts. Use your hands to shape each one into a log, then fold up the long sides of the dough over the ends of the chicken mixture. This will help seal them up when rolled. Starting at the end with the meat mixture, roll each one up tight, then seal the seam with your fingers. Place on baking sheet with seam down, bake for 15-20 minutes or until starting to brown. Cut each one in half on an angle and serve!

HOBBIT'S IRON GIANT CRAB RANGOONS (WITH KETO FRIED RICE)

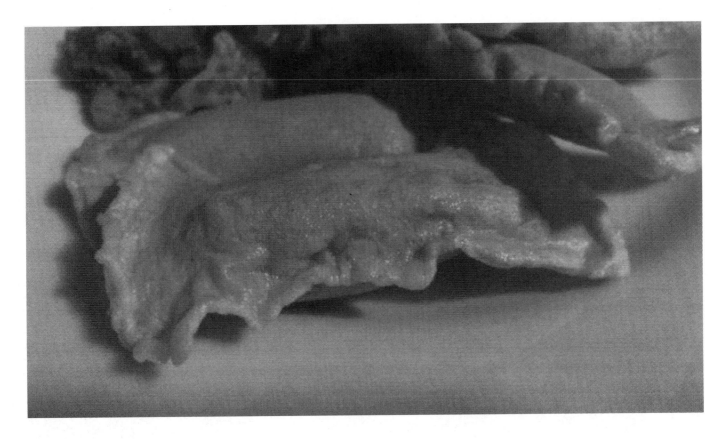

Hobbit's Crab Rangoon
Servings=16
Time=45mins

Ingredients:

Iron Giant Dough (see first chapter for basic recipe)
Cover in plastic wrap, store in the fridge for at least 30 minutes while you make the filling.

Filling:

4oz cream cheese, softened
1/2 can (2.5oz) of minced crabmeat, drained
1/2 tsp soy sauce (or coconut aminos if you have them)
1 tsp Worcestershire sauce
1 tsp minced garlic
1 tsp onion powder
Mix all the ingredients thoroughly in a bowl until well combined. Get out your Iron Giant dough. Flatten out as best you can, then place between two sheets of parchment or silicon mat and roll out to about as thick as a dime. Using a straight edge and pizza cutter, trim to a rectangle, saving the cast offs in a plastic bag for another recipe, then cut the rectangle into even squares (do a better job than me, not one was a square. lol). Slide or lift the squares apart for filling. Get a small bowl of warm water ready. Put about 1 to 1.5 tsp of the crab mixture in the middle of each square. Take your finger, get it wet in the bowl

of water, then wet all four edges. Fold one side over the top and press the edges together firmly. Repeat for each square. If you MADE squares and not rectangles like I did, you can do the traditional triangle shape.. Let them sit for 2-3 minutes for the water to start bonding the edges, then crimp with a fork or pastry crimper around the seams. Let them sit out on the counter for 30 minutes to dry a little and let the seams bond. When the 30 minutes are up, start a pot of boiling water, add 1/4 cup salt to the water. drop the rangoons in a couple at time for 2-3 minutes or until they start to puff a little. Remove with a slotted spoon to a towel and let air dry 5-10 minutes. Start your deep fryer or a small pan with 1" of hot oil in it (about 350F). Drop the rangoons in to the oil, making sure you don't do too many at a time as to cool the oil too much. They will cook QUICKLY so watch them. As soon as the edges start to brown, flip them so the other side browns. When the bubbles almost stop, remove to a paper towel-covered plate to remove excess oil. Serve with your favorite keto Asian dish, like the fried rice recipe below:)

Nutritional information per rangoon (based off my ingredients, double-check!): Calories: 49, Fat: 2g, Protein: 7g, Carbs: 2g, Fiber: 1g, Net Carbs: 1g

Hobbit's Cauliflower Fried Rice
Servings=4
Time=30mins

Make the rice:
1 bag of frozen cauliflower
2 tbsp soy sauce
2 tbsp vinegar (white, rice, red, doesn't matter)
1/2 tsp Oriental Five Spice powder (or a dash of cinnamon, cardamon, ginger, nutmeg mixed together)
1/4 cup diced onions

Nuke cauliflower for 7-8 minutes until cooked. Rice up in food processor. Dump in the hot skillet. Mix the spices and liquids together in a bowl. Return to cauliflower, stir and mix until the cauliflower starts to brown just a little, Add onions. Continue mixing until the cauliflower is uniformly brown and the onions just a little soft. Add seasoning mixture and stir well so all the 'rice' is coated and wet. Continue to stir until all liquid gone. Serve.

HOBBIT MAKES ZERO CARB, HIGH-PROTEIN FISH KAKES (NO CARBS WERE HARMED IN THIS RECIPE)

Hobbit's Fish Kakes
Servings=2
Time=15mins

Ingredients:

1 can (5oz) tuna (or fish of your choice)
1 egg
1 scoop (1/4 cup) of unflavored protein powder.
1/8 tsp salt
1/8 tsp dill
1/4 tsp onion powder

Heat up a skillet, use a little oil if it isn't a non-stick. Beat the egg with a fork, then add drained fish, mix well. Add spices and protein powder. Mix again with fork until well combined. Form into two equal sized patties. Place in skillet (no need to chill these puppies ▢). Brown one side. Flip. Brown the other. Serve on a roll, with cocktail sauce or tartar sauce, cauil-tots, whatever.

Nutritional information (based off my ingredients, double-check!): Calories: 145, Fat: 6g, Protein: 24g, Carbs: 0g, Fiber: 0g, Net Carbs: 0

KETO FRIED 'RICE' MATCHES NICELY WITH RULED.ME'S GENERAL TAO'S CHICKEN

General Tao's Chicken
Servings=4
Time=45mins

Chicken
1lb Chicken Breasts
1/2 cup Crushed pork rinds or keto tortillas chips
2 tbsp unflavored whey protein powder
2 tbsp Cup Almond Flour
1 Large Egg
2 tbsp heavy cream
2 Tbsp. Olive Oil
1 Tbsp. Coconut Oil
1/4 cup diced onions and peppers

Sauce
1/4 Cup Water
2 Tbsp. Rice Vinegar
2 1/2 Tbsp. Soy Sauce
1 Tbsp. concentrated tomato paste
1 tsp. Stevia
2 tsp. Hemp Oil
1 tsp. Hoisen Sauce
1 tsp. Red Chili Paste
1 tsp. Red Pepper Flakes
1 tsp. Garlic Powder
1/2 tsp. Minced Ginger
1/4 tsp. Xanthan Gum

Preheat oven to 325F. Heat the oils together in a skillet on med-high. Get a casserole dish out and handy.
Cut the chicken into cubes. In a bowl or large (1 gallon) plastic bag, mix together the crushed rinds and almond flour. In another bowl, whisk together the egg and cream. A couple at a time, dunk the chicken chunks in the egg mixture, coating all sides, then either roll in the crumb bowl, or if you lazy….errrr…efficient like me, drop them in the bag and shake them. Once you have all of them coated, arrange as many as you can in the hot oil, making sure you leave a little room around each so they cook instead of just soak up the grease. Turn until all sides are a little crisped up but try not to overcook. Place them in the baking dish. Repeat until all the chicken is cooked, then sprinkle the onions and peppers around the gaps between the chicken. Keep the pan warm, you can use it for frying the 'rice' Now, let's make the sauce. Toss it all in a bowl, whisk it up so it is all combined. Dead simple, huh? Now pour over the chicken, trying to hit each one if possible. If you can't, don't fret (you'll see why in a minute). Put in the oven for 15 minutes. Remove. Turn each piece of chicken over.

Put back in the oven for 15 minutes. At this point, start the fried rice (below) Take out. Using tongs, remove the chicken piece by piece to a bowl. then pour the sauce over the top, give a gentle stir and plate up (or if you are really in the Date Night mood, into some of those little white boxes).

Hobbit's Cauliflower Fried Rice
Servings=4
Time=30mins

Make the rice:

1 bag of frozen cauliflower
2 tbsp soy sauce
2 tbsp vinegar (white, rice, red, doesn't really matter)
1/2 tsp Oriental Five Spice powder (or a dash of cinnamon, cardamom, ginger, nutmeg mixed together)
1/4 cup diced onions

Nuke cauliflower for 7-8 minutes until cooked. Rice up in food processor. Dump in the hot skillet. Mix the spices and liquids together in a bowl. Return to cauliflower, stir and mix until the cauliflower starts to brown just a little, Add onions. Continue mixing until the cauliflower is uniformly brown and the onions just a little soft. Add seasoning mixture and stir well so all the 'rice' is coated and wet. Continue to stir until all liquid gone. If the chicken isn't done yet, turn to low. Otherwise, serve it up!!!

WTH TO DO WITH THE CABBAGE EDITION - HOBBIT'S KETO CHICKEN ALFREDO. HONEST, IT'S GOOD!

Hobbit's Keto Chicken Alfredo
Servings=4
Time=30mins

Ingredients:
1 small green cabbage
1 lb chicken breast
1/2 cup mushrooms (optional but hey, they are all fiber so why not?)
1/2 cup chopped kale
1 tbsp minced garlic
3 tbsp salt
2 oz cream cheese
2 oz Monterrey Jack cheese, shredded
1/2 cup Parmesan grated cheese
2 tbsp butter

Preheat oven to 375F. Yeh, the oven. Bear with me. You trust me, right?
Good:).

Thinly slice your cabbage, about the thickness of fettuccine noodles. Put them in a pot, fill with water then dump the salt in. Bring to boil on high. Stir a couple of times then turn off the heat and move the pot to a back burner and let it sit while you get the chicken ready. Heat up a cast iron skillet (or if you don't have one, use a regular one) on medium heat. Once hot, add the butter until melts, then add the chicken. Cook the chicken until not pink on all sides, then add the 'shrooms. Cook them for a few minutes until you get a little liquid building up, then add the cream cheese and garlic, stir a few times to melt the cheese, then turn down to med-low. Grab that pot of cabbage and drain it well. Add the other cheeses and kale to the cabbage and stir to combine. Go back to the stove (hey, it's kitchen cardio!) and get the chicken mixture. Pour into the cabbage and stir well until it's all coated with the 'sauce' from the chicken mixture. Dump the entire thing back into the cast iron (or, if you used a regular skillet, into a baking dish) and tamp down the mixture.

Put in the oven for 45 minutes. Remove and let rest for 5 minutes. Scoop and serve. Makes 4 servings.

Nutritional information: Calories each 372, Fat: 20g, Protein: 42, Carbs: 2, Fiber: 1, Net carbs: 1

HOBBIT'S SPECIAL DATE NIGHT DINNER - KETO CHICKEN MARSALA WITH RISOTTO

Marsala and risotto
Servings=4
Time=30mins

Risotto

1 package frozen cauliflower
2 tbsp diced onions
1 tbsp minced garlic
1/2 cup chicken broth
1/4 cup grated Parmesan cheese
1/2 cup heavy cream
2 tbsp olive oil
2 tbsp butter

Nuke cauliflower until cooked (7-8 minutes). Rice the cauliflower in food processor or blender. Heat sauce pan on Med-High, then add olive oil. Let oil get hot. Add onions and cauliflower, stir frequently until the onions are transparent and the cauliflower soft. Add butter. Stir until melted, then let simmer for about 5 minutes. Add rest of the ingredients, reduce to Med and let reduce until creamy.

Chicken Marsala (makes 4 servings):

1lb cut chicken breast
2 tbsp diced onion
1.5 cups sliced mushrooms
2 tbsp minced garlic
3 tbsp rice vinegar
1/2 cup chicken broth
1/2 tsp thyme
1/4 tsp salt
2 tbsp butter
1/2 tsp Xanthan Gum Powder

In a large skillet at Med-High melt butter until gets foamy. Add chicken. Cook the chicken until no more pink shows, then add onions and mushrooms. Cook until mushrooms are soft and not rubbery any more. Add rest of ingredients except xanthan gum. Let cook until liquid about half reduced. Sprinkle xanthan gum over the mixture and stir in. Let simmer until sauce thickens. Serve and enjoy!!

Nutritional info risotto (based off my ingredients, check yours!): Calories: 254, Fat: 25g, Protein: 4g, Carbs: 4, Fiber: 1, Net Carbs: 3
Nutritional info Marsala (based off my ingredients, check yours!): Calories: 255, Fat: 10g, Protein: 36g, Carbs: 3, Fiber: 1, Net Carbs: 2

KETO MEXICAN KABOCHA-KALE CABBAGE ROLLS - YEH, THAT'S A MOUTHFULL, ISN'T IT?

Keto Mexican Kabocha-Kale Cabbage Rolls
Servings=4
Time=60mins

Ingredients:

1/2lb ground beef (or turkey, pork, brains, eye of newt)
2 tbsp taco seasoning
1/4 cup water
1 cup kabocha squash
1/2 cup chopped kale
6 cabbage leaf
4 oz shredded cheddar

Taco seasoning (mix together, store in a jar):

2 tablespoons chili powder
1 tablespoon ground cumin
1 teaspoon xanthan gum
2 teaspoons salt
1 1/2 teaspoons hot smoked paprika
1 teaspoon ground coriander
1/2 teaspoon cayenne pepper

Preheat oven to 325F

Brown the meat in a skillet. Add taco seasoning, water, mix well, and turn to med-low until reduced. Mix kabocha and kale in a bowl. Set aside. Place the cabbage in a saucepan, fill with water until leaves are covered. Bring to a boil. Turn down to simmer until the cabbage is soft and pliable. Remove from heat. Drain and let cool. Spoon a layer of meat into the bottom of each leaf, add some cheese, then top with the squash mixture until you have it evenly distributed between the cabbage. Starting with the stem side of the cabbage, roll up each one, tucking in the ends. Place in a baking dish, seam side down. I find a standard glass bread loaf dish works well for this. Bake for 40 minutes, I like to use the juices to baste the tops about every 10 minutes to keep the tops from overcooking. At 40 minutes, top with a little more cheese and return to the oven just long enough to melt.

Nutritional information (per serving of 2 rolls) : Calories: 381, Fat: 26, Protein: 30, Carbs: 5, Fiber: 1, Net carbs: 4

CHICKEN-BACON ENCHILADAS - KETO-STYLE

Chicken-bacon Enchiladas – keto-Hobbit-style!
Servings=4
Time=30mins

Ingredients:

6 oz boneless chicken thighs (or breast if you want) – cut to strips and cooked.
4 strips of bacon (I used turkey bacon because we've had it for a while and needed to get used, pork bacon could take this to next level) – cooked and diced
1 chipotle, diced
1/4 cup shredded mozzarella cheese
1/4 cup diced tomato (fresh or canned, your call)
4 tortillas – low carb
1/4 cup shredded mozzarella cheese
1/4 cup butter
2 oz cream cheese
1/4 cup heavy cream
2 oz cheddar (or jack or cheese of your choice)
1 tsp minced garlic
2 chipotles, diced
1/4 cup mozzarella for topping

Preheat oven to 350F.

In a bowl, mix the single diced chipotle, tomato, chicken, bacon, and 1/4 cup cheese together. Set aside.

In a sauce pan on low to med-low heat, melt the butter. Once completely melted, add the cream cheese (if you nuke it for about 30 seconds, it will melt quicker in the pan) and stir until combined. Add the garlic, the 2 diced chipotles, and cream to the pan. Stir until combined and the mixture starts to steam lightly. Add shredded cheddar (or Jack, Pepper Jack, etc.). Stir over the same heat until smooth (for me that was about 5 minutes). Turn off the heat, leave the pan on the burner so doesn't cool too much while you stuff the tortillas. Lay out 4 tortillas on the counter (put something under it like parchment, cutting mat, etc. Food safety, people!!). Take 1/4 of the chicken-bacon mixture and run it up the middle of each tortilla. Roll each one up snug (I didn't on a few, yeh, Hobbits don't follow directions well, even their own...), putting the seam on the bottom so they don't unravel while you move to the next one. Once all 4 are wrapped, take a couple of big spoonful's of the cheese sauce and completely cover the bottom of an 8×8 or 9×9 baking dish. Lay the wrapped tortillas – seam-side down – on the cheese. Top with the remaining cheese mixture, spreading with a spoon so that the tops of the tortillas are all covered. Sprinkle the topping mozzarella over the pan. Put in the oven for 20 minutes or until the cheese starts to brown. Remove, let stand 5 minutes. Serve!

Nutritional information (per serving with homemade tortillas): Calories: 450, Fat: 38, Protein: 24, Carbs: 8, Fiber: 4, Net carbs: 4

CRISPY ASIAN-STYLE NOODLES

You can make this wide and flat or thin like chow mein noodles, it's all in how you cut them (more on that in the recipe).

Crispy Asian-style noodles
Servings=4
Time=30mins prep, 120mins rest

Get your cold ball of Iron Giant (see first section of this book for the basic recipe) out of the fridge. Kneed it for 2-3 minutes to soften it up. Form into a log. If you have a pasta roller, this would be a good time to use it. Otherwise, place on parchment or silicone mat and press down with your hand and flatten as much as possible. Cover with another sheet, and using a rolling pin, roll out as thin as possible (this is a pretty stiff dough, would be a good time to cash in on payback if you have a teen that has misbehaved). Roll out flat to about the thickness of one blade of your kitchen shears. Again, you have a pasta roller, this would be a good time to use it. If not, get out a pizza cutter or sharp knife and cut the dough into strips. You don't have to be precise, just cut to widths between spaghetti or fettuccine, depending on the noodle style you want. Thin will be chow mein, wider the wide noodles (Hello, Hobbit is Captain Obvious, huh?). Lay on a wire rack to dry for about an hour. You back? Has it been an hour? Are the strips a little dry but not hard? Good. Now heat up your oil in the fryer, small sauce pan, or small skillet. Bring it to about 350F. Heat up a couple of cups of water with 2-3 tablespoons of salt in it. Bring to a rolling boil. Drop the dried noodles into the boiling water and drop temp down to a slight boil. Stir several times so they don't stick, then let them boil for 10 minutes or so. Remove the noodles from the water and place on a kitchen towel to dry for 5-10 minutes so when you drop in the oil, you don't end up going to the ER with grease burns. Ask me how I know... Using the knife or cutter again, cut the dough into 1-1.5" strips toss around so they don't stick. Take 8-10 cut strips and drop into the hot oil. You will need to move quickly, these fry in less than a minute. As soon as they hit the oil, they should start to quickly brown. Stir constantly to make sure all surfaces are getting hit with the oil. As soon as the get dark but not burnt, remove them, and move to a plate covered with a paper towel to cool. Once they are all done, drop in a bowl and enjoy, or put on top or bottom of your favorite Asian dish!!

Nutritional information (based off my ingredients, double-check!): Calories: 103, Fat: 2g, Protein: 20g, Carbs: 0g, Fiber: 0g, Net Carbs: 0g

HOW ABOUT A SAMMICH?

FAIR SEASON CALLS FOR PHILLY CHEESE...CHOPS? YES. CHEESECHOP. AND IT'S KETO!

Philly Cheese Chop Sandwich
Servings=2
Time=30mins

Ingredients:

2 Keto dogs rolls – sliced and toasted (recipe in Breads section of this book)
1/2lb pork loin chop (or any lean pork)
1 tsp thyme
1 tbsp garlic powder
1 tbsp onion powder
1 tsp salt
1 cup water
1/4 cup sliced onions (optional)
1/4 cupe sliced peppers (optional)
1/4 cup sliced mushrooms (optional)
4 slices of cheese of your choice (I used provolone)

Mix up the seasonings in the water, then pour into your crockpot. Add the pork. Set it on high for one hour, then turn down to low for 5-6 hours or until pork is soft and falls apart easy when poked with a fork. Remove lid. Sauté up the veggies if so desired and add them to the crockpot. Let cook on HIGH for 30 more minutes. Lay out your sliced rolls on a baking sheet. Mound up the pork mixture then top with cheese. Place under the broiler for a few minutes until cheese is melted. Put top on roll, slice in half, serve with tots or your side of choice, and channel your inner fair-goer!!

Nutrition info (1 sandwich with roll): Calories: 380, Fat: 23g, Protein: 42, Carbs: 2, Fiber: 1, Net Carbs: 1

SHREDDED PORK SAMMICH, HOBBIT STYLE, NO CARB PORK RECIPE ON KETO ROLL. KILL THOSE CARBS!

Pulled pork keto-style (enough to cover about 3lbs of pork)

Servings=4 -6

Time=8hrs

a honking piece of pork (I used pork loin because that's what I had on hand, but shoulder works well)

1.5 tsp onion powder

1.5 tsp garlic powder

1 tbsp crushed garlic

1.5 tsp Light Salt (or sea salt – for the potassium)

1 tsp black or white pepper

1.5 tsp smoked (or regular if that is what you have) paprika

1 tsp allspice

1 tsp mustard powder

1 tsp cloves

0.5 tsp cumin

3/4 cup water

Mix all the dry together well, then take the rub and, well, rub all over the pork, covering it all. Mix the water in with any remaining spices, pour into bottom of crock pot. Put pork in, turn on and let it do its thing. After the proper time, remove the pork and shred it with a couple of forks, then add back to the crock, stirring it up well so all the pieces are coated. If you used the 'low heat' method, kick it up to high for 15 minutes, if not leave it on high for 15 minutes with the COVER OFF. Toast the buns while waiting, then brush with a little melted butter for that extra oomph. Pile on the pork, serve, and ENJOY!!

The pork depends on what pork you use, I used 6oz of loin chops since there's just two of us, so factored on a 3oz serving of pork.

Nutritional information (sandwich): Calories each 346, Fat:24g, Protein: 31, Carbs: 2, Fiber: 1, Net carbs: 1

FATHEAD CORNDOGS. YES. CORNDOGS

"Corn" wrap recipe:

User fathead dough recipe from Pizza section of this book.

Preheat oven (or deep fryer) to 375F

Roll out dough into rectangle about double the width of two hotdogs plus about 2". Slice lengthwise down the middle. Roll individual hotdogs up in dough in each section of fathead, cutting off when each dog covered. Pinch the ends to seal. If deep frying, insert kebab skewers into the dogs to aid in frying. Deep fry until golden brown or bake for 20 minutes in the oven.

BREADS

GETTING READY FOR THE HOLIDAYS - WHO WANTS KETO DINNER ROLLS?

Hobbit's Keto Dinner Rolls
Servings=6
Time=40 mins

Ingredients (makes 6 rolls):

5 tbsp Organic Coconut Flour
4 tbsp unflavored whey isolate
2 tbsp butter (melted)
2 tsp bacon grease (melted)
1.5 tsp baking powder
1 tsp salt
1/2 tsp Xanthan Gum Powder
1.5 tsp apple cider vinegar
4 eggs
1/8 cup warm coconut or almond milk
1/2 envelope (about 1tsp) of fast-rising yeast

Preheat oven to 350F
Warm the milk to a little above body temp, then dissolve the yeast in it. Get out a muffin tin and spray down with cooking spray (I use coconut oil spray). Dump all the ingredients (including milk\yeast mixture) into a blender or food processor. Melt the grease, add that as well, then blend\process until well combined and a little thick – think cake batter consistency. Pour\spoon equal amounts in each cup, then spread smooth with spatula or back of a spoon. Pop in the oven for about 15 minutes or until the top browns. Take them out and let them cool completely before unwrapping. Look, nice, light colored and tasting dinner rolls!!

Nutritional information: Calories each 140, Fat:12g, Protein: 8, Carbs: 2, Fiber: 1, Net carbs: 1

HOBBIT DOES KORNBREAD - CORNBREAD. KETOFIED

Hobbit does Kornbread – Cornbread. Ketofied.
Servings=8
Time=90 min

Ingredients:

1/4 cup almond flour
2 tbsp Pea Protein Isolate
2 tbsp whey isolate
1 tbsp butter. melted
2 eggs
1/2 tsp xanthan gum
1/2 tsp salt
1 tbsp apple cider vinegar
1/4 cup pureed kabocha (or pumpkin)
1/2 tbsp baking powder
1 tsp baking soda
2 tbsp flax meal
1 tsp sweetener
1 tsp vanilla extract

Preheat oven to 325F
Spray loaf pan (I used 7×3.5) with cooking spray. Dead. Simple. So simple it should be illegal. Dump everything in the blender, putting in the vinegar last. Pulse until smooth. Pour\scrape into pan, place in the oven for 30 minutes or until the top is a nice brown. Remove. Let cool for a few minutes (hot enough to melt butter, not hot enough to burn you). Slice. Slather with butter. Eat.

Nutritional information (per serving slice) : Calories: 122, Fat: 7, Protein: 5, Carbs: 2, Fiber: 1, Net carbs: 1

AN NEW ENGLAND TRADITION - STEAMED BROWN BREAD. KETOFIED

Hobbit's Steamed Brown Bread – Ketofied
Servings=8
Time=90 min

Ingredients:

1/3 cup almond flour
2 tbsp Pea Protein Isolate
2 tbsp whey isolate
3 tbsp butter, melted
2 eggs
1/2 tsp xanthan gum
1/2 tsp maple extract
1 tbsp cocoa powder
(unsweetened)
3 tsp sweetener
1/4 cup pureed kabocha (or
pumpkin)
1 tbsp cottage cheese
1/4 tsp allspice
2 tbsp flax meal

This takes a little planning but it's not too bad. You will need a 15oz (or larger, just double recipe) metal can, cleaned well with top removed. Preheat oven to 300F. Take can, place something underneath it in a pot that is oven-safe, like a mason jar rim or upside down tuna can (empty). Pour enough water in the pot to come half-way up the can. Remove the can, spray with oil, set aside. Bring water to a boil. While waiting for the water to boil, dump all the ingredients in your blender and blend until smooth. Should be a thick batter. Pour\scrape into the can, smoothing out the top. Should be about 2/3rds full. Cover the top of the can with aluminum foil and secure with cooking twine.

Once the water is boiling remove from heat, put the can in on the 'base', place in oven. Bake for 1 hour. Remove from oven and remove foil. Let cool for 10 minutes before removing bread from can. Slice into 8 slices, butter, EAT!

Nutritional information (per serving slice) : Calories: 102, Fat: 8, Protein: 6, Carbs: 2, Fiber: 1, Net carbs: 1

AHHH. KETO BURGER OR BULKY ROLLS. YESSSSSS

Hobbit's Keto Burger or bulky rolls
Servings=8

Time=45 min
Ingredients:

1 cup(s) plus 2tbsp Almond Flour
2 tbsp unflavored whey isolate
2 tsp baking powder
2 large Eggs
1/2 tsp salt
4 tbsp Psyllium husk powder
3/4 cup boiling water
Small bowl of water to wet your hands with

Optional:
sesame, fennel, poppy seeds for toppings.

Preheat oven to 350F
Prepare a baking sheet, lined with parchment or silicone mat (or lightly greased if neither of those are available).
Beat the eggs whisk until well combined. Add all the dry, mix well with a spoon or rubber spatula. This will result in a crumbly mess that looks like there's no way this is going to work. Bear with me:). Grab the hot water and pour it into the mixture while stirring until you have a soupy mess. Wait 5 minutes, the dough will become a dough instead of soup. Using wet hands (that's what the bowl of water is for ⬚), roughly shape the dough into a rectangle. Cut the rectangle into 8 squares. Wet hands again, shape into circles. Place on sheet and repeat until all 8 are done. Space them out with room to at least double in size. While still wet, sprinkle your toppings on if you are using them, then pat lightly to make sure they are attached. Place in the oven for 15-20 minutes or until the tops are dry and bounce back when lightly touched. Remove. Let cool. STUFF WITH MEAT AND CHEEEEEEEESE!!!

Nutritional information pr roll: Calories each 113 , Fat: 8g Protein: 6g, Carbs: 6g Fiber: 3g Net: 3g

KETO DOG ROLLS - ONLY 1 NET CARB EACH!

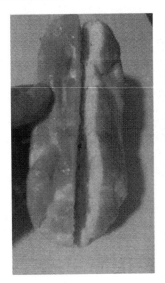 

Hobbit's Keto Sub rolls
Servings=4
Time=30mins

Ingredients (makes 4 rolls):

6 tbsp coconut flour
3 tbsp unflavored whey isolate
1 tsp Coconut Oil
1 tbsp butter
2 tbsp bacon grease
1 tsp baking powder
1 tsp salt
1/2 tsp Xanthan Gum Powder
1 tsp apple cider vinegar
4 eggs

Preheat oven to 350F

Make 4 dog roll shaped forms out of aluminum foil (I formed mine around a box from tomato paste but you can just eyeball it if you want). Place forms on baking sheet, spray down with cooking spray (I use coconut oil spray).
Dump all the ingredients into a blender or food processor except the vinegar. Melt the grease, add, then top with the vinegar. Blend on high until well combined and a little thick – think cake batter consistency. Pour equal amounts in each form, then spread smooth with spatula or back of a spoon. Pop in the oven for about 15 minutes or until the top browns. Take them out and let them cool completely before unwrapping. Stuff them with meat and enjoy!!!

Nutritional information: Calories each 240, Fat:22g, Protein: 8, Carbs: 2, Fiber: 1, Net carbs: 1

HOBBIT'S KETO BREAD (GREAT FOR STUFFING TOO!)

Hobbit's Protein Bread
Servings=10
Time=40 mins

Ingredients (makes 10 slices):

5 tbsp coconut flour
4 tbsp Whey Protein Isolate Powder
2 tbsp butter (melted)
2 tsp bacon grease (melted)
1.5 tsp baking powder
1 tsp salt
1/2 tsp Xanthan Gum
1.5 tsp Apple Cider Vinegar
4 eggs
1/8 cup warm coconut or almond milk
1/2 envelope (about 1tsp) of fast-rising yeast

Preheat oven to 350F

Warm the milk to a little above body temp, then dissolve the yeast in it. Get out a bread pan – I used a 4×8. If not silicone, lightly grease. Dump all the ingredients into a blender or food processor except the vinegar. Melt the grease, add, then top with the vinegar. Blend on high until well combined and a little thick – think cake batter consistency. Pour into your bread pan, then spread smooth with spatula or back of a spoon. Pop in the oven for about 25 minutes or until the top browns. Take it out and let it cool completely before turning onto a cooling rack. Look at them nooks and crannies!!!!!

Nutritional information: Calories each 84, Fat:7g, Protein: 4, Carbs: less than 1

KETO TORTILLAS

Ingredients
1/2 cup coconut flour
1/4 cup crushed pork rinds
5 tbsp psyllium husk powder
1 tsp sea salt
4 eggs
1 cup water

Instructions

In a bowl, combine the coconut flour, pork rinds, psyllium powder, and salt. Add in the eggs and combine until i thickens up then add water into the bowl. Mix until well and then let it chill in the bowl for a few minutes while the psyllium does it's thing. Separate into 8 balls (I make one big ball, cut in half, then again and again so I get even sized pieces) and place the dough onto a piece of parchment paper or silicon mats. Top with another parchment, plastic wrap, or mat. Using a rolling pin, roll the dough out in a circle shape with even thickness throughout (about as thick as a quarter). If your circle is a little rough, you can use your hands to tweak your tortilla.
Heat a large pan to medium-high heat with coconut oil, olive oil or spray. Once hot, place an unbaked tortilla on the pan,

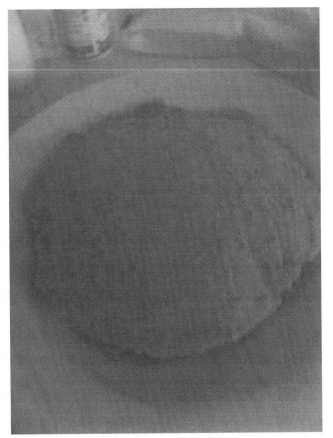

I find it easiest to flip the paper upside down, get the tortilla in contact with the pan, and then in a second or two, it will peel right off as the tortilla heats up. Sauté until light brown, then flip and bake through. Makes 8 servings.

NUTRITION COUNT PER wrap (based off my ingredients, double-check your numbers!): Calories: 114, Protein: 5g, Fat: 8 g, Carbs: 6g, Fiber: 4g, NET CARBS: 2g

POLLY WANT A CRACKER (OR CHIPS?)

HOBBIT'S KETO DORITOS REBOOTED (KICKING TORTILLAS TOO!)

Hobbit's Tortillas and Doritos Reboot
Servings=4
Time=45 min

Ingredients:

2 tbsp coconut flour
2 tbsp Unflavored Whey Protein
Isolate.
1/4 cup crushed pork rinds
5 tbsp psyllium husk powder
1 teaspoon salt
2 eggs
1 cup water
1/4 cup nutritional yeast
1 heaped tablespoon miso (use
chickpea miso if you are sensitive to soy)
1 teaspoon onion powder
1 teaspoon dry ground mustard powder
1 teaspoon smoked paprika
2 teaspoon chili powder
1/2 teaspoon turmeric
dash cayenne

Instructions

Heat a non-stick skillet or seasoned cast iron on medium heat.

In a bowl, combine the coconut flour, pork rinds, psyllium powder, and salt. Add in the eggs and combine until it thickens up. In a separate bowl, whisk the miso, nutritional yeast, onion powder, mustard, paprika, chili powder, turmeric, and cayenne until well mixed. Pour into the other bowl and mix until well combined, let it chill in the bowl for a few minutes while the psyllium does its thing. It will firm up into a slightly sticky mass that you can pick up with your hands. Separate into 16 balls (I make one big ball, cut in half, then again and again so I get even sized pieces) about 1 oz each for chips (16), 2 oz for tortillas (8). Place a ball of dough onto a piece of parchment paper or silicon mats. Top with another parchment, plastic wrap, or mat. Using a rolling pin, roll the dough out in a circle shape with even thickness throughout (about as thick as a quarter). Peel off the top sheet. If your circle is a little rough, you can use your hands to tweak your tortilla. Take the parchment\mat over to the skillet, flip the paper\mat upside down, get the tortilla in contact with the pan, use a spatula to gently press all around the tortilla until you see it change color through the sheet (get lighter), in a second or two, it will peal right off as the tortilla heats up. Saute until light brown, then flip and bake through. Move off the skillet, repeat with the rest of the balls.

If you want to make the Doritos, there's a few more steps:

Preheat oven to 350F
Once tortillas cooled, slice into 6 or 8 wedges. place as many wedges on a baking sheet as will fit without overlapping. Put in the oven for 5 minutes. Flip each one. Put back in for 5 minutes, watching to make sure they don't burn on the edges. Move off the sheet to a spot to cool. Repeat until all the chips are baked. Toss with a little nutritional yeasts and smoked paprika to taste. EAT! Yes. You can dip with these.

NUTRITION COUNT PER wrap or 12 chips (based off my ingredients, double-check your numbers!): Calories: 36, Protein: 3g, Fat: 2g, Carbs: 3g, Fiber: 3g, NET CARBS: 0g

AHH, TORTILLA CHIPS, I'VE MISSED YOU

Keto tortilla chips
Ingredients:
1/2 cup Coconut Flour
2 tbsp Psyllium Husks
4 Eggs
1 tbsp, Olive Oil
4 tbsp golden flax meal
1/2 oz., Pork Rinds crushed
1 cup water
1 tsp salt
1 tsp garlic powder
1 tsp onion powder

In a bowl, combine the coconut flour, pork rinds, psyllium powder, seasonings, and salt. Add in the eggs and combine until i thickens up then add water into the bowl. Mix until well and then let it chill in the bowl for a few minutes while the psyllium does its thing. Separate into 8 balls (I make one big ball, cut in half, then again and again so I get even sized pieces) and place the dough onto a piece of parchment paper or silicon mats. Top with another parchment, plastic wrap, or mat. Using a rolling pin, roll the dough out in a circle shape with even thickness throughout (about as thick as a quarter). If your circle is a little rough, you can use your hands to tweak your tortilla. Heat a large pan to medium-high heat with coconut oil, olive oil or spray. Once hot, place an unbaked tortilla on the pan. I find it easiest to flip the paper upside down, get the tortilla in contact with the pan, and then in a second or two, it will peel right off as the tortilla heats up. Sauté until light brown, then flip and bake through. Let cool for a few minutes and preheat your oven to 400F. Spray each one with the oil of your choice (or rub both sides with an oil dampened paper towel) to lightly coat with oil, then stack them on top of each other. Cut down the stack so you have 6 stacks of wedges. Place as many as you can on parchment or silicon mat on a baking sheet without overlapping and sprinkle salt over them. Put in oven for about 5 minutes or until the edges start to get crisp, then flip them and bake for another 3-4 minutes. Remove and place on cooling rack. EAT THEM!!

NUTRITION COUNT PER 6 chips (based off my ingredients, double-check your numbers!): Calories: 114, Protein: 5g, Fat: 8 g, Carbs: 6g, Fiber: 4g, NET CARBS: 2g

HOBBIT'S KETO SESAME KRACKERS

Hobbit's Keto Sesame Krackers
Servings=48
Time=30mins

Ingredients:

3/4 cup almond meal flour
1 egg
2 tbsp butter softened
2 tbsp Ground Flax Meal
3 tbsp sesame seeds
1/2 tsp salt
1/2 tsp black pepper

Preheat oven to 400F

Whisk egg until well combined. Add the rest of the ingredients, stir and fold with a large spoon or rubber spatula until you have a solid ball of dough. Put it in the fridge for about 15 minutes to rest and firm up. Remove the dough. Place on a piece of parchment or silicone mat. Place another on top, then roll out the dough into a rectangle about the thickness of a quarter or a little thicker. You don't want these too thin, they won't puff up a bunch when baked, so think the size of a commercial cracker. Use a pizza cutter or long knife to cut them into squares (or use a cooking cutter for fun shapes). Hopefully you cut straighter than Hobbits. Place the parchment on a baking sheet. Put in the oven for 8-10 minutes. Take them out, flip them over, and bake for another 5 minutes or until the edges start to brown. Remove from oven, let cool on sheet, then break apart. Crackers. Keto. Krackers.

Nutritional information: Calories each 34, Fat:3g, Protein: 1, Carbs: 1,Fiber:1, Net carbs: 0

HOBBIT'S KEETOS! KETO CHEETO'S KNOCKOFFS (IRON GIANT DOUGH)

Hobbit's Keetos!
Servings=4
Time=30mins prep 60min rest

Ingredients:

One batch Iron Giant dough from first section of this book

6 tbsp of your favorite hard cheese, grated (Asiago, Parmesan, etc – I used 3 tbsp nutritional yeast and 3 tbsp Parmesan)
About 1/2 cup of your preferred frying oil (or a deep fryer if you have one)
1/2 tsp salt

** *If making dough specifically for this recipe, when adding the first 1/2 cup of protein, also add 1/2 of the cheese. You can skip adding cheese during the rolling process.*

Get your cold ball of Iron Giant out of the fridge. Knead it for 2-3 minutes to soften it up. Form into a log. If you have a pasta roller, this would be a good time to use it. Otherwise, place on parchment or silicone mat and press down with your hand and flatten as much as possible. Cover with another sheet, and using a rolling pin, roll out as thin as possible (this is a pretty stiff dough, would be a good time to cash in on payback if you have a teen that has misbehaved). If pre-made dough, sprinkle half of the cheese over the dough, otherwise, continue. Fold over and over like an envelope. Roll out flat again to about the thickness of one blade of your kitchen shears. Again, you have a pasta roller, this would be a good time to use it. If not, get out a pizza cutter or sharp knife and cut the dough into strips. You don't have to be precise, just cut to widths between spaghetti and fettuccine. Lay on a wire rack to dry for about an hour. You back? Has it been an hour? Are the strips a little dry but not hard? Good. Now heat up your oil in the fryer, small sauce pan, or small skillet. Bring it to about 350F. Using the knife or cutter again, cut the dough into 1-1.5" strips toss around so they don't stick. Doesn't look like much, does it? Oh, but wait! Take the rest of the cheese mixture and dump into a plastic bag. Add salt and shake to combine. Take 8-10 cut strips and drop into the hot oil. You will need to move quickly, these fry in less than a minute. As soon as they hit the oil, they should start to puff up, then quickly brown. Stir constantly to make sure all surfaces are getting hit with the oil. As soon as they get dark tan, remove them, drop into the bag with the cheese and salt, shake, then move to a plate covered with a paper towel to cool. Once they are all done, drop in a bowl and enjoy!!

Nutritional information : Calories: 103, Fat: 2g, Protein: 20g, Carbs: 0g, Fiber: 0g, Net Carbs: 0g

HOBBIT'S KETO GARLIC CHIVE CRACKERS...SNACK TIME!

Hobbit's Garlic Chive Crackers
Servings=48
Time=30mins

Ingredients:

3/4 cup almond meal flour
1 egg
2 tbsp butter softened
2 tbsp Ground Flax Meal
1 tsp garlic powder
2 tsp chopped or dried chives
1/2 tsp salt
1/2 tsp black pepper

Preheat oven to 400F

Whisk egg until well combined. Add the rest of the ingredients, stir and fold with a large spoon or rubber spatula until you have a solid ball of dough. Put it in the fridge for about 15 minutes to rest and firm up. Remove the dough. Place on a piece of parchment or silicone mat. Place another on top, then roll out the dough into a rectangle about the thickness of a quarter or a little thicker. You don't want these too thin, they won't puff up a bunch when baked, so think the size of a commercial cracker. Use a pizza cutter or long knife to cut them into squares (or use a cooking cutter for fun shapes). Place the parchment on a baking sheet. Put in the oven for 8-10 minutes. Take them out, flip them over, and bake for another 5 minutes or until the edges start to brown. Remove from oven, let cool on sheet, then break apart. Crackers. Keto. Krackers.

Nutritional information: Calories each 34, Fat:3g, Protein: 1, Carbs: 1,Fiber:1, Net carbs: 0

CAKES. CAKES!!!

LOSE WEIGHT, EAT CAKE!! HOBBIT'S KETO MOCHA CAKE

Lose weight, eat cake!! Hobbit's Keto Mocha Cake (If you want to use a traditional round cake pan for a LARGE cake, double the recipe.)

Servings=12
Time=45 min

Cake ingredients:

4 tbsp butter, melted
4 eggs
2 tbsp cup cocoa powder
1 cup sweetener
1 tsp vanilla extract
1 cup almond meal or flour
1/4 cup unflavored whey isolate
1 tsp baking soda
1/4 cup instant coffee

Glaze:

2 tbsp. melted butter
1 tbsp. cocoa powder
2 tbsp. sweetener of your choice
2 tbsp. heavy cream

Preheat oven to 350F

For the Cakes:

Using your mixer or by hand (I go by hand as I make a mess usually with cocoa powder and a mixer, lol), beat or whisk the wet until well combined. Slowly add cocoa powder, then the rest of dry. Continue mixing until you have a smooth batter. You can use a deep square or round layer pan for this, or since I made these as a special treat for The Lady, use a fancy pan like I did. If using a traditional cake pan, lightly grease the pan, dust with coconut flour or almond meal. Pour into a cake pan. Put in the oven for 30 minutes or until it passes the toothpick test. Remove and let cool until cold.

For the Glaze:

Using your whisk, beat the wet until it combined, then slowly add dry, scraping sides of bowl often. Set aside to firm up while the cakes cool, shooting for a thick syrup consistency. Once cake is cool, drizzle the glaze over the top and sides of the cake. Put in fridge for 15 minutes to harden glaze. Slice. Eat. Rinse. Repeat:).

Nutritional information: Calories each slice 95 , Fat: 8g Protein: 4g, Carbs: 1g Fiber: 0g Net: 1g

THERE ISN'T A BAD TIME OF YEAR TO HAVE CHOCOLATE CAKE

Servings=16
Time=30mins

{Photo and cake by Deliaha Lamberts}

Ingredients:

- 1/4 cup almond flour
- 1/4 cup oat fiber (NOT OAT FLOUR)
- 1/4 cup baking cocoa powder (increase to 1/2 cup if using unflavored whey)
- 4 Tbsp. butter
- 4 Egg
- 1/2 cup (1 scoop (33.6 g), chocolate whey protein isolate (I use This one often for flavored).
- 1/2 cup (cooked), Kabocha Squash
- 1/2 cup brewed coffee (for less intense chocolate taste, use 1/2 cup water instead)
- 1 Tbsp. baking powder
- 1 tsp glucomannan powder
- 1 Tbsp. vanilla extract
- 1/3 cup or equivalent of sweetener of your choice

Pre-heat oven to 375F. Grease cake pan (or cupcake tins if making cupcakes instead of a cake-cake).

Mash up the kabocha until it is free of chunks, I like to zip it in the blender quick. Combine the butter, kabocha, sweetener, extract in a bowl and mix well with mixer until smooth. Add everything else to bowl and stir with a spoon until wet, otherwise when you use the mixer, you'll have cocoa and oat fiber flying all over the place. Ask me how I know.... Ok, is it wet? Good. Beat well for about 30 seconds until you have a smooth batter. Pour into your cake pan and pop in the oven for 45 minutes for cake (or until a tooth pick comes out dry, whichever comes first) or 30 minutes for cupcakes. Remove and let cool to touch before releasing from pan. Let cool all the way before frosting (if you so desire). I've included the frosting recipe I used below, this is not included in the nutrition count so adjust accordingly if you chose

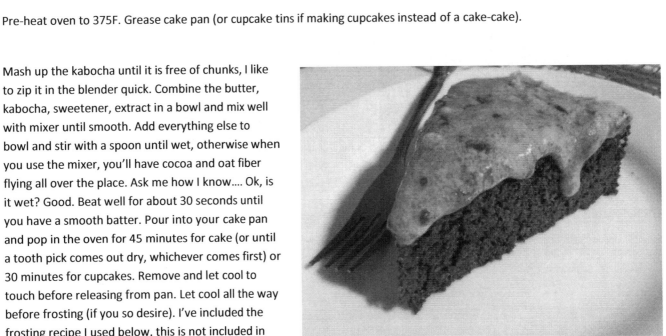

to frost. You could also glaze with some sugar-free syrup or dust with dutch chocolate powder or powdered sweetener. Or screw that, eat it just the way it is and smile a brown grin of chocolate cake teeth.

FROSTING:

1/2 cup (1 stick) softened butter
1/2 cup or equivalent of sweetener of your choice
1.5 tsp raspberry extract
1 tsp vanilla extract
Couple of drops of red food coloring just to make it look purdy...
Whip the butter until starts to get fluffy. Add rest of ingredients, whip until smooth. Spread on cake once cooled.

Nutritional info per slice (based off my ingredients, check yours!): Calories: 60, Fat: 5g, Protein: 2g, Carbs: 3.5, Fiber: 3, Net Carbs: 0.5

HOBBIT CHURNS OUT SOME KETO PEANUT BUTTER CUPCAKES

Servings=6
Time=30mins

Ingredients for Cupcakes:

1/4 cup coconut flour
1/2 Scoop (about 2 tbsp.) Unflavored Whey Isolate
*1 Cup, Baked Kabocha Squash
1/2 cup sweetener of your choice

1/4 cup Almond Milk

2 tbsp. Butter, melted

3 large Eggs

1 tsp(s), Vanilla extract

**1/4 cup PBFit Peanut Butter Powder

1.5 tsp(s), Baking Powder

1/2 tsp(s), Salt

* You can replace the kabocha with pumpkin puree or butternut squash, adjust the carb count as needed.

** You can replace PBFit powder with 1/4 cup unsweetened natural peanut butter, reduce the almond milk to 2tbsp. Preheat your oven to 350F. Get out a muffin pan and lightly grease all with coconut oil (I use the spray type because not only do I like simple, I'm freaking lazy too). Combine all the wet ingredients (including the kabocha) for the in a bowl, beat until smooth. Put all the dry ingredients in a different bowl, then whisk to combine\break up clumps. Add the dry to the wet, and beat until smooth, scraping down the sides. Using a 1/3 cup measuring cup or large soup spoon, drop the batter into your muffin tin and fill each one to just below the top. Place in oven for 25-30 minutes or until the tops puff up and start to brown. Let cool to touch before removing from tin, then put on rack to finish cooling...

While cooling, make the frosting:

4 tbsp. butter, softened

1/2 cup sweetener of your choice

**2 tbsp. PBFit Peanut Butter Powder

** You can replace with 2 tbsp unsweetened natural peanut butter

Beat the butter until fluffy, while continuing to beat, add the sweetener and PBFit powder. Continue to beat until well combined and a smooth frosting. Once cupcakes are cool to the touch, frost and enjoy!

Nutritional info (based off my ingredients, check yours!): Calories: 101, Fat: 7g, Protein: 7g, Carbs: 6, Fiber: 4, Net Carbs: 2

HOBBIT'S DEATH BY CHOCOLATE HAND CAKES - NANA'S RECIPE KETO-HACKED :)

Hobbit's Death By Chocolate Hand Cakes.

Servings=4
Time=45 min

Ingredients:

3 tbsp. butter, melted
4 eggs
1/2 cup cocoa powder
1 cup sweetener
1 tsp vanilla extract
1/2 cup almond meal
1 tsp baking soda
2 tbsp Unflavored Whey Protein

Frosting:

1/4 cup softened butter
1/4 cup softened (not melted) coconut oil
2 squares (0.5oz\14g) unsweetened baker's chocolate, melted
2 tbsp. cocoa powder
1 cup or equivalent sweetener
1 tsp vanilla extract
2 tbsp. heavy cream

Preheat oven to 350F

For the Cakes:

Using your mixer or by hand (I go by hand as I make a mess usually with cocoa powder and a mixer, lol), beat\whisk the wet until well combined. Slowly add cocoa powder, then the rest of dry. Continue mixing until you have a batter of brownie batter consistency. Spoon onto a baking sheet (or if you have one of those cool pans for muffin tops or pancakes, use that instead). Put in the oven for 15 minutes. Remove and let cool until cold.

For the Frosting:

Using your mixer, beat the wet until it starts to get creamy, then slowly add dry, scraping sides of bowl often. Continue mixing until combined, then beat on high for 2-3 minutes or until the frosting comes together. Set aside to firm up while the cakes cool. Once cool, slap a big, ol' dollop on one cake, top with another. Resist temptation to lick the edges:)
Ah, screw that! EAT ONE. Or three.

Nutritional information: Calories each 522 , Fat: 49g Protein: 13g, Carbs: 7g Fiber: 4g Net: 3g

CAKE. HOBBITS LOVE CAKE. CHOCOLATE FUDGE, GANACHE, AND PEANUT BUTTER BUTTERCREAM KETO CAKE. YES, THIS JUST MIGHT BE HEAVEN

DISCLAIMER!!

Be forewarned, this is rich. Very rich. Very high in calories. The quantity of some of the ingredients (butter, sweetener, baker's chocolate) is high. Wait, calories? HA! WHO CARES! This is for special occasions, right? BRING IT!! In the end, it's 1 net carbs per slice. The original one? Over 100g carbs. Yeh. Oh, and no special ingredients! While I used PBFit powder, you could swap for no-sugar-added creamy peanut butter (one cup instead of the PBFit and coconut oil). It also has more ingredients and steps than I usually do, but trust me, it will be worth it and seriously, it's a cake. WITH GANACHE AND FROSTING!!! I will have you note that the one I made is small (1/3rd recipe) because we have a bunch of goodies still in the freezer and there's only two of us. The recipe below will make 3 8×8 or 8in round cakes, plus enough ganache and frosting to do it up right for the whole family (12 slices) or a gathering (trust me, they will have NO CLUE it is low carb!). If you want to make a small one like I did, cut all the ingredients to 1/3rd, make one cake layer, slice into 4 equal parts, and make a 4-layer small cake of 4 serving total. Same nutritional values. Soooooooooooo....

WHO WANTS CAKE????

Servings=12
Time=45 min

Cake Ingredients:

1 cup butter
6 eggs
1.5 cups sweetener (stevia bulk or erythritol\blends)
12 squares of baker's chocolate (unsweetened, I used 100% cacao)
1 tbsp. vanilla extract
1 tbsp. instant coffee (optional but helps the chocolate 'pop')
1/2 tsp salt
1/2 cup cocoa powder

Ganache Ingredients:

12 squares baker's chocolate (unsweetened, I used 100% cacao)
1/4 cup cocoa powder
1/2 cup butter
1 cup sweetener equivalent (stevia bulk or erythritol\blends)

Frosting Ingredients:

3/4 cup PBFit powder
2 tbsp. melted coconut oil
1 cup butter
2 tsp vanilla
1.5 cups sweetener equivalent (stevia bulk or erythritol\blends)
4 tbsp. heavy cream

Preheat oven to 350F

Grease three 8 inch cake pans, line bottom with parchment paper. Melt the butter and baker's chocolate in the microwave or on the stove top, starting with the chocolate first until starts to soften, then include the butter. Break out your stand mixer if you have one, yes, I even used my old beast :). Beat together the eggs, vanilla, and sweetener for about five minutes at high speed until pale and more than doubled in size. Add the cocoa, coffee, and salt and mix again until combined. Stream in the melted chocolate and butter and beat until combined, then switch to medium high for one minute. Divide into prepared cake pans and bake for about 20-25 minutes or until toothpick comes out clean. Let cakes cool in pans until completely cooled. Remove.

Make Ganache:

Melt chocolate and butter like you did for the cake. Whisk well. Add cocoa and sweetener. Use mixer on med-high to mix well until becomes consistency of frosting. Spread over the top of each cake, using all of it.

Make the Frosting:

Cream together the peanut butter, vanilla, oil and butter until smooth, then add sweetener and cream. Beat on high until fluffy. Refrigerate for 5-10 minutes. Put a layer over each layer of ganache. Assemble cake into 3 layers. Frost remainder of cake. Lick frosting spatula. Smile. Scrape inside of bowl to get last bit. Smile. Oops. I mean put cake in fridge for at least 15 minutes before cutting and serving. I calculated macros on 12 slices of the whole recipe.

Nutritional information (based off 12 pieces of cake): Calories each 531, Fat: 53g, Protein: 9, Carbs: 7 Fiber: 6 Total carbs: 1

HOBBIT HACKS YELLOW CAKE - KETOFIED

Servings=8
Time=30 min

Preheat oven to 350F

Ingredients:

1/2 cup almond flour
1/2 cup Unflavored Whey
Protein,
6 tbsp. butter, softened
3 eggs
1 tsp xanthan gum
1.5 cups sweetener
1.5 tsp vanilla

Put the butter and sweetener
in a bowl, beat with your mixer until creamed. Add eggs. Beat until fluffy. Add dry. Beat on low until combined. Should be a slightly thick dough that is a little elastic. Pour into your cake pan, smooth the top. Drop a few times lightly on the counter to even out. Put in the oven for 15-20 minutes or until passes toothpick test. Do not overbake so it doesn't dry out. Let cool completely in the pan before frosting or cutting.

Nutritional information (based off 16 pieces of cake): Calories each 85, Fat: 7g, Protein: 5, Carbs: less than 1

KETO PUMPKIN-MAPLE WHOOPIE PIES...OK, THIS AUTUMN THING MIGHT NOT SUCK AFTER ALL :)

SReady for a New England treat, KETO STYLE? GO! (makes 5)

Ingredients (cookie part):

- 1/4 cup + 2 tbsp. Coconut Flour
- * 0.5 Scoops (33g) vanilla whey protein powder (we use Dymatize Elite, YMMV)
- 1.5 Cup, Baked Kabocha Squash
- 0.5 cup sweetener
- 0.25 cup Almond Milk
- 2 tbsp. Butter – Salted
- 3.00 large, Eggs
- 0.5 tsp Xanthan Gum
- 1.00 tsp(s), Vanilla extract
- 1 tsp maple extract
- ** 1.00 tsp(s), Spices – Cinnamon, ground
- 1 tsp(s), Baking Powder
- 1 tsp(s), Apple Cider Vinegar
- 0.50 tsp(s), Salt, table
- ** 0.50 tsp(s), Spices, ginger, ground
- ** 0.25 tsp(s), Spices, cloves, ground

* If dairy-sensitive or do not have whey protein, increase coconut flour by 2 tbsp. and oil by 1 tbsp.

** You can replace the ginger, cinnamon, and cloves with 2 tsp of pumpkin spice

Filling:

3/4 cup coconut oil (refined, softened)

1.5 cup granulated stevia

.75 cup coconut (or almond) milk

1 tsp vanilla extract

1 tsp maple extract

1/4 tsp xanthan gum

Make the cookie-cakes:

Preheat your oven to 350F. Get out a 10×17 baking pan, line with parchment or silicon mat and lightly grease all with coconut oil (I use the spray type because not only do I like simple, I'm freaking lazy too). Combine all the wet ingredients (including the kabocha) for the cake part in a bowl, beat until smooth. Put all the dry ingredients in a different bowl, then whisk to combine\break up clumps. Add the dry to the wet, and beat until smooth, scraping down the sides. This is a little thicker than the cake recipe to make it easier to drop the cookie cakes. Using an ice cream scoop or a couple of large soup spoons, drop the batter on the parchment, should make 10 cookies about the size of a regular cookie, just raised up a bit. Don't press down! You want them raised. Use the back of one of the spoons or a spatula to smooth the tops a little. We like smooth cookie-cakes. Drop the pan a few times from an inch or two height to level pop in the oven for 15-20 minutes or until the center of a cookie-cake is firm but spongy, not browned (edges will be a little browned, that's good) and no longer wet. Remove, put on racks to cool. Now, let's make the filling. Using your mixer (preferably with the whisk attachment but regular beaters will get the job done), put all the ingredients except the thickening agent in the bowl and whisk\beat until it combined. If the coconut oil is too clumpy, toss in the microwave for 10 seconds or so. If too runny, toss in the fridge. You are looking for a thick consistency, about equal to cake batter. Once that is achieved, add the thickening agent and beat the hell out of it until it is well mixed. It should now look and feel like soft frosting. Pop in the fridge while the cookie-cakes are cooling so it will firm up a little. Once they are cool, get your filling and spread a generous dollop on one and top with another. Yes, this should squish out the sides a little. Oh yes it should :). Once you have all of them made, cover with wrap and put back in the fridge until it is time to DIG THE HELL IN!!!

Nutritional info (based off my ingredients, check yours!): Calories: 234, Fat: 22g, Protein: 5g, Carbs: 6, Fiber: 5, Net Carbs: 1

LET'S TUMBLE INTO FALL WITH A PUMPKIN JELLYROLL, HOW'S THAT SOUND? AND YES, LOW CARB!!

Not Traditional Pumpkin, not quite jelly, roll

Servings=8

Time=45mins

Cake Ingredients:

0.75 cup Organic Coconut Flour

1.00 Scoops (33g) vanilla whey protein powder
0.75 Cup, Baked Kabocha Squash
0.75 cup sweetener
0.50 cup Almond Milk
0.25 cup, Butter – Salted
6.00 large, Eggs
1 tbsp. Psyllium Husk
1 tsp Xanthan Gum Powder
0.50 Envelope, Gelatin, Unflavored
1.00 tsp(s), Vanilla extract
1.00 tsp(s), Spices – Cinnamon, ground
0.50 tsp(s), Baking Powder
0.50 tsp(s), Apple Cider Vinegar
0.50 tsp(s), Salt, table
0.50 tsp(s), Spices, ginger, ground
0.25 tsp(s), Spices, cloves, ground

Filling Ingredients

4.00 tbsp.(s), Butter – Salted – softened
2.00 tbsp.(s) Coconut Oil – softened
8.00 oz.(s), Cream cheese – Plain – softened
0.25 cup(s) sweetener

Preheat your oven to 350F. Get out a 10×17 baking pan, line with parchment or silicon mat and lightly grease all with coconut oil (I use the spray type because not only do I like simple, I'm freaking lazy too). Combine all the wet ingredients (including the kabocha) for the cake part in a bowl, beat until smooth, then slowly add the gelatin\water mix while beating until incorporated (10-15 seconds). Put all the dry ingredients in a different bowl, then whisk to combine\break up clumps. Add the dry to the wet, and beat until smooth, scraping down the sides. Pour into the pan, smooth with a spatula, then drop the pan a few times from an inch or two height to level and smooth out the cake batter. Pop in the oven for 15-20 minutes or until the center is firm but spongy, not browned (edges will be a little browned, that's good) and no longer wet. SET ASIDE UNTIL COMPLETELY COOLED! DO NOT RUSH THIS PART! You don't want your filling to melt all over the place, do you? Didn't think so.

Let's whip up the filling.

Put everything in a bowl, whip it up good with your mixer until fluffy and spreadable. Spread evenly from one edge to the other on the cake, making sure you go to all the edges. Now, for the fun part – rolling the roll. First, lay out a sheet of plastic wrap the same length as your unrolled cake, putting one end right up to the edge of the cake. Grab the parchment or mat on the OTHER end of the cake and lift it. Fold a short roll of the cake over (if it cracks, no worries, it will still taste good 🙂) onto the filling to start your roll, then slowly continue to lift the parchment\mat while rolling the cake with your other hand until you have a nice log. Go slow

(I didn't this time around and below you can see a small crack, not that it is going to make it taste bad) and be gentle.

Now, roll that log over onto the plastic wrap, then roll it up TIGHT in the wrap and seal it up (you might need another sheet to cover the ends). Pop it in the fridge for 2-3 hours so the filling 'firms' up. Take it out and cut it into 10 one inch slices. Done! 10 slices? But what if you have a family of 4? Eat two to make it even, you're the baker, there are privileges of being the baker :). Want something simpler? Try my Pumpkin (Kabocha) whoopee pies!

Nutritional information (based off my brand of ingredients, double-check yours!): Calories – 263, Fat: 23, Protein: 9, Carbs: 6, Fiber: 2, Net Carbs: 4

C IS FOR COOKIE, THAT'S GOOD ENOUGH FOR ME!

ANTHONY'S GOODS NOW HAS OAT FIBER, SO I MADE CHOCOLATE CHIP COOKIES IN THE NAME OF SCIENCE

So, are you ready for some chocolate chip cookies that don't suck? (makes 12 big'uns)??

Servings: 12
Time: 30mins

Ingredients:

1/4 cup **almond flour**
1/2 cup **oat fiber** (NOT OAT FLOUR)
1/4 cup water
4 Tbsp. SOFTENED butter (not melted, NO NOT MELTED)
1/2 cup or equivalent of sweetener of your choice
1 tbsp. protein isolate
1/2 tsp. salt
1/2 cup sugar-free (**or my homemade**) chocolate chips\chunks

1 tbsp. baking powder
1 tsp baking soda
1 Tbsp. vanilla extract

Pre-heat oven to 375F. Get a baking sheet lined with silipat or parchment.

Cream (that means beat on medium speed until smooth and fluffy) butter, sweetener, and vanilla. Stop mixer. Add the dry ingredients, then the water. Take a spoon or rubber spatula and hand mix just long enough to knock down some of the powder from the oat fiber. While this isn't critical in the making of the cookies, unless you like fine oat fiber powder all over everything – including stuff three rooms away – do this step :). Turn mixer back on and beat on low until you have a good cookie dough. Fold in the chocolate chips (I added some sliced almonds to mine just for fun, that is not reflected in the nutritional count or ingredients list). Scoop out onto your baking sheet. Once all are scooped out, wet your hands and press each one down a little. This will help them spread out instead of UP when they bake. Put in the oven for 15 minutes or until the edges brown. Remove from oven and move immediately to cooling rack. Let them cool. When they first come out of the oven, they will still be soft. The cooling process finalizes the crispy texture we are looking for :).

Nutritional info per slice (based off my ingredients, check yours!): Calories: 60, Fat: 5g, Protein: 2g, Carbs: 3.5, Fiber: 3, Net Carbs: 0.5

HOBBIT CREATES KETO SKILLET SUGAR COOKIE PIE

Servings=8
Time=30mins

Crust:

1 cup almond meal\flour
1/4 cup ground pumpkin seeds (or 2 tbsp. coconut flour)
4 tbsp. Butter, melted
1 Eggs
1/4 Cup sweetener of your choice

Preheat oven to 350F

Blend together everything until well combined. Grease a cast iron skillet (or if you don't have one, make this in a pie plate), then spread the mixture evenly on the bottom of the skillet\plate. Put in preheated oven until it starts to firm up, about 7-8 (5-6 if using pie plate) minutes. You will know when it is no longer wet to the touch. Remove and let it cool a little while you make the top part.

For the cookie part:

2 tbsp. softened butter
1/2 cup almond meal\flour

2 tbsp. Unflavored Whey Isolate (or flavored whey isolate for a different taste).
1/2 cup sweetener of your choice
2 tsp vanilla extract
1 egg
1 tsp baking powder
1/2 haas avocado, mushed.

Brownies:
Combine the butter, sweetener, vanilla extract, egg, and avocado, beat until creamed and fluffy. Add the rest of the ingredients, stir slowly by hand until fully combined – don't beat or whip or you'll end up with a much cakey-er texture. Spread over the top of your prepared crust. Bake for about 12-13 minutes, or until the edges start to brown. Cool. Slice into wedges. Eat as is or top with some keto caramel.

(Optional caramel topping)
For the caramel:

3 Tbsp. salted butter
1/3 cup sweetener of your choice
1/4 cup heavy cream
1/4 tsp xanthan gum

To make the caramel:

Melt the butter and sweetener together in a small saucepan over medium heat. Cook, stirring constantly for about 2 minutes or until bubbling. Add the cream and, xanthan then whisk continually, 3-5 minutes over medium heat. It will get darker in color the longer you cook it. Remove from heat when your desired color is reached. Let it cool slightly to thicken.

Nutritional info (based off my ingredients, check yours!)for 1 slice: 206 calories, 14g fat, 7g protein. Total Carbs: 4, Fiber: 3, Net Carbs: 1

HOBBIT CREATES DEATH BY COCONUT

Servings=6
Time=30mins

Crust:

Crust	
1/2 cups almond meal	
cup coconut flour	.25
shredded	.25
flaked	.25
tbsp. coconut oil, melted	2
cocoa powder	1/4
Eggs	1
Cup sweetener of your choice	.25

Blend together everything and pour   in 8×8
pan. Put in preheated 350F oven until sides start to lightly brown. Let cool.

For the brownies:

4 tbsp. melted butter
1/4 cup almond flour
2 tbsp. whey protein isolate
1/2 cup sweetener of your
1 tsp vanilla extract
2 egg
1 tsp baking powder
.25 cup coconut flour
.25 shredded
.25 flaked
2 tbsp. coconut milk

Brownies:

Combine the melted butter, almond flour, coconut flour, sweetener, vanilla extract, eggs , cocoa powder, chopped chocolate in a medium bowl. Stir slowly by hand until fully combined – don't beat or whip or you'll end up with a much cakey-er texture. Pour into an 8×8 square pan. Bake in a preheated 375 degree oven for about 12-13 minutes, or until the center no longer jiggles. Cool.

For the caramel:
3 Tbsp. salted butter
1/3 cup sweetener of your choice
1/4 cup heavy cream
1/4 tsp xanthan gum

To make the caramel:

Melt the butter and sweetener together in a small saucepan over medium heat. Cook, stirring constantly for about 2 minutes or until bubbling. Add the cream and, xanthan then whisk continually, 3-5 minutes over medium heat. It will get darker in color the longer you cook it. Remove from heat when your desired color is reached. Let it cool slightly to thicken. Remove the brownies from the pan. Spread the caramel over the bottom crust, making sure to cover the crust entirely. Carefully place the brownie sheet on top, press lightly to 'cement' it all together. Place in fridge for 30 minutes. Slice into 16 squares. EAT!

Nutritional info (based off my ingredients, check yours!)for 1 brownie: 166 calories, 10g fat, 2.5g net carbs, 3g protein. Total Carbs: 6, Fiber: 4.5, Net Carbs: 2.5

I KNOW IT'S NOT GS COOKIE SEASON BUT ANYONE WANT SOME KETO SAMOAS?

Ready?
Servings=15
Time=45 min

Ingredients:
For the cookie base:

1/2 cup Almond Flour
2 tbsp. coconut flour
1/3 cup cooked kabocha puree (or pumpkin\butternut squash)
1/2 tsp salt
2 tbsp. melted coconut oil
1/2 cup sweetener of your choice or equivalent measure.
1 tsp vanilla extract
Preheat oven to 350F

Prepare a baking sheet, lined with parchment or silicone mat (or lightly greased if neither of those are available). Using a mixer on low speed or with a spoon, mix the wet along with the sweetener until combined and smooth. Add the flours, mix until completely combined but do not over mix it. Scoop or spoon out 15 portions, flatten with your hand, then use a finger or handle of wooden spoon to make a hole in the center (or not, that's up to you) or spread on the bottom of a 8×8 baking dish. Place in the oven for 12-15 minutes or until the edges brown.

The Caramel layer:
My keto caramel sauce
1/2 cup unsweetened shredded coconut

Heat sauce over medium heat until starts to lightly steam. Add coconut, stir frequently until about half the liquid is gone. Immediately scoop equal portions on top of each cookie. Refrigerate for 15 minutes or until cool to touch.

Chocolate topping:

1/4 cup Hobbit Chocolate Chips

Melt in microwave. Drizzle over top of cookies (or mound it if you are like me). Return immediately to fridge to harden. Once set... EAT!!!!!!

Nutritional information per cookie: Calories each 66 , Fat: 6g Protein: 0g, Carbs: 2g Fiber: 1g Net: 1g

HOBBIT'S KETO CHOCOLATE CRINKLE COOKIES

Servings=16
Time=30mins

Ingredients:

2/3 cup almond flour
1/4 cup coconut flour
1/4 cup butter, softened
14g baker's unsweetened chocolate, melted
1/4 cup unsweetened cocoa powder
3 tbsp. heavy whipping cream
1 tsp baking powder
1 egg
2 tsp vanilla extract
1 cup sweetener of your choice
** For a nut-free version, replace the almond flour with 1/3 cup more coconut flour, increase the butter by 2tbsp, cream by 1 tbsp.

Preheat oven to 350F.

Combine in a large bowl the butter, baker's chocolate, and sweetener, beat until creamy. While beating, add cream and extract, beat until smooth, then add the egg, continue to beat until well combined. While beating on low speed, gradually add the dry ingredients, starting with the cocoa powder, then flours, until you have a thick, spoon able dough.

**If you can use granulated sweeteners like Swerve, erythritol, etc, you could roll the dough balls in some to take them up another level.

Let sit for 5 minutes while you line a baking sheet with parchment or silicone mat. Roll into 16 one inch balls onto the baking sheet, Press down with your knuckles or back of a spoon to flatten them out a little, then pop in the oven for 12-15 minutes or until they no longer spring back to the touch and the tops start to crack. Remove from oven, move to cooking rack. Eat with a nice glass of almond or coconut milk, or maybe a chai latte :).

Nutritional information per cookie (based off my brand of ingredients, double-check yours!): Calories – 96, Fat: 8, Protein: 2, Carbs: 3, Fiber: 2, Net Carbs: 1.

HOBBIT'S KETO SWEET AND SOFT PECAN PIE COOKIES

Servings=15
Time=30mins

Preheat oven to 350F

Making the cookies:

0.50 cup Unflavored Whey Isolate
0.5 cup, Almond Meal/flour
1 egg
0.50 cup(s), Butter, melted
1 cup sweetener
2 tbsp. heavy cream
0.50 tsp, Baking Powder
1/4 cup pecans, roughly chopped
1.50 tsp Maple extract

Combine all the dry ingredients except sweetener in a small bowl and whisk to combine, breaking up any clumps. In a larger bowl, with your mixer quickly combine the sweetener and butter until completely incorporated. Add the egg, cream and extract, beat again until smooth. While beating on low speed, gradually add the dry ingredients until you have a thick, spoon able dough. Add your nuts to the bowl and fold in with a spoon or spatula. Let sit for 5 minutes while you line a baking sheet with parchment or silicone mat. Spoon or scoop 15 balls onto the baking sheet, press down with your knuckles to flatten them out a little, then pop in the oven for 12-15 minutes or until they lightly start to brown around the bottom edges. Remove...and unlike I usually suggest, eat these puppies as soon as they don't burn your mouth! One MUST have sweet goodness while still warm at least once (though these are tasty cool as well). ENJOY!

Nutritional information (based off my brand of ingredients, double-check yours!): Calories – 111, Fat: 10, Protein: 5, Carbs: 1, Fiber: 0, Net Carbs: 1

KETO KNUTTER BUTTERS - HOBBIT HACKS NUTTER BUTTERS

Servings=12
Time=30mins

Ingredients (cookie dough):

1/4 cup Organic Coconut Flour
1/2 cup Almond Flour
1/4 cup whey protein isolate
1/8 cup butter – melted
1/4 cup natural (unsweetened) peanut butter *
2 eggs
1 tsp baking powder
1 tsp vanilla extract
1/2 cup Stevia (concentrated – use 1tsp=1cup) or equivalent sweetener like Swerve
1/8 tsp salt

You can sub in 1/4 PBFit or PB2 powder instead of the peanut butter, if so, increase the butter by 2 tbsp.

Preheat oven to **300F**

Get out your biggish mixing bowl. Whisk the eggs, butter and extract together until eggs are well-beat and a little frothy. Add the rest of the ingredients and mix well with a spoon or my favorite tool, a silicon spatula. It will seem dry at first and look like it just isn't going to come together. Keep mixing. When it comes together without crumbling apart, pick it up in your hands and kneed it for a few seconds like you would pizza dough. Let it sit for a few minutes – go get a cup of coffee or something. All caffeinated? Ready? OK! Next, plop it on a sheet of parchment and put another sheet (or plastic wrap or sandwich between two silicon mats) over the top and press it down flat. Get out your rolling pin and roll it out in a rectangle to about the thickness of a couple of stacked quarters. Even it up with your hands if you need to, this is very easy-to-work with dough. Cut the shapes you want. Put the cut pieces on a parchment or mat-lined cookie sheet, leaving a little space between to allow them to puff a little.Pop in the oven for about 20 minutes, checking occasionally to make sure they don't overcook. You want them to just start to brown on the edges. Once done, remove from the oven and move to a rack to cool.

While the cookies are cooling, let's make the filling.

Ingredients (filling):

1/4 cup butter – softened
1/2 cup sweetener
1/2 tsp vanilla extract
2 tbsp. heavy cream
Put the butter in a bowl and with your mixer, start blending it. SLOWLY ADD SWEETENER! That is, unless you like looking like a toddler that found the baby powder, ask me how I know… 🙂 Once the two are combined (don't worry if it looks lumpy and dry), add the other ingredients, then mix until combined. Kick it up to whip for a few seconds to make it nice and fluffy. Spread some filling on half the cookies. Top with the other half. Hide half for you for later. Share the rest. Ok. Hide 3/4 for you for later and share the rest. Tell them it was a small batch:).

Nutritional information (per cookie sandwich) : Calories: 129, Fat: 10, Protein: 6, Carbs: 3, Fiber: 1, Net carbs: 2[

SWEET, OH SO SWEET KETO WALNUT BARS - LESS THAN ONE NET CARB EACH!

Servings=16
Time=30mins

Ingredients:

1 tbsp (9.00 g), Organic Coconut Flour
4 tablespoon, Butter
1 Egg
1/2 cup Vanilla whey protein isolate
1/2 cup Unflavored Whey Protein isolate
1/4 cup heavy cream
1 tsp baking powder

1 cup sweetener
1 tsp vanilla extract
1/2 cup chopped walnuts (pecans would be good too)

Pre-heat oven to 350F

Put the cream, butter, egg, sweetener, vanilla in a bowl and mix well with a spoon. NO ELECTRIC MIXER! You don't want to work this batter too much or it will be a cake, not a bar (of course, if you WANT a cake, add 3 eggs to this recipe and beat it up good in a mixer – yes, that's all you need to do :)). Add everything else to the butter-cream-egg mixture and stir with a spoon until all the wet and dry are combined. Fold in the walnuts. Pour into your brownie pan and pop into the oven for 15-20 minutes or until the bars don't jiggle when you gently shake the pan. Don't cook too long, remember, protein powder-based recipes can dry out fast if overcooked. Remove and let cool before slicing and removing from the pan. EAT!!

Nutritional info (based off my ingredients, check yours!): Calories: 88, Fat: 6g, Protein: 4g, Carbs: 1, Fiber: 0.5, Net Carbs: 0.5

OHHH, APPLE-CRANBERRY BARS. LOW CARB. APPLE LOW CARB??? THINK. PURPLE

Servings=16
Time=30mins
Ingredients:

1 tbsp. (9.00 g), coconut flour
1/4 cup Almond Flour
4.00 tablespoon, Butter, melted
2 Eggs
1/2 cup whey protein isolate.
1 cup cubed and pealed eggplant
1/4 cup fresh or frozen cranberries
1 tsp baking powder
1/3 cup sweetener plus 2 tbsp. for dusting the eggplant
2 tsp cinnamon – one for the bars,

one

for dusting

Pre-heat oven to 350F

Peel and cube your eggplant. Rinse quick in cold water, then put on a paper towel to dry for 2-3 minutes. You want them moist but not wet. Take your 2 tbsp granulated or powdered sweetener and 1 tsp cinnamon, put in a ziplock bag and shake to mix. Dump in the eggplant and shake until they are all coated. Remove and let sit while you do the batter. Add the butter and eggs to a bowl and mix well with a spoon, whisk, or electric mixer on low speed. Add everything else to the butter and eggs (except the berries and eggplant) and stir with a spoon until all the are combined. Gently fold in the eggplant and cranberries. Pour into your 8×8 brownie pan and pop into the oven for 15-20 minutes or until the edges brown and a toothpick inserted in the center comes out clean. Let cool for a few minutes, then cut and serve!!

Nutritional info (based off my ingredients, check yours!): Calories: 57, Fat: 5g, Protein: 3g, Carbs: 2, Fiber: 1, Net Carbs: 1

THE KETO IRON CHEF JOINS THE HOBBIT AND WE ARE OFF AN RUNNING! LET'S CELEBRATE WITH KETO MAPLE WALNUT COOKIES, LESS THAN ONE CARB EA. :)

Servings=15
Time=30mins
Preheat oven to 375F

Ingredients:
1/2 cup + 1/4 cup whey protein isolate
1 egg
0.50 cup(s), Butter, melted
1 cup sweetener
2 tbsp. heavy cream
1 tbsp. water
0.50 tsp, Baking Powder

0.50 tsp baking soda
0.50 tsp Vanilla extract
0.50 tsp Maple Extract
2 tbsp. chopped walnuts (optional)

Combine all the dry ingredients in a small bowl and whisk to combine, breaking up any clumps. In a larger bowl, with your mixer quickly combine the sweetener and butter until completely incorporated. Add the egg and vanilla and maple, beat again until smooth. While beating on low speed, gradually add the dry ingredients until you have a thick, spoon able dough. Add your nuts to the bowl and fold in with a spoon or spatula. Let sit for 5 minutes while you line a baking sheet with parchment or silicone mat. Spoon or scoop 15 balls onto the baking sheet, then pop in the oven for 8-10 minutes or until the lightly start to brown. Do NOT overcook these, they will dry out and be like eating chalk. They should look like below, a little tan on the bottom edges. Remove...and unlike I usually suggest, eat these puppies as soon as they don't burn your mouth! One must have maple while still warm (though these are tasty cool as well). Notice there are two missing? The Lady couldn't wait :). BTW, these freeze excellent. ENJOY!!

Nutritional information (based off my brand of ingredients, double-check yours!): Calories – 76, Fat: 2, Protein: 2, Carbs: 0, Fiber: 0, Net Carbs: 0.

THE KETO IRON CHEF JOINS THE HOBBIT, SO I CELEBRATED WITH KETO CHOCOLATE CHIP COOKIES:)

Servings=15
Time=30mins

Preheat oven to 375F

I recommend making the chips prior to starting the cookies, they take about an hour to set up.

Making the cookies:

0.50 cup Whey Isolate
0.25 cup, Almond Meal/flour
1 egg
0.50 cup(s), Butter, melted
1 cup sweetener
2 tbsp. heavy cream
0.50 tsp, Baking Powder
0.50 tsp baking soda
1.50 tsp Vanilla extract

Combine all the dry ingredients in a small bowl and whisk to combine, breaking up any clumps. In a larger bowl, with your mixer quickly combine the sweetener and butter until completely incorporated. Add the egg and vanilla, beat again until smooth. While beating on low speed, gradually add the dry ingredients until you have a thick, spoon able dough. Add your chips to the bowl and fold in with a spoon or spatula. Let sit for 5 minutes while you line a baking sheet with parchment or silicone mat. Spoon or scoop 15 balls onto the baking sheet, then pop in the oven for 12-15 minutes or until the lightly start to brown. Remove...and unlike I usually suggest, eat these puppies as soon as they don't burn your mouth! One must have gooey chocolate chips while still warm (though these are tasty cool as well). ENJOY!!

Nutritional information (based off my brand of ingredients, double-check yours!): Calories – 120, Fat: 12, Protein: 3, Carbs: 3, Fiber: 1, Net Carbs: 2.

COCONUT-CRANBERRY COOKIES...KETO-TWISTED :)

Servings=24
Time=30mins

Ingredients:

1/2 cup whey protein isolate
2 Eggs
1/2 cup Kabocha Squash
1/2 cup sweetener
1 tsp Baking Powder
3 tbsp Butter – Salted
2 tbsp Coconut Flour
1/2 cup Flaked Coconut, Unsweetened
1/2 cup Unsweetened Shredded Coconut
1/2 cup Whole fresh or frozen cranberries
1 tsp Almond Extract

Preheat oven to 350F. Get a baking sheet ready with parchment or silicone mat.

Melt the butter in the microwave, then stir into the kabocha, mixing vigorously until smooth. Add the eggs, mix again until all the eggs are incorporated. Add all the other ingredients except cranberries, mix until you get a nice, drop-cookie dough (not runny or loose). Fold in the cranberries. Using a scoop or two spoons, drop mounds of dough on the baking sheet, no need to leave much room between as with the limited butter, they will not spread. Put in oven for 12-15 minutes or until the bottom edges brown. Remove and let cool to touch on sheet before moving to cooling racks (or your mouth). Done!!!

Nutritional info per cookie (based off my ingredients, check yours!): Calories: 61, Fat: 5g, Protein: 3g, Carbs: 2, Fiber: 1, Net Carbs: 1

HOBBIT'S PUMPKIN COOKIE BARS. YUP. WITH KABOCHA :) ONE NET CARB

Servings=12
Time=30mins

Ingredients:

2 tbsp. coconut flour
½ cup vanilla whey protein powder
1.5 Cup, Baked Kabocha Squash
0.5 cup granulated sweetener
0.25 cup Almond Milk (or 1 tbsp. heavy cream and 1 tbsp. water)
2 tbsp. Butter – Salted
3.00 large, Eggs
1.00 tsp(s), Vanilla extract
1 tsp(s), Baking Powder
0.50 tsp(s), Salt, table
** 1.00 tsp(s), Spices – Cinnamon, ground
** 0.50 tsp(s), Spices, ginger, ground
** 0.25 tsp(s), Spices, cloves, ground

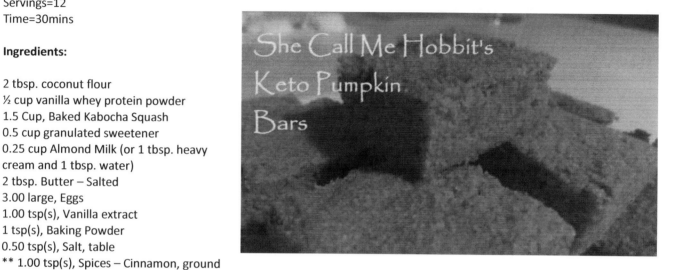

* If dairy-sensitive or do not have whey protein, increase coconut flour by 4 tbsp. and oil by 1 tbsp.
** You can replace the ginger, cinnamon, and cloves with 2 tsp of pumpkin spice

Let's make the bars!!

Preheat your oven to 350F. Get out a 8×8 or 9×9 baking dish, lightly grease all with coconut oil (I use the spray type because not only do I like simple, I'm freaking lazy too). Combine all the wet ingredients (including the kabocha) for the in a bowl, beat until smooth. Put all the dry ingredients in a different bowl, then whisk to combine\break up clumps. Add the dry to the wet, and beat until smooth, scraping down the sides. You should get a thick batter, like brownie batter. Pour into your baking dish, smooth the top with a spoon or spatula. Place in the oven for 20-30 minutes or until the sides start to brown and a toothpick inserted in the center comes out clean. Let cool completely before slicing. This is critical with any recipe using coconut flour or protein powder to make sure the final product doesn't crumble. These two ingredients like to cool slowly to finish binding up.I think these would be really good with some protein and cream cheese frosting, I didn't do that this time as today is a lazy day and I'm taking full advantage of it!! If you try it, let me know!

Nutritional info per bar (based off my ingredients, check yours!): Calories: 56, Fat: 4g, Protein: 4g, Carbs: 2, Fiber: 1, Net Carbs: 1

JOY TO THE WORLD...A LITTLE TOO EARLY FOR THAT??? WHAT IF I PLY YOU WITH ALMOND JOY COOKIES? KETO ONES?

Servings=24
Time=30mins

Ingredients:

24 whole almonds
4.00 Tablespoons, Organic Coconut Flour
0.50 cup(s), Shredded Unsweetened Coconut
0.50 cups(s) Unsweetened Coconut Flakes
2.00 tbsp.(s), Coconut Butter
0.50 cup(s), Butter melted
2.00 large, Eggs
1.00 tsp(s), Baking Powder
2.00 tsp(s), Vanilla extract
1 cup granulated sweetener

Preheat oven to 350F

Mix until well combined the butter, eggs, vanilla, and stevia. Add the rest of the dry ingredients except the nuts. Mix well, you should get a thick dough. LET STAND FOR 10 MINUTES. This is important as coconut (flour and shredded) absorb a lot of liquid. To make these easiest to form, let them sit before spooning them out. Spoon onto parchment or silicon mat on a baking sheet. Flatten slightly, then press one almond into the top of each cookie. Place in the oven for 8-12 minutes or until the edges brown. Remove from oven, let cool to the touch before removing off sheet to finish cooling on a rack (or on the way to your belly).

Nutritional information (per serving cookie) : Calories: 72, Fat: 7, Protein: 1, Carbs: 2, Fiber: 1, Net carbs: 1

STILL THE PUMPKIN-EVERYTHING SEASON RIGHT? PUMPKIN PIE BARS?

Servings=16

Time=30mins

Ingredients (top and bottom layers):

1/2 cup kabocha (or pumpkin puree)
1/2 cup whey protein isolate
1/2 cup sweetener
1/2 cup Coconut Flour
1/2 cup coconut or almond milk
2 eggs
1 tsp vanilla extract
2 tsp cinnamon

Preheat oven to 350F

In classic Hobbit fashion, nothing needed here. Put everything in a fancy bowl, stir or use a mixer until well combined and a thick batter like cake. Pour half of it in the bottom of an 8×8 baking dish. Level out the top if needed.

Ingredients (filling):

1/2 cup whey protein isolate
3 tbsp. plain Greek yogurt
1 egg
1/3 cup sweetener
1 tsp vanilla extract
1/4 cup heavy cream
1/2 cup coconut or almond milk

Again, add everything to a bowl, mix until well combined and creamy. Scoop all of it onto the first layer prepped above. Smooth out. Spoon the remaining pumpkin batter on top, smooth out as needed (wet hands work really well for this step). Put in the oven for about 15-20 minute or until the top layer cracks slightly and pulls away from the edge of the pan. The goal here is firm enough to eat with our hands, soft enough not to choke on them :). LET COOL COMPLETELY before cutting. This will give you nice, clean squares instead of mush. Not that mush tastes bad, but let's be serious, they taste better when they LOOK better:).

NUTRITION COUNT PER bar (based off my ingredients, double-check your numbers!): Calories: 90, Protein: 5g, Fat: 5 g, Carbs: 3g, Fiber: 1g, NET CARBS: 2g

MOIST AND SOFT BROWNIES - LESS THAN ONE NET CARB EACH!

So, are you ready for some brownies (makes 16 1" brownies)??

Servings=16
Time=30mins

Ingredients:

1 tbsp (9.00 g), Coconut Flour
1/4 cup Baking Cocoa powder
4.00 tablespoon, Butter
1 Egg
1/2 cup whey protein isolate
1/2 cup (cooked), Kabocha Squash
1/4 cup brewed coffee
1 tsp baking powder
1/3 cup granulated sweetener

Pre-heat oven to 350F.

Mash up the kabocha until it is free of chunks. Add the butter and mix well with a spoon. NO ELECTRIC MIXER! You don't want to work this batter too much or it will be a cake, not a brownie (of course, if you WANT a cake, add 3 eggs to this recipe and beat it up good in a mixer – yes, that's all you need to do :)). Add everything else to the butter\kabocha mixture and stir with a spoon until all the egg and dry are combined. Pour into your brownie pan (8×8 is what I used) and pop into the oven for 15-20 minutes or until the brownies don't jiggle when you gently shake the pan. Remove and let cool before slicing and removing from the pan. Get your brownie eating on and enjoy!!

Nutritional info (based off my ingredients, check yours!): Calories: 42, Fat: 3g, Protein: 2g, Carbs: 1.5, Fiber: 1, Net Carbs: 0.5

MMMM. MAPLE. THE SWEETHEART OF NEW ENGLAND. KETO MAPLE CREAM COOKIES. LESS THAN ONE CARB

Servings=12
Time=30mins

Ingredients:
(cookie dough)

1/4 cup Organic Coconut Flour
1/2 cup Almond Flour
1/2 cup whey protein isolate
1/4 cup butter – melted
2 eggs
1 tsp baking powder
1 tsp maple extract
1 tsp vanilla extract
1/2 cup sweetener
1/8 tsp salt

Preheat oven to **300F**

Get out your biggish mixing bowl. Whisk the eggs, butter and extract together until eggs are well-beat and a little frothy. Add the rest of the ingredients and mix well with a spoon or my favorite tool, a silicon spatula. It will seem dry at first and look like it just isn't going to come together. Keep mixing. When it comes together without crumbling apart, pick it up in your hands and kneed it for a few seconds like you would pizza dough. Let it sit for a few minutes – go get a cup of coffee or something. Now plop it on a sheet of parchment and put another sheet (or plastic wrap or sandwich between two silicon mats) over the top and press it down flat. Get out your rolling pin and roll it out in a rectangle to about the thickness of a couple of stacked quarters. Even it up with your hands if you need to, this is very easy-to-work with dough. Cut the shapes you want. Put the cut pieces on a parchment or mat-lined cookie sheet, leaving a little space between to allow them to puff a little. Pop in the oven for about 20 minutes, checking occasionally to make sure they don't overcook. You want them to just start to brown on the edges. Once done, remove from the oven and move to a rack to cool.

While the cookies are cooling, let's make the filling.

Filling ingredients:

1/4 cup butter – softened
1 cup sweetener
1/2 tsp vanilla extract
1/2 tsp maple extract
2 tbsp heavy cream

Put the butter in a bowl and with your mixer, start blending it. SLOWLY ADD SWEETENER! That is, unless you like looking like a toddler that found the baby powder, ask me how I know... Once the two are combined (don't worry if it looks lumpy and dry), add the other wet ingredients, then mix until combined. Kick it up to whip for a few seconds to make it nice and fluffy. Spread some filling on half the cookies. Top with the other half. Hide half for you for later. Share the rest. Ok. Hide 3/4 for you for later and share the rest. Tell them it was a small batch:).

Nutritional information (per cookie sandwich): Calories: 123, Fat: 12, Protein: 4, Carbs: 1, Fiber: 1, Net carbs: 0

IS IT TOO EARLY FOR THESE YET? KETO GINGERBREAD MEN?

Servings=24
Time=30mins

Ingredients:

1/2 cup plus 3tbsp whey isolate powder
1/4 cup butter, melted
1 tbsp Coconut Flour
1/2 tsp vanilla extract
3 drops or so of maple extract
3/4 tsp ginger
1/2 tsp cinnamon
1/2 tsp cloves
1/2 tsp allspice
1 egg
1 tsp baking powder

Preheat oven to 350F. Prepare a cookie sheet with parchment or silicon mat.

You know I like simple, and this simple. Beat the egg until frothy.
Whisk in the butter until combined, then add everything else. Stir with spoon or rubber spatula until completely combine. You should get a stiff, heavy dough that you can easily roll into a ball without it crumbing. If too wet, add a little more protein powder. Once you can roll into a ball, wrap up the ball in plastic wrap and put in the fridge for 30 minutes. Remove and press into a flat rectangle, cover with plastic wrap and use a rolling pin to roll out a rough rectangle about 1/4 in thick. Cut out your shapes, remove the excess, re-roll the excess and use it up :). Put the little men on the cookie sheet and bake 12-15 minutes or until the edges brown. Remove and let cool.

Frost* if desired.
EAT!

*Easy keto frosting:

2 tbsp. butter, melted
2 tbsp. whey protein isolate, vanilla flavor
1 tsp milk

Whisk until fluffy and smooth. Done:)

Nutritional information (cookie): Calories: 56, Fat: 4, Protein: 4, Carbs: 1, Fiber: 0.5, Net carbs: 0.5

NO CARB 'SUGAR' COOKIES? IS THIS FOR REAL??

Servings=12
Time=30mins

Ingredients:

1/4 cup Coconut Oil or 1/4 cup butter – MELTED
1/2 cup vanilla whey protein isolate
1 tsp baking powder
1 tsp coconut milk (or almond, you pick)

OR

1/4 cup Coconut Oil or butter – MELTED
1/2 cup unflavored whey protein isolate
1/4 cup sweetener
1.5 tsp vanilla extract
1 tsp baking powder
1 tsp coconut milk (again, feel free to use almond if you want)

Preheat oven to 350F

You know I like simple and I'm lazy, this recipe hits both those points :). Melt the oil\butter in the microwave, add extract if using the unflavored whey recipe. Mix the dry together, then mix into the wet until all combined. Should have a nice dough that you can form into balls – these are not drop cookies. If the dough is a little dry, add a little water and remix. Again, you want something you can roll, not spoon out. Once combined, take about a tablespoon of dough at a time, roll into a ball, then put it on a cookie sheet lined with parchment or silicon baking mat. Flatten out on the sheet, this is forgiving dough so don't be afraid to shape and round the edges as needed to form the cookies. Should make about 12 cookies. Pop in the oven for 5-8 minutes or until the edges start to brown. These cook up rather quickly so watch them. Remove from oven, let cool to touch before moving to rack to completely cool. DONE!!

Nutritional information (per cookie using flavored powder) : Calories: 65, Fat: 5, Protein: 4, Carbs: 0.2, Fiber: 0, Net carbs: 0.2.
Nutritional information (per cookie using unflavored powder) : Calories: 65, Fat: 5, Protein: 4, Carbs: 0, Fiber: 0, Net carbs: 0

YOU KNOW WHAT GOES GREAT WITH COOKIES? COOKIES!!! FAUX OATMEAL KETO COOKIES!

Ingredients:

1 cup smooth almond butter (no sugar added!!)
1/3 granulated stevia
2 tsp vanilla extract
5 tbsp. water
1 tbsp. flax meal
2 tsp cinnamon
1/8 tsp nutmeg
1/2 tsp salt
1/2 tsp baking soda
1/4 cup shredded unsweetened coconut
1/2 tsp maple extract
1/4 cup hemp seeds
2 tbsp. egg whites

Preheat oven to 350F.

Prep your cookie sheet with parchment or silicon mat. By now, you should know how we roll in the House of Hobbit. Nothing is a ton of steps. We like simple. We like basic. We hate too much work. Dump everything in a bowl. Stir until combined. Drop on cookie sheet with a spoon or small ice cream scoop (which reminds me, need to get a new one of those. Our's is not doing the sweep-dump-scrape thing any more). Pop in your oven for 10 minutes or until the edges start to lightly brown. Take them out of oven and leave them on the cookie sheet until they are cool to the touch. Move them to your mouth...errr...I mean move them to a cooling rack to finish cooling. Then move to your mouth. Or both. Screw it, eat them whenever you feel like it

Nutritional information (per cookie) : Calories: 143, Fat: 12, Protein: 6, Carbs: 4, Fiber: 3, Net carbs: 1

OHHHH, BROWNIES WITH CARAMEL AND NUTS!!!

Ingredients:
For the brownies:

1/2 cup melted butter
3/4 cup almond flour
1 tbsp. coconut flour
1/3 cup sweetener
1 tsp vanilla extract
3 large eggs
1 egg yolk
1 tsp baking powder
1/4 cup cocoa powder
1/4 cup 90% cacao dark chocolate, chopped

For the caramel:
3 tbsp. salted butter
1/3 cup sweetener
1/4 cup heavy cream
1/4 tsp xanthan gum

Extras on top:)
1/3 cup chopped walnuts

Preheat oven to 350F.

Brownies:
Combine the melted butter, almond flour, coconut flour, sweetener, vanilla extract, eggs (and yolk), cocoa powder, chopped chocolate in a medium bowl. Stir slowly by hand until fully combined – don't beat or whip or you'll end up with a much cakey-er texture. Pour into an 8×8 square pan. Bake for about 12-13 minutes, or until the center no longer jiggles. Cool.

To make the caramel:
Melt the butter and sweetener together in a small saucepan over medium heat. Cook, stirring constantly for about 2 minutes or until bubbling. Add the cream and, xanthan then whisk continually, 3-5 minutes over medium heat. It will get darker in color the longer you cook it. Remove from heat when your desired color is reached. Let it cool slightly to thicken. Remove the brownies from the pan and peel off the parchment or foil. Add the cooled caramel to a small plastic Ziploc baggie, then cut about 1/8 inch off of one of the bottom corners of the bag. Gently squeeze the caramel over your brownies and sprinkle your chopped nuts evenly over the top of the brownies. Cut into 16 brownies.

Nutrition information: 1 brownie: 166 calories, 10g fat, 2.5g net carbs, 3g protein

PASTRIES AND OTHER STUFF TO MAKE YOU HAPPY...

HOBBIT'S KETO FATHEAD PIE CRUST

Servings=2x9in crusts
Time=30mins

Ingredients:

1.5 cups (145g) low moisture, part skim mozzarella cheese
4 tbsp almond flour
3 tbsp coconut flour
4 tbsp butter melted
1 tsp vanilla extract
1/4 cup or equivalent sweetener
1 egg

Let's make the crust. Mix all the dry ingredients in a bowl, then add one well-beaten egg, vanilla, and butter. Stir until well combined. Set aside. In a separate bowl, melt your mozzarella in the microwave on 30-40% (depending on power) for 2 minutes, stirring and blending after 1 minute. Immediately add this to the rest of the mixture and fold it over and over to incorporate as much of the cheese with the others. Nuke it for 10 seconds on high, then fold\kneed it until you have a uniform color with no obvious 'cheesy' spots. Repeat the nuke if you if it starts getting hard to work the cheese. Once you have it uniform, roll it into a ball, then nuke one more time for 10 seconds on high. Cut the ball in half and set one half aside. Place it between two sheets of parchment or silicon baking mats. Press down with your hand to flatten it out as much as you can, then working from the center-out, use your hands to spread and press it into a circle. Use your pie plate to check the size, you want it about 1.5" bigger than the plate so you have room to up the sides as well as fold over to form that edge on the crust. Once you have it the right size, peel off the top silicone mat\parchment. Lay it centered over the top of your pie plate, then slowly peel the other mat\parchment off. Using your hands, gently press and shift the dough so it fills the bottom and goes up the sides. This is very forgiving dough, if it rips or wrinkles, just use your fingers to press and fix :). Trim if needed, then fold over, pressing with your fingers or knuckles to form the top edge of the crust. It is now ready for filling\baking\freezing. Yes, this freezes excellent.

I have a video walk-through on our YouTube channel if you are a visual person :).

Nutritional information (based off my ingredients, double-check!): Calories: 152, Fat: 12g, Protein: 8g, Carbs: 3g, Fiber: 2g, Net Carbs: 1g

DONUT. WHAT? DONUTS? ON KETO? YEH. DONUTS!!!!

Servings=8
Time=45 min

Ingredients:
1 cup(s) plus 2 tbsp Almond Flour
2 tbsp. unflavored whey isolate
2 tsp baking powder
2 tsp vanilla extract
3/4 cup sweetener of your choice
2 large Eggs
4 tbsp. Psyllium husk powder
3/4 boiling water

Small bowl of water to wet your hands with

Preheat oven to 350F

Prepare a baking sheet, lined with parchment or silicone mat (or lightly greased if neither of those are available). Beat the eggs and vanilla with a whisk until well combined. Add all the dry, mix well with a spoon or rubber spatula. This will result in a crumbly mess that looks like there's no way this is going to work. Bear with me:). Grab the hot water and pour it into the mixture while stirring until you have a soupy mess. Wait 5 minutes, the dough will become a dough instead of soup. Using wet hands (that's what the bowl of water is for), roughly shape the dough into a rectangle. Cut the rectangle into 8 squares. Wet hands again, poke your thumb through the middle of each square, spin on your thumb and use your hands to make a rough donut shape. Place on sheet and repeat until all 8 are done. Space them out with room to at least double in size. Place in the oven for 15-20 minutes or until the tops are dry and bounce back when lightly touched. Remove. Be patient, let them cool on a rack and save for later.
Yeh. Ok. I tried that. Eh.
They didn't make it 15 minutes 😁

Optional toppings – chocolate glaze, frosting, shredded coconut, whatever you can think of.

Nutritional information per donut: Calories each 113 , Fat: 8g Protein: 6g, Carbs: 6g Fiber: 3g Net: 3g

HOBBIT'S KETO APPLE-NO-APPLE PASTRY

Servings=12
Time=45mins

Crust:

My Fathead pie crust from beginning of this chapter (add 1 tbsp. protein powder to the dry ingredients)

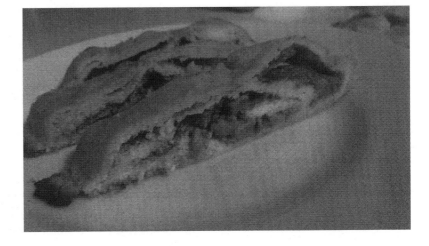

Filling base:

2 tbsp. butter, melted
3 tbsp. heavy cream
1 tbsp. water
3 tbsp. sweetener
1/2 tsp Xanthan Gum Powder
2 tbsp. Unflavored Whey Protein isolate
1.5 tsp cinnamon

"Apples"

1 cup eggplant (raw), peeled, sliced thin and cut into strips
2 tbsp. butter, melted
1 tsp cinnamon
2 tbsp. lemon juice
2 tbsp. sweetener

Preheat oven to 350F

Let's do the 'apples' first. Add everything but the eggplant together and mix until combined. Put the eggplant in a bowl, then pour the mixture over it. Stir until completely coated. Microwave for 20 seconds on high. Should be warm to the touch. Let it sit while getting the rest done. In another bowl (I know, more than one bowl for a Hobbit recipe?? It's worth it ⬚), mix the butter, cream, and water together with a whisk. Once combined, whisk in the stevia and cinnamon. Slowly add the protein powder while whisking, stopping when it is smooth. Get ready, since once you get the crust done, you are going to want to move fast :). Make the crust, if you need a video walkthrough on it, check out our YouTube channel, it's linked from our website, so you can see how it is made. Roll it out like you would a Stromboli. Spread the base over one half of the dough (lengthwise). Using a slotted spoon so you don't pick up too much liquid, spoon the eggplant over the top of the base. Fold over the edges of the dough about 1-1.5" so it covers the edges of the base and eggplant. Starting at the end that is 'loaded,' roll the dough up into a roll – it's easiest to get the first fold started, then use the parchment\mat to do the rest by lifting the edge and guiding the dough with your hands. Seal the edge and set on the parchment\mat, then move to baking pan. Bake for 30 minutes or until top browns. Remove and let cool to the touch before slicing and serving. Makes 12 slices\servings (unless you are The Lady and Hobbit, then it makes 2 servings ☺).

Nutritional information (based off my ingredients, double-check!): Calories: 92, Fat: 7g, Protein: 3g, Carbs: 2g, Fiber: 1g, Net Carbs: 1g

HOBBIT'S KETO PUMPKIN PIE (WITH KABOCHA, OF COURSE, BUT YOU CAN USE PUMPKIN)

Servings=8
Time=1hr 30mins

Ingredients – makes one 9", 8 slice pie:

Hobbit's fathead pie crust
1.5 cups baked kabocha or pumpkin puree
1/2 cup sweetener of your choice
1 tbsp. pumpkin pie spice
3 eggs
1 tsp vanilla extract
Preheat oven to 350F.

Put all the ingredients in a bowl, using a whisk, spoon, or rubber spatula, mix the hell out of it until you have a smooth, well-mixed batter. We like chunks in ours, if you don't, then run the squash through the blender or food processor first :). Pour into crust (it will be a little thick so might need some help). Smooth the top. Place in the oven for 40 minutes, take out at 20 minutes and use strips of tin foil to cover up the top edge of the crust so it doesn't burn. It is done when a toothpick comes out clean when inserted in the center. Let cool.

Nutritional information including crust (based off my ingredients, double-check!): Calories: 184, Fat: 14g, Protein: 11g, Carbs: 5g, Fiber: 3g, Net Carbs: 2g

HOBBIT'S NEW ENGLAND PECAN PIE

Servings=8
Time=1hr 30mins

Ingredients – makes one 9", 8 slice pie:

Hobbit's fathead pie crust
1 cup Hobbit's light 'corn' syrup
1 cup sweetener of your choice
1.5 cups chopped or whole pecan halves
3 eggs
1 tsp vanilla extract

Preheat oven to 350F.

Put all the ingredients in a bowl except pecans, using a whisk, spoon, or rubber spatula, mix the hell out of it until you have a smooth, well-mixed batter. Fold in 1 cup of the pecans. Pour into crust (it will be a little thick so might need some help). Smooth the top. Sprinkle the other 1/2 cup of pecans on the top of the pie. Place in the oven for 40 minutes, take out at 20 minutes and use strips of tin foil to cover up the top edge of the crust so it doesn't burn. It is done when the top is firm and bounces back when you lightly touch it.

Nutritional information including crust (based off my ingredients, double-check!): Calories: 336, Fat: 31g, Protein: 16g, Carbs: 6g, Fiber: 4g, Net Carbs: 2g

CINNAMON ROLLS THE KETO WAY

Servings=4
Time=30mins

Dough:

3 eggs
1/2 cup softened butter, salted
1 cup sweetener
1/4 cup coconut flour
1/2 cup almond flour\meal (or pepita flour)
1/4 cup Whey Isolate
1 tsp baking powder
1 tsp vanilla extract

Preheat oven to 350F.

In one bowl, whip the eggs, butter, vanilla, and sweetener until it is well combined and smooth. In another bowl, put all the dry in, then whisk to combine and break up clumps. Pour the dry into the wet and with a rubber or silicone spatula or spoon, stir and fold until a thick dough forms. It will be a little sticky, don't fret. Cover with plastic wrap and place in fridge to chill overnight. Once it's chilled, get out two sheets of parchment or silicon mats, spray or rub both down with coconut oil. Place dough on greased parchment, push the dough down a bit and form a rough rectangle with your hands. Top with the other sheet of parchment. Roll the dough out with a rolling pin into a rectangle, about 1/4 to 1/2 inch thick. The thicker you make it, the less dense the final rolls will be. Carefully peel off the top parchment. Square up the rectangle with your hands.

Now, let's make the inner goodness:)

3 tbsp. melted butter
1 tbsp. cinnamon
1 tbsp. sweetener

With a brush or spoon, cover the dough with the melted butter, making sure you get it from edge to edge across the shorter part of the rectangle and leave about 1/2" without butter on the two ends that you are going to roll from (you will roll this down the longer length of the dough). Mix the sweetener and cinnamon together and sprinkle evenly over the dough. Roll up dough, start by folding over with your hands one end, then I found it easiest to lift the parchment over the top, pull it towards the other end, and use that to roll up the dough. Cut into 1 1/2 inch pieces. Place the rolls into a greased muffin tin or baking dish (made a small batch so I used muffin tins but with the larger rolls, I recommend baking dish – 8x8 should be good). Bake for 12-15 minutes, you want the tops of the rolls to just get a little brown, not too much or they will be dry. Remove from the oven and let cool for about 10-15 minutes or until they are warm to the touch but not hot enough to burn you.

Let's make the glaze:

1/4 cup water
2 tbsp cup whey (or veggie!) protein isolate
1tsp vanilla extract
3 tbsp heavy cream

Place all ingredients into a medium sized bowl and whisk the hell out of it until smooth. drizzle over cinnamon rolls. Chow down!!!

Nutritional information (based off my ingredients, double-check!): Calories: 229, Fat: 21g, Protein: 19g, Carbs: 5g, Fiber: 4g, Net Carbs: 1g

NUTRI-GRAIN KNOCK-OFFS VERSION 2.0 - STILL LOW CARB!

Servings=8
Time=30mins

Crust:

8.00 tbsp(s), Raw Pepitas (roasted then ground)
2.00 tsp(s), Ground Flax Meal
1 tsp(s), baking soda
0.50 tsp, Spices – Cinnamon, ground
0.25 tsp(s), Sea Salt
0.25 cup(s), Coconut Oil (melted)
1.00 tsp(s), Vanilla extract
3.00 tbsp(s), Water
2.00 egg, Brown, Large
½ cup whey protein isolate.

Preheat oven to 350F

You know how I work – simple and as little steps as possible. Whisk the eggs with the coconut oil until combined, don't need to go nuts here, just mix it up well. Add the rest of the ingredients to the bowl, then using a rubber spatula or good spoon, mix it together until you get a solid, firm dough. Should be able to roll into a ball without sticking too much to your hands. Wrap in plastic wrap and put in the fridge while making your filling. I made the cranberry-orange, but you can use a variety of fillings like I show below:

Filling

1 cup water
1/2 cup sweetener
1/4 cup frozen blueberries, strawberries, cranberries, cherries, etc
1/2 tsp xanthan gum

While dough is setting, mix stevia in with water, then bring to a gentle boil on the stove. Add blueberries and let boil until reduced by half. Add xanthan gum while whisking briskly until all dissolved. Remove from heat and let cool for about 10 minutes. Get your dough out, place between two sheets of parchment or silicon mat, then roll out into a large rectangle. Using a pizza cutter, cut into even segments. I used a total of 16 rectangles to make 8 bars. Put some filling up the middle of every other rectangle, keeping it about 1/4" from the edges all the way around. Place one piece without filling over the top of one with filling until all of the bars are covered, then using a fork (or pastry crimper if you have one...obviously, I don't), crimp the edges down. Pop in the oven for about 15 minutes or until the edges start to brown. Place on a rack to cool, then EAT!!

NUTRITION COUNT PER BAR (based off my ingredients, double-check your numbers!): Calories: 171, Protein: 9g, Fat: 15g, Carbs: 3g, Fiber: 1g, NET CARBS: 2g

WE DO LOVE OUR FATHEAD... CRANBERRY-ORANGE, PUMPKIN, CHEESE, OR EGGNOG CUSTARD KETO DANISH

Servings=8
Time=30mins

Pumpkin Filling (fills 8 Danishes):

1/2 cup kabocha (or pumpkin puree)
1 egg
1 tbsp. heavy cream
1 tsp pumpkin spice
2 tbsp. sweetener

Put everything in a blender, pulse a few times until smooth-ish. Done.
HA! You know me, I like SIMPLE AND EASY. How freaking easy is that??

Cranberry-Orange (fills 8 Danishes):

1/4 cup fresh or frozen cranberries
1 cup water
3 tbsp granulated sweetener
1/4 tsp xanthan
1/8 tsp orange extract

Put the cranberries and water in a saucepan on the stove on high until comes to boil, then reduce heat to simmer. Stir in the stevia. Let the water reduce to about half, stirring occasionally and crushing the berries as they get soft until they are all broken down. Remove from heat, whisk in the orange extract and xanthan gum, let cool.

Eggnog Custard (fills 8 Danishes):

1 egg
1 tbsp. coconut or almond milk
1 tbsp. heavy cream
1/8 tsp nutmeg
1/4 tsp Xanthan Gum Powder

Put all ingredients except xanthan gum in blender, pulse until well mixed and egg is frothy. Pour into a small saucepan and heat on low to med-low until it starts to thicken, stirring or whisking frequently so it doesn't clump up. When it coats a spoon, remove from heat and whisk in the xanthan gum. Let cool. This should be pudding consistency once cooled. If still a little too runny, nuke it for 30 seconds and let cool again.

Cheese Filling:

8 oz cream cheese
1 tsp lemon juice
1 tsp vanilla extract
1/4 cup Stevia
1 egg

Soften cream cheese and combine with lemon juice, vanilla, and sweetener and egg yolk using a whisk or electric mixer. Set aside in the fridge until you are ready with the dough.

Now let's make the dough:

Ingredients:

1.5 cups low moisture, skim milk mozzarella
4 tbsp. Almond Flour
3 tbsp. Coconut Flour
4 tbsp. butter, melted
1 egg
1 tbsp. sweetener

Preheat oven to 350F

Mix all the dry ingredients in a bowl, then add one well-beaten egg and butter. Stir until well combined. Set aside. In a separate bowl, melt your mozzarella in the microwave on 30-40% (depending on power) for 2 minutes, stirring and blending after 1 minute. Stir again to make sure it is good and blended. Immediately add this to the rest of the mixture and fold it over and over to incorporate as much of the cheese with the others. Nuke it for 10 seconds on high, then

fold\knead it until you have a uniform color with no obvious 'cheesy' spots. Repeat the nuke if you if it starts getting hard to work the cheese. Once you have it uniform, roll it into a ball, then nuke one more time for 10 seconds on high. Place the ball of dough between two sheets of parchment or silicon baking mats. Press down with your hand to flatten it out as much as you can, then using a rolling pin to roll out the dough in a large rectangle of uniform thickness (about the thickness of two quarters stacked). Trim if needed. Using a knife or pizza cutter, cut the dough into 8 equal squares, then fold each corner of each square in towards the middle, leaving about 1/4-1/2 inch between the folds. Hopefully you are more consistent than I am, lol. This should give you 8 Danish 'bases.' Plop a generous spoonful of the filling of your choice in the center of each Danish base. I did 2 ea. of cranberry-orange and pumpkin, and 4 of the eggnog (I got a little mess with the eggnog as I got distracted, hopefully yours look prettier). Slide onto a baking sheet and put in the oven for about 20 minutes or until the edges of the pastry start to brown. Remove and move to a cooling rack to cool.

Nutritional information – **Pumpkin** (based off my ingredients, double-check!): Calories: 95, Fat: 4g, Protein: 9g, Carbs: 4g, Fiber: 1g, Net Carbs: 3g. **Cranberry-orange**: Calories: 91, Fat: 4g, Protein: 7g, Carbs: 3g, Fiber: 1g, Net Carbs: 2g. **Eggnog Custard**: Calories: 77, Fat: 4g, Protein: 7g, Carbs: 3g, Fiber: 1g, Net Carbs: 2g

THE POP TART HACKED - TAKE THAT!

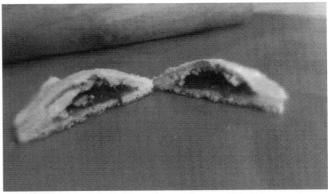

Servings=8
Time=30mins

Crust:

1 cup whey protein isolate
1/4 cup Coconut Flour
1/4 cup melted coconut oil
1 egg
2 tbsp. coconut milk (or 1 tbsp heavy cream mixed with 1 tbsp water)
2 tbsp. sweetener
1 tsp baking powder

In a small bowl, beat the egg, coconut milk (or cream and water). and coconut oil together until well combined. In a separate bowl, mix all the dry together, making sure you destroy any clumps. Pour the wet into the dry and mix well with a rubber spatula or good spoon. This is going to be a thick dough, very much like pie crust or fathead, you will get your kitchen cardio in with this one :). Once you have the dough so it can be rolled into a ball without being sticky, wrap it in plastic wrap and toss it in the fridge for 30 minutes while you make the filling.

Fillings:
Cranberry:

1/4 cup fresh or frozen cranberries
1 cup water
3 tbsp sweetener
1/4 tsp xanthan gum
1/8 tsp orange extract

Put the cranberries and water in a saucepan on the stove on high until comes to boil, then reduce heat to simmer. Stir in the stevia. Let the water reduce to about half, stirring occasionally and crushing the berries as they get soft until they are all broken down. Remove from heat, whisk in the orange extract and xanthan gum, let cool.

Pumpkin:

1/2 cup kabocha (or pumpkin puree)
1 egg
1 tbsp heavy cream
1 tsp pumpkin spice
2 tbsp granulated sweetener
Put everything in a blender, pulse a few times until smooth-ish. Done. HA! You know me, I like SIMPLE AND EASY. How freaking easy is that??

Preheat oven to 350F.

Get your dough out of the fridge. Place it on a piece of parchment or silicon mat and flatten it out. Cover with another mat or parchment, then using a rolling pin, roll it out in a rectangle to the thickness of about a nickel. Decide how you want to cut the pieces, then cut them. Remember, there is a top and bottom so make sure you end up with an equal number :). If you have dough left over, roll out again and repeat. Using a spoon, drop about a tablespoon for the round or 2 tbsp

for the rectangle, filling half the pastries. Spread GENTLY to even out, keeping about 1/4" from the edge untouched. You don't want any filling too close to the edge or it won't seal well when you put the tops on and leak out. Likewise, you don't want it too high or it will squish out just from the weight of the top piece. Place the tops on, then using a fork, crimp all the way around the edges, make sure it is sealed well. FYI, this is very forgiving dough, if the tops tear or get deformed lifting them, you can patch them back up easily with your fingers :). Plop in the oven for 12-15 minutes or until the edges start to brown. Remove, move the pastries to a cooling rack.

Glaze:

1 tbsp. whey protein isolate
1 tbsp. coconut oil, melted
1 tsp vanilla extract
1 tsp sweetener

Mix all the ingredients together until smooth. Once the pastries are cool to the touch, use a spoon or small rubber spatula to 'frost' the pastries.

NUTRITION COUNT PER pastry CRANBERRY: Calories: 128, Protein: 8g, Fat: 9 g, Carbs: 3g, Fiber: 1g, NET CARBS: 2g. PUMPKIN : Calories: 139, Protein: 8g, Fat: 10 g, Carbs: 3g, Fiber: 1g, NET CARBS: 0.2g

KETO GRAHAM CRACKERS, HOBBIT LOVES SWEET, LOW-CARB TREATS!!

Servings=36
Time=30mins

1/2 cup Whey Protein Isolate
2 tbsp. Coconut Flour
1/4 cup Butter, melted
2 Eggs
4 tsp Vanilla extract
1.50 tsp Cinnamon, ground
1/3 cup sweetener

In a bowl, combine the eggs and melted butter, whisk until well combined and the eggs a little frothy. Add the dry, then with a rubber spatula or large spoon, mix well while scraping the sides. You want this to all combine into a stiff dough. Wrap it in plastic wrap, put in fridge for 15 minutes while you go get a cup of coffee and pat yourself on the back :). Once chilled, remove and place between two silicon mats or sheets of parchment. Roll out the dough into a rectangle about the thickness of 2 quarters. Now here's a great hack for making these. Traditionally, graham crackers come in sheets and you snap them apart, hell, that's half the fun. So, instead of cutting these with knife or pizza cutter, break out your serrated bread knife. Press it down (not slice) on the dough in rectangles that look right to you. This will perforate the dough without cutting it up. Toss in the oven for 15 minutes or until the edges brown. Once cooled, break them up and store in a bag for eating!

Nutritional info per cracker (based off my ingredients, check yours!): Calories: 19, Fat: 2, Protein: 1g, Carbs: 0.4, Fiber: 0.2, Net Carbs: 0.2

THERE ARE NO FAILURES, ONLY UNEXPECTED RESULTS - BREAD BOWL THAT TURNED TO KETO BISCOTTI

NOTE* *This does use a small amount of molasses, but doesn't get any carbs from it. The yeast eats the sugar and converts it to carbon dioxide for the air bubbles. Yes, the yeast 'farts' in your bread. You're welcome for that visual :). I did not exclude the molasses or yeast carbs from my values just to be totally transparent, but they technically do not count.*

Ingredients (makes 8 slices):

1/2 cup unflavored whey isolate

1/2 cup vanilla whey protein

1/4 cup coconut flour

1 tbsp. olive or coconut oil (melted)

1 tsp molasses

1 pkg of yeast

1.5 cup of water

1 tsp xanthan gum

|Preheat oven to 325F

Proof the yeast with the molasses in the water (a little warmer than body temp) until it foams and bubbles. While waiting for it to proof, mix the dry ingredients together in a large bowl, then mix in the oil, then add the proofed water\yeast mixture and stir until well combined and you have a slightly sticky dough. If too wet, wait a few minutes for the dry to absorb the wet (coconut flour and protein powder will do that). If still too wet after 5 minutes, add another tsp of coconut flour. I didn't have to do this but just in case... Dump the dough onto parchment or silicon mat-lined baking sheet. Pat it into a roughly 8" round mound. Put in oven for 20 minutes or until the sides start to brown and crust up. Removed and let stand until cool enough to lift with hands, then move to a cooling rack to finish cooling. Cut into strips once cool, return to the oven on 350F for 10 minutes to dry the cut edges. BAMM! Biscotti. Dust with whatever you feel like using or dip in keto chocolate and cool. ENJOY!

Nutritional info (based off my ingredients, check yours! 1 slice, undipped): Calories: 69, Fat: 3g, Protein: 9g, Carbs: 5, Fiber: 3, Net Carbs: 2

5-LAYER BARS WITHOUT 500,000 LAYERS OF CARBS!

Servings=16
Time=30mins

Ingredients:

My keto graham crackers
My keto chocolate
My keto butterscotch
My keto sweetened condensed milk
1 cup shredded or flaked coconut (unsweetened)

Preheat oven to 350F

Line the bottom of a baking dish with one or two layers of graham crackers. Alternatively, you could crush them and make a crust. I chose not to as I figured there is enough oils in the rest of the recipe that adding more butter was probably not that important. Take your chocolate and butterscotch out of the freezer and cut into chunks. Put the chunks in a bag or bowl, mix together by shaking, then dump on top of graham crackers. Cover the chunks with about 1/2 cup of flaked or shredded coconut. Pour the cooled condensed milk over the top, making sure to cover it all, cover with remaining coconut. It will soak down when baking so don't worry about stirring it up. Put in the oven for about 30 minutes at 350F or until the edges firm up and it starts to brown on top. Remove from oven, let cool in pan. Once cool enough to touch pan without burning, put in fridge to finish cooling. Do not put in the fridge hot, it will collect moisture and get all nasty. Ask me how I know…. Once cooled, slice up and enjoy!!

Nutritional info per bar – 16 total (based off my ingredients, check yours!): Calories: 210, Fat: 20g, Protein: 2g, Carbs: 6, Fiber: 3, Net Carbs: 3

I LIKE CANDY...

HOBBIT'S KETO CHOCOLATE COCONUT BALLS

Servings=28
Time=45mins

Ingredients:
Coconut balls:

2 tbsp. Coconut milk
1/2 cup, Flaked Coconut, Unsweetened
2 tbsp. golden flax meal
2 tbsp. Coconut Flour
1 egg
3/4 cup Shredded Unsweetened Coconut
4 table spoon, Coconut Oil – melted
3/4 cup sweetener
1 tsp vanilla extract

Preheat oven to 350F. Line baking sheet with parchment or silicon mat

Combine in a large bowl whisk egg, oil, vanilla, milk, and sweetener until combined. Add rest of ingredients, stir until you have a thick, solid dough. Roll dough into 28 small balls, about the size of a melon ball. Place on sheet. Put in the oven for 15-20 minutes or until solid and a starting to toast on the top. Remove and let cool to touch.

Chocolate coating:

2 tbsp. Coconut milk
2 tbsp. Cocoa powder, unsweetened
4 tbsp. Coconut Oil
1 Piece (1/16th of bar) Unsweetened Baking Chocolate Bar
1/2 cup sweetener

While balls cooling, in a double-boiler or a glass bowl fitted into a simmering pot of water, melt coconut oil. Whisk in coconut milk until combined. Add sweetener and cocoa powder. Whisk until smooth. Add baker's chocolate. Whisk constantly. The chocolate will melt and then appear to separate, don't worry, continue to whisk. As the baker's chocolate equalizes in temp with the rest of the ingredients, it will come together into a thick sauce. Turn off heat. Once balls cooled, roll them one at a time in the chocolate sauce, then move to parchment or plate. Once all have been coated, you could sprinkle more shredded coconut, chopped nuts, etc. over the top or leave as is. I left as is. Place in the fridge to firm up. Enjoy!!

Nutritional information per cookie (based off my brand of ingredients, double-check yours!): Calories – 69, Fat: 6, Protein: 1, Carbs: 1, Fiber: 1, Net Carbs: 0.

HOBBIT'S KETO COCONUT CRACK

Servings=16
Time=15 min

Ingredients:

1.5 cups unsweetened shredded coconut
3 tbsp. butter, melted
2 tbsp. virgin coconut oil, melted
1 tsp vanilla extract
1/2 cup sweetener
2 tbsp. chopped nuts (I used pecans)

Dead. Stupid. Simple. Mix everything in a bowl until well coated. Press into an 8×8 pan. Set in fridge for 15 minutes. Cut. Eat. Repeat. Over. And. Over:)

Nutritional information: Calories each 91 , Fat: 9g Protein: 1g, Carbs: 2g Fiber: 1g Net: 1g

KETO PUMPKIN FUDGE. MMMMM

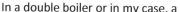

Servings=24
Time=30mins

I recommend a silicon baking dish for this if you have one. I used a bread loaf pan which was just the right size. Alternatively, use a regular pan but first grease with a little butter.

2 sticks butter, unsalted
1 cup kabocha (or pumpkin puree)
1 cup of sweetener
1/4 cup heavy cream
2 tbsp. whey protein isolate
1 tsp vanilla extract
1.5 tsp pumpkin spice

In a double boiler or in my case, a glass bowl over a pot of simmering water, melt the butter. Whisk in your sweetener and continue to whisk until completely dissolved. In your blender, put the kabocha, cream and spices, then puree. You want it to be as smooth as possible. Depending on your blender, this might be a few pulses or a run on the 'puree' setting. You want a smooth 'batter.' Pour and scrape the pumpkin into the butter, then whisk quickly and vigorously until it is all smooth and combined. Continue to let it simmer for about 5-10 minutes, you want the mixture to get hot to the touch. Gently sprinkle the protein powder on the top while whisking to avoid clumps. Whisk continuously for a couple of minutes, the mixture should thicken a little more. Remove from heat. Let cool 3-4 minutes, then pour into your pan. Put in the fridge for 3-4 hours to set, then you can remove from pan, cut, and enjoy!!!

Nutritional information per 1" piece: Calories each 141, Fat:20g, Protein: 4, Carbs: 2, Fiber: 1, Net carbs: 1

KETO FUDGE? YES. YES THERE IS SUCH A THING AND IT'S AWESOME (1 NET CARB)

Servings=12
Time=30mins

LET'S MAKE FUDGE!! (makes 12 1x1x1.5 pieces with my baking dish)

I recommend a silicon baking dish for this if you have one. I used a bread loaf pan which was just the right size. Alternatively, use a regular pan but first grease with a little butter.

2 sticks butter, unsalted
1/4 cup cocoa powder
1 cup of sweetener
1/4 cup heavy cream
2 tbsp. whey protein isolate (use chocolate flavored if you wish)
1 tsp vanilla extract

In a double boiler or in my case, a glass bowl over a pot of simmering water, melt the butter. Whisk in your sweetener and continue to whisk until completely dissolved. Whisk in cocoa, again until completely dissolved. Whisk in cream. Continue whisking as the cream initially will try to separate with the butter. Continue until smooth. Sprinkle whey protein while whisking vigorously, this is key as the protein shouldn't clump up. This will immediately thicken the mixture. Whisk for 5-6 minutes, then turn off heat and whisk 3 more minutes. It should be good and thick now. If not, return to heat and continue whisking until consistency of pudding. Pour into pan. Set in fridge for 2-3 hours until set. Remove and cut into squares (mine are still a little soft in the pics, I took them out early so I could snap the pics before I ran out of ambition).

Nutritional information per 1" piece: Calories each 206, Fat:20g, Protein: 4, Carbs: 2, Fiber: 1, Net carbs: 1

JUST IN TIME FOR HALLOWEEN, HACKING THE TWIX BAR - KETO-STYLE!

NOTE**: The cookies are modified to specifically work with this recipe due to the oils in the caramel and chocolate. If you want to make just the shortbread cookies as a snack, eliminate the eggs, replace with 2 tbsp cream (heavy, light, h&h, coconut\almond milk, your choice) and drop the baking temp to 325F.

Ready to get cracking?
Keto Hacked Twix Clones (makes 24 in my trays, you're results will vary based off the size of your 'molds.':
Servings=24
Time=45mins

Ingredients:

Keto caramel from this book.

Cookie:

1 cup whey protein isolate
2 tbsp. Organic Coconut Flour
1 tsp baking powder
1/3 cup butter (or Coconut Oil), melted
2 tbsp. sweetener of your choice
1 tsp vanilla extract
1 egg

Preheat oven to 350F and prep a cookie sheet with parchment or silicon mat. Whisk the egg into the melted oil until combined. Add in the rest of the ingredients, then stir with a rubber spatula or spoon until you get a nice, firm dough that will roll into a ball without being too sticky. Wrap in plastic wrap, toss in the fridge while we make the chocolate.

Chocolate:

1/3 cup Coconut Oil
2 tbsp. cocoa powder
1/3 cup sweetener
2 tbsp. heavy cream

Melt the coconut oil in the microwave until completely liquid. Wisk in the cocoa powder until smooth. Add stevia slowly while whisking until smooth. Add heavy cream, whisk until incorporated. Let sit for a couple of minutes, then whisk again. Get out what you are going to use for a mold and put a small amount in the bottom of each to use as a 'base' for the candy bars. In my mold that was about a teaspoon each. Put the mold in the freezer. Take out the cookie dough and roll it out so it is about the thickness of your pinky. Cut it to the shape you need to fit in the mold with a little room on all sides. These will puff up a little in baking so make sure you give a little room for that. Move them to the cookie sheet and bake for 6-7 minutes or until the edges brown. Remove and cool. Once cool to touch, drop each cookie into your mold on top of the chocolate base. Top with a dollop of caramel, then spoon more chocolate over them until completely covered. Put back in the freezer to firm up. Once solid, pop out of the molds and store in the fridge. Put a label on them that says 'nuclear waste, do not touch!' so you can have them all to yourself :).

NUTRITION COUNT PER bar (based off my ingredients, double-check your numbers!): Calories: 191, Protein: 1g, Fat: 19 g, Carbs: 0.1g, Fiber: 0g, NET CARBS: 0.1g

HOBBIT CREATES KETOBURSTS - STARBURST FRUIT CHEWS KETOFIED

Servings=about 12 chews
Time=30mins

1/4 cup Unflavored Whey Protein
1 tbsp. butter, melted
1/4 tsp citric acid
1.5 tbsp. water
3 tbsp. sweetener
1 tsp of flavored extract (berry, citrus)
couple of drops of food coloring
Whisk all the wet together. Whisk in stevia and citric acid. Add the protein powder. Mix and fold until all combined. Should have be a firm mess :). Pull out the powdery mass and kneed with your hands until smooth. Should be a little oily but not sticky. Form into a log. Yes, it's supposed to be greasy, no fear, that will go away. Put the greasy block in the fridge for 15 minutes. Remove. Slice to thickness. Enjoy.

Nutritional information per chew: Calories: 15, Fat: 1g, Protein: 2g, Carbs: 0g, Fiber: 0g, Net Carbs: 0g

HOBBIT'S QUICK AND EASY LOW-FAT, HIGH PROTEIN BARS

Servings=4
Time=45mins
Fat-Free (almost – 1g per bar) Protein bars.

1 tbsp. chia seeds, soaked overnight in 3 tbsp. water
1 tsp choice of extract
1 tbsp. sweetener
1 cup of unflavored whey isolate or skip the extract and sweetener and use flavored isolate

Mix well. Form into 4 bars. Refrigerate for 30 minutes.

Nutritional Information per bar: 135 calories, 1g fat 1g fiber 28g protein (using Z Nutrition Ultimate whey – 27g protein per 33g scoop)

HOBBIT MAKES PROTEIN BARS THAT TASTE GOOD AND ARE LUNCHBOX SAFE!

Servings=3
Time=30mins

Ingredients:

3/4 cup of your favorite flavored Whey Isolate
3 tbsp. butter, melted
1 large egg
1 tbsp. water

Preheat oven AND BAKING SHEET OR A PIZZA STONE to 375F

Whisk the egg, butter, and water together until frothy. Add 1/2 cup of the protein powder. Mix and fold until all combined. Should have a gooey, almost firm mess :). Slowly add the last 1/4 cup of protein powder while folding until you get a solid mass (you probably will need to scrape the sides and bottom of the bowl a few times). Pull out the powdery mass and kneed with your hands until smooth. Should be a little oily but not sticky. Roll into a log, then cut into 3 equal sized chunk. Flatten out into bar shapes on a piece of parchment or silicon mat that matches your baking tray or pizza stone that is in the oven. Quickly transfer to the sheet or stone and close oven door. At 2 minutes, check the bars. If they have doubled in size and are looking almost dry on top, remove and IMMEDIATELY move to a cooling rack. You want to stop the baking as soon as possible, so once on the rack, put right in the fridge. Let cook for 15 minutes until cool to the touch. They are done :). You can store them in a plastic bag outside of the fridge for up to 10 days.

Nutritional information (based off my ingredients, double-check!): Calories: 247, Fat: 14g, Protein: 29g, Carbs: 1g, Fiber: 0g, Net Carbs: 1g

HOBBIT WHIPS UP SOME CHOCOLATE BROWNIE PROTEIN BARS

Servings=3
Time=15mins

¾ cup whey protein isolate
4 sections of Baker's chocolate, melted
1 tsp Coconut Oil, melted
3/4 cup sweetener
3 tbsp. water

Add all your liquids to a bowl and well so that the oil at least tries to combine with the others (the chocolate will help). Now, get out rubber spatula, add ONE scoop at a of the protein powder, the first will easy. The next will take some folding. The last will take some STRONG folding. Once you get as folded in as you can with the spatula, remove it from the bowl. probably will have about 1/2 scoop the bowl of powder. Kneed the lump

whisk

your
time
mix

much

You
left in
of

'dough' with your hands until it gets smooth and sticky, then roll it around in the leftover powder, then kneed some more. Repeat until you cannot pick up any more and have it smooth out. Cut the lump into 3 pieces. Form a bar with each piece. Done. These are dense enough that you don't even need to refrigerate unless you want to store them. Perfect for taking to the gym or work.

Nutritional information (based off my ingredients, double-check!): Calories: 189, Fat: 7g, Protein: 23g, Carbs: 6g, Fiber: 3g, Net Carbs: 3g

PUMPKIN SPICE HOMEMADE PROTEIN BARS

Servings=2
Time=15mins

1/2 tbsp. melted Coconut Oil
1 scoop whey protein isolate
2 tsp water
2 tbsp. finely chopped almonds
2 tbsp. fresh or frozen cranberries, chopped
2 tbsp. keto chocolate chips

Dump protein powder in a bowl, add water little at a time while mixing with a fork. Once all the water is mixed in, add your nuts or berries and stir. Now slowly add the coconut oil and continue to mix with a fork. It will be crumbly and not like a dough at this point, think more pie crust or puff pastry. Pour the crumbs onto one end of a big piece of plastic wrap then fold the other side of the wrap on top. Using your hands, kneed the crumbs through the wrap until you get a solid 'dough,' then flatten it out to about 1/4" thick rectangle. Unfold the wrap, put any additional items on one side (if using chocolate chips or soft berries, this would be the time). Fold over and seal the edges, then pat down a few times to make sure the fillers are pressed good into the dough. Toss in the fridge for 15-20 minutes, then slice up into bar shapes. Also, you could roll this into a log before refrigerating and after set, cut in to bite-sized nuggets. Sometimes she melts more keto chocolate and coats them as well:)

Nutritional information: Calories each 180, Fat:2g, Protein: 25, Carbs: 2, Fiber: 0, Net carbs: 0

Hobbit's Pumpkin Spice Protein Bars
Servings=2
Time=15mins

Ingredients:

1/2 tbsp. melted Coconut Oil
1 scoop whey isolate
1.5 tbsp. kabocha or pumpkin puree
1 tsp pumpkin pie spice

Dump protein powder in a bowl, add melted oil little at a time while mixing with a fork. It will be crumbly and not like a dough at this point, think more pie crust or puff pastry. Stir in the kabocha (or pumpkin) well, mixing until you have a soft dough. Dump half a scoop of protein powder onto parchment, cutting board, or baker's mat. Plop the dough right on top of it, then with a rubber or silicone spatula, start working and folding in the extra powder until you get a smooth and not sticky dough. If it seems still too sticky, add a little more powder (I didn't need to do this but just in case...). Form into a log with your hands. Now flatten it out to about 1/4-inch-thick, then using a flat side of a knife of spatula, even it up. Slice down the center to make two bars about 1.25" wide and 4" long. Place in fridge for 30 minutes to set. Done.

Nutritional information: Calories each 240, Fat:2g, Protein: 37.5, Carbs: 3, Fiber: 1, Net carbs: 2

THE HOBBIT TAKES A CRACK AT...KOOTSIE ROLLS - KETO TOOTSIE ROLLS

Servings=4
Time=45mins

Ingredients:

1/2 cup + 1/4 cup whey (or veggie!) flavored protein powder
3 tbsp. water
1 tsp melted coconut oil
1/4 cup cocoa powder (optional)
1-2 tsp flavored extract (optional)

Add 1/2 cup of protein powder. Mix well to combine. You will get a sticky dough. Let rest for 15 minutes at room temp. Trust me, it will look even stickier when you come back :). Add the coconut oil. Mix well. Add your extras now, such as cocoa powder for traditional 'tootsie rolls' or flavored extracts (1 tsp for a creamsicle taste, 2 tsp if you want that sharper, stronger taste like you get from the wonderful flavored 'tootsies'). Mix until very well combined. Add the additional powder now, stirring and folding until you have a dusty mass. Remove from bowl and kneed by hand until you have a smooth, non-sticky ball. If still a little sticky, roll it around in the bowl with the leftover powder until covered, then repeat. Refrigerate for an hour to let the protein set up. Remove from fridge. Kneed for a minute to soften, then form a log about 1/2" square and 12" long (or to make it easier on yourself, cut the ball in half and do two 1/2" by 6" logs). Slice into 1" long blocks. Roll the blocks in your hand until they are about 3"-4" long. Cut in half. Toss in a bag or bowl for eating! I made one batch (1/2 batch of each) of strawberry and one of chocolate.

Nutritional information per 6 rolls (based off my ingredients, double-check!): Calories: 87, Fat: 3g, Protein: 18g, Carbs: 2g, Fiber: 0g, Net Carbs: 2

SHE'S DROPPING THE BOMB... WMDS. WEAPONS OF MASS DECADENCE. THE LADY'S FAT BOMBS TO THE NEXT LEVEL

good, don't get me wrong, but what I'm about to share is how The Lady took these staples to the next freaking level.

Operation Fat Bomb!
In search of WMDs!

Creamsicle Fatbombs
Strawberry Shortcake Fatbombs
Lemon Curd Fatbombs
BPC (Bullet Proof Coffee) Fatbombs
Chocolate Caramel Fatbombs
White Chocolate Fatbombs

The process to make any of these is the same, so I'm going to run through the basics first, then I'll list the different recipes after. Melt the coconut oil\butter\cream cheese in the microwave, mix in the other ingredients, whisking them up good do they don't separate before you can get them into your mold. Once all mixed well, give a little taste to see if you need to adjust any of the sweetness or flavor. If not, pour into your mold and pop in the freezer for about 15 minutes, then you can store them in the fridge. They will last several weeks if not eaten is my guess, can't promise you that because they never last that long around here:)

Servings=16
Time=30mins

Creamsicle Fatbomb:

- 1/4 cup Coconut Oil, melted
- 2 tbsp butter, melted
- 1/4 cup heavy cream
- 1 tsp orange extract
- 5 tbsp sweetener

Strawberry Shortcake Fatbomb:

- 1/4 cup Coconut Oil, melted
- 2 tbsp butter, melted
- 1/4 cup cream cheese, softened
- 1 tsp strawberry extract
- 5 tbsp sweetener

Lemon Curd Fatbombs:

- 1/4 cup Coconut Oil, melted
- 4 tbsp butter, melted
- 2 tbsp heavy cream
- 1 tsp lemon extract or 3 TBSP lemon juice concentrate
- 5 tbsp sweetener

BPC (Bullet Proof Coffee) Fatbombs:

- 1/4 cup Coconut Oil, melted
- 2 tbsp butter, melted
- 1/8 cup heavy cream
- 1/4 cup very strong brewed coffee or espresso
- 5 tbsp sweetener

Chocolate Caramel Fatbombs:

- 1/4 cup Coconut Oil, melted
- 2 tbsp butter, melted
- 1/8 cup heavy cream
- 2 tbsp cocoa powder
- 1 tsp vanilla extract
- 5 tbsp sweetener
- keto caramel

(follow basic fat bomb instructions at top but only fill part way with chocolate mixture, put in freezer for 15 minutes, then drop about a tsp on caramel in each hole on top of the cooled chocolate, return to freezer for 15. Remove, fill up rest of way with more chocolate. Return to freezer for 15 before popping out of mold and storing in fridge)

White Chocolate Fatbombs:

- 1/4 cup Coconut Oil, melted
- 2 tbsp cocoa butter, melted
- 1/4 cup heavy cream
- 1 tsp vanilla extract
- 5 tbsp sweetener

BREAKFAST

YES, IT'S BEEN A WHILE, HOW ABOUT SOME KETO BISCUITS TO GET BACK INTO THE SWING OF THINGS?

Servings=4-6
Time=45 min

Ingredients:

1/4 cup(s), Mayonnaise
1/2 cup(s), Almond Flour
1/4 cup(s), Coconut Flour
1 tsp baking powder
1/2 tsp baking soda
1 tsp(s) Apple Cider Vinegar
2 large Large Egg – room temp
2 tbsp, Butter, salted and melted
1/4 cup(s), Greek Plain Yogurt

Small bowl of water to wet your hands with

VARIATION (Jalapeno-cheese biscuits):
4 oz chopped\diced pepper jack cheese

Preheat oven to 350F

Prepare a baking dish, lined with parchment or silicone mat (or lightly greased if neither of those are available). Cool butter to room temp but still liquid. Quickly wisk in eggs. Once combined, add the yogurt, mayo, and vinegar. Whisk again until smooth. Add the almond flour, coconut flour, baking powder, and soda. Mix thoroughly with a large spoon or rubber spatula. You should have a wet and sticky dough. Get both hands good and wet. Break up the dough into 4 or 6 lumps, depending on the size you want your results to be. They will spread out to about 1.5 the size pre-baked. Wet your hands again. Quickly, roughly shape each lump into a round or square shape (you can pick ▨) and place in your dish, slightly separated if you like your biscuits to have a soft edge (easier to slice to use as a sandwich bread) or well-spaced for browned edges that will be slightly more crumbly. Place in the oven for 15-20 minutes or until the tops start to brown in a few spots. Remove. Slice and butter the hell out of them, stuff with some cheese and homemade keto sausage, chow down...or be patient, let them cool on a rack and save for later. Yeh. Ok. I tried that. Eh. They didn't make it 15 minutes/

Nutritional information for SIX BISCUITS (adjust accordingly for 4 larger ones): Calories each 207 , Fat: 18g Protein: 6g, Carbs: 6g Fiber: 3g Net: 3g

HOBBIT'S PUMPKIN MUFFINS

Servings=6
Time=30mins

1/4 cup coconut flour
¼ cup Scoops whey protein powder isolate
1 Cup, Baked Kabocha Squash
0.5 cup sweetener
0.25 cup Almond Milk
2 tbsp Butter, melted
3.00 large, Eggs
1.00 tsp(s), Vanilla extract
** 1.00 tsp(s), Spices – Cinnamon, ground
1.5 tsp(s), Baking Powder
0.50 tsp(s), Salt, table
** 0.50 tsp(s), Spices, ginger, ground
** 0.25 tsp(s), Spices, cloves, ground

** You can replace the ginger, cinnamon, and cloves with 2 tsp of pumpkin spice

Preheat your oven to 350F. Get out a muffin pan and lightly grease all with coconut oil (I use the spray type because not only do I like simple, I'm freaking lazy too). Combine all the wet ingredients (including the kabocha) for the in a bowl, beat until smooth. Put all the dry ingredients in a different bowl, then whisk to combine\break up clumps. Add the dry to the wet, and beat until smooth, scraping down the sides. Using a 1/3 cup measuring cup or large soup spoon, drop the batter into your muffin tin and fill each one to just below the top. Place in oven for 25-30 minutes or until the tops puff up and start to brown. Let cool to touch before removing from tin, then put on rack to finish cooling...

or slab some butter in them and eat warm!!

Nutritional info (based off my ingredients, check yours!): Calories: 101, Fat: 7g, Protein: 7g, Carbs: 6, Fiber: 4, Net Carbs: 2

START YOUR DAY RIGHT...COCONUT KETO PANCAKES :)

Servings=2
Time=15 min

Ingredients:

2 eggs
½ cup unflavored whey isolate
**1 tbsp unsweetened coconut (shredded)
**1/2 tsp coconut extract
1/2 tsp vanilla extract
1 tbsp sweetener
1/2 tsp xanthan gum
1 tsp baking powder
2 tbsp water or coconut milk for more flavor

**Leave out the coconut items for regular pancakes, add nuts or berries if you like.

Preheat a skillet (use a cast iron if you have one for best results) on med-high heat. Whisk the eggs, liquid, and extract together. Add the dry, whisk until well combined. Heat some coconut oil in the skillet until it gets a nice sheen. Add 1/4 cup of batter. Watch the edges, when you get a nice line of bubbles coming up, gently flip. Watch it rise :). When the edges look dry, flip onto a plate, add a pat of butter to the top, and repeat. A short stack of 3 is what we go for, then top with some Hobbit Syrup from my pumpkin pancake recipe elsewhere in this book. Toss some bacon or homemade sausage (also in this book) on the side, chow down. I promise you, you will never know these are not made with wheat flour :).

Nutritional information: Calories each 75 (per pancake), Fat:4g, Protein: 10, Carbs: less than 1

HOBBIT'S LOW CARB PROTEIN PANCAKES THAT DON'T SUCK :)

Servings=6 x 6in pancakes or 2 x 8in waffles
time=15mins

1/2 cup whey isolate protein powder
2 eggs

1 tsp baking soda
1 tsp vanilla extract
1 tsp baking soda
½ tsp xanthan gum
1 tsp sweetener.

Heat up a skillet on med-high heat. It's hot enough when a drop of water bounces around before it evaporates. Whisk the eggs until frothy, then add the rest of the ingredients and whisk to a batter. Pour a little oil of your choice in the skillet, let it heat up for 30-45 seconds, then using a measuring cup or ladle, pour about 1/4 cup worth of batter per pancake in the skillet. When you start to see bubbles pop up in the middle and there's a good line of them around the edges, flip. They should puff up nicely. Remove and repeat when the bottom is a nice brown.

Nutritional information: Calories each 65, Fat:2g, Protein: 10, Carbs: less than 1

DEAR ABBY, I HAVE A PROBLEM... KETO PUMPKIN SPICE PANCAKES. ONE CARB EACH. WAIT, WHAT'S THE PROBLEM?

servings=4
Time=30mins

To make the syrup, it's dead simple.

2 tbsp sweetener
1/4 cup water

1/4 tsp maple extract
1/4 tsp xanthan gum

Heat the water in the microwave for about 30 seconds, then stir in stevia until all dissolved. add extract and taste, adjust as needed. Sprinkle xanthan gum over the top while whisking. Once all combined, nuke for another 30 seconds, whisk again then set in fridge while making the pancakes.

The Pancakes (makes 6 4" pancakes):

½ cup whey protein isolate
1 tbsp coconut flour
1 tsp baking powder
pinch of salt
1/4 c almond\coconut milk (or 1/8 cup cream and 1/8 cup water)
2 large egg
1 tsp pumpkin spice (or 1/4 tsp ginger +1/4 tsp nutmeg + 1/2 tsp cinnamon)
1/4 cup cooked kabocha squash (or pumpkin puree)
1 tsp vanilla extract

Preheat a skillet on the stove to medium heat. It's ready when a drop of water dances on the surface of the pan before evaporating. If it just sizzles, turn the heat up a little bit more and try again. Mix all the dry together in one bowl. In a separate bowl, whisk the eggs until well combined, then whisk in the milk, extract, and kabocha until well blended. Pour into the dry, then whisk again until all the lumps are gone. Grease your pan with your choice of oil and let it warm up for few seconds and get thin. Scoop the batter into the pan 1/4 cup at a time. My pan is small so I only do one at a time. I recommend trying one first to make sure the temp of the pan is correct. IF the edges of the batter immediately get, turn the heat down just a little, let it adjust, and try again. When you see bubbles form all around the batter like above, it's time to flip. Flip the pancake over gently, it should start to rise in seconds. Watch the edges of the side facing down. When a nice golden brown, flip it onto a plate and start with the next one. Top with butter and the homemade sugar-free syrup, toss bacon on the plate, and watch the family (or the Lady in my case) love you over, and over again!

Nutritional information (per serving of 3 pancakes) : Calories: 202, Fat: 12, Protein: 19, Carbs: 5, Fiber: 2, Net carbs: 3

QUICK AND DIRTY SUNDAY - KETO BREAKFAST SAUSAGE

Servings=6
Time=30mins

1 lb ground pork (or turkey, beef, or combination)
1 tsp ground sage
1 tsp salt
1 tsp rosemary
1 tsp black pepper
1/8 tsp crushed red pepper
1/2 tsp fennel (optional)

With a couple of forks, break up the ground meat. Sprinkle your spices over the meat. Using the forks, combine well, making sure the spices are all distributed evenly. Make into 6 patties. Brown in a skillet. You can eat them right away, or freeze for a quick nuke-and-eat in the morning.

HOBBIT'S KETO CRISPY BREAKFAST CEREAL - ZERO CARBS, YOU PICK THE FLAVORS!

- Use one of the many flavored protein powders to make fruit, chocolate, cookie, cake, or cinnamon roll flavors

- Use PB2 to make Peanut Butter Capt'n Crunch ⍰

- Use flavored extracts to make a variety of berry or even maple flavored cereals

I'm going to outline the steps I used to make Cinnamon Life Clones, but the process is the same if you want a different flavor – I'll indicate where you need to make the changes, don't worry ☺,

Servings=4
Time=30mins

Ingredients:

1/2 cup + 1/4 cup whey protein isolate powder
1 tsp olive or Coconut Oil (melted if coconut oil)
1 egg
1 tbsp cinnamon (or 1/4 cup cocoa powder, PB powder, or 1 tbsp extract)
2 tbsp sweetener

Whisk egg and oil together until frothy. Add 1/2 cup of protein powder and your flavoring. Mix well to combine. You will get a sticky dough. Let rest for 15 minutes. Trust me, it will look even stickier when you come back :). Dump the additional 1/4 cup of protein on top. With a rubber spatula, mix and fold until you have a kinda dry dough with some powder still on the outside. Using your hands, knead the dough for about 5 minutes until you get a smooth, not sticky ball of dough. If the ball still sticks to your hands, put back in the bowl and roll it around until it is covered in protein again and repeat the kneading until you get a smooth ball. Get out your parchment paper or silicon mat. Do yourself a favor, cut the ball in half first and repeat this step twice, your arms will thank you :). Kneed again it for 2-3 minutes to soften it up. Form into a log.

PREHEAT OVEN TO 375F

If you have a pasta roller, this would be a good time to use it. Otherwise, place on parchment or silicone mat and press down with your hand and flatten as much as possible. Cover with another sheet or mat, and using a rolling pin, roll out as thin as possible (this is a pretty stiff dough, would be a good time to cash in on payback if you have a teen that has misbehaved). Put another sheet on top, roll it out until it is the thickness of about a penny. Take your pizza cutter or long knife, cut it into strips (if using a knife, PRESS DOWN, do not slice so you don't cut your mat). Now, cut it in the other direction into small squares. I baked mine instead of frying it this time. So much easier and better suited for cereal. Drop your mat\sheet on a baking pan. Place in the oven on the LOWER RACK for 3-4 minutes. Remove, shake the pan to mix them up a little, then put back in on the TOP RACK, switch to BROIL (if you have convection oven, you might be able to skip this step. Let me know if you try it) for 1-3 minutes until the tops brown. Remove and let cool. Dump into a bowl and let cool for a minute or two before scooping some out into a bowl of milk (or in my case 1/2 scoop protein powder and 1 cup water). If you are not going to eat right away, let it sit out for a few hours before bagging up. Should keep at least a week this way.

Nutritional information (based off my ingredients, double-check!): Calories: 103, Fat: 2g, Protein: 20g, Carbs: 0g, Fiber: 0g, Net Carbs: 0g

HOBBIT'S HOLIDAY HARVEST BREAKFAST BRAID - 3 NET CARBS PER SERVING!

Servings=8
Time=30mins

Crust ingredients:

4 tbsp(s), Raw Pepitas
3 Tbls coconut flour
1 egg Egg
4 tbsp(s), Butter – Salted
1.5 cup, Mozzarella, part skim milk
1 tsp vanilla extract

Filling:

0.25 cup, Fresh Fruit – Cranberries
1/2 tsp sweetener
1/2 tsp xanthan gum
1/2 tsp orange extract
0.50 cup(s), Cheese, cheddar shredded
0.25 lb(s), Pork (or turkey) breakfast sausage, browned and cooled
40.00 g(s), Apples, raw, without skin, sliced thin (about 1/4 of an apple, I used pink lady)

Let's make the filling:

Put the cranberries and water in a saucepan on the stove on high until comes to boil, then reduce heat to simmer. Stir in the stevia. Let the water reduce to about half, stirring occasionally and crushing the berries as they get soft until they are all broken down. Remove from heat, whisk in the orange extract and xanthan gum, let cool.

Let's make the crust:

Preheat oven to 425F

Mix all the dry ingredients in a bowl, then add one well-beaten egg, melted butter and vanilla. Stir until well combined. Set aside. In a separate bowl, melt your mozzarella in the microwave on 30-40% (depending on power) for 2 minutes, stirring and blending after 1 minute. Immediately add this to the rest of the mixture and fold it over and over to incorporate as much of the cheese with the others. Nuke it for 10 seconds on high, then fold\kneed it until you have a uniform color with no obvious 'cheesy' spots. Repeat the nuke if you if it starts getting hard to work the cheese. Once you have it uniform, roll it into a ball, then nuke one more time for 10 seconds on high. Place it between two sheets of parchment or silicon baking mats. Press down with your hand to flatten it out as much as you can, then using a rolling pin to roll out the dough in a large rectangle of uniform thickness (about the thickness of two quarters stacked). Trim if needed. Starting at one end, make slices down each side about 1/3rd of the way across. This will let you braid\wrap the dough across the top of the filling. Working quickly, lay the apple slices up the center of the dough, then top with generous amount of the cranberry-orange 'jam'. Spread over this the shredded cheddar, then sprinkle the sausage on top of the cheese. Fold the dough over the top to give a braid appearance, alternating sides all the way down, sealing the ends.

Put on a baking sheet and put in the oven for 15 minutes or until the tops are brown. Remove and let cool for about 5 minutes, then slice into 8 pieces, sit back and watch the joy on your family and guests' faces as they chow down:)

Nutritional information (based off my ingredients, double-check!): Calories: 209, Fat: 18g, Protein: 9g, Carbs: 4g, Fiber: 1g, Net Carbs: 3g

KETO BAGELS. BAGELS!! OH, LIFE IS GOOD

Servings=8
Time=45 min

Ingredients:

 1 cup(s) plus 2tbsp Almond Flour
2 tbsp unflavored whey isolate
2 tsp baking powder
3/4 tsp salt
2 large Large Eggs
4 tbsp Psyllium husk powder
3/4 cup boiling water
5-6 ice cubes
Small bowl of water to wet your hands with

Preheat oven to 350F

Prepare a baking sheet, lined with parchment or silicone mat (or lightly greased if neither of those are available). Beat the eggs with a whisk until well combined. Add all the dry, mix well with a spoon or rubber spatula. This will result in a crumbly mess that looks like there's no way this is going to work. Bear with me:). Grab the hot water and pour it into the mixture while stirring until you have a soupy mess. Wait 5 minutes, the dough will become a dough instead of soup. Using wet hands (that's what the bowl of water is for ⊡), roughly shape the dough into a rectangle. Cut the rectangle into 8 squares. Wet hands again, poke your thumb though the middle of each square, spin on your thumb and use your hands to make a rough bagel shape. Place on sheet and repeat until all 8 are done. Space them out with room to at least double in size. Place in the oven and set your timer for 5 minutes. When the timer goes off, open the door and toss the ice cubes into the bottom of the oven. Yeh, the bottom where the burner element is (no, it won't short it out) and quickly close the door again. Back for another 15 minutes or until the tops are brown to your liking and bounce back when lightly touched. Remove. Let cool. Ok. Screw that, let them cool so they don't burn your hands, slice them in half, slather with butter or cream cheese and channel your inner NYC Bagel fiend. Yes, you can put toppings on these before baking. Brush lightly with some coconut or almond milk and then sprinkle poppy seeds, coarse salt, etc before baking

Nutritional information pr bagel: Calories each 113 , Fat: 8g Protein: 6g, Carbs: 6g Fiber: 3g Net: 3g

STUFF THAT DIDN'T FIT ANYWHERE ELSE

SUMMERTIME, SUMMERTIME... WITH KETO ICE CREAM - 3NET CARBS PER SERVING

A few things to note:

- If you don't have a dairy issue, you can use 1 pt of heavy cream instead of the coconut milk

- The inulin is NOT required, but if you have some... use it. It helps slow down the melting as well as gives you some prebiotics. Yeh, $#!#$ HEALTHY ICE CREAM EVEN!!

- For softer ice cream, add 1 tbsp of vodka or Everclear to the mix before putting into the maker. No worries, it's not enough to affect the taste, get you hammered, or kill your progress ⏂

Servings=4
Time=120 min

Ingredients:

1 can (15oz) full-fat coconut milk (or 2 cups heavy cream)
1 cup whey protein isolate (unflavored or flavored)
3/4 cup sweetener of your choice or equivalent
2 tsp vanilla extract (for vanilla ice cream)
1 tbsp inulin (optional – see article above)
1 tbsp vodka or Everclear (optional – see article above)

Warm coconut milk in a sauce pan on low heat. Whisk in vanilla, sweetener, inulin until well combined and the temp is just slightly above body temp. Remove from heat. Pour into blender. Add whey. Pulse until all combined. Pour into your ice cream maker and follow directions for 'traditional' ice cream. Variations: add 1/4 cup cocoa powder (or use chocolate isolate) for chocolate ice cream. Replace vanilla extract with strawberry, cherry, blueberry, etc extract or use a flavored isolate for different flavors. Once ice cream has set up, you can cut in nuts or other add-ins of your choice. Slap a little bit between Hobbit Chocolate Cookies for a freaking DELICIOUS Ice Cream Sammich!!!

Nutritional information per 1/2 cup serving (vanilla, as written): Calories each 254 , Fat: 15g Protein: 29g, Carbs: 5g Fiber: 2g Net: 3g

HOBBIT AND THE LADY TEAM UP FOR SANKAYA - THAI PUMPKIN CUSTARD

Servings=8
Time=45 min

1 1.5-2lb kabocha
5 eggs
3/4 cups coconut milk
1/2 cup sweetener
pinch of salt
1/2 tsp cinnamon
1 tsp. vanilla extract

Instructions:

Get a pot of water with steamer basket in it on the stove, get some steam going (not boiling!). Cut the 'plug' out of the kabocha, scrape out the seeds and stringy crap. Toss all the other ingredients in the blender, pulse until well combined and a little foamy. Pour into the kabocha. Put the kabocha in the steamer, cover. Steam for 30-45 minutes or until a fork stuck in the custard comes out clean and the skin is soft on the kabocha when you press on it. Remove from heat. When cool enough to lift out with your hands, move to fridge to finish cooling. Slice into 8 pieces. Eat as is or top with whipped cream.

Nutritional information (based off my brand of ingredients, double-check yours!): Calories – 98, Fat: 8, Protein: 5, Carbs: 3, Fiber: 2, Net Carbs: 1.

KETO IRON CHEF

The Keto Iron Chef joined us in 2015. We partnered on the first Ketofy Everything! Cookbook. After the terrorist attack in Jakarta, Indonesia, he changed his focus from recipes to using Keto as a therapeutic and medical tool for men, women, and children in his home country. Being blunt, his work with them is more important than any cookbook. I've included all of his recipes in this book as translated with no modification out of respect for his time and dedication to his current endeavor. Many of the pictures I had on file for his recipes are of low resolution and unsuitable for a print medium. I apologize up front for the lack of photos. I've included what I could but many pictures of dishes could not be used, and with what he has going on, there was no way I was going to ask him to take time away from the important work he is doing to not only reproduce the pictures in high resolution, but recreate each dish for photographing as well. I hope you understand and appreciate the work he did to get us so many wonderful, ketofied international dishes.

MAIN COURSE

KETO-IRON CHEF LO BAK GO (CHINESE SAVORY TURNIP CAKE)

Keto-Iron Chef Lo Bak Go (Chinese Savory Turnip Cake)
Servings=1-2
Time=60mins

Ingredients
20g Pea Protein Isolate
15g Egg White Powder
15g Inulin Powder
1,5g Salt
1g Pepper Powder
1g Onion Powder
(Whisk and sift all the ingredients above together)
100g Chinese turnip/daikon radish (grated)
1/4 cup wate
1 teaspoon dried shrimp (washed, soaked and chopped)
3-5 dried Chinese black mushrooms (washed, soaked, and chopped)
1 Chinese sausage (diced)
1/2 scallion, chopped

Directions

Grate the turnip. Use the largest holes on a box grater. Add grated turnip and water to a wok or sauce pan and bring to a simmer. Simmer for about 10 minutes, stirring occasionally so the turnip does not brown. The turnip will produce liquid, some of which will evaporate. Cook it until you have about half liquid left in the pan with the radish. Pour everything (including the liquid) into a large mixing bowl. Heat your pan over medium heat and add a couple tablespoons coconut oil. Add the shrimp, mushrooms, and sausage and cook for about 5 minutes. Stir in the chopped scallion and remove from the heat to cool. Add the whisked dry ingredients to the mixing bowl with the radish and cooking liquid. Mix well until the dry ingredients are well-incorporated. Add in the cooked shrimp, mushrooms and sausage, and be sure to scrape the oil from the pan into the batter. Mix well and let sit for about 15 minutes. Give the batter a final stir and pour it into a well-oiled loaf pan. Place the pan into a steamer with plenty of water and steam over medium-high heat for 30 minutes. Remove the pan from the steamer and let your turnip cake set for about 30 minutes. Once cooled, loosen the sides with a spatula and turn it out onto a cutting board. It should come out quite easily. Use a sharp knife dipped in water to slice ½-inch thick pieces. Add a couple tablespoons oil to a non-stick or seasoned cast iron pan over medium-low heat. Fry the cakes on both sides until golden and crispy and serve with red hot chilli sauce.

KETO-IRON CHEF TUMIS KANGKUNG (INDONESIAN SPICY STIR FRIED SPINACH)

Servings=4-6
Time=60mins
Ingredients

1 kilogram water spinach, clean the water spinach and shake it dry
1/2 tablespoon tamarind paste liquefy in 1 tablespoon lukewarm water
1 tablespoon coconut aminos
200 grams medium prawn/shrimp, cleaned and disposed of the heads
1 tablespoon coconut oil for stir frying
salt to taste
Spices to be ground:

6 shallots
3 cloves garlic
1/2 teaspoon shrimp paste, toasted.
5 red long cayenne peppers

Directions
Prepare the veggie by breaking off the leaves at the base, and after that breaking the stems with your hands at about 1,5 inch periods. Leave the top tail end of stem undamaged with the leading 2 leaves on
Heat your wok to truly high. The secret of stir fry is a hot wok. If you're utilizing an electrical stove, leave the stove on high for about 3-5 minutes with the frying pan loaded with oil resting on top. Stir fry ground spices and shrimps till fragrance
Add water spinach, tamarind mix, coconut aminos and salt. Turn the veggies and expanded a couple of times to make certain they equally prepare. They're done when the leaves are dark green and wilted and the stem is medium green. Do not overcook, or they'll taste bad. Get rid of from heat and serve hot

KETO IRON CHEF'S KETO-DHOKLA (INDIA STREET FOOD - STEAMED SAVORY CAKE)

Keto Iron Chef's Keto-Dhokla (India Street Food – Steamed Savory Cake)
Servings=2-3
Time=60mins

Ingredients
20g Pea Protein Isolate
15g Egg White Powder
15g Inulin Powder
3g Turmeric or Curry Powder
1,5g Salt
1,5g Baking Powder
1,5g Baking Soda
(Whisk and sift all the ingredients above together)

Seasoning
2 green chiles (sliced)
1/4 inch Ginger (peeled and chopped)
Garnish
Cilantro sprigs
Dessicated Coconut

Directions
Set up a steamer large enough to hold an 4-inch cake pan on a rack, with sufficient room above and below
Add water to just below rack. Bring to a boil over high heat, then reduce to a brisk simmer
Grease a 4-inch cake pan with a little coconut oil and set aside
Combine all the dry ingredients in a mixing bowl. Set aside
Put the ginger and chiles in a mortar with a pinch of salt and pound them to a rough paste
Put the ginger-chile paste onto the mixing bowl and mix together with the dry ingredients using spatula
Add yogurt and coconut oil, stirring vigorously, to make a smooth lump-free batter
Gradually thin with more water, as necessary, until mixture resembles thick pancake batter
Beat well, then pour batter into oiled cake pan. Put pan in steamer and cover pot with a clean dish towel, then place a lid on top
Steam for 15 minutes, until a skewer, inserted, emerges dry. Carefully remove pan from steamer
Let dhokla cool in pan for a few minutes, run a knife along sides of pan, then invert bread onto a serving plate

When completely cool, sprinkle dessicated coconut and cilantro sprigs over the cake and serve with yogurt as the dipping sauce

KETO-CHAR SIU BAO (CHINESE STEAMED PORK BUNS WITH POOLISH METHOD)

Keto Iron Chef's Keto-Char Siu Bao (Chinese Steamed Pork Buns with Poolish Method)
Servings=2-3
Time=60mins

Ingredients
Dry Ingredients

30g Casein Protein Isolate
20g Whey Protein Isolate
15g Egg White Powder
15g Egg Yolk Powder
20g Inulin Powder
5g Psyllium Husk
3g Xanthan Gum
2g Salt
5g Sweetener
3g Instant Dry Yeast
(Whisk & sift all these ingredients together)
* Note : The first 7 ingredients above are the Keto-Flour formula for this recipe

Wet Ingredients

30g Coconut Milk
30g Warm Water
5g Apple Cider Vinegar
8g Coconut Oil

* For The Filling

50g Diced Shrimps (The Original Recipe is Using Pork)
1 clove Garlic (minced)
1 stalk Green Onion (chopped)
10g Inulin Powder
10g Casein Protein Isolate
50g Water
2g Sweetener
1/4 tsp Fish Oil
1/4 tsp Sesame Oil
1 tsp Coconut Aminos
1 tsp Oyster Sauce (Fermented)
1 tbsp Coconut Oil for Sautee
Salt & Pepper to taste
* Note : The original recipe is using Pork for the filling, but since I'm a moslem and I can't eat Pork, then I substitute this recipe using shrimps

Direction

On a medium bowl, whisk and sift all the dry ingredients together into Keto-Flour Mix

Scale 30g of Keto-Flour Mix, then transfer into another bowl to make "Preferment Batter" (Poolish)

Combine coconut milk and the Poolish Flour, then stir with spatula until thoroughly combines and forming a thick batter consistency

Rest the Poolish batter on a warm spot for 20 minutes, until it rise to almost double in size

* For The Filling

Mix inulin powder, casein protein isolate, sweetener, salt, pepper and 50ml of water. Stir until there is no more lump, set aside

Mix coconut aminos, fermented oyster sauce, fish oil and sesame oil in a small bowl, as the seasoning. Set aside

Heat 1 tablespoon of coconut oil on a sauce pan. Add the minced garlic and sautee till fragrance

Add the chopped shrimps (or Pork) and cook until the color change into bright red

Pour the seasoning over the shrimp, followed by the chopped green onion, stir well

Add the slurry, and stir until the mixture thicken. Taste for perfection, and add more salt or pepper if needed

Transfer the filling into a bowl, and let it cool for at least 10 minutes. Set aside

* For The Dough

Combine the risen Preferment Batter (Poolish) with the rest of the Keto-Flour Mix

Add water and vinegar gradually, then stir using spatula until a rough dough formed.

Switch using hand your to knead the dough, until it become elastic

Add coconut oil and knead again until the dough become smooth

Divide the dough into 2 equal size and shape each dough into balls

Rest the dough balls on a warm spot for 15 minutes, using plastic wrap to cover the dough so that the dough surface won't dry out

The dough balls should rise to almost double in size

* Assemble

Flatten each balls into flat circle with the center being thicker than the edges

Spoon the filling equally onto the center of each dough

Use your hand to wrap the dough over the filling, then seal the dough by making a seam but leaving a small hole opening on the top of the buns

Repeat once again for the other dough

Steam the buns for 12 minutes, then serve warm with a chilli sauce

KETO IRON CHEF'S KETO-HOTTEOK (KOREAN STREET FOOD - FRIED SWEET PANCAKE)

Keto Iron Chef's Keto-Hotteok (Korean Street Food – Fried Sweet Pancake)
 Servings=2-3
Time=60mins
2 Serving Size

Ingredients
Dry Ingredients

15g Casein Protein Isolate
10g Whey Protein Isolate
7.5g Egg White Powder
7.5g Egg Yolk Powder
10g Inulin Powder
3g Psyllium Husk
2g Xanthan Gum
1g Salt

3g Sweetener
2g Instant Dry Yeast
(Whisk & sift all these ingredients together)
* Note : The first 7 ingredients above are the Keto-Flour formula for this recipe
For softer crumbs the Keto-Flour can be changed into this formula : 15g Wheat Protein Isolate 8000, 5g Casein Protein Isolate, 5g Whey Protein Isolate, 7,5g Egg White Powder, 7,5g Egg Yolk Powder, 10g Inulin Powder
Wet Ingredients
10g Coconut Milk
30g Warm Water
3g Coconut Oil

* For The Filling
40g Diced Almonds
5g Inulin Powder
5g Sweetener
2g Cinnamon Powder
1g Salt

Direction
* For Keto-Hotteok Dough

On a medium bowl, whisk and sift all the dry ingredients together
Add coconut milk and water gradually, then stir using spatula until a rough dough formed.
Switch using hand your to knead the dough, until it become elastic
Add coconut oil and knead again until the dough become smooth
Rest the dough on a warm spot for 20 minutes, using plastic wrap to cover the bowl so that the dough surface won't dry out
The dough should rise to almost double in size

* For The Filling

Combine all the filling ingredients onto a blender or food processor
Blitz until the filling ingredients turns into a paste consistency. Set aside

* Assemble

Transfer the risen dough onto a silicone pad and divide the dough into 2 equal balls
Flatten each balls into rounds and spoon the filling equally onto the center of each dough
Use your hand to wrap the dough over the filling, then seal the dough by making a seam and turning the dough back into a ball shape
Repeat once again for the other dough
Rest these dough in a warm spot for another 30 – 45 minutes and use plastic wrap to cover them
These dough balls should rise to double in size and the skin will become very soft to the touch and leave a finger mark when pressed

* Cooking Keto-Hotteok

Heat up your non-stick pan over medium heat and add some coconut oil
Place 1 ball on the pan and let it cook for 30 seconds
When the bottom of the dough ball is light golden brown, turn it over and press the dough with a spatula to make a thin and wide circle (about the size of a CD)
Let it cook about 1 minute until the bottom is golden brown

Turn it over again and turn down the heat very low. Place the lid on the pan and cook 1 more minute
Repeat these cooking step for the other dough ball
Serve hot with black coffee or green tea
* Note : You could use mozzarella cheese for stuffing. Invent your own fillings with your favourite ingredients

KETO IRON CHEF'S IKAN CAKALANG PEDAS (INDONESIAN SPICY SMOKED TUNA FROM MANADO PROVINCE)

Keto Iron Chef's Ikan Cakalang Pedas (Indonesian Spicy Smoked Tuna from Manado Province)
Servings=2-3
Time=60mins

2 – 3 Serving Size
Ingredients

500 gram Smoked Tuna Fish – Cut into pieces
2 kafir lemon leaves
1 cup coconut milk
1 huge shallot (sliced)
2 lemon turf (squashed the white part)
2 white basil leaves
2 green onion (sliced)
* Put into a blender/food processor or grind it:
5-8 cloves garlic
2 cm ginger root
5-10 Red Chili Pepper (according to your choice).
salt & pepper
5 -7 cloves candle light nuts

Direction
Stir fry shallot till it scent
Bring in minced/smooth spices, stir till the color altered
Include lemon turf as well as Kafir lemon leaves
Stir the smoked fish into the sauteed flavoring, blend it well
Pour the coconut milk into the fish mixtures, remain to prepare it up until the liquid decreased. Prior to the liquid decreased, include green onion and White Basil leaves
Serve with other Keto-Meal dishes

KETO-KHAO SOI GAI (THAILAND STREET FOOD CHICKEN CURRY NOODLES WITH FRIED & BOILED KETO-EGG NOODLES)

Keto-Khao Soi Gai (Thailand Street Food Chicken Curry Noodles with Fried & Boiled Keto-Egg Noodles)
Servings=1-2
Time=60mins
1 – 2 Serving Size

Keto-Egg Noodles
Dry Ingredients

10g Egg Yolk Powder
20g Egg White Powder
20g Inulin Powder
1g Salt

Wet Ingredients

20g Egg White
3g Coconut Oil
Keto-Khao Soi Gai

Ingredients

2 whole red chilli pepper
1 small shallots, peeled and minced
2 whole cloves garlic
1 stalk lemongrass, bottom 4 inches only, chopped
1 teaspoon makrut lime zest
1 (1 inch) knob fresg turmeric, chopped
2 thin slices ginger
1 small bunch cilantro stalks, cut from the very base of the stalks
1/2 teaspoon whole coriander seed
3 pods cardamom, inner seeds only
Pinch of salt
1 tablespoon shrimp paste
1 cup coconut oil, for frying
1 cup fresh coconut milk
1/2 cup chicken broth
1/2 teaspoon sweetener
4 chicken legs
Fish sauce to taste

* For Garnish
Sliced shallots, lime wedges, mung bean sprouts and bok choy

Direction
* For Keto-Egg Noodles

Whisk all dry ingredients on a medium bowl. Add Egg and stir using spatula until a rough dough formed, then switch using hand to knead the dough until elastic
Add coconut oil and knead until the dough become smooth
Shape the dough into round. Flatten the dough using rolling pin on a silicone pad. Fold the vertical edges to the center, turn 90 degree then roll it again. Repeat the steps one more time until forming a rectangle with a smooth edges
Then using a pasta machine, roll the dough up to stage 6 – 7 setting on the pasta machine.
Rest the rolled dough for 30 minutes, then continue to cut the dough using noodles cutter on the pasta machine. Set aside

* For Keto-Khao Soi Gai

Place chillies, shallots, garlic, lemon grass, cilantro stalks, coriander seed and cardamom in the center of aluminium foil pouch mould
Place pouch directly over the flame of a gas burner and cook, turning occasionally, until aromatic and wisps of smoke begin to

rise

Allow content to cool slightly and transfer to a large mortar and pestle

Add a large pinch of salt to the aromatics. Pound until a very fine paste is formed, about 10 minutes. Add shrimp paste and pound to incorporate. Set curry paste mixture aside

Separate out 1/3 of the Keto-Egg Noodles and set the remaining noodles aside

Heat coconut oil in large wok over high heat until shimmering. Add noodles to oil and fry, stirring and flipping until golden brown and crisp. Drain with a spider strainer then transfer to a paper towel to remove excess oil. Set aside

Discard all but 1 tablespoon coconut oil from wok. Using spoon, skim 2 tablespoons of creamy fat of the top of the coconut milk and add to the wok

Heat wok over high heat, stirring constantly, until coconut oil breaks and oil begin to lightly smoke, about 2 minutes

Add curry paste mixture and cook, stirring and smearing the paste into the oil, until aromatic, about 45 seconds

Slowly whisk in the coconut milk, followed by the chicken broth and sweetener. Add chicken legs and bring to a simmer. Cook, turning chicken occasionally, until chicken is tender and soup is very flavorful, about 30 minutes. Season to taste with fish sauce

Bring a pot of salted water to a boil. Add remaing uncooked Keto-Egg noodles and cook until al dente about 1 minute

Drain noodles and divide between 2 warmed bowls

Top noodles with 2 pieces of chicken. Divide soup evenly between bowls. Top with the fried noodles and serve immediately with sliced shallots, lime wedges, mung bean sprouts and bok choy on the side

KETO-TTEOKBOKKI (KOREAN STREET FOOD - HOT & SPICY RICE CAKE USING KETO-TTEOK & KETO-EOMUK)

Keto-Tteokbokki (Korean Street Food – Hot & Spicy Rice Cake using Keto-Tteok & Keto-Eomuk)

Servings=1-2

Time=60mins

Ingredients

1 cup Keto-Tteok (Korean Rice Cake)

1/2 cup Keto-Eomuk (Korean Fish Cake)

2 cups Water

8 large size Dried Anchovies

1 cup Dried Kelp

2 tablespoon Red Chilli Paste

2 teaspoon Red Chilli Flakes

1/4 teaspoon Sweetener

1 Green Onion (cut into 3 inches long pieces)

1 clove Garlic (chopped)

1/2 cup Enoki Mushroom (shredded)

Direction

Add the water, dried anchovies, and dried kelp to a shallow pot or pan

Boil for 15 minutes over medium high heat without the lid

Combine red chilli paste, red chili flakes, and sweetener in a small bowl. Remove the anchovies and kelp from the pot and add the rice cake (Keto-Tteok), the mixture in the bowl, green onion, minced garlic, shredded enoki mushroom and the fish cake (Keto-Eomuk). The stock will be about 1,5 cups

Stir gently with a wooden spoon when it starts to boil. Keep stirring until the rice cake turns soft and the sauce thickens and looks shiny, which should take about 10 -15 minutes

If the rice cake is not soft enough, add more water and continue stirring until soften

Remove from the heat and serve hot

KETO-IRON CHEF'S KETO-TTEOK & KETO-EOMUK (KOREAN RICE CAKE & FISH CAKE)

Keto-Iron Chef's Keto-Tteok & Keto-Eomuk (Korean Rice Cake & Fish Cake)
Servings=1-2
Time=60mins
For Keto-Tteok (Korean Rice Cake)

Ingredients

20g Egg White Powder
10g Inulin Powder
1g Salt
120g Coconut Milk

For Keto-Eomuk (Korean Fish Cake)

20g Egg White Powder
10g Inulin Powder
150g Fresh White Fish Fillet (Cod, Pollock, Flounder or Snapper)
1 cloves Garlic
1/3 medium Onion
1/4 tsp Salt
1/8 tsp Ground White Pepper
1/8 tsp Sweetener
1 medium Egg
2 cup Coconut Oil for frying

Direction
* For Keto-Tteok (Korean Rice Cake)

Combine the egg white powder, inulin powder, salt, and coconut milk in a bowl
Line a lightly greased baking pan with parchment paper. Add the rice cake batter and steam for about 15 minutes over high heat
Let the steamed rice cake cools for 10 minutes then transfer into a silicone pad
Cut the rice cake into match stick size

* For Keto-Eomuk (Korean Fish Cake)

Inspect the fish fillet and remove any remaining fish bones
Cut the fish fillets into chunks and put them into a food processor. Add the garlic, onion, salt, sweetener, ground white pepper and egg. Blend for a couple of minutes until the mixture turns into a smooth paste
Transfer the paste to a medium bowl, then add inulin powder and egg white powder. Stir the mixture until thoroughly combines
Heat 2 cups coconut oil in a skillet over medium high heat for about 5 minutes. Lower the heat to medium (about 330F)
Use a spoon to scoop up some of the paste, and then another one to shape the paste into small ball and push it off into the hot oil
Repeat shaping and pushing the fish mixture to hot oil, 4 to 5 balls in the skillet, and be sure not to to crowd them
Stir the fish cakes occasionally to fry all sides evenly. Let them cook about 5 to 7 minutes over medium heat until golden brown

Take the fish cakes out and put them in a strainer over small bowl. Pat the fish cakes with paper towel to remove the excess oil

THE KETO IRON CHEF'S "BAKWAN" THE ASIAN VEGETABLES FRITTER

The Keto Iron Chef's "Bakwan" the asian vegetables fritter
Servings=4
Time=30mins
Good Morning (my time 7am)
Yeay its thursday, my veggies day.. (vegs only from thursday to sunday)
When I'm about to leave for work.. I remember my past high carbed life, which I was always had a simple breakfast with "Bakwan" the asian vegetables fritter.
And for had been posting keto-dessert cuisines yesterday, reminds me of this food again
I'm going to make this again once again to be taken for my 28h IF feast today ☺
Well here it goes

BAKWAN SAYUR (Ketofied Vegetables Fritter)

Ingredients
The Vegetables

250 gram shredded cabbage
150 gram shredded carrot
2 scallions, thinly sliced
The Keto-Flour
60g Inulin Fiber (Chicory Root) – LC Foods
40g almond flour
20g Golden Flax Seeds
40g Isopure Whey Protein Isolate, Unflavored
40g Micellar Casein
10g Psyllium Husk
10g gelatin powder
5g baking soda
(Sift all these ingredients together as the keto-flour)

The Seasonings

1 teaspoon salt
1/8 teaspoon splenda
1 teaspoon ground pepper
1/2 teaspoon nutmeg powder
1/2 teaspoon curry powder
5 cloves garlic, peeled and grated
(Mix all these ingredients together in a small bowl)

The Wet Ingredients

1 egg
50ml full fat yogurt
100ml coconut milk

200ml water
Coconut Oil for deep frying
The Peanut Butter Sauces
2 tablespoon Natural peanut butter
1 teaspoon Chilli paste
1 teaspoon Butter (melted)
2 tablespoon Coconut milk
3 to 5 tablespoon of water (I use 3 tbsp to make it thick)
(Mix all these ingredients together untill well combined)

Direction

In a mixing bowl, combine the Keto-Flour with the seasonings and mix well.
Add water, yogurt, coconut milk and mix well, make sure there are no lumps.
Add grated garlic and egg into the batter. Mix well.
Add shredded cabbage, shredded carrot, and sliced scallions into the batter and mix well.
Pour enough coconut oil in a pot for deep frying. Once a bit of batter dropped into the oil bubbles immediately, the oil is ready.
Use a small laddle and drop a laddleful of vegetables mixture into the hot coconut oil. Deep fry until the fritter is crispy and turns golden brown on both sides, remove and drain on a wire rack/paper towel.
Repeat until all batter is used up then serve immediately with some green chilies and the hot peanut butter sauce
* Be creative by adding small prawns or sliced bacons to the batter. I used to add grated cheese to make them crispier

TELUR DADAR PADANG (PADANG THICK OMELLETE)

Telur Dadar Padang (Padang Thick Omellete)
Servings=2-4
Time=30mins

Ingredients

5 Large Duck Eggs
2 tbsp Dessicated Coconut
1 Tbsp Inulin Powder
1 Tbsp Whey Protein Isolate
2 stalk Spring Onion
* For Spice Paste
6 pcs Shallots
2 cloves Garlic
4 pcs Red Chillies
1/2 tsp Salt
1/4 tsp White Pepper

Direction

Whisk the eggs slowly with a fork (don't over do it and make the mixture foamy) on a medium bowl, set aside
Grind the spice paste ingredients on a food processor, then put the paste in a large mixing bowl.
Mix inulin powder, whey protein isolate and dessicated coconut with the spice paste, until well combined
Add the egg and spring onion into the mixture, whisk to combine
Heat the coconut oil on a frying pain on low heat, then pour the egg mixture

Cover the frying pan with a lid for 30 second, so the steam will make the egg puffs
When the edge has starting to brown, flip the egg to the other side and cook until done
Cut into 6 – 8 pieces when served

KETO-IRON CHEF'S KETO-EGG NOODLES & KETO-RED CHILLI NOODLES

Keto-Iron Chef's Keto-Egg Noodles & Keto-Red Chilli Noodles
Servings=1-2
Time=60mins
(Hongkong Street Food Red Chilli Noodles with Keto-Egg Noodles & Keto-Iron Crispy Chicken)
1 – 2 Serving Size
Warning : VERY HOT, Dare to take the HEAT

Keto-Egg Noodles
Dry Ingredients

20g Egg Yolk Powder
20g Egg White Powder
20g Inulin Powder
1g Salt

Wet Ingredients

40g Egg
3g Coconut Oil

Keto-Iron Crispy Chicken
Ingredients

200g Chicken Skins or Boneless Chicken Breast (cut into 1/2 inch pieces)
2 Egg Whites (Beat into stiff peak)
2 cup Coconut Oil for deep frying

* For Breading The Chicken
Keto-Flour Mix Ingredients

20g Egg White Powder
10g Egg Yolk Powder
20g Inulin Powder
1g Baking Soda
1g Salt
0,5g Garlic Powder
0,5g Pepper Powder
0,5g Nutmeg Powder
0,5g Coriander Powder
(Whisk & sift all these ingredients together)

Keto-Red Chilli Noodles
Ingredients

3 tbsp Coconut Oil
1 tsp Minced Garlic
1 tsp Chopped Onion
1 tbsp Red Chilli Pepper Paste
1 cup Keto-Iron Crispy Fried Chicken
1 (60g) Large Egg
1/2 cup Sliced Chanterelle Mushroom
1/2 cup Enokitake Mushroom

* For Seasoning

1/4 cup Red Chilli Powder
1 tbsp Shao Xing Wine
1 tsp Fish Sauce
1 tbsp Coconut Aminos
1 tbsp Oyster Sauce (Fermented)
1 tsp Sweetener

* For Garnish
Red Chilli Pepper Slices
Roasted Sesame Seeds

Direction
* For Keto-Egg Noodles

Whisk all dry ingredients on a medium bowl. Add Egg and stir using spatula until a rough dough formed, then switch using hand to knead the dough until elastic
Add coconut oil and knead until the dough become smooth
Shape the dough into round. Flatten the dough using rolling pin on a silicone pad. Fold the vertical edges to the center, turn 90 degree then roll it again. Repeat the steps one more time until forming a rectangle with a smooth edges
Then using a pasta machine, roll the dough up to stage 6 – 7 setting on the pasta machine.
Rest the rolled dough for 30 minutes, then continue to cut the dough using noodles cutter on the pasta machine
Cook the noodles on a boiling water, strain when the noodles are already floating. Sprinkle 2 tbsp coconut oil over the drained noodles to keep them from sticking, set aside

* For Keto-Iron Crispy Chicken

whisk and sift the Keto-Flour mix ingredients. Beat the egg white on a standing mixer into stiff peak. Add the chicken pieces and fold with spatula to coat
Using chopsticks, bread all chicken pieces with Keto-Flour mix until covered thoroughly, then transfer to a plate
Heat the coconut oil in a large skillet over medium heat. Sprinkle any left over Keto-Flour mix into the hot oil, then place chicken into the skillet, and fry for 5 – 6 minutes on each side to brown. Drain with a spider strainer and remove the excess oil with paper towel

* For Keto-Red Chilli Noodles

Heat the coconut oil in a wok. Add the onion, garlic and chilli paste, stir fry until golden brown. Add the crispy chicken then stir to coat. Break the egg next to the chicken and scramble the egg to combine with the chicken
Add the mushrooms and bok choy, then stir to mix. Drop the noodles. They will stick together so stir fast and try to separate them. Add a little water, stirring a few times.
Add the shaoxing wine, coconut aminos, oyster sauce, fish sauce, and sesame oil. Stir fry everything together until the

noodles get an even brown color

Sprinkle the sweetener and red chilli powder over then mix until thoroughly combine. Turn off the heat then remove the fried noodles into a serving plate

Garnish with red chilli pepper slices and roasted sesame seeds

KETO IRON CHEF KETO-THANKSGIVING STUFFING

Keto-Thanksgiving Stuffing

Thanksgiving will not become a suffer anymore on the Keto-Lifestyle

As a request from a member on the Keto-Group, I'm making this traditional stuffing for Thanksgiving, and I hope this will help fellow ketoers on celebrating the event in old fashion way of dinner using ketofied recipes for Thanksgiving dishes (Keto-Stuffing, Keto-Mashed Potato, Keto-Buns) from this recipe and my previous recipes.

Well I hope you like this one Jason Pitzer

Happy Thanksgiving for all fellow ketoers that celebrate it (indonesian doesn't celebrate this, but wishing you all the best for the Keto-Lifestyle)

Keto-Thanksgiving Stuffing Servings=4
Time=60mins

Keto-Bread for Stuffing

200g Loaf (with 10% Baking Loss)
(Net Carb 7,2g / Protein 44,3g / Fat 26,4g)
(Energy 517cal / Fiber 48,7g / Insulinogenic 25%)
Suggested Serving Size : 2 – 3 serving

Dry Ingredients
50g Inulin Fiber (Chicory Root) – LC Foods
20g Micellar Casein
20g Isopure Whey Protein Isolate, Unflavored
10g Dried Egg Whites
3g Psyllium Husk
2g Xanthan Gum
2g Salt
(whisk all these ingredients together on a medium bowl)

Wet Ingredients
30g Egg
10g Heavy Whipping Cream
10g Coconut Milk
30g Warm Water
Yeast Solution
3g Instant Dry Yeast
2g Honey (consumed by the yeast)
20g Warm Water
(Mix all these ingredients on a small glass and wait until bubbles before adding to the mixed dough)

Fat Ingredient
10g Virgin Coconut Oil

Direction
Preheat oven to 200C
Sift all the dry ingredients onto a mixer bowl
Add the egg and turn on the mixer to level 1, by also using spatula to scrap the dry ingredients into the egg
Add the heavy whipping cream and coconut milk all at once, and keep scraping until a rough dough formed
Pour the water gradually by seeing the dough consistency stages becoming more elastic
As soon as dough has become elastic, add the yeast solution and raise the speed into level 2 until combined
Add coconut oil and raise the speed to level 3 until the dough become smooth.
Turn the dough into balls and shape into loaf, then move to the matched & greased loaf pan
Rise the loaf for 30 minutes or until it is 1,5x from the original size, on a warm spot
Brush the loaf surface with an egg wash and bake for 20 – 30 minutes.

Slice the cooled loaf, and arrange the loaf on a tray
Dry the sliced loaf in the sun for 3 to 4 hours (depends on the sunlight) until the crumbs feels very dry
Cut the dry bread into cubes

For the Thanksgiving Stuffing
477g (with 10% Baking Loss)
(Net Carb 16,7g / Protein 65,1g / Fat 103,2g)
(Energy 1451cal / Fiber 51g / Insulinogenic 25%)
Suggested Serving Size : 3 – 4 serving

Ingredients
Dry Bread cubes
1/2 medium onion, diced (55g)
50g Cheddar Cheese, grated
50g Butter, melted
30g Egg, beaten
60g Heavy Whipping Cream
60g Coconut Milk
4g Salt
15g Oregano, Thyme, Basil, Rosemary, Sage mix
2g Garlic Powder
2g Curry Powder
2g Pepper

Direction
Mix all the seasoning, grated cheese, butter and egg in a Pyrex bowl, stir
Add the dry bread cubes and stir with a spatula to evenly distribute the mixture
Slowly drizzle heavy whipping cream and coconut milk over bread cubes while stirring until bread cubes are moist but not soggy.

Bake at 200C for 30 – 40 minutes or until bread cubes on top are crispy

KETO IRON CHEF - KETO-PORTUGUESE EGG TART

This Keto-Portuguese Egg Tart is the best recipe I ever made, for pastries.
Since it's only take me less than an hour to made this one.

The folding method for the pie dough is adapted from the previous Keto-Bakpia recipe (simple envelope folding), with also suspending the butter with the Keto-Flour to avoid the need for refrigerating
And what makes this recipe awesome is the higher fat ratio that can be easily tailored on this recipe, since we can modified the custard to meet the Fat macro needed
Here goes the recipe

Keto-Portuguese Egg Tart Servings=5 Time=60mins
5 serving size @94,6g
(Net Carb 2,2g / Protein 10,5g / Fat 15g)
Ingredients
For The Pie Dough
Dry Ingredients
25g Inulin Fiber (Chicory Root) – LC Foods
10g Micellar Casein
10g Isopure Whey Protein Isolate, Unflavored
5g Dried Egg Whites
1,5g Psyllium Husk
1g Xanthan Gum
1,5g Salt
2,5g Splenda (Optional)
1g Vanilla Extract (0,1/0/0)
(Whisk all the ingredients above in a medium bowl)

Wet Ingredient
10g Heavy Cream (0,3/0,2/3,7)
30g Warm Water
5g Butter (0/0,1/4,1)

For The Pastry Batter
10g Inulin Fiber (Chicory Root) – LC Foods
10g Micellar Casein
20g Butter (0/0,2/16,2)
(Mix all the ingredients above with a spatula until forming a thick batter consistency, set aside)

For The Custard
50g Egg (0,4/6,3/5)
30g Egg Yolk (1,1/4,8/8)
200g Heavy Cream (2,8/2,1/37)
20g Keto-Flour (10g Inulin Powder & 10g Casein Protein Isolate) (0,6/8,6/0,2)
20g Splenda
5g Vanilla Extract (0,6/0/0)
5g Salt

Topping (Optional)
Cinnamon Powder for sprinkling
Direction

For The Custard:
Whisk egg yolks and egg with heavy cream, salt, splenda and Keto-Flour in a large saucepan and set over medium. Continue whisking until mixture thickens, 7 to 10 min. Whisk in vanilla, then scrape into a medium bowl. Lay a piece of plastic wrap directly on surface to prevent skin from forming. Chill in freezer until very cold, but not frozen, about 1 hour.

For The Pie Dough:

Sift the dry ingredients in the bowl of a stand mixer that is fitted with a dough hook. Turn on the mixer on low speed, gradually stir in water and heavy cream until the dough holds together enough to clean the sides of the bowl.

Add the butter and move to medium speed until smooth dough is forming.

Shape into a flat ball, and allow to rest for at least 10 minutes.

Divide the pie dough into 5 equal parts, then flatten it using rolling pin into circles.

Divide the pastry batter into 5 equal parts, then take 1 part of pastry dough and spread it on one of the pie dough. Fold it like an envelope and set aside (see pictures for details).

Repeat the process for the other pie dough and pastry batter.

Preheat the oven into 200C

Lay one of the pastry dough on a silicone pad and roll with a rolling pin until it is 4 in. across. Pastry will be very thin. Repeat with remaining rounds. Gently push each round into a muffin cup, pressing along the bottom, then up the sides until it reaches the rim.

Spoon the chilled custard into each muffin cup, reaching 3/4 of the cup heights.

Optional : Sprinkle cinnamon powder evenly over each custard.

Bake in centre of oven until tops are brown, but not burnt, 13 to 15 min. If tops have not browned, continue baking and check at 2-min intervals. Cool in pan on a rack for 5 min. Remove from pan and let cool slightly on rack, about 15 min.

Serve with black coffee or green tea.

KETO IRON CHEF'S KETO-MOCHI

As a request from my friend at Keto-Group, I'm going to show you how to ketofied the famous Mochi that comes from Japan

This snack is also my previous cracks when I was so so Fat and diabetic.. LOL

Can't stop eating this even when I want to.. just can't get enough for the moist and rubbery textures coated with sesame seeds

(12pcs Mochi @15g)

Keto-Mochi Servings=12 Time=30mins

Nutrition Fact (without topping)

*1 serving 180g of Mochi (5,4g Net Carb : 23,8g Protein : 50g Fat)

* Per Mochi 15g (0,5g Net Carb : 2g Protein : 4,2g Fat)

Ingredients

* Mochi Dough

Dry Ingredients

35g Inulin Fiber (Chicory Root) – LC Foods

10g Micellar Casein

5g Dried Egg Whites

1g Xanthan Gum

1g Salt

5g Splenda

Wet Ingredients

65g Coconut Milk

5g Virgin Coconut Oil

* Mochi Filling

30g Grated Cheddar Cheese

15g Coconut Milk

5g Splenda
5g Egg Yolk Powder
5g Butter

* Mochi Topping
Roasted sesame seeds
Dessicated coconut
Egg yolk powder

Direction
For Mochi Dough : Sift all dry ingredients together until well combines (except for splenda) on a mixer bowl
Add coconut milk gradually with speed 1 on the mixer until rough dough formed
Proceed to speed 2 on the mixer, by also adding the coconut oil until an elastic and smooth dough is formed
Steam the dough using low heat for 30 minutes
Remove the steamed dough back into the mixer bowl and mix it again with coconut oil and splenda until a smooth dough formed
Remove the dough to a sill plate and continue to knead with your hand until the dough become smooth and just a little tacky
Divide the dough into small balls (@10g), set aside
For Mochi Filling : Heat the butter on a sauce pan with low to medium heat until melt, then add the coconut milk by also stirring to combine
Add the grated cheddar cheese and keep stirring until dissolved and the batter start to bubbles
Turn off the heat, and add the egg yolk powder then splenda, stir until a thick batter formed, set aside to cool
Divide the Mochi filling into 10 small balls (@5g) and keep the left over on the refrigerator if you are making larger batch (up to 2 weeks on refrigerator & 1 month on the freezer)
Assemble : using roller pin, flatten each Mochi dough into circle and put the filling balls on the center of each flattened Mochi dough
Wrap the dough and lightly assemble into smooth balls
Coat the Mochi with the chosen topping, such as sesame seeds, dessicated coconut or egg yolk powder using a little warm water as the dipping before coating
Serve with black coffee or green tea
* Note : be creative with the filling by using peanut butter, dark chocolate or other keto compatible filling ingredients

KETO IRON CHEF'S KETO-ALMOND PIE

Keto-Almond Pie Servings=4 Time=60mins

Ingredient
* For Pie Dough
Dry Ingredient
10g Micellar Casein
10g Isopure Whey Protein Isolate, Unflavored
5g Dried Egg Whites
5g Egg Yolk Powder
20g Inulin Fiber (Chicory Root) – LC Foods
1g Xanthan Gum Powder
1g Salt
5g Sucralose
* Note : The first 6 ingredients above are the Keto-Flour formula for this recipe

Wet Ingredient
35g Butter
15g Egg White
* For Pie Filling
5g Egg Yolk Powder
5g Inulin Fiber (Chicory Root) – LC Foods
5g Micellar Casein
0,5g Vanilla Extract
0,5g Nut Meg
1g Salt
2g Dark Rum
5g Sucralose
15g Egg
25g Heavy Whipping Cream
10g Butter
Note : if using "Torani Sugar Free Vanilla Syrup", omit Heavy Whipping Cream, Inulin Powder, Casein Protein Isolate, Vanilla Extract & Sucralose. Use 35g of the syrup to substitutes

* Topping
30g Roasted Almonds (diced) or Shelled Pecans

Direction
* For Pie Dough
Preheat the oven into 300F
Whisk all the dry ingredients together on a medium bowl
Add butter, then mix with a spatula until the dough comes together
Add egg white, then mix again until the dough become smooth
Divide the dough into 2 equal dough balls then roll each dough into flat circle with 1/2 inch thickness

Ease each dough into the bottom of 2 lightly greased 3 inch aluminium pie shell, and crimp the top edge. Pierce the bottom in several place with fork
Bake the pie dough for 15 minutes
* For Pie Filling
Melt butter on a sauce pan over low to medium heat
Add heavy whipping cream, Inulin Powder, Casein Protein Isolate, Egg Yolk Powder and sucralose and stir to combine.
Add egg the last and stir until the mixture thickens, then turn off the heat, set aside
Fill each half-baked pie dough with diced roasted almonds (or shelled pecans),then scrape in the pie filling until level with the top edge of the pie dough
Bake again for 15 – 20 minutes, until the nuts are lightly browned and filling is just about set. The filling will puff up and may be bubbling, but it will settle as it cools.
Serve with black coffee or green tea
* Note : The ingredients of this recipe can be multiply to larger serving size with larger single pie pan. This recipe is using 2 x 3" pie mould and to fit into 9" round pie pan, the ingredients quantity can be multiplied by 8

KETO-IRON CHEF'S MONGOLIAN BEEF (CHINESE SWEET FRIED BEEF)

Keto-Iron Chef's Mongolian Beef (Chinese Sweet Fried Beef) Servings=2-3 Time=60mins
The Keto-Iron Chef's Mom Holiday Cooking
Mongolian Beef

(Chinese Sweet Fried Beef)
2 – 3 Serving Size

Ingredients
300g Flank Steak (thinly sliced) or Fatty Brisket (cut into dice)
1/2 medium Onion (sliced)
2 cloves Garlic (mashed)
2 cm Ginger (peeled, sliced)
2 tbsp Chilli Paste (or Chilli sauce)
3 tbsp Tomato Puree (or Tomato sauce)
2 tbsp Butter
200ml Water
2 pcs Bok Choy / Chinese Cabbage (shredded)
Salt, Pepper & Sweetener to taste

Ingredients to Ferment
3 tbsp Oyster Sauce
2 tbsp Hoisin Sauce
2 tbsp Coconut Aminos
1/8 tsp Instant Dry Yeast
For Garnish
Roasted Sesame seeds
Small Red Chillies slices
Fried shallots
Scallions

Direction
In a small bowl, add 3 tbsp oyster sauce, 2 tbsp hoisin sauce, 2 tbsp coconut aminos and 1/8 tsp instant dry yeast. Stir to combine
Rest the oyster/hoisin/amino sauce mixture for 2 hour at a warm spot to ferment. Set aside
Melt butter on a wok with low-medium heat
Sautee garlic and ginger until fragrant. Add the sliced flank steak or diced fatty brisket, then cook until the color start to change
Pour 200ml water and let it cook until the water evaporates and the sliced flank steak or diced fatty brisket become tender
Add the fermented oyster/hoisin sauce, chilli paste and tomato puree, stir to combine
Stir in the shredded bok choy and onion slices, then sprinkle salt, pepper and sweetener to taste. Simmer for 2 more minutes
Turn off the heat, then taste for perfection. Add more salt, sweetener or pepper if needed
Serve immediately with sprinkles of roasted sesame seeds, red chilli slices, fried shallots and scallions as the garnish

KETO-IRON CHEF'S KETO-YOUMIAN NOODLES & KETO-GENERAL TSO'S CHICKEN

Keto-Iron Chef's Keto-Youmian Noodles & Keto-General Tso's Chicken Servings=1-2 Time=60mins
Keto-Youmian Noodles & Keto-General Tso's Chicken
(Hongkong Thin Noodles & Chinese Sweet Spicy Chicken with Iron Style Crispy Chicken)
2 – 3 Serving Size
Keto-Youmian

Dry Ingredients
15g Casein Protein Isolate
10g Whey Protein Isolate

5g Egg White Powder
5g Egg Yolk Powder
15g Inulin Powder
2g Psyllium Husk
1g Xanthan Gum
1g Salt
0,5g Garlic Powder
0,5g Pepper Powder
* Note : The first 7 ingredients above are the Keto-Flour formula for this recipe
For more chewy noodles the Keto-Flour can be changed into this formula : 15g Wheat Protein Isolate 8000, 10g Casein Protein Isolate, 10g Whey Protein Isolate, 5g Egg White Powder, 5g Egg Yolk Powder, 5g Inulin Powder

Wet Ingredients
30g Egg
3g Sesame Oil

* For Noodles Sauce
1 tbsp Sesame Oil
Keto-General Tso's Chicken
Ingredients

* For The Chicken Marinate
1/4 cup Water
1 tbsp Shao Xing Wine
1 tbsp Coconut Aminos
1 tsp Garlic Powder
1 tsp Ginger Powder
1 tsp Salt
1/4 tsp Pepper Powder

* For Keto-Iron Crispy Fried Chicken
300g Chicken Skins or Boneless Chicken Breast (cut into 1/2 inch pieces)
2 Egg Whites (Beat into stiff peak)
* For Breading The Chicken
Keto-Flour Mix Ingredients
30g Casein Protein Isolate
20g Whey Protein Isolate
20g Egg White Powder
10g Egg Yolk Powder
20g Inulin Powder
2g Baking Soda
2g Salt
1g Garlic Powder
0,5g Pepper Powder
0,5g Nutmeg Powder
0,5g Coriander Powder
(Whisk & sift all these ingredients together)

* For The Sauce
3/4 cup Chicken Stock
2 tbsp Coconut Aminos

1 tbsp Vinegar
2 tsp Sweetener
1 tsp Minced Garlic
1 tsp Minced Ginger
2 tbsp Chopped Green Onion
1 tbsp Chopped Red Chilli Pepper

* For Sauce Slurry
2 tbsp Keto-Flour Mix
1/4 cup Coconut Milk

* For Garnish
Sesame seeds

Direction
* For Keto-Youmian
Whisk all dry ingredients on a medium bowl. Add egg and stir using spatula until a rough dough formed
Add sesame oil, then switch using hand to knead the dough until elastic and smooth
Shape the dough into round. Flatten the dough using rolling pin on a silicone pad. Fold the vertical edges to the center, turn 90 degree then roll it again. Repeat the steps one more time until forming a rectangle with a smooth edges
Then using a pasta machine, roll the dough up to stage 8 – 9 setting on the pasta machine. The pasta sheet must be very thin, just like a phyllo pastry sheet
Rest the rolled dough for 30 minutes, then continue to cut each dough using noodles cutter on the pasta machine
Cook the noodles on a boiling water, strain when the noodles are already floating. Sprinkle 1 tbsp sesame oil over the drained noodles to keep them from sticking, set aside

* For Keto-Iron Crispy Fried Chicken
On a small bowl, mix all the chicken marinate ingredients together
Place the chicken pieces into a medium bowl. pour the marinate into the bowl and cover with plastic wrap. Rest the chicken in the refrigerator for at least 1 hour
In another bowl, whisk and sift the Keto-Flour Mix ingredients. Beat the egg white on a standing mixer into stiff peak. Add the marinated chicken pieces and fold with spatula to coat
Using chopsticks, bread all chicken pieces with Keto-Flour mix until covered thoroughly, then transfer to a plate
Heat the coconut oil in a large skillet over medium heat. Sprinkle any left over Keto-Flour mix into the hot oil, then place chicken into the skillet, and fry for 5 – 6 minutes on each side to brown. Drain with a spider strainer and remove the excess oil with paper towel

* For General Tso's Chicken
On a small bowl, 2 tbsp Keto-Flour Mix with 1/4 cup coconut milk. Stir using spatula to combine, until the mixture become thick and no more lumps appears
Heat 2 tbsp coconut oil on a wok with low heat. Sautee the minced garlic and ginger until fragrant, then stir in the chopped green onion and red chilli pepper
Pour 3/4 cup chicken stock into the wok and set over medium-high heat. Bring to a boil. Stir the slurry mixture into the sauce. Reduce heat to medium low, add the crispy chicken pieces followed by coconut aminos and sweetener then simmer, about 5 minutes, stirring occasionally until the sauce absorp to the chicken
Spread the Keto-General Tso's chicken over Keto-Youmian noodles and serve with sprinkles of sesame seeds

THE KETO IRON CHEF'S SAYUR LODEH (ASIAN VEGETABLES CURRY)

SAYUR LODEH (Asian Vegetables Curry)
Servings=4
Time=60mins
SAYUR LODEH (Asian Vegetables Curry)

Ingredients
5 Shallots
3 Garlic cloves
4cm Ginger
2 stalks Lemon Grass (if available)
1/2 teaspoon Turmeric powder
2 teaspoons Cumin Powder
2 teaspoons Coriander Powder
1 teaspoon Sea Salt (or to taste)
1/2 teaspoon Pepper powder (or to taste)
Splenda / Stevia to taste
1 big Onion (chopped)
2 big Tomatoes (diced)
200g Green Beans (chopped)
200g Pumpkin (diced)
200g Cabbage (shredded)
200g Cucumber (diced)
500ml (2 cups) Coconut milk (heavy cream will be a fine substitutes)
4 tablespoons Coconut oil Virgin Coconut Oil
Curry leaves, bay leaves – for seasoning
A handful of roasted cashews or almonds
Red chillies & Fried chopped shallots – for decoration

Direction
Peel and finely chop the shallots and garlic, peel and finely grate the ginger, trim and wash the lemon grass and finely chop the thick, lower ends.
Put the shallots, garlic, ginger, lemon grass in a bowl with turmeric, cumin powder, coriander powder, salt, pepper powder, and splenda / stevia
Stir together to form a thick paste
Wash and trim the green beans, then cut diagonally into 4cm pieces. Cut the pumpkin, tomatoes, onion and cucumber into small cubes. Trim and wash the cabbage, removing the stalks and tough ribs. Cut the leaves into strips about 1cm wide.
Heat the coconut oil or VCO in a pan. Stir fry the curry paste over a medium heat for 3 – 5 minutes.
Add the green beans and continue to fry for another 5 minutes.
Stir the diced pumpkin, cucumber and shredded cabbage.
Pour the coconut milk, add the curry and bay leaves, then cover the pan and cook over medium heat for about 30 to 35 minutes.
Stirring occasionally to distribute the vegetables
Garnish with red chilies, cashews/almonds and fried shallots, then serve with Omelette, Fried Fish or Fried Chicken.

THE KETO IRON CHEF'S OPOR AYAM (ASIAN CHICKEN STEW)

The Keto Iron Chef's OPOR AYAM (Asian Chicken Stew)
Servings=4
Time=30mins
The Keto Iron Chef's OPOR AYAM (Asian Chicken Stew)

Ingredient
4 Chicken legs or breast, cut into large chunks
270ml Coconut milk
1/2 teaspoon of turmeric
1 teaspoon Salt
1 teaspoon Ground black pepper
1 teaspoon Ground ginger
2 teaspoons Cayenne
3 tablespoons Natural peanut butter
1 tablespoon Coriander
1 tablespoon Water
2 medium Onions, finely chopped
2 Garlic cloves, crushed
1 tablespoon Coconut oil or VCO
1 tablespoon grated Lemon rind
Direction
Combine turmeric, salt, ginger, pepper, cayenne, peanut butter, coriander and water, mix to a paste consistency
Sauté onions and garlic in a little coconut oil until tender, add the peanut butter paste, sauté 2 minutes
Remove from heat, combine well with chicken. Refrigerate in a covered bowl for at least 1 hour
In a large pan, bring coconut milk to the boil. Add chicken pieces, paste and lemon rind. Stir until all combined.
Reduce the heat and simmer for 20 minutes
Remove the chicken pieces from the pan and place under the grill until browned. Spoon remaining chicken sauce over the chicken to serve

THE KETO IRON CHEF'S TONGSENG KAMBING (LAMB CURRY)

The Keto Iron Chef's Tongseng Kambing (Lamb Curry)
Servings=6-8
Time=30mins
Tongseng Kambing (Lamb Curry)
For 6 – 8 serving

Ingredients
1 kg lamb (with bone is ok)
5 tablespoons coconut oil for sautéing

For the spice paste
2 tablespoons coriander, toasted
10 shallots (can be replaced by 2 large onions)
6 cloves garlic
1 tsp cumin
½ teaspoon nutmeg

3 tbs bone broth or 2 tbs beef stock
(Blend these ingredients in the food processor or blender)

Other spices
6 lime leaves
2 bay leaves
1 lemongrass stalk, crushed
1 ltr curry sauce (can be replaced by water +1 tsp curry powder / 1 tbs Thai curry paste + coconut milk).
1 tablespoons of splenda or 1 tsp of stevia (optional)
5 cabbage leaves, chopped
2 tomatoes, sliced in quarters
5 green chilies, diced (optional)

Direction
Heat the cooking oil, sauté ground spices until fragrant, add lamb meat and stir spice paste evenly while meat changes color.
Add the curry sauce, lime leaves, bay leaves and lemongrass, stir well, continue to boil and cook the meat tender.
When the meat is tender, add the cabbage and tomatoes. You can also add a little sweetness by adding Splenda at this step, then cover the pan briefly until cabbage is done.
Garnish with deep fried shallots and diced green chilies

THE KETO IRON CHEF'S SOP KONRO (BEEF RIBS SOUP)

The Keto Iron Chef's Sop Konro (Beef Ribs Soup) Servings=4-6" difficulty="easy"]
Ingredients
1 kg beef ribs (I used beff short-ribs)
6 cloves

Paste (grind all ingredients):
5 – 6 tbsp of natural peanut butter or almond butter
1 tsp peppercorn, roasted
1 tbsp corriander, roasted
1 tsp minced turmeric (I used ground turmeric)
1 tsp seedless tamarind
3 cloves garlic
7 shallots
salt and splenda to tasteDirections

Saute the ground ingredient and clove until fragrant, add beef ribs, stir and cook meat until lightly browned. Add 1 litre of water, and cook until meat tender. (Add water again, if you need it but I like to keep my soup thick)Add salt and splenda as desired, simmer over low heat 15 to 20 minutes. Serve with fresh cabbage and chilli paste sauce Grilled Konro (Grilled Beef Ribs)
If you wanna make Grilled Konro, just take some beef short-ribs of the soup, then grill with my Asian Keto-BBQ sauce – 2 tbsp peanut butter sauce, 5 tbsp coconut milk and 1 tbsp coconut oil , blend all ingredient into a sauce mixture (add splenda & salt to taste)

THE KETO IRON CHEF'S GULAI UDANG (PRAWNS THICK CURRY)

The Keto Iron Chef's GULAI UDANG (Prawns Thick Curry)
Servings=4-6
Time=30mins
GULAI UDANG (Prawns Thick Curry)

Ingredient
1,5 Lbs Large shrimp, cleaned and defined
1 onion, chopped
1 – 2 tablespoon of chilli paste (ground 10 red chiles with 1 cloves of garlic, a little salt, 1 teaspoon of VCO or coconut oil, and a little Splenda / Stevia to taste – Food processor can be used) – I have this ready all the time coz it's being use in many of my Asian keto recipes
4 Garlic cloves
2 teaspoons ground cumin
2 teaspoons ground coriander
8 macadamia nuts
1 teaspoon of fish sauce (Chinese Sauce, find without added sugar)
1 teaspoon of ground nutmeg
2 tablespoons of VCO or Coconut oil
2 Lime leaves
2 Basil leaves
2 cups Coconut milk or cream (can be substituted with heavy / whipping cream)
A little Sea Salt & Splenda/Stevia to taste

Direction
Put the following into your food processor : onion, chilli paste, garlic, cumin, coriander, macadamia, fish sauce, nutmeg and process until you have a paste
Heat the coconut oil and fry the paste for approx 5 minutes, then add the lime leaves and the basil leaves
Add the coconut milk and bring to the boil, then simmer for 15 – 20 minutes
Add the prawns and cook until they turn pink, do not overcook them
Taste the sauce and add salt and sucralose/stevia to your liking
Serve with steamed or raw cabbage (steamed & riced cauliflower would definitely be the best companion replacing rice as the original authentic meals)

KETO IRON CHEF'S INDONESIAN TELUR BALADO (SPICY CHILLIES EGGS)

Indonesian Telur Balado (Spicy Chillies Eggs) Servings=4 Time=30mins
2 – 3 Serving Size
Ingredients
6 pcs Hard Boiled Duck Eggs (shell removed)
6 pcs Red Chillies (seeded and chopped)
4 cloves Garlic
4 pcs medium Shallots
2 pcs Tomatoes (quartered)
1 tsp Shrimp Paste
1,5 Tbsp Macadamia Oil / Peanut Oil
1 tsp White Vinegar
Salt & Pepper to taste

1 cup Coconut Oil (for frying)

Direction
Heat 1 cup coconut oil in a small saucepan over medium high heat
Deep fry the duck eggs in the hot oil until they are golden brown (5 to 7 minutes), set aside
Combine the chillies, garlic, shallots, tomatoes, and shrimp paste in a food processor, blend into a paste
Add in macadamia oil, process again until smooth
Heat 1 tablespoon coconut oil in a large skillet over medium heat, then pour the chillies mixture into the skillet
Stir the vinegar, salt and pepper into the mixture
Add the fried eggs to the mixture, turning to coat
Reduce heat to medium-low, simmer until fragrant, about 5 minutes
Serve with other Keto-Meal dishes

KETO IRON CHEF'S INDONESIAN ASAM PADEH (HOT & SOUR FISH)

Indonesian Asam Padeh (Hot & Sour Fish) Servings=4 Time=30mins
3 – 4 Serving Size

Ingredients
1/2 kg Skip Jack Tuna
3 tbsp Lime Juice
300ml Water
Coconut Oil for Stir Frying

* For Non Grinding Spices
3 pcs Asam Kandis (can be substituted with Gorakha or Kodampuli)
2 stalk Lemon Grass (take the white parts & bruised)
3 pcs Bay Leaves
3 pcs Lime Leaves (teared)
1 pcs Turmeric Leaf (teared)
2 pcs Cardamom

* For Spices to grind into paste
10 pcs Red Chillies
5 cloves Garlic
8 pcs Shallots
5 cm Ginger (scrapped)
5 cm Galangal
2 pcs Candlenuts
Salt & Pepper to taste
(Grind all these ingredients into paste in a food processor)

Direction
Clean the skip jack tuna stomach cavity, remove the gills and surrounding tissue
Cut into pieces, then drizzle lime juice over, set aside
In a medium high heat, stir fry non-grinding ingredients and paste spices until fragrant
Add water and cook until boiling and the liquid starts to thicken
Add skip jack tuna pieces, reduce the heat to low and cook until fish done and the liquid has evaporated
Taste to perfection (add more salt or pepper to your liking) then remove from heat.
Serve with other Keto-Meal dishes

KETO-IRON CHEF'S KETO-RICE NOODLES & KETO-PAD THAI

Keto-Iron Chef's Keto-Rice Noodles & Keto-Pad Thai
Servings=1-2
Time=60mins
(Thailand Street Food Fried Noodles with Ketofied Rice Noodles / Rice Vermicelli)
1 – 2 Serving Size

Keto-Rice Noodles (Keto-Rice Vermicelli)
Dry Ingredients
40g Egg White Powder
20g Inulin Powder
1g Salt

Wet Ingredients
30g Egg White
10g Coconut Milk
3g Coconut Oil

Keto-Pad Thai
Ingredients
2 tbsp Coconut Oil
1/2 tsp Minced Garlic
1/2 tsp Minced Ginger
2 tsp Dried Shrimp
1/4 cup Chicken Skins or Boneless Chicken Breast (cut into pieces)
1/4 cup Whole Shrimp (peeled & deveined)
2 tsp Preserved Radish (chinese salted radish)
1 (60g) Large Egg
1 tsp Ground Red Chiles
1 tbsp Ground Roasted Almonds or Peanuts
1/4 cup Sliced Green Onion (or Garlic Chives) 1 cup Mung Bean Sprouts
1/2 cup Sliced Mushroom (I'm using white chanterelle mushroom)
3 tbsp Pad Thai Sauce (see recipe below)

* For Pad Thai Sauce
1/2 cup Tamarind Juice
1/2 cup Water
1/4 cup Fish Sauce
1 tsp Salt
2 tsp (10g) Sweetener

* For Garnish
Lime Wedges
Raw Mung Bean Sprouts

Direction
* For Keto-Rice Noodles
Whisk all dry ingredients on a medium bowl. Add coconut milk and stir using spatula until a rough dough formed
Add egg white, stir to combine, then switch using hand to knead the dough until elastic
Add coconut oil and knead until the dough become smooth

Divide the dough into 2 equal part. Shape each dough into round. Flatten each dough using rolling pin on a silicone pad. Fold the vertical edges to the center, turn 90 degree then roll it again. Repeat the steps one more time until forming a rectangle with a smooth edges

Then using a pasta machine, roll each dough up to stage 8 – 9 setting on the pasta machine. The pasta sheet must be very thin, just like a phyllo pastry sheet

Rest the rolled dough for 30 minutes, then continue to cut each dough using noodles cutter on the pasta machine

Cook the noodles on a boiling water, strain when the noodles are already floating. Sprinkle 2 tbsp coconut oil over the drained noodles to keep them from sticking, set aside

* For Pad Thai Sauce

Mix all ingredients in a sauce pan for about 10 minutes until it is well mixed and syrupy. Stir occasionally to prevent burning. Set aside

* For Keto-Pad Thai

Heat the coconut oil in a wok. Add the garlic and ginger, stir fry until golden brown. Add the chicken pieces and shrimp and keep stirring until the shrimp changes color

Add the noodles. They will stick together so stir fast and try to separate them. Add a little water, stirring a few times. Then add the Pad Thai sauce, and keep stirring until everything is thoroughly mixed. The noodles should appear soft and moist

Push the contents of the wok up around the sides to make room to fry the eggs. If the pan is very dry, add 1 more tablespoon of coconut oil. Add the eggs and spread the noodles over the eggs to cover. When the eggs are cooked, stir the noodles until everything is well mixed-this should result in cooked bits of eggs, both whites and yolk, throughout the noodle mixture

Add chiles, almond, green onion, preserved radish, mushroom, dried shrimp and bean sprouts. Mix well. Remove to a platter

Serve with more raw mung bean sprouts and a few drops of lime juice

* Note : You can buy premixed tamarind concentrate or make your own tamarind juice. Buy a package of compressed tamarind pulp at any Asian market, cut off 3 tablespoons of paste and soak in 1 1/2 cups of warm water for 20 minutes. Squeeze out the pulp and discard; the remaining liquid is tamarind juice. Store any leftover juice or noodle sauce in a tightly sealed container in the refrigerator or freezer

KETO-IRON CHEF'S KETO-ROYAL MEE KROB

Keto-Iron Chef's Keto-Royal Mee Krob
Servings=1-2
Time=60mins

(Thailand Royal Crisp Noodles with Ketofied Rice Noodles / Rice Vermicelli)
1 – 2 Serving Size
Keto-Rice Noodles (Keto-Rice Vermicelli)

Dry Ingredients
40g Egg White Powder
20g Inulin Powder
1g Salt

Wet Ingredients
30g Egg White
10g Coconut Milk
3g Coconut Oil

Keto-Mee Krob

Ingredients

1 1/2 cup coconut oil

1 cup Mung Bean Sprouts

1 cloves garlic (chopped)

1/2 ginger root (minced)

1/2 shallots (sliced)

1/2 teaspoon ground chilli pepper

2 teaspoon (10g) sweetener

1 tablespoons fish sauce

2 tablespoon tamarind juice

2 teaspoon lime juice

2 teaspoon orange zest (use the green one)

1/4 cup water

1 1/2 teaspoon Yellow Bean Sauce

1/4 cup chicken skin or boneless chicken breast (cut into pieces)

1/4 cup shrimp

1 ounces mushroom (the original recipe is using pressed tofu)

1 large egg

1/8 cup dried shrimp

1/4 cup preserved radish

* For Garnish

Lime Wedges

Raw Mung Bean Sprouts

Garlic Chives

Cilantro

Direction

* For Keto-Rice Noodles

Whisk all dry ingredients on a medium bowl. Add coconut milk and stir using spatula until a rough dough formed

Add egg white, stir to combine, then switch using hand to knead the dough until elastic

Add coconut oil and knead until the dough become smooth

Divide the dough into 2 equal part. Shape each dough into round. Flatten each dough using rolling pin on a silicone pad. Fold the vertical edges to the center, turn 90 degree then roll it again. Repeat the steps one more time until forming a rectangle with a smooth edges

Then using a pasta machine, roll each dough up to stage 8 – 9 setting on the pasta machine. The pasta sheet must be very thin, just like a phyllo pastry sheet

Rest the rolled dough for 30 minutes, then continue to cut each dough using noodles cutter on the pasta machine

Cook the noodles on a boiling water, strain when the noodles are already floating. Sprinkle 2 tbsp coconut oil over the drained noodles to keep them from sticking, set aside

* Frying the Noodles

This step should be fast. Heat up your wok and add coconut oil. It's very crucial that oil is at the right temperature. Test the oil by dip a strand of Keto-Rice Noodles in the hot oil. If the noodle puffs up immediately, the oil is hot enough

Take a handful of noodles and drop them into hot oil. The noodles should puff up instantly. Immediately, flip the noodles to get all strands submerged in oil. If you drop too much in, some strands will not get a chance to puff up in the oil. The fried noodles should be white or slightly brownish. Then, immediately, remove the noodles from hot oil into a strainer. Set aside

* Frying The Shrimp, Chicken & Egg

Using the same oil from frying the previous noodles, drop the shrimp into the hot oil and stir just for 2 minutes until the color change into bright red. Strain the shrimp, set aside

Follow by frying the chicken pieces. The chicken should be fried longer until crisp. It will took 5 minutes to fry them. When they has turn brown, strain immediately, set aside

Fry the mushroom just for 1 minutes until the color start to turn golden, then strain and set aside

Remove the oil into a bowl, and spoon back 2 tablespoon into the wok. Beat the egg until the white and yolk mix well. Again the oil should be hot. Pour the beaten egg slowly through a strainer over the wok. Shake the strainer to drizzle thin streams of the egg into the hot oil. The egg will puff up right away. You don't want a big patch of egg but small drops and thin strands. Fry until the egg is golden brown and crispy on both sides, about 5 minutes. Strain the egg out the oil and set aside

* Making The Sauce

Pour another 2 tablespoons of the oil. Add chopped garlic, minced ginger and sliced shallot in the wok, over medium heat. When they turn brown, add ground chilli, yellow bean sauce, sweetener, water, lime juice, lime zest, tamarind juice and fish sauce. Stir to mix until dissolve

Let the sauce reduce until it is at a soft crack stage (much thicker than molasses – almost to warm peanut butter consistency). Sauce that's too thin will make the noodles soggy. Sauce that's too thick will risk burning the sauce and having difficulty in spreading the sauce on the noodles evenly. Taste the sauce, you want a balance of sweet, sour and salty. Add the fried shrimp, chicken and mushroom to the sauce and stir to coat with the sauce. Reduce the sauce back to thick consistency

* Assemble

Turn off the heat or keep on lowest setting (to keep the sauce fluid). Add the mung bean sprout, mix into the sauce then followed by the fried noodles. Gently mix the noodles with the sauce using spatula. Stir to get the sauce on all the noodles. Gently break up clumps. Mee Krob should be brownish orange. Add the crispy fried egg stir to combine.

Scoop Mee Krob into a serving plate and garnish with more raw mung bean sprouts, garlic chives, cilantro and lime wedge on the side

* Note : You can buy premixed tamarind concentrate or make your own tamarind juice. Buy a package of compressed tamarind pulp at any Asian market, cut off 3 tablespoons of paste and soak in 1 1/2 cups of warm water for 20 minutes. Squeeze out the pulp and discard; the remaining liquid is tamarind juice. Store any leftover juice or noodle sauce in a tightly

KETO-IRON CHEF MAIN COURSE RECIPE - GULAI DAUN SINGKONG

Keto-Iron Chef Main Course Recipe – Gulai Daun Singkong
Servings=2-3
Time=30mins
Keto-Iron Chef Main Course Recipe – Gulai Daun Singkong
(Indonesian Cassava Leaves Stew)
2 – 3 Serving Size

Ingredients
2 bunch of cassava leaves (about 250 gram), washed and drained
2 tablespoon cooking oil
5 bay leaves

1 lemongrass (chopped into 4 pieces)
750 ml water
250 ml coconut milk
Grind the following into spice paste
5 red chilies
8 shallots
2 cloves garlic
3 candlenuts
2 fresh turmeric (each about 1 inch length)
1 inch Ginger
1 inch Galangal
1/2 tbsp Ground Coriander
1/2 tbsp salt

Direction
Heat coconut oil in a deep skillet (or a pot) and fry the spice paste until fragrant, about 3-5 minutes
Add bay leaves and lemongrass and cook for another 2 minutes
Toss in the cassava leaves and pour water into the skillet. Cook until boiling. Reduce heat and simmer for 15 minutes
Add coconut milk, mix well, and simmer for another 5 minutes. Adjust salt as needed
With a scissor, cut the cassava leaves into smaller pieces so they are easier to scoop with a spoon when consumed
Turn off heat and serve hot with other Keto-Meal dishes

KETO-IRON CHEF'S KETO-PESARATTU DOSA

Keto-Iron Chef's Keto-Pesarattu Dosa
Servings=6-8
Time=60mins
Keto-Pesarattu Dosa
(Indian Mung Bean Crepes)
1 Serving Size
Nutrition Fact per Serving (without the sauce)
(3,5g Net Carb : 12,5g Protein : 18g Fat : 12g Fiber)

* For Dosa Batter
30g Mung Bean (soaked overnight with water) – 3,5
200ml Water
50ml Coconut milk
10g Inulin Powder
10g Casein Protein Isolate
0,5g Pepper (grounded)
0,5g Ginger Powder
1g Salt

* For Coconut Chutney Sauce
50ml Coconut Milk
2g Ginger Powder
1g Curry Powder
1g Salt
0,5g Pepper (grounded)

5g Butter

Direction
Soak 30g mung bean overnight with some water. Drained mung beans on the next day
Boil the mung bean with 50ml coconut milk and 100ml water until tender
Drain the mung bean then grind it into a smooth paste with a blender or food processor
Whisk inulin powder, casein protein isolate, chilli powder, ginger powder and salt in a small bowl, then mix with the mung bean paste until completely combine
Add 100ml water gradually and stir well into a thick batter consistency
On a griddle, smear a little coconut oil. With a big spoon, pour the batter on the griddle and use the same spoon for spreading the batter into a round shape
Optional : Sprinkle some of the finely chopped onions, green chilies and coriander leaves
Drizzle coconut oil at the sides and in the center
Flip the crepe a couple of times till both sides are well cooked and browned

* For Coconut Chutney Sauce
Melt butter on a sauce pan with low heat. Pour coconut milk and stir well
When the mixture starts to bubbles, turn off the heat then sprinkle the seasoning. Stir well
Serve the Keto-Pesarattu Dosa with coconut chutney sauce

KETO-IRON CHEF'S MOM HOLIDAY COOKING - BUBUR KACANG HIJAU (INDONESIAN MUNG BEAN PORRIDGE)

Keto-Iron Chef's Mom Holiday Cooking – Bubur Kacang Hijau (Indonesian Mung Bean Porridge)
Servings=3-4
Time=60mins
Keto-Iron Chef's Mom Holiday Cooking
Bubur Kacang Hijau
(Indonesian Mung Bean Porridge)
3 – 4 Serving Size
Nutrition Fact per Serving (without the sauce)
(5,8g Net Carb : 3,5g Protein : 0,2g Fat : 4g Fiber : 52 Cal)

Ingredients
* For Mung Bean Porridge
150g Mung Bean
1,5 liter Water
1 cm Ginger
1 pcs Pandan Leaf (cut into 3 cm long)
2g Salt
Sweetener to taste

* For Coconut Milk Sauce
30g Butter
200g Coconut Milk
60g Cream Cheese
10g Sweetener

* For Compliment
2 – 3 slices Keto-Bread

(I'm using Keto-Corn Bread)
For Keto-Corn Bread, refer to this link
Direction

* For Mung Bean Porridge
Wash the mung beans and soak overnight in 1,5 liter
The next day cook the mung beans in the same water with 1 pcs pandan leaf, until they are soft
Rinse the ginger and slightly bruise the ginger with the flat of a meat mallet
Add ginger, sweetener and salt to the cooking mung beans

* For Coconut Milk Sauce
Melt butter on a medium sauce pan with low heat
Add coconut milk and cream cheese, stir to combine
When the mixture start to bubbles, add in sweetener and stir to dissolve
Turn off the heat, and drizzle the sauce over each served porridge
Serve the Keto-Bubur Kacang Hijau with shredded Keto-Corn Bread dipped into the porridge

THE KETO-IRON CHEF'S MOM HOLIDAY COOKING - SAYUR LABU PADANG

The Keto-Iron Chef's Mom Holiday Cooking – Sayur Labu Padang
Servings=3-4
Time=60mins
The Keto-Iron Chef's Mom Holiday Cooking
Sayur Labu Padang
(Indonesian Spicy Chayote Curry)
3 – 4 Serving Size

Ingredients
4 tablespoon coconut oil
2 bay leaves
4 red chillies, sliced diagonally
1 chayote, about 300 to 400 gram, peeled and cut into match sticks
2 teaspoon salt
500 ml coconut milk
Grind the following into spice paste
6 shallots
4 cloves garlic
10 red chillies
4 candlenuts
1 inch galangal

Direction
Heat oil and sauté spice paste and bay leaves until fragrant, about 4 to 5 minutes
Add sliced chillies and cook until slightly wilted, about 2 minutes
Add chayote, season with salt. Stir so everything is mixed well
Pour coconut milk, stir, and cook on medium heat until boiling. Stir every 2 minutes or so, this is to prevent the coconut milk from curdling
Once the chayote is cooked, make sure it is still slightly crunchy, then bring to a boil. Reduce heat and simmer for 3 minutes
Turn off heat and serve immediately

KETO IRON CHEF'S KETO-MEE GORENG

Keto Iron Chef's Keto-Mee Goreng
Servings=1-2
Time=60mins
Keto-Mee Goreng
(Malaysian Spicy Fried Noodles)
1 – 2 Serving Size

Ingredients
* For Keto-Noodles
Dry Ingredients
15g Micellar Casein
10g Isopure Whey Protein Isolate, Unflavored
5g Dried Egg Whites
5g Egg Yolk Powder
15g Inulin Fiber (Chicory Root) – LC Foods
2g Psyllium Husk
1g Xanthan Gum Powder
1g Salt
* Note : The first 7 ingredients above are the Keto-Flour formula for this recipe

Wet Ingredients
15g Egg
15g Water
3g Coconut Oil

* For Keto-Mie Goreng
100g Chicken Thigh and Skins (shredded)
1 Large Egg
3 tbsp Virgin Coconut Oil
2 cloves Garlic (diced)
2 pcs Asian Bok Choy (shredded)
1 cup Water
1 tsp Chilli Paste
2 tbsp Coconut Aminos
2 tsp Fish Sauce
Sweetener, Salt & Pepper to Taste

Direction
* For Keto-Noodles
Whisk all dry ingredients on a medium bowl. Add egg and stir using spatula until a rough dough formed
Add water gradually then switch using hand to knead the dough until elastic
Add coconut oil and knead until the dough become smooth
Shape the dough into round, then roll into rectangle with a rolling pin on a silicone pad. Fold the vertical edges to the center, turn 90 degree then roll it again. Repeat the steps one more time until forming a rectangle with a smooth edges
Then using a pasta machine, roll each dough up to stage 7 – 8 setting on the pasta machine
Rest the rolled dough for 1 hour, then continue to cut each dough using the noodle cutter on the pasta machine
Cook the noodles on a salted boiling water, strain when the noodles are already floating. Sprinkle some coconut oil over the drained noodles to keep them from sticking, set aside

* Cooking Keto-Mie Goreng

Heat 3 tablespoon of coconut oil in a wok over high heat. Add garlic, shredded chicken thigh and skins, then stir-fry until browned

Add the egg and continue to fry with the chicken until the egg cooks

Spread the shredded bok choy, cook for a while then pour the water. Cook until the water evaporates

Break up the boiled noodles gently with your hands and add them to the wok noodles, then season with chilli paste, coconut aminos, fish sauce, sweetener, salt and pepper

Stir-fry everything together until the noodles get an even brown color

Serve while it's still hot

KETO IRON CHEF'S KETO-WONTON SOUP

(Chinese Dumpling Soup)
1 – 2 Serving Size
Ingredients
* For Wonton Dough

Dry Ingredients
15g Micellar Casein
10g Isopure Whey Protein Isolate, Unflavored
5g Dried Egg Whites
5g Egg Yolk Powder
15g Inulin Fiber (Chicory Root) – LC Foods
1,5g Psyllium Husk
1g Xanthan Gum Powder
1,5g Salt
1g Garlic Powder

* Note : The first 7 ingredients above are the Keto-Flour formula for this recipe
For more chewy Wonton, the Keto-Flour can be changed into this formula : 15g Wheat Protein Isolate 8000, 10g Casein Protein Isolate, 10g Whey Protein Isolate, 5g Egg White Powder, 5g Egg Yolk Powder, 5g Inulin Powder

Wet Ingredients
15g Sour Cream
15g Water
3g Coconut Oil
* For Wonton Filling
50g Prawns (peeled)
30g Cabbage (shredded)
5g Egg Yolk Powder
1 tsp Coconut Amino
1 tsp Oyster Sauce
1/4 tsp Salt
1/4 tsp Garlic Powder
1/4 tsp Onion Powder

* For Wonton Soup
1 liter Homemade Chicken Broth
1 tbsp Fish Sauce

1 stalk Ginger (diced)
2 stalk Onion Spring (chopped)
Salt & Pepper to Taste

* For Wonton Compliment
20g Shitake Mushroom
20g Enokitake Mushroom
2 stalk Bok Choy
2 stalk Celery

Direction
* For Wonton Dough
Whisk all dry ingredients on a medium bowl. Add sour cream and water gradually, then stir using spatula until a rough dough formed, then switch using hand to knead the dough until elastic. Add the coconut oil and knead again until smooth
Shape the dough into a balls, then flaten the dough using rolling pin on a silicone pad. Fold the vertical edges to the center, turn 90 degree then roll it again. Repeat the steps one more time until forming a rectangle with a smooth edges
Then using a pasta machine, roll the dough into stage 5 – 6 setting on the pasta machine
Rest the rolled dough for 10 minutes, before cutting

* For Wonton Filling :
Grind the peeled shrimps with a blender or food processor into a paste
Combine the shrimp paste, with the rest of the wonton filling ingredients on a medium bowl. Set aside

* Assemble & Cooking Wonton Soup
Spoon some Wonton filling into the center of the squares, then fold into triangle. Fold each side of the triangle into the center, making a wonton shape pattern. Press to seal the junction (refer to the attached pics for details)
Heat the chicken broth on a boiler pan with medium heat, then add all the soup ingredients.
Drop all the shaped wonton into the boiling soup, and cook until tender
Add all wonton compliments and cook for just 1 minutes
Serve The Keto-Wonton Soup while it's still hot

KETO IRON CHEF'S KETO-APPLE PASTRY HAND PIE

Keto Iron Chef's Keto-Apple Pastry Hand Pie Servings=4 Time=60mins
(Danish Apple Pastry Hand Pie using "Juicy" Mexican Yam Bean / Jicama / Xicama)
1 – 2 Serving Size
Ingredients
* For Pie Dough

Dry Ingredients
15g Micellar Casein
10g Isopure Whey Protein Isolate, Unflavored
5g Dried Egg Whites
5g Egg Yolk Powder
15g Inulin Fiber (Chicory Root) – LC Foods
2g Psyllium Husk
1g Xanthan Gum Powder
1g Salt
1g Vanilla Extract

3g Sweetener

* Note : The first 7 ingredients above are the Keto-Flour formula for this recipe
For more crisper pastry, the Keto-Flour can be changed into this formula : 15g Wheat Protein Isolate 8000, 10g Casein Protein Isolate, 10g Whey Protein Isolate, 5g Egg White Powder, 5g Egg Yolk Powder, 5g Inulin Powder

Wet Ingredients
15g Egg
15g Water
3g Butter
* For Pastry Batter
25g Keto-Flour
25g Butter

* For Apple Pie Filling
80g Sliced Mexican Yam Bean (Jicama / Xicama)
Nutrition Fact for 80g Yam Bean
(3g Net Carb : 0,6g Protein : 0g Fat : 30 Cal)
15g Butter
4g Inulin Fiber (Chicory Root) – LC Foods
2g Cinnamon Powder
2g Sweetener
Direction

* For Pie Dough
Whisk all dry ingredients on a medium bowl. Add egg and stir using spatula until a rough dough formed
Add water gradually then switch using hand to knead the dough until elastic
Add butter and knead the dough until the surface become smooth
Shape the dough into round, then rest for 5 minutes
Divide the dough into 4 equal dough balls, then roll each dough into a rectangle using roller pin
On a pasta machine, roll each dough into a long thin pasta sheet (up to stage 6 – 7 setting), then rest the dough back for 1 hour until the surface feels almost dry to the touch

* For Pastry Batter
On a small bowl, combine Keto-Flour with butter using spatula, until a smooth batter forms
Rest the pastry batter for 10 minutes at the refrigerator

* For Apple Pie Filling
Peel the yam bean, quarter and core it. Chop every quarter into 1/8 to 1/4 inch thick slices
Melt butter on a sauce pan using low medium heat, then add the chopped yam bean
Cook for 5 – 8 minutes until the yam bean looks tender and the butter absorb, then add inulin powder, cinnamon powder and sweetener, stir to combine.
Turn off the heat, then let the apple pie filling cools for 10 minutes in the refrigerator

* Assemble
Preheat the oven into 300F
Spread the pastry batter evenly over each rolled dough
Fold each pastry dough from one side into the other side, making 4 – 5 folds into square shape (see the attached pics for details)
Roll each folded dough into a larger square, using roller pin. Roll gently in one direction at a time, do not roll back and forth which will make the thin pastry dough easy to tear

Spoon the filling onto 2 pastry dough. Leave a space on edges for making a seam

Cover the filling with the other 2 pastry dough, and press the edges to make layer adhere

Seam the pastry edges using a fork to make a danish pastry pattern, then transfer them into a greased baking pan

Brush the pastry surface with an egg wash, then use a knife to score 3 small slice over the pastry, so the steam can escape during baking

Bake for 15 – 20 minutes, until the pastry edges turns brown and crispy

Serve warm with black coffee or green tea

* Note : This Keto-Apple Pastry Hand Pie dough can also be cooked with a deep fry method

KETO IRON CHEF'S KETO-MLINCI

Keto Iron Chef's Keto-Mlinci Servings=4 Time=60mins

(North Croatian Pasta with Roasted Chicken Skins)

1 – 2 Serving Size

Ingredients

* For Mlinci Dough

Dry Ingredients

15g Micellar Casein

10g Isopure Whey Protein Isolate, Unflavored

5g Dried Egg Whites

5g Egg Yolk Powder

15g Inulin Fiber (Chicory Root) – LC Foods

2g Psyllium Husk

1g Xanthan Gum Powder

1g Salt

0,5g Garlic Powder

0,5g Pepper

* Note : The first 7 ingredients above are the Keto-Flour formula for this recipe

For more chewy pasta, the Keto-Flour can be changed into this formula : 15g Wheat Protein Isolate 8000, 10g Casein Protein Isolate, 10g Whey Protein Isolate, 5g Egg White Powder, 5g Egg Yolk Powder, 5g Inulin Powder

Wet Ingredients

15g Egg

15g Water

3g Virgin Coconut Oil

* For Roasted Chicken Skins

200g Chicken Skins

1/4 tsp Pepper

2 Cloves Garlic

1/2 tsp Salt

2 cups Water

Direction

Whisk all dry ingredients on a medium bowl. Add egg and stir using spatula until a rough dough formed

Add water gradually then switch using hand to knead the dough until elastic

Add coconut oil and knead the dough until the surface become smooth

Divide the dough into 2 equal dough balls, then roll each dough into a thin tortilla shape

Warm a large, flat cast iron griddle or skillet over medium-high heat. When ready, a few drops of water flicked onto the surface should sizzle immediately

Cook for 1 to 2 minutes, until the edges are starting to curl up and the bottoms look dry and pebbly

Flip and cook another 1 to 2 minutes on the other side. When done, both sides should be dry to the touch and beginning to show some brown, toasted spots

Break Keto-Mlinci into pieces, then put in a bowl. Set aside

Ground garlic, pepper and salt, then mix it with the chicken skins

Roast the seasoned chicken skins on a skillet without oil for 10 minutes on low heat, until the chicken fat melting out

Add 2 cup of water and let it boil until the water evaporates into half

Add the Keto-Mlinci pieces into the chicken soup, and let it cook until all the water evaporates and leave the chicken fat covering the pasta

Serve while it's still warm

KETO-IRON CHEF'S KETO-ORANGE CHICKEN & KETO-IRON CRISPY CHICKEN

Keto-Iron Chef's Keto-Orange Chicken & Keto-Iron Crispy Chicken Servings=3-4 Time=60mins

Keto-Orange Chicken & Keto-Iron Crispy Chicken

(Chinese Orange Chicken with Iron Style Crispy Chicken)

3 – 4 Serving Size

Ingredients

* For The Crispy Fried Chicken

500g Chicken Skins or Boneless Chicken Breast (cut into 1/2 inch pieces)

3 Egg Whites (Beat into stiff peak)

* For Breading The Chicken

Keto-Flour Mix Ingredients

30g Casein Protein Isolate

20g Whey Protein Isolate

20g Egg White Powder

10g Egg Yolk Powder

20g Inulin Powder

2g Baking Soda

2g Salt

1g Garlic Powder

0,5g Pepper Powder

0,5g Nutmeg Powder

0,5g Coriander Powder

(Whisk & sift all these ingredients together)

* For Orange Chicken Sauce

1,5 cup Water

2 tbsp Water + 1/8 tsp Orange Essence

1/4 cup Lemon Juice

1/3 cup Vinegar

2 tbsp Coconut Aminos

1 tbsp Grated Orange Zest

2 tsp Sweetener

1 tsp Minced Garlic

1 tsp Minced Ginger

2 tbsp Chopped Green Onion

* For Thickening the Sauce
3 tbsp Keto-Flour Mix
Direction
Pour 1,5 cups water, orange essence mixture, lemon juice, vinegar, and coconut aminos into a saucepan and set over medium-high heat. Stir in the orange zest, sweetener, ginger, garlic and chopped onion. Bring to a boil. Remove from heat, and cool 10 to 15 minutes
Place the chicken pieces into a medium bowl. When contents of saucepan have cooled, pour 1 cup of sauce into the bowl. Reserve the remaining sauce. Cover with plastic wrap, and refrigerate at least 2 hours
In another bowl, whisk and sift the Keto-Flour Mix ingredients. Beat the egg white on a standing mixer into stiff peak. Add the marinated chicken pieces and fold with spatula to coat
Using chopsticks, bread all chicken pieces with Keto-Flour mix until covered thoroughly, then transfer to a plate
Heat the coconut oil in a large skillet over medium heat. Sprinkle any left over Keto-Flour mix into the hot oil, then place chicken into the skillet, and fry for 5 – 6 minutes on each side to brown. Drain with a spider strainer and remove the excess oil with paper towel
Wipe out the skillet, and add the remaining orange chicken sauce. Bring to a boil over medium-high heat. Stir 3 tbsp Keto-Flour mix into the sauce. Reduce heat to medium low, add the chicken pieces, and simmer, about 5 minutes, stirring occasionally
Serve with sprinkles of sesame seeds

KETO-IRON CHEF'S KETO-UMM ALI

Keto-Iron Chef's Keto-Umm Ali Servings=2 Time=60mins
(Egyptian Phyllo Pastry Pudding)
2 serving size
Ingredients
* For Umm Ali Phyllo Dough
Dry Ingredients
15g Casein Protein Isolate
10g Whey Protein Isolate
5g Egg White Powder
5g Egg Yolk Powder
15g Inulin Powder
1.5g Psyllium Husk
1g Xanthan Gum
1g Salt
* Note : The first 7 ingredients above are the Keto-Flour formula for this recipe
For crisper crust the Keto-Flour can be changed into this formula : 15g Wheat Protein Isolate 8000, 10g Casein Protein Isolate, 10g Whey Protein Isolate, 5g Egg White Powder, 5g Egg Yolk Powder, 5g Inulin Powder
Wet Ingredients
20g Egg
10g Sour Cream
3g Coconut Oil
* For Brushing Phyllo Dough
10g Melted Butter
* For Umm Ali Topping
20g Diced Almonds
20g Dessicated Coconut
20g Egg Yolk
50g Heavy Cream
2g Salt

3g Cinnamon Powder
15g Sweetener
Direction
* For Umm Ali Phyllo Dough
Whisk all dry ingredients on a medium bowl
Add egg gradually, stir using spatula until a rough dough formed
Add sour cream, stir again to combine then switch using hand to knead the dough until elastic
Add coconut oil and knead again until smooth
Rest the dough for 10 minutes
Divide the rested dough into 2 equal parts. Using roller pin, flaten each dough into rectangle, then fold the vertical edges into the center of the dough. Roll again to flaten, then repeat the folding from the horizontal edges into the center of the dough and flaten to make smooth edges of rectangles.
Rest the rolled dough back for another 10 minutes
Continue rolling each dough using a pasta machine up to the thinnest setting, so that the sheet would be very thin and transparent (stage 7 – 8 setting on the pasta machine)
Preheat the oven into 300F
On a silicone pad, spread the melted butter thinly using brush, over each rolled phyllo sheet
Fold the longest side of each phyllo sheet into 4 folds, making a belt shape
Brush the surface once more with butter, then fold 3 times to shorten the length
(see the attached pictures for details)
Rest the phyllo pastries on the freezer for 5 minutes, then roll them gently into thick rectangles with rolling pin
Cut them into pieces, then transfer the pieces into a greased baking pan
Bake for 10 – 15 minutes, until golden brown
Cool the baked phyllo pieces on the pan for 10 minutes
* For Umm Ali Topping
Mean while, combine all Umm Ali topping ingredients except for cinnamon powder, into a medium bowl, then stir to combine using spatula
Arrange the cooled phyllo pieces into 2 baking mould equally, then pour the topping mixtures to submerges the pieces
Dust the cinnamon powder evenly, then bake for another 10 – 15 minutes, until the puddings are set
Serve while still warm as a Keto-Dessert

KETO-IRON CHEF'S DENDENG BALADO (INDONESIAN SPICY FRIED BEEF)

Keto-Iron Chef's Dendeng Balado (Indonesian Spicy Fried Beef) Servings=2-3 Time=60mins

2 – 3 Serving Size
Ingredients
250g Beef, thinly sliced
1 tbsp Lime Juice to marinate
3 Shallots
8 – 10 Red Chillies, seeded and roughly grind
2 Lime leaves
Salt to taste
Direction
Marinate the meat with lime juice. Leave it for 10 minutes
Put the meat into oven tray pan and bake until half dry
When it's done, fry the meat. Set aside
In remaining oil, sauté the shallots until fragrant, then add lime leaves and chillies. Stir well
Add the lime juice, salt and the meat. Continue cooking. Add a little of water if necessary

sealed container in the refrigerator or freezer

KETO IRON CHEF'S KETO-GRITS

Keto Iron Chef's Keto-Grits Servings=1-2 Time=45mins
(Southern US Corn Base Porridge using Bean Sprouts)
1 – 2 Serving Size
* Refer to this Link for Asian Bean Sprout
https://en.m.wikipedia.org/wiki/Bean_sprout

Ingredients
30g Bean Sprout
Nutrition Fact for 30g Asian Bean Sprouts
(1,2g Net Carb : 0,9g Protein : 0g Fat : 9 Cal)
http://nutritiondata.self.com/facts/custom/509870/2
10g Inulin Fiber (Chicory Root) – LC Foods
10g Micellar Casein
20g Egg Yolk Powder
60g Coconut Milk
30g Heavy Cream
15g Butter
Salt, Garlic Powder & Pepper to taste

Direction
Whisk and sift inulin powder, casein protein isolate and egg yolk powder on a medium bowl, set aside
On a small sauce pan, boil the bean sprouts until floats with medium heat
Strain the cooked bean sprout, and let it cool for 15 minutes
Grind the cooled bean sprouts with a blender or a food processor into grits coarse texture, set aside
Melt the butter on a medium pan with low heat, then pour coconut oil and heavy cream. Stir to combine
Add the bean sprouts into the mixture and stir combine
When the mixture start to bubbles, pour the dry ingredients all at once and stir until a porridge consistency formed
Turn off the heat, and add salt, garlic powder and pepper to taste
Serve the Keto-Grits with egg, bacon (I'm using salami) and fried chicken (I'm using my own hot chicken curry recipe)

THE KETO IRON CHEF TACKLES KETO-MAC & CHEESE (AMERICAN MACARONI & CHEESE) DEDICATED TO ALL MY AMERICAN KETO-FELLOWERS

Keto-Mac & Cheese
(American Macaroni & Cheese)
Dedicated to All my American Keto-Fellowers

Keto-Mac & Cheese
(American Macaroni & Cheese)
Dedicated to All my American Keto-Fellowers Servings=4 Time=30mins

Ingredients
* For Macaroni Dough
Dry Ingredients

15g Micellar Casein
10g Isopure Whey Protein Isolate, Unflavored
5g Dried Egg Whites
5g Egg Yolk Powder
15g Inulin Fiber (Chicory Root) – LC Foods
1,5g Psyllium Husk
1g Xanthan Gum Powder
1g Salt

Wet Ingredients
10g Egg
20g Sour Cream
3g Coconut Oil
* For Mac & Cheese
15g Butter
1 cloves Garlic (diced)
1/4 medium Onion (diced)
2 tsp Egg Yolk Powder
50g Grated Cheddar Cheese
50g Heavy Whipping Cream
Salt & Pepper to taste

* For Garnish
Italian Seasoning (diced dry Oregano, Basil & Thyme leaves)
Direction

* For Macaroni Dough
Whisk all dry ingredients on a medium bowl. Add egg and sour cream gradually, then stir using spatula until a rough dough formed, then switch using hand to knead the dough until elastic. Add the coconut oil and knead again until smooth
Shape the dough into a balls, then flaten the dough using rolling pin on a silicone pad. Fold the vertical edges to the center, turn 90 degree then roll it again. Repeat the steps one more time until forming a rectangle with a smooth edges
Then using a pasta machine, roll the dough into stage 5 – 6 setting on the pasta machine
Rest the rolled dough back for another 10 minutes
On a silicone pad, cut the rolled dough with square cookies cutter until all used, with minimal left over (roll the left over dough with the pasta machine again to get more squares)
Fold each squares over into hollow rectangles and press to seal the edges
Insert a round chop stick into one of the dough hole, and press the seam against the chop stick to make the seam smoother and become a cylinder macaroni shape
Repeat until all dough are shaped into cylinder macaroni shape
Dry the macaroni over the sunlight for 2 to 3 hours until all the moisture evaporated, and the macaroni become stiff

* Cooking Keto-Mac & Cheese
Bring a large pot of lightly salted water to a boil. Drop the dried macaroni one at a time. They are done when they float to the top. Do not boil too long, or they will be soggy. Remove with a slotted spoon.
Drain the cooked macaroni on spider strainer, set aside
On a medium frying pan, heat 1 tablespoon (15g) of butter with low heat.
Sautee the diced garlic and onion until fragrant, then pour the heavy whipping cream and keep stirring until it start to boil
Add the egg yolk powder, stir until the mixture thicken, then add the grated cheddar cheese until melts
Pour the macaroni over then cook until done
Serve with sprinkle of diced dry oregano, basil and thyme

KETO IRON CHEF'S BREAKFAST PIZZA NUMBER 1

My Home made ketogenic pizza
Starch Free, Gluten Free, Sugar Free & Very Low Carbohydrate

Keto-Dessert Pizza Servings=8 Time=45mins
Pizza Crust
Dry Ingredient :
30g Inulin Fiber (Chicory Root) – LC Foods
20g Almond Flour
20g Golden Flax Seeds
20g Isopure Whey Protein Isolate, Unflavored
20g Micellar Casein
5g Psyllium Husk
5g Gelatin Powder
2g Salt
1g Garlic Powder
1g Pepper
1g Nutmeg Powder
2g Baking Powder
1g Baking Soda

Wet Ingredient
30g Eggs
20g Cream Cheese
50g Coconut Milk
50g Warm Water
Cheese Sauce
30g Butter
30g Cream Cheese
30g Grated Cheddar Cheese
1 egg yolks
30g Splenda or 5g Stevia
20g Inulin Fiber (Chicory Root) – LC Foods
5g Lemon Zest
20g Lemon Juice
2g Gelatin Powder
Topping
Sugar Free Blueberry Jam + Grated Mozarella
Or
Sugar Free Strawberry Jam + Grated Mozarella
Or
Cinnamon Powder + Cocoa Powder + Sesame Seeds + Granulated Sucralose / Erythritol + Grated Mozarella
Direction
Preheat the oven at 300F
Mix all dry ingredients on a standing mixer and add the wet ingredient, mix for 5 minutes at speed 1 to 3 until forming a dough (a little tacky)
Form a round dough with roller pin (I use plastic wrap over the dough), aim as thin as possible, I use 32cm Pizza Pan or 20cm x 20cm cookies pan, which result 5mm to 8mm thick dough
bake for 15 minutes at 300F or until the edges has just starting to brown, set aside and let it cooling down for about 10 minutes
Mix all the cheese sauce ingredients with a mixer until thick and creamy (I start with creaming the butter, followed by gelatin powder, inulin powder and splenda until the mixtures thicken, then add the rest of the ingredients)
spread the sauce evenly over the half baked Pizza dough
Add your choice of Pizza topping and bake again for another 10 to15 minutes until the mozarella cheese has melt
Optional : you can give the dessert Pizza a cream cheese frosting (3tbsp cream cheese, 3tbsp coconut milk, 1tbsp butter, a pinch of salt and splenda to taste)

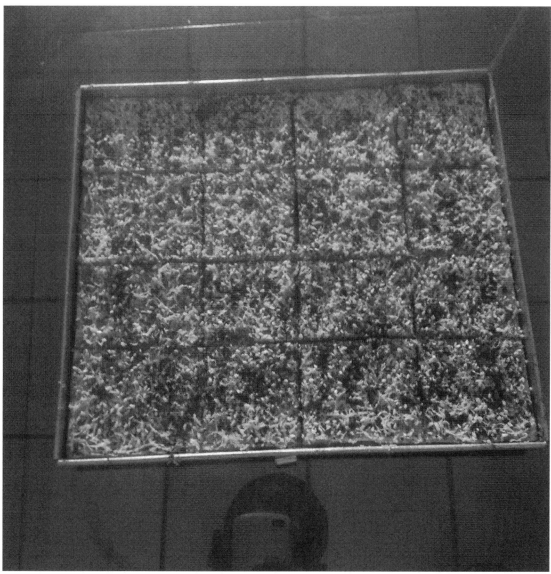

Serve with Black Coffee or Green Tea

KETO-IRON CHEF'S MOM HOLIDAY COOKING - PEPES IKAN GURAME

Keto-Iron Chef's Mom Holiday Cooking – Pepes Ikan Gurame Servings=2-3 Time=60mins
Keto-Iron Chef's Mom Holiday Cooking
Pepes Ikan Gurame
(Indonesian Steamed Fish in Banana Leaf)
2 – 3 Serving Size
Ingredients
Half a kilogram of Carp Fish (Gurame Fish)
7-10 onions
5-7 cloves of garlic.
1 candlenut fruit
2 thumbs of turmeric

2 cm ginger
Additional Ingredients
Chopped onion leaf 0,5 – 1 cm long
3-5 chillies
A tomato, chopped into at least 6 to 10 slices, to easily wrap it later
2-3 bay leaves, basil
One piece of long lemongrass
A small pinch of salt and a spoonful of lime juice
Direction
Remove scales as well as internal part of fish; mark the skin slightly with knife, but keep it intact without breaking the bone
Grind the main ingredients in a mortar and pestle
Mix the finely pounded main ingredients with the additional ingredients excluding the basil and tomato
Smear the fish with the spices, tear the bay leaves and put them inside the fish
Wrap the fish tightly in a banana leaf and close off with a tooth pick. Make sure the fish and spices is sealed off completely so the parcels don't leak
Don't forget to add the basil and tomato slices as well as the shattered lemongrass
Steam the wrapped fish for at least 30 minutes until cooked
Burned the ripe wrapped fish on small fire stove, flipping it up and down and taking it out when its aromatic smell emerges
Serve with other Keto-Meal dishes

KETO IRON CHEF'S KETO-HUMINTAS, KETO-TAMALES & KETO-CORN BREAD

Keto Iron Chef's Keto-Humintas, Keto-Tamales & Keto-Corn Bread Servings=1-2 Time=60mins
(Bolivian or Mexican Tamales & Corn Bread using Mung Bean Sprouts)
Ingredients
* For Humintas/Tamales/Corn Bread Dough
Dry Ingredients
10g Micellar Casein
10g Isopure Whey Protein Isolate, Unflavored
5g Egg White Powder
5g Egg Yolk Powder
20g Inulin Powder
1g Xanthan Gum Powder
2g Baking Powder
1g Salt
Wet Ingredients
50g Egg
50g Coconut Milk (or Sour Cream for Tamales)
50g Cheddar Cheese (grated)
30g Butter
* For Corn Meal Texture
40g Mung Bean Sprouts
10g Egg Yolk Powder
* For Keto-Humintas (Bolivian Tamales)
Cinnamon Powder, Chilli Powder, Salt & Anise to taste
2 pcs Dry Corn Husk
* For Keto-Tamales (Mexican Tamales)
Cooked pork loin with onion, garlic and chilli sauce as the filling
2 pcs Dry Corn Husk
* For Keto-Corn Bread

Sweetener to taste
Small Loaf Pan
* For Keto-Mexican Corn Bread
Jalapeno and onion
Cooked ground beef
Small Loaf Pan
Direction
Whisk and sift all the dry ingredients in a mixing bowl
In a food processor or a blender, pulse the mung bean sprouts into paste, then mix with egg yolk powder until completely combine and forming corn meal textures
Whisk the egg until frothy then add butter and coconut milk gradually. Whisk the mixture until creamy
Add the mung bean mung bean mixture and grated cheddar cheese, then stir until forming a lumpy batter
Add in the whisked dry ingredients all at once, then stir the batter until completely combines and thick
* For Keto-Humintas or Keto-Tamales
To make Bolivian Humintas, take 3 – 4 tablespoon of the batter and season with chilli powder, salt and anise to taste
To make Mexican Tamales, take 3 – 4 tablespoon of the batter and flatten the dough in your hand. Add the pork filling then wrap it back by joining each side of the dough into the center
Take two husks, join them by the wide parts, then place the Humintas or Tamales dough in the middle
Close them by doubling first the husk on top and later the one at the bottom and finally the sides
Tie them using a string made of husks
Steam the dough in a double boiler for 15 – 20 minutes
Serve while it's still warm
* For Keto-Corn Bread
Preheat the oven into 300F
To make Corn Bread, mix in sweetener into the dough to taste
To make Mexican Corn Bread spread the cooked beef, jalapeno, onion into the base of a loaf pan, before adding the remaining dough
Spoon the batter into greased small loaf pan and level the batter surface with a rubber spatula
Bake for 20 – 25 minutes, until the bread looks brown on the edges and an inserted tooth pick comes out clean
Let cool for 10 minutes on the loaf pan, then remove to a serving plate

KETO IRON CHEF'S KETO-YOUTIAO (CHINESE OIL STICK / CHINESE CRULLER)

Keto-Youtiao (Chinese Oil Stick / Chinese Cruller) Servings=4 Time=30mins
1 Serving Size
Ingredients
Dry Ingredients
15g Micellar Casein
10g Isopure Whey Protein Isolate, Unflavored
5g Dried Egg Whites
5g Egg Yolk Powder
15g Inulin Fiber (Chicory Root) – LC Foods
2g Psyllium Husk
1g Xanthan Gum Powder
0,3g Baking Powder
0,3g Baking Soda
0,3g Bakers Ammonia
1g Salt
1g Sucralose
1g Instant Dry Yeast

* Note : The first 7 ingredients above are the Keto-Flour formula for this recipe
For crisper crust the Keto-Flour can be changed into this formula : 15g Wheat Protein Isolate 8000, 10g Casein Protein Isolate, 5g Whey Protein Isolate, 5g Egg White Powder, 5g Egg Yolk Powder, 10g Inulin Powder
Wet Ingredients
10g Coconut Milk
30g Water
Direction
Whisk all dry ingredients on a medium bowl. Add sour cream then stir using spatula until forming a rough dough
Add water gradually while folding with spatula to combine, then switch using hand to knead the dough until elastic. The dough will be a little tacky after knead.
Shape the dough into a balls, then rest the dough for 20 minutes on a warm spot, until rise to almost double in size
The dough should become soft to the touch, and bounce back when pressed leaving a slight finger print
On a silicone pad, divide the risen dough into 4 balls. Using your palm, roll each dough back and forth forming a long rope
Stack 2 ropes together, then press the center length wise with a spatula or chop stick on both side
Let the shaped dough rest for another 10 minutes, mean while heat the coconut oil with low medium heat, slowly bring the oil up to 400F
Deep fry the dough until light golden brown on each side, and the bubbles almost disappear
Transfer to a paper towel using chop stick to remove excess oil
Serve with coconut milk as the dipping sauce

THE KETO IRON CHEF'S KETO-PIEROGI (POLISH DUMPLING - COOKED WITH ITALIAN STYLE)

The Keto Iron Chef's Keto-Pierogi (Polish Dumpling – Cooked with Italian Style) Servings=1 Time=60mins
Ingredients
* For Pierogis Dough
Dry Ingredients
15g Micellar Casein
10g Isopure Whey Protein Isolate, Unflavored
5g Dried Egg Whites
5g Egg Yolk Powder
15g Inulin Fiber (Chicory Root) – LC Foods
1,5g Psyllium Husk
1g Xanthan Gum
1g Salt
5g Sucralose
* Note : The first 7 ingredients above are the Keto-Flour formula for this recipe
For more chewy pasta dough (Al Dente) the Keto-Flour can be changed into this formula : 15g Wheat Protein Isolate 8000, 10g Casein Protein Isolate, 10g Whey Protein Isolate, 5g Egg White Powder, 5g Egg Yolk Powder, 5g Inulin Powder
Wet Ingredients
10g Egg
20g Sour Cream
3g Butter
* For Pierogis Filling (Keto-Mashed Potatos)
Dry Ingredients
25g Keto-Flour (half the quantity from the Keto-Flour formula listed above)
1g Salt
0,5g Garlic Powder
0,5g Pepper
Wet Ingredients
50g Coconut Milk

25g Keto-Cheese Filling (12g Grated Cheddar Cheese, 5g Egg Yolk Powder, 1g Salt, 2g Sucralose, 5g Butter)
15g Ricotta
15g Egg Yolk
5g Butter
* For Italian Style Pierogis Dish
50g Bolognese Sauce (Store bought without added sugar and starch, or make your own)
5g Diced Onion
15g Coconut Oil (for Sautee)
* For Pierogis Dish Garnish
Grated Cheddar Cheese
Italian Seasoning (diced dry Oregano, Basil, Thyme & Rosemary leaves)
Direction
* For Pierogis Dough
Whisk all dry ingredients on a medium bowl. Add egg and sour creamgradually, then stir using spatula until a rough dough formed, then switch using hand to knead the dough until elastic. Add the softened butter and knead again until smooth
Shape the dough into a balls, then flaten the dough using rolling pin on a silicone pad. Fold the vertical edges to the center, turn 90 degree then roll it again. Repeat the steps one more time until forming a rectangle with a smooth edges
Then using a pasta machine, roll the dough into stage 5 – 6 setting on the pasta machine
Rest the rolled dough back for another 10 minutes
* For Pierogis Filling (Keto-Mashed Potatoes)
On a small sauce pan, melt butter on a low heat. Add coconut milk, cheese sauce and ricotta, then stir with a rubber spatula to combines.
When the mixture starts to bubbles, add in the Keto-Flour while keep stirring until the mixture starts thicken.
Turn off the heat then drop the egg yolk and stir until completely combines
Rest the batter for 10 minutes to cools at room temperature
* Assemble
On a silicone pad, cut the rolled dough with circle cookies cutter until all used, with minimal left over (roll the left over dough with the pasta machine again to get more circles)
Spoon some Pierogis filling into the center of the circles, then fold the circles over into half circles and press to seal the edges
Place Pierogis on a cookie sheet, and freeze. Once frozen, transfer to freezer storage bags or containers.
* Cooking Pierogis (Italian style)
Bring a large pot of lightly salted water to a boil. Drop Pierogis in one at a time. They are done when they float to the top. Do not boil too long, or they will be soggy. Remove with a slotted spoon.
Drain the cooked Pierogis on spider strainer, set aside
On a medium frying pan, heat 1 tablespoon (15g) of coconut oil with low heat.
Sautee the diced onion until fragrant then add the Pierogis by keep stirring until the Pierogis starts to brown
Pour the bolognese sauce over and cook until it's done
Serve with sprinkles of grated cheddar and Italian seasoning

THE KETO IRON CHEF'S KETO-CRAMOSA (INDIAN SAMOSA PASTRY) A HYBRID OF CROISSANT AND SAMOSA IN A KETOFIED WAY

Keto-Cramosa (Indian Samosa Pastry) A hybrid of Croissant and Samosa in a Ketofied Way Servings=4 Time=60mins
Ingredients
* For Cramosa Dough
Dry Ingredients
15g Casein Protein Isolate Hardcore Micellar Casein
10g Isopure Whey Protein Isolate, Unflavored
5g Dried Egg Whites
5g Egg Yolk Powder

15g Inulin Fiber (Chicory Root) – LC Foods

1,5g Psyllium Husk

1g Xanthan Gum

1g Salt

1g Sucralose

0,5g Pepper Powder

0,5g Garlic Powder

0,5g Curry Powder

0,5g Cumin Powder

* Note : The first 7 ingredients above are the Keto-Flour formula for this recipe

For crisper crust the Keto-Flour can be changed into this formula : 15g Wheat Protein Isolate 8000, 10g Casein Protein Isolate, 10g Whey Protein Isolate, 5g Egg White Powder, 5g Egg Yolk Powder, 5g Inulin Powder

Wet Ingredients

10g Coconut Milk

15g Water

5g Virgin Coconut Oil

* For Pastry Batter

Dry Ingredients

25g Keto-Flour (half the quantity from the Keto-Flour formula listed above)

0,5g Salt

0,25g Pepper Powder

0,25g Garlic Powder

Wet Ingredients

5g Virgin Coconut Oil

20g Butter

* For Cramosa Filling

100g Goat Meat (diced)

15g Onion (diced)

1/2 stalk Lemon Grass ; the white parts (sliced)

1 pcs Turmeric Leaf (sliced)

1 pcs Lime Leaf (sliced)

50ml Coconut milk

2g Curry Powder

0,5g Cumin Powder

* For Cramosa Grounded Spice

1 pcs Shallots

1 clove Garlic

1 pcs Candlenut

2 pcs Red Chillies

1g Ginger Powder

1g Coriander Powder

1g Salt

1g Sucralose

Direction

* For Cramosa Dough

Whisk all dry ingredients on a medium bowl. Add coconut milk and water gradually, then stir using spatula until a rough dough formed, then switch using hand to knead the dough until elastic. Add the softened butter and knead again until smooth

Rest the dough for 10 minutes

Divide the rested dough into 2 equal parts. Then using a pasta machine, roll each dough into stage 5 – 6 setting on the pasta machine

Rest the rolled dough back for another 10 minutes
* For Pastry Batter
On a small bowl, combine Keto-Flour with butter using spatula, until a rough batter formed. Add the coconut oil and mix again until completely combines
Rest the batter for 10 minutes at the refrigerator
* For Cramosa Filling
Sautee all grounded spices with onion, lemon grass, turmeric leaf and lime leaf until fragrant
Add the goat meats and stir until the colour changes
Pour in coconut milk with curry powder and turmeric powder, stir to combine
Cook until the coconut milk evaporates, set aside
* Assemble
On a silicone pad, spread the pastry batter evenly over each rolled dough
Fold each rolled dough from one side to the other side, making at least 4 – 5 fold into a square shape
Roll the folded dough to flatten it into 1/2 cm thick, by rolling it vertically and horizontally on both side of the dough
Cut each dough into squares (10 x 10cm) using pastry cutter or a knife
Take half of the Cramosa filling and put on the center of the dough
Fold into triangle and seam the edge with egg white or water
Repeat with the second dough and the rest of the filling
Deep fry the dough using coconut oil on a low medium heat, until golden brown
Serve as a Keto-Snack or as a side dish for Keto-Meals

THE KETO IRON CHEF'S RENDANG (ASIAN BEEF STEW)

Rendang (Asian Beef Stew) Servings=4 Time=30mins
INGREDIENTS
1.5kg Fatty Beef cut into 12 pieces
500ml Coconut Milk (2 cups)
110g Toasted coconut paste (kerisik) Taylor & Colledge Extract Paste, Coconut, 1.40 Ounce
Salt to taste
Splenda (sucralose) to taste
1 Turmeric leaf, sliced
2 Red chillies, composed of flowers
1 Handful lime leaves, torn
For Spice Paste
8 Shallots, skin peeled
3 cloves Garlic, skin peeled
8 stalks Lemon grass, sliced
¾ inch Ginger, skin peeled
¾ inch Fresh turmeric, skin peeled
6 Red chillies, deseeded
1½ tbsp Coriander powder
1 tsp Cumin powder
2 tbsp Chilli paste
Direction
Combine the spice paste ingredients in a blender and blend until smooth.
Combine Beef, spice paste and coconut paste into the pot and simmer for 30 min or until the broth is almost dry.
Lower heat and stir in coconut milk. Season with salt and sugar.
Add turmeric and stir well before turning off the fire.
Decorate with red chilli and lime leaves

THE KETO IRON CHEF'S GULAI AYAM (CHICKEN CURRY)

The Keto Iron Chef's Gulai Ayam (Chicken Curry) Servings=4 Time=45mins
Gulai Ayam (Chicken Curry)
(4 – 6 Serving Size)
Ingredients
2 tsp Coriander Seeds
1 tsp Cumin Seeds
1 tsp Fennel Seeds
1 tsp Nutmeg (grated)
5 pcs Candlenuts
1 tsp Turmeric (grounded)
1/2 tsp Cloves
1/4 tsp Cardamom Seeds
10 pcs Red Chillies
4 cloves Garlic (peeled)
3 pcs Shallots (peeled)
1 (2 inch) Ginger (peeled and sliced)
2 cups Coconut Milk
3 tbsp Coconut Oil Virgin Coconut Oil
5 pcs Kaffir Lime Leaves
2 stick Cinnamon
1 stalk Lemon Grass (trimmed and knotted)
1 (1,8 kg) Chicken (cut into 8 – 10 pcs)
Salt to taste
Direction
Purée coriander, cumin, fennel, nutmeg, turmeric, cloves, cardamom, chiles, candlenuts, garlic, shallots, ginger, and 2 tbsp water in a food processor into a paste, set aside.
Heat coconut oil in a 12 inch skillet over medium-high heat.
Cook paste with lime leaves, cinnamon, and lemongrass until golden, 5–7 minutes.
Add chicken; cook until browned, 8–10 minutes.
Stir in half the milk and 1,5 cups water, until boil.
Reduce heat to medium, cook, while stirring, until tender, 10–12 minutes.
Stir in remaining milk and salt, cook until slightly thick for 2 minutes more.
Serve with other Keto-Meals dishes

THE KETO IRON CHEF'S CREATION - KETO-CROZZA!

A hybrid of Croissant and Pizza in a Ketofied Way
Keto-Crozza Servings=4 Time=60mins" difficulty="moderate"]
Ingredients
* For Crozza Dough
Dry Ingredients
45g Micellar Casein
30g Isopure Whey Protein Isolate, Unflavored
15g Dried Egg Whites
15g Egg Yolk Powder
45g Inulin Fiber (Chicory Root) – LC Foods
5g Psyllium Husk
3g Xanthan Gum
3g Salt
1,5g Garlic Powder
1,5g Pepper Powder
3g Instant Dry Yeast
* Note : The first 7 ingredients above are the Keto-Flour formula for this recipe
For crisper crust the Keto-Flour can be changed into this formula : 45g Wheat Protein Isolate 8000, 30g Casein Protein Isolate, 15g Whey Protein Isolate, 15g Egg White Powder, 15g Egg Yolk Powder, 30g Inulin Powder
Wet Ingredients
90g VERY COLD WATER (to suspend the yeast leavening action over the dough, during the rolling & folding process)
12g Virgin Coconut Oil

* For Pastry Batter
Dry Ingredients
50g Keto-Flour (half the quantity from the Keto-Flour formula listed above)
1g Salt
0,5g Garlic Powder
0,5g Pepper Powder
Wet Ingredients
10g Virgin Coconut Oil
40g Butter
* For Crozza Sauce
1 tbsp Butter
3 tbsp Cream Cheese
5 slice Salami (diced)
100g Tomato Puree
1 tsp Basil (dry)
1 tsp Oregano (dry)
1 tsp Rosemary (dry)
1/2 tsp Fennel (dry)
1/4 tsp Salt
1/8 tsp Black Pepper
1/8 tsp Nutmeg
1/8 tsp Sucralose
* For Crozza Topping
20g Ricotta Cheese
50g Mozzarella Cheese (grated)
11 slice Salami
Direction
* For Crozza Dough
Whisk all dry ingredients on a medium bowl. Add water gradually and stir using spatula until a rough dough formed, then switch using hand to knead the dough until elastic. Add the coconut oil and knead again until smooth

Rest the dough for 10 minutes at the refrigerator
Divide the rested dough into 4 equal parts. Then using a pasta machine, roll each dough into stage 5 – 6 setting on the pasta machine
Rest the rolled dough back in the refrigerator for another 10 minutes
* For Pastry Batter
On a small bowl, combine Keto-Flour with butter using spatula, until a rough batter formed. Add the coconut oil and mix again until completely combines
Rest the batter for 10 minutes at the refrigerator
* For Crozza Sauce
On a small sauce pan, melt butter using low to medium heat, then sautee the diced salamis until almost fully cooked. Add cream cheese, then followed by tomato puree and the rest of the sauce seasoning. Cook until the sauce thickens, set aside
* Assemble
On a silicone pad, seam each end of the rolled dough forming a long sheet, then spread the pastry batter evenly over the sheet
Fold the dough from the longest side forming a very long rope. Fold the rope from one side into the other side, forming a large spiral shape by seaming the end beneath the dough
Remove the spiral dough onto a round greased baking pan or a Pizza Stone
Flatten the dough using a roller pin, by keeping the round pizza shape maintained. The dough should be rolled into 1,5x wider from its original size, then rest the dough in a warm spot for 20 – 30 minutes until it rise

Preheat the oven into 300F

Bake the risen dough for 10 – 15 minutes until the edge has just starting to brown, then remove the half baked crust out from the oven

Spread the ricotta cheese thinly over the crust, then spread the cooked Crozza sauce evenly. Sprinkle the grated mozzarella cheese, then arrange the salamis to cover almost all of the surface neatly

Bake again for another 15 – 20 minutes, until the crust edges are completely browned and the salamis are cooked

Slice and serve the Keto-Crozza into 4 – 8 serving size

THE KETO IRON CHEF'S GULAI LELE (SPICY CAT FISH CURRY)

My Asian Keto-Meals
Gulai Lele (Spicy Cat Fish Curry) Servings=2-3 Time=30mins
Ingredients:
For The Fish ;
Cat fish – 6 pieces
Marinate with lemon juice for 30 minutes
Fry the fish over medium heat until crispy
For Dry Roast & Grind into paste ;
Dessicated coconut – 2 tbsp
Fenugreek seeds – 1 tsp
Groundnuts – 1tbsp
Sesame seeds – 1 ½ tbsp
For Grinding ;
Red onion (large) – 1 nos
Tomato (large) – 1 nos
Garlic – 6 nos
Tempering:
Coconut Oil – 2 tbsp
Mustard seeds – ½ tsp
Cumin seeds – 1 tsp
Curry leaves – 3 to 4 leaves
Onion – 1 (chopped finely)
Turmeric powder – 1 tsp
Red chili powder – 2 tsp
Coriander powder – 2 tsp
Green chilies – 6 nos (small)
Garlic – 6 to 7 nos (chopped)
Tamarind – lemon size (soaked in water & extracted)
Garnishing:
coriander leaves – 1/4 cup (chopped)
Direction
Dry roast the fenugreek seeds, dessicated coconut, sesame seeds, groundnuts, till the raw flavor goes off and grind it into paste by adding little amount of water and keep it aside.

Ground the ingredients onion, tomato, garlic and keep aside.Keep the pan on low flame, add 2 tablespoon of oil and start to tempering with mustard, cumin seeds and curry leaves.

After that add finely chopped onions, garlic, green chilies & sauté it for 2- 3 minutes. And then add all the spices like turmeric, red chili, coriander powder and sauté until the raw flavor goes off.

Now add the grounded onion, tomato & garlic paste, tamarind extract, dry roasted paste and add enough water to boil it for 15 more minutes on high flame till the raw smell goes off.

After that add the crispy fried fish , cover with lid and cook it for 10 more minutes and switched off the flame and garnish with chopped coriander, mint and curry leaves.

Another option is just to pour the curry over the fried cat fish to keep the crisp

Serve it hot and enjoy!!!

THE KETO IRON CHEF'S KETO-DIM SUM (CANTONESE AUTHENTIC DIM SUM)

Keto-Dim Sum (Cantonese Authentic Dim Sum) Servings=1-2 Time=60mins

Ingredients

* For Dim Sum Wrapper

Dry Ingredients

15g Micellar Casein

10g Isopure Whey Protein Isolate, Unflavored

5g Dried Egg Whites

5g Egg Yolk Powder

15g Inulin Fiber (Chicory Root) – LC Foods

1,5g Psyllium Husk

1g Xanthan Gum Powder

1,5g Salt

1g Garlic Powder

1g Pepper Powder

1g Sucralose

* Note : The first 7 ingredients above are the Keto-Flour formula for this recipe

Wet Ingredients

10g Egg White

20g Sour Cream

3g Butter (or sesame oil)

* For Dim Sum Filling

Dry Ingredient

10g Micellar Casein

10g Inulin Fiber (Chicory Root) – LC Foods

10g Egg Yolk Powder

2g Salt

1g Garlic Powder

1g Pepper Powder

1g Sucralose

Wet Ingredients

100g Shrimp or Crab meat (softened on a food processor)

15g Egg Yolk

5g Butter (or sesame oil)

* For Dimsum Topping

Tong Cai (Salted Cabbage) or Grated Carrot

Direction

* For Dim Sum Wrapper

Whisk all dry ingredients on a medium bowl. Add egg and sour cream gradually, then stir using spatula until a rough dough formed, then switch using hand to knead the dough until elastic. Add the softened butter (or sesame oil) and knead again until smooth

Shape the dough into a balls, then flaten the dough using rolling pin on a silicone pad. Fold the vertical edges to the center, turn 90 degree then roll it again. Repeat the steps one more time until forming a rectangle with a smooth edges

Then using a pasta machine, roll the dough into stage 5 – 6 setting on the pasta machine

Rest the rolled dough for 10 minutes, before cutting

* For Dim Sum Filling

On a medium bowl, whisk and sift all the ingredients together

Combine the softened shrimp with the dry ingredient using spatula, until a rough dough formed

Add the egg yolk and butter (or sesame oil), then stir to combine, until a tacky thick batter formed, set aside

* Assemble & Cooking

On a silicone pad, cut the rolled dough with pastry cutter or a knife into large squares

Spoon some Dim Sum filling into the center of the squares, then fold each 4 side of the squares making hexagonal folding pattern and leaving some Dim Sum filling exposed on the center. Press to seal the edges (refer to the attached pics for details)

Give Tong Cai or grated carrot over the Dim Sum as the topping

Steam the Dim Sum on a steamer pan with low medium heat for 15 – 20 minutes, or use a rice cooker with steamer option

Serve the Keto-Dim Sum with chilli sauce or peanut butter sauce

DESSERTS

THE KETO IRON CHEF'S MARTABAK BANGKA

Had just finished the chest day with reverse pyramid..so exhausting and reach muscles failure faster

Thinking of making another keto-dessert.. ☺
Martabak Bangka.. Thats it 😀

Have been dreaming of it since starting ketogenic.. but now I want to make the Martabak Bangka in the Keto-Cuisine Style
BOOM
Here goes the recipe
Martabak Bangka (Thick Pancakes) Servings=6 Time=30mins

Dry Ingredient :
40g Inulin Fiber (Chicory Root) – LC Foods
20g Almond Flour
30g Isopure Whey Protein Isolate, Unflavored
20g Micellar Casein
5g Psyllium Husk
5g Gelatin Powder
2g Salt
15g Splenda
3g Baking Soda
Wet Ingredient
200ml Water
100ml Coconut Milk
100g butter
1 egg
50g Cream Cheese
Topping
Grated cheddar cheese
Cocoa Powder
Almond Slices
Splenda
Cinnamon powder
Direction
In a large bowl, sift all the dry ingredients, except for the baking soda
Mix in coconut milk and water
Beat eggs with cream cheese and melted butter. (make sure the melted butter is not hot so it does not cook the eggs)
To the egg mixture, add baking soda dissolved in a little water and mix well. Then add the sifted dry ingredients and mix into crumbles
Combine the crumble batter mixture with coconut milk mixture, beating for about 30 seconds on medium / low speed until well blended and no more lumps.
Pour the batter about 1 – 2 inch thick, wait until you can see bubbles start to form around 5 minutes, then sprinkle with splenda evenly. Immediately cover with the lid and check every 30 second or 1 minutes until the surface is full of holes. This will take approximately 10 minutes
Ensure that your heat is LOW so that the skin doesn't burn. The level of the batter should not exceed half the height of the skillet.
Turn off the heat and spread butter on top using spatula, while the surface is still hot and finally sprinkle with grated cheddar cheese, cocoa powder, cinnamon powder, almond slices, splenda and coconut cream
Remove from the pan and fold it in half immediately like the shape of a semicircle. This will prevent the cake from cracking. Spread the outer surface with more butter to keep the cake moist.
Slice the cake into 6 part and serve while it still warm

THE KETO IRON CHEF'S KETO-BAKPIA (FLAKY SWEET CHEESE PIE)

Good Morning (in my time again)
It's the Keto-Iron Chef again.. LOL.. don't you laugh @David Wood

If you guys ever go to Yogyakarta, Indonesia which is a beautiful city with all those tourist attraction site & for the "BATIK" clothes.. you will find this famous souvenir snack called "Bakpia Pathok" (mung bean pies). They are all over the place and can be easily bought with a reasonable price.

This pastry have a flaky textures similar to croissant, but much more crisper and dryer. The difference is at the pastry filling for the layer, which use flour and vegetable oil combination instead of cold butter like croissant does. And the folding method is much more easier and takes shorter time to make than croissant method, since the flour will be the one that hold the oil moisture without the need of refrigerating to prevent the meltdown.

Eureekaa

Hmm.. what about that.. Nice trick right, this will shock any professional pastry chef around, by knowing how easy to create the flaky textures for pastries.. LOL, I may make my croissants, cronuts, pie crust, egg tarts and danish pastry with this method next time, so so easy.

The original recipes use mungbeans for the pies filling, but as you already know we can't use that beans for their high carb content. So I decide to substitutes the filling with my own sweet cheese filling, and the result taste much more better than I remember back in the days when I was still lost with the High Carbs Lifestyle and ate that mungbean pies every week.. LOL

Well my sweet high carb snacks in the past memory is hitting me back all over again, just love to be able to ketofied this snack.. it's awesome

* God Help me, this pie that I'd bake yesterday is tempting me in the morning while I'm still on IF (Fasting) hours.. LOL

Well here it goes, I hope you're not drooling as much as I do

Keto-Bakpia (Flaky Sweet Cheese Pie) Servings=10 Time=60mins

Ingredients:
For Keto-Flour
185g Inulin Fiber (Chicory Root) – LC Foods
27g Isopure Whey Protein Isolate, Unflavored
53g Micellar Casein
For Pie Dough
200gr Keto-Flour
20g Splenda
1/2 tsp salt
100ml water
25ml Virgin Coconut Oil
150ml Coconut Oil
for Pastry Dough
65g Keto-Flour
25ml coconut oil
1 tsp butter
for the Cheese Filling
100gr grated cheddar cheese
50g softened cream cheese
150ml coconut milk
20g Splenda
30gr Inulin Fiber (Chicory Root) – LC Foods
a pinch of salt
1 pandan leaf / few drops of the essence
1 tbsp coconut oil
Direction
For the filling: on a food processor mix grated cheddar cheese and cream cheese until combines. Transfer to a bowl and use wooden spatula to mix with splenda, inulin powder, coconut milk, pinch of salt and pandan leaf. When everything is well combined, add coconut oil. Mix again then set aside
For the Pie Dough: Warm up the water (until it almost reach boiling point). Take off from the heat. Add splenda, stir. Place flour and salt in a food processor bowl. Pour warm water into the bowl. Pulse until it holds together. Add 25ml coconut oil, and pulse it some more until nice and smooth. Divide and weigh the dough into 10g each (2 tsp size). Set aside.

For the Pastry Dough: Mix all the ingredients. Divide it into as many pastry dough you have.
Assemble: Take one 10g pie dough, flatten it using rolling pin. Take 1 part of pastry dough (around 1/2 tsp size) and spread it on the pie dough. Fold it like an envelope. And form into ball shape. (see pictures for details)
Pour 150ml coconut oil into a bowl, and place the assembled balls into the oil. Let it rest for 15 minutes.
After 15 minutes, take 1 assembled ball and flatten it again using rolling pin. Take 3/4 tsp – 1 tsp of cheese filling. Shape it into ball again and flatten it a bit. Place the messy part (the seam) downside in the baking tray.

Bake in the oven 200°C for around 15 to 20 minutes (until light brown). You can also flip them over after 7 to 10 minutes in the oven so that the both side will have browned surface, and creates an equal flaky texture within.

If you make the filling very well, it can last up to a week in the refrigerator.
I know it looks quite tricky to make, but it's actually easy and took me only an hour to make. This recipe is so tasty and you will love the flaky texture which create a crisper taste & appearance more than the croissant method.
Not to mention the sweet cheese filling, yumm
It's a must try for you Keto-Baking Lovers

KETO IRON CHEF'S KETO-CROCINNABUNS

Well this is the 3rd attempt I had ever made to make a hybrid of croissant pastry with cinnamon rolls in a ketofied way, which unfortunately always fails before

And yesterday I finally succeed ...Eurekaaaa...LOL

The trick was using a very cold water for making the croissant dough, so the yeast will be suspended on the leavening action without having to refrigerate many time between each folding process, just like what bakers did on making croissant. Coz if the yeast leaven too soon then the dough will became to soft to be rolled and tear easily

And to simplify the flaky effect, I suspend the butter liquidity by mixing it with the Keto-Flour as the coagulator and using 1 : 1 ratio of Butter : Keto-Flour, so the butter will still bring the flakes comes out between layers after bake, and dries out the moisture from the thin layers of dough to get the crispness

Then another trick to simplify the rolling, I use a Pasta Machine to roll this dough into a pasta sheet, so that I won't need to roll the dough many time between folding. And just spread the pastry batter over the rolled sheet and fold it like an envelopes (4 – 5 folds) without having to worry for the leaking butter just like on the traditional way of making croissant dough

Damn.. I finally nailed this one

So I'm naming this Keto-Bread

Keto-Crocinnabuns Servings=4 Time=1:30mins

A marriage of Croissant & Cinnamon Rolls in a Ketofied Way

May I call this the world first Ketofied Crocinnabuns??.. LOL

Well here goes the recipe..

Keto-Crocinnabuns

6 serving size

Ingredients

* For Crocinnabuns Dough

Dry Ingredients

60g Micellar Casein

40g Isopure Whey Protein Isolate, Unflavored

20g Dried Egg Whites

20g Egg Yolk Powder

60g Inulin Fiber (Chicory Root) – LC Foods

6g Psyllium Husk

4g Xanthan Gum

2g Salt

2g Vanilla Extract

5g Sucralose

4g Instant Dry Yeast

* Note : The first 7 ingredients above are the Keto-Flour formula for this recipe

For crisper crust the Keto-Flour can be changed into this formula : 60g Wheat Protein Isolate 8000, 40g Casein Protein Isolate, 20g Whey Protein Isolate, 20g Egg White Powder, 20g Egg Yolk Powder, 40g Inulin Powder

Wet Ingredients

40g Cold Egg White

60g VERY COLD WATER (to suspend the yeast leavening action over the dough, during the rolling & folding process)

10g Virgin Coconut Oil

* For Pastry Batter

Dry Ingredients

100g Keto-Flour (half the quantity from the Keto-Flour formula listed above)

2g Salt

2g Vanilla Extract

5g Sucralose

Wet Ingredients
15g Virgin Coconut Oil
75g Butter
* For Cinnamon Spread
30g Butter
20g Cinnamon Powder
10g Sucralose
* For Egg Wash
1 Egg Yolk
1 tsp Coconut Milk
Direction
* For Crocinnabuns Dough
Whisk all dry ingredients on a mixer bowl. Using low speed stage, mix in egg white until crumbly dough formed, then add water gradually while raising the mixer speed into medium stage until a dough completely formed

Rest the dough for 10 minutes at the refrigerator
Divide the rested dough into 6 equal parts. Then using a pasta machine, roll each dough into stage 5 – 6 setting on the pasta machine

Rest the rolled dough back in the refrigerator for another 10 minutes
* For Pastry Batter
On a standing mixer, cream butter until light with low speed. Then add coconut oil until combined and gradually add the Keto-Flour using spoon until the batter thicken
Rest the batter for 10 minutes at the refrigerator, then divide the rested batter into 6 equal parts.

* Assemble
On a silicone pad, spread the rolled dough with the pastry batter evenly
Make 3 – 4 fold from one side to the other end of the rolled dough, then fold one more time to the opposite direction (just like closing a book)
Roll the dough at one direction to flatten and seaming the pastry batter within.
Brush the butter over the rolled dough, then sprinkle cinnamon powder and sucralose evenly
Roll the dough into a log and make a seam at the end by pinching it to combines
Repeat the procedure with the rest of the rolled dough until 6 Crocinnabuns are formed

Proof the dough on a warm spot for 20 – 30 minutes until double in size
Preheat the oven into 300F
Give an egg wash over the risen dough, then bake for 30 – 40 minutes, until brown
Served with black coffee or green tea

KETO IRON CHEF NAILS KETO-LÁNGOS

Keto-Lángos Servings=3 Time=60mins
Ingredients
* For The Keto-Flour Mix
Dry Ingredients
30g Micellar Casein
20g Isopure Whey Protein Isolate, Unflavored
10g Dried Egg Whites
10g Egg Yolk Powder
30g Inulin Fiber (Chicory Root) – LC Foods

3g Psyllium Husk
2g Xanthan Gum Powder
2g Salt
1g Garlic Powder
1,5g Baking Powder
1g Baking Soda
* Note : The first 7 ingredients above are the Keto-Flour formula for this recipe
For crisper crust the Keto-Flour can be changed into this formula : 45g Wheat Protein Isolate 8000, 30g Casein Protein Isolate, 15g Whey Protein Isolate, 15g Egg White Powder, 15g Egg Yolk Powder, 30g Inulin Powder
* For Preferment (Sponge)
30g Keto-Flour Mix
1g Instant Dry Yeast
10g Sour Cream
20g Water
* For Lángos Dough (Dough)
The Rest of the Keto-Flour Mix
The Risen Preferment (Sponge)
2g Instant Dry Yeast
10g Sour Cream
40g Water
* For Lángos Topping
Sour Cream
Grated Cheddar Cheese
Direction
Whisk and sift all the ingredients for the Keto-Flour Mix on a medium bowl
* For Preferment
Whisk 30g Keto-Flour Mix with 1g Instant dry yeast on a small bowl
Mix 10g sour cream with 20g water on a cup
Add the sour cream mixture into the flour then mix using spatula until a tacky dough formed
Rest the sponge for 30 minutes, until rise into double in size
* For Lángos Dough
Whisk the rest of the Keto-Flour Mix with 2g Instant dry yeast on a medium bowl
Mix 10g sour cream with 40g water on a cup
Combine the risen sponge with the flour using spatula, until a rough dough formed
Add the sour cream mixture gradually into the dough, then switch using hand to knead the dough until soft and elastic
* Shaping & Cooking
On a silicone pad, divide the dough into 3 balls and flat them with your palm
Stretch out each dough with your fingers into a round shape with the centre being thinner than the edges
Let the dough rest for another 30 minutes on the silicone pad, until they rise again (the edges should feel soft and bouncy when pressed, leaving a slight mark on the dough surface)
Deep fry each dough using coconut oil on a low medium heat until both side are golden brown
Serve while it's hot, with a spread of sour cream and sprinkle of grated cheddar cheese

THE KETO IRON CHEF'S DOES KETO-KLENÄT (SWEDISH DOUGHNUT KLEJNER / KLENÄTER)

Keto-Klenät (Swedish Doughnut Klejner / Klenäter) Servings=1-2 Time=45mins
Ingredients
Dry Ingredients
15g Micellar Casein
10g Isopure Whey Protein Isolate, Unflavored
5g Dried Egg Whites
5g Egg Yolk Powder
15g Inulin Fiber (Chicory Root) – LC Foods
1,5g Psyllium Husk
1g Xanthan Gum Powder
1g Salt
1g Lemon Zest
0,8g Ground Cardamom
3g Sucralose
* Note : The first 7 ingredients above are the Keto-Flour formula for this recipe

For crisper crust the Keto-Flour can be changed into this formula : 15g Wheat Protein Isolate 8000, 10g Casein Protein Isolate, 5g Whey Protein Isolate, 5g Egg White Powder, 5g Egg Yolk Powder, 10g Inulin Powder

Wet Ingredients

10g Egg

20g Sour Cream

5g Butter

Dusting

Cinnamon Powder

Sucralose

Direction

Whisk all dry ingredients on a medium bowl. Add egg and sour cream gradually, then stir using spatula until a rough dough formed, then switch using hand to knead the dough until elastic. Add the softened butter and knead again until smooth. Shape the dough into a balls, then rest the dough for 1 hours before shaping. On a silicone pad, roll the dough to thin tortilla, approximately 1/4 inch (5 mm) thin. Using pastry cutter or a knife, cut the flaten dough into diamond / rhombus shape. And then cut out the incision in the middle, and fold one tip through the incision to form a knot. Repeat until all dough are used. Rest the shaped dough for 10 minutes before frying. Deep fry the shaped dough in a batch, using coconut oil on low medium heat. Fry for about 1 – 2 minutes one each side, until evenly brown and the release of bubbles is almost over. Drain with spider strainer then transfer to a paper towel to remove excess oil.

Serve with a generous dust of cinnamon powder and sucralose

KETO-IRON CHEF CRISPY CHOCOLATE ICE CREAM CONE RECIPE

Keto-Iron Chef Crispy Chocolate Ice Cream Cone Recipe

Keto-Iron Ice Cream Cone Servings=12 Time=60mins

(Keto-Iron Chef Crispy Chocolate Ice Cream Cone Recipe)

* Dedicated to all children on Therapeutic Ketogenic Diet

Ingredients
Dry Ingredients
15g Micellar Casein
10g Isopure Whey Protein Isolate, Unflavored
5g Dried Egg Whites
5g Egg Yolk Powder
15g Inulin Fiber (Chicory Root) – LC Foods
1,5g Psyllium Husk
1g Xanthan Gum Powder
1g Baking Soda
1g Bakers Ammonia
3g 100% Dark Cocoa Powder
1g Salt
5g Sucralose
* Note : The first 7 ingredients above are the Keto-Flour formula for this recipe
Wet Ingredients
10g Egg White
20g Sour Cream
3g Butter
Direction
Whisk all dry ingredients on a medium bowl. Add egg and sour cream gradually, then stir using spatula until a rough dough formed, then switch using hand to knead the dough until elastic. Add the softened butter and knead again until smooth
Shape the dough into a balls, then flaten the dough using rolling pin on a silicone pad. Fold the vertical edges to the center, turn 90 degree then roll it again. Repeat the steps one more time until forming a rectangle with a smooth edges
Then using a pasta machine, roll the dough into stage 6 – 7 setting on the pasta machine
Rest the rolled dough for 10 minutes, before shaping and cutting
Preheat the oven into 300F
Cut the rested dough into triangles until all dough are used up
Brush one side of the triangle with an egg white (1/2 cm width), then fold into a cone shape
Seam the cone edges by pressing with finger and also insert a chop stick to seam the inner part of the cone
Trim the cones edges using scissor to make a smooth round circle for the cone top
Arrange all shaped cones into a cookie baking pan, with the cone facing downward
Bake for 10 – 15 minutes, until it's done
Serve the cones with a scoop of Keto-Iron Chocolate Ice Cream

KETO-IRON CHOCOLATE ICE CREAM (KETO IRON CHEF RICH, FLUFFY & SILKY CHOCOLATE ICE CREAM SECRET RECIPE)

Keto-Iron Chocolate Ice Cream (Keto Iron Chef Rich, Fluffy & Silky Chocolate Ice Cream Secret Recipe)
Keto-Iron Chocolate Ice Cream Servings=2 Time=60mins
(Keto Iron Chef Rich, Fluffy & Silky Chocolate Ice Cream Secret Recipe)
* Dedicated to all children on Therapeutic Ketogenic Diet

Ingredients
30g 100% Dark Cocoa Powder
30g Butter
200ml Coconut Milk
2 Egg Yolks
10g Isopure Whey Protein Isolate, Unflavored
10g Inulin Fiber (Chicory Root) – LC Foods
10g Sucralose
2g Xanthan Gum Powder
200ml Heavy Whipping Cream
Direction
Beat the butter and egg yolks in a mixer bowl until pale and thick
Add inulin powder and sucralose into the mixture until creamy and fluffy
Stir in the dark cocoa powder until the mixture starts harden into a chocolate paste, set aside
On a sauce pan, heat coconut milk and casein protein isolate on a very low heat
Pour in the chocolate paste, then continuously stir the mixture until it thickens and coats the back of a spatula
Don't allow the mixture boil or it will curdle. Pour into a bowl and leave to cool, stirring occasionally.
Whip the heavy cream into soft peaks, then pour the cooled chocolate mixture until completely combine
Sprinkle xanthan gum over the ice cream mixture, until it start to become very thick and fluffy
Churn in an ice-cream machine, according to the manufacturer's instructions, until it's frozen or just use a glass bowl with sealed cover to store the ice cream for at least 3 hours in the freezer
Serve the ice cream with sprinkle of diced roasted almonds

THE KETO IRON CHEF'S ONDE-ONDE (ASIAN FRIED DUMPLINGS)

My Asian Keto-Meals
Good morning (at my time)
Its time to make some new "ketofied" recipes
This time I want to share about one of indonesian most favorite snack which called onde-onde

This snack is actually very high carbed insulin spiker snack that I had been avoiding for 2 years.. but now using my New Keto-Dough formula and ketofied fillings for this snack.. I can remake them all over again ☺
Here it goes

Onde-Onde (Asian Fried Dumplings) Servings=20 Time=1:30mins
INGREDIENTS
for Onde-Onde dough
Dry Ingredients
Keto-Flour 100g
* 50g Inulin Fiber (Chicory Root) – LC Foods
* 15g Isopure Whey Protein Isolate, Unflavored
* 15g Micellar Casein
* 20g Egg Yolk Powder
(Sift all these ingredients together)
5g Psyllium Husk
2g salt
5g Stevia (concentrated – use 1tsp=1cup) * This one is good too. * I test with bulk using this, can be used with listed measurement
2g baking powder
(Add to the Keto-Flour and mix well)
Wet Ingredients
30g coconut milk/cream

30g warm water

(Combine this wet ingredients to the dry ingredients / Keto-Flour mix and knead until a dough is formed, then rest the dough for 30 minutes)

for Onde-Onde fillings

30g grated cheddar cheese

20g cream cheese, softened

20g Egg Yolk Powder

10g Stevia (concentrated – use 1tsp=1cup) * This one is good too. * I test with bulk using this, can be used with listed measurement

2g salt

2g garlic powder

(Mix all these ingredients in a food processor or blender and form a 2g balls until all the fillings are used)

For Onde-Onde toppings

50g sesame seeds or dessicated coconuts

A small bowl of cold water for dipping the onde-onde dough

DIRECTION

from the rested Onde-Onde dough, scale 10g of small dough balls until all used up

Flaten each dough balls on your palm and add the filling ball, then wrap it to make a perfect shape of ball again

Do this until all doughs and fillings are used up

Use the cold water in a small bowl to wet the onde-onde dough and roll it over a plate that have been spread with sesame seeds or dessicated coconuts. Roll carefully until each dough is covered with the sesame seeds or dessicated coconuts

Heat the frying pan with low heat and fill with coconut oil for deep frying

Test the oil with some sesame seeds to see if its ready, then fry all the dough until golden brown

Dont stir to much during frying otherwise the sesame seeds will detach from the dough

Drain them and serve while still warm, with black coffee or green tea

Note : be creative for the fillings, such as using peanut/almond butter and mix with grated cheese.

THE KETO IRON CHEF'S KETO-MOLLEN

Keto-Mollen

3 – 6 serving size

Keto Mollen Servings=3-6 Time=1:30mins" difficulty="moderate"]

Ingredients

* For Mollen Dough

Dry Ingredients

30g Micellar Casein

20g Isopure Whey Protein Isolate, Unflavored

10g Dried Egg Whites

10g Egg Yolk Powder

30g Inulin Fiber (Chicory Root) – LC Foods

3g Psyllium Husk

2g Xanthan Gum

2g Salt

2g Vanilla Extract

5g Sucralose

* Note : The first 7 ingredients above are the Keto-Flour formula for this recipe

For crisper crust the Keto-Flour can be changed into this formula : 30g Wheat Protein Isolate 8000, 20g Casein Protein Isolate, 10g Whey Protein Isolate, 10g Egg White Powder, 10g Egg Yolk Powder, 20g Inulin Powder

Wet Ingredients
50g Water
15g Butter
* For Pastry Dough
Dry Ingredients
50g Keto-Flour (from the Keto-Flour Formula above ; the first 7 ingredients of Mollen Dough dry ingredients)
1g Salt
2g Sucralose
Wet Ingredient
5g Virgin Coconut Oil
40g Butter
* For Cheese Filling
50g Cheddar Cheese (grated)
30g Egg Yolk Powder
5g Sucralose
30g Butter
5g Lemon Juice
* For Chocolate Filling
50g 100% Cocoa Powder (or 30g 90% Dark Chocolate + 20g 100% Cocoa Powder)
10g Egg Yolk Powder
10g Sucralose
50g Butter
* For Mollen Filling
6 pcs of Hard Cheese of your choice cut into long cubes
* The original recipe is using banana as the mollen filling
* For Mollen Topping
1 egg yolk + 2 tsp coconut milk for egg wash
20g of grated cheddar cheese
Direction
* For Mollen Dough
Whisk all the dry ingredients together on a medium bowl
Add water gradually while stirring with spatula to combines. When a rough dough has formed, switch using your hand to knead until almost elastic then add the softened butter to make the dough smoother. Rest the dough for 10 minutes

Divide the mollen dough into 6 equal parts, set aside
* For Pastry Dough
Whisk all the dry ingredients together on a medium bowl
Add butter and coconut oil all at once, then stir with spatula to combine.
Divide the pastry dough into 6 equal parts, set aside

* For Cheese Filling
Mix all the cheese filling ingredients until completely incorporated
* For Chocolate Filling
Mix all the chocolate filling ingredients until completely incorporated
* For Mollen Filling
Cut hard cheese of your choice into long cubes (approximately 4 x 1 x 1 cm)
Preheat the oven into 300F
* Assemble
Roll each mollen dough into pasta sheet thickness with a roller pin, or use pasta machine to roll the dough up to the 5th – 7th setting level

Spread the pastry dough evenly over the rolled mollen dough, then fold 3 times from the left or the right longest side of the dough

Roll the folded dough gently (one direction rolling only on each 4 side of the square shaped dough) to make it wider

Fill the flattened dough with hard cheese cubes then slip in the cheese and chocolate filling on each side of the hard cheese cubes

Fold the dough from each 4 side to the center and make a seam

Move all the assembled dough onto a greased baking pan, then gives an egg wash and sprinkle of grated cheddar cheese

Bake for 25 – 30 minutes until browned

Serve while they're still warm

THE KETO IRON CHEF'S KETO-CHAPATI DESSERT

As a request from a friend on the ketogenic group, today I'm making Keto-Chapati (Roti Canai), which origin from India

This bread is usually eaten with Lamb Curry or other spicy curry dishes

I'm excited to try this one, coz the bread will have flaky appearance and texture almost similar to those croissant and danish pastry, but of course this one is cooked on a skillet instead of baking in the oven

Ok guys.. Let's go to the recipes

Keto-Chapati (Roti Canai) Servings=4 Time=1:30mins

Dry Ingredient

100g Keto-Flour

* 50g Inulin Fiber (Chicory Root) – LC Foods
* 15g Isopure Whey Protein Isolate, Unflavored
* 15g Micellar Casein
* 20g Egg Yolk Powder

5g Psyllium Husk or 2g Xanthan Gum or 2g Guar Gum Powder

2g Salt

1g Garlic Powder

1g Curry Powder

1g Nutmeg Powder

2g Baking Powder

1g Baking Soda

(sift all these ingredients together)

Wet Ingredients

30g Egg

10g Heavy Cream

10g Coconut Milk

20g Warm Water

(Mix all these ingredients together)

Pastry Ingredients

Some butter for brushing the dough and for frying

Alternative Topping (I'm making Keto-Chapati Dessert)

Keto-Cheese Sauce

* 2 tbsp Butter
* 2 tbsp Keto-Flour (Inulin powder, Whey protein isolate, Casein protein isolate, Egg yolk powder)
* 30g grated cheddar cheese / parmesan cheese
* 1 cup Heavy cream
* 1 egg yolk
* Salt, Pepper, Cayenne, nutmeg to taste

(Heat the butter on a sauce pan with low heat, then add the keto-flour and mix until combines. Add the heavy cream then grated cheese and mix until the cheese dissolve and the sauce start bubling. Turn off the heat then add egg yolk & the spices, mix until combines)

Cocoa Powder, for sprinkling

Cinnamon Powder

Splenda

Grated Cheddar Cheese

Cream Cheese Frosting

2 tbsp Butter

2 tbsp Cream Cheese

1/2 tsp Stevia (concentrated – use 1tsp=1cup) * This one is good too. * I test with bulk using this, can be used with listed measurement

1 tsp Inulin Fiber (Chicory Root) – LC Foods

1/2 cup Heavy Cream

(Beat butter, cream cheese, splenda, inulin powder until creamy, then add heavy cream and mix until combines)

Direction

Mix all the dry ingredients and add wet ingredient one at a time until a rough dough is form with spatula

Knead the dough using hand until it smooth and elastic, then divide into 4 equal dough balls

Roll each dough with roller pin to make flat round dough (as thin as you can)

Brush each dough with butter evenly, and make a rolling fold from 1 edge to the end of the circle, then do the rolling fold again to make a spiral dough with the seam beneath each dough

Press the spiral dough using palm to make flat round dough again, but not to thin (5mm thick)

Fry each pressed dough on a skillet using "VERY LOW HEAT" and turn to each side every 2 – 3 minutes until golden brown

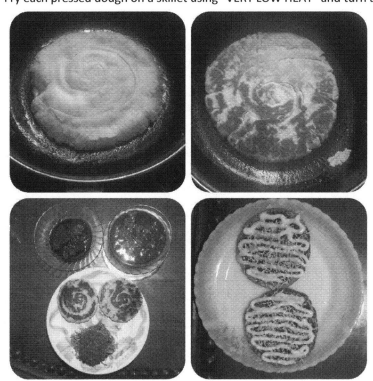

For Keto-Chapati Dessert

Preheat oven into 300F

Spread the keto-cheese sauce evenly over the Keto-Chapati

Sprinkle cocoa powder, cinnamon powder, splenda and inulin powder evenly over the keto-cheese sauce

Spread grated cheddar cheese and bake for 10 minutes

Turn off the oven, and let the Keto-Chapati Dessert cools for 10 minutes, then spread the cream cheese frosting using piping bag

Serve the Keto-Chapati with Lamb Curry and the Keto-Chapati Dessert with black coffee or green tea

KETO IRON CHEF'S KETOFIED CRONUT

Keto Iron Chef's Ketofied cronut

This pastry recipe is dedicated to all keto-baking lovers.

Making cronut is achievable without the gluten, and I had succeed making the ketofied cronut without it. And I also find a new way to make this pastry dough to be folded like a croissant method but without the need of refrigerating. Coz I'm suspending the butter with the Keto-Flour so they won't easily melt during the folding. Awesome huh.. LOL

It is the trick that I duplicate from making the previous recipe for Keto-Bakpia (Cheese Filling Pies)

So pastry is going to be easier now for you ketoers.

Let's see how this Keto-Cronut created, here it goes

Keto-Cronut Servings=1 Time=30mins" difficulty="moderate"]

(Net Carb 3,9g / Protein 40,7g / Fat 46,4g)

Ingredient

For The Dough

Dry Ingredients

25g Inulin Fiber (Chicory Root) – LC Foods

10g Micellar Casein

5g Isopure Whey Protein Isolate, Unflavored

10g Dried Egg Whites

5g Egg Yolk Powder

2,5g Psyllium Husk

1g Xanthan Gum

2g Instant Dry Yeast

1,5g Salt

1,5g Vanilla Extract

2,5g Splenda (Optional)

Wet Ingredients

25g Egg

1g Honey (consumed by the yeast on proofing)

10g Heavy Cream

10g Warm Water

5g Virgin Coconut Oil

For The Pastry Batter

10g Inulin Fiber (Chicory Root) – LC Foods

10g Micellar Casein

20g Butter

(Mix all the ingredients above with a spatula until forming a thick batter consistency, set aside)

* Topping

10g Butter

5g Cream Cheese

5g Splenda

5g Egg Yolk Powder

10g Grated Cheddar Cheese

Direction

Sift all the Dry ingredients together onto a standing mixer bowl

Add egg, honey, then mix with low speed until a crumble dough formed
Add heavy cream and warm water gradually, raise into medium speed until the dough getting elastic
Add the coconut oil and raise into high speed until the dough become smooth, then start using your hand to knead the dough, until a smooth elastic dough has formed.

Roll out the dough into rectangle shape, then spread the pastry butter on half side of the rectangle.
Fold the dough into quarter then roll again into rectangle. Fold one more time into quarter then roll again into rectangle.
Make one last fold into quarter, then shape the dough into doughnut shape.

(see the post pictures for the folding method)
Proof (ferment) the dough on a warm spot for 30 minutes until 1,5x its original size.
Deep fried the risen dough with coconut oil on medium to low heat for 2 minutes on each side, until golden brown
Drain the Keto-Cronut on a strainer, set aside.
Mix butter, cream cheese, egg yolk powder and splenda on a medium bowl using spatula.
Spread the butter mixture onto the Keto-Cronut evenly, then sprinkle grated cheddar cheese by also pressing them lightly over the butter mixture.

Serve with black coffee or green tea

KETO IRON CHEF'S KETO-DUMPLING

More ketofied Asian foods today..LOL

I'm sorry for not making spring rolls as a single recipe, coz this recipe also represent the whole spring rolls recipe too, so if you want to make the Keto-Spring Rolls, just fold the dumpling skins with spring rolls method and then deep fry them.

I'm also making the deep fried method for this Keto-Dumplings beside of course steaming them like the original dumpling version. And there's also another way to cook this Keto-Dumpling which is Pan Fried method.

Keto-Dumplings Servings=1 Time=30mins

Nutrition Fact (without the sauces)

* 1 serving 200g (5,9g Net Carb : 19,5g Protein : 14,6g Fat)
* Per Dumpling 25g (0,7g Net Carb : 2,4g Protein : 1,8g Fat)

Ingredients

* Dumpling Dough

Dry Ingredients
35g Inulin Fiber (Chicory Root) – LC Foods
10g Micellar Casein
5g Dried Egg Whites
1g Xanthan Gum
1g Salt
1g Garlic Powder
Wet Ingredients
40g Warm Water
5g Virgin Coconut Oil
* Dumpling Filling (150g)
50g Skinless Prawns, diced
50g Cabbage, shredded
20g Shitake Mushroom, sliced
5g Egg Yolk Powder
1 tsp Coconut Amino
1 tsp Oyster Sauce
1/4 tsp Salt
1/4 tsp Garlic Powder
1/4 tsp Onion Powder
1 tbsp Virgin Coconut Oil (for sautee)
* Dumpling Topping
Chilli Sauce
Peanut Butter Chilli Sauce
Coconut Amino
Direction
For Dumpling Dough : Sift all dry ingredients together until well combines on a mixer bowl
Add warm water gradually with speed 1 on the mixer until rough dough formed
Proceed to speed 2 on the mixer, by also adding the coconut oil until an elastic and smooth dough is formed
Remove the dough to a sill plate and continue to knead with your hand until the dough become smooth and just a little tacky
Divide the dough into small balls (@15g), set aside

For Dumpling Filling : Heat 1 tablespoon coconut oil on a sauce pan with medium heat then add the diced prawns until golden, followed by the shredded cabbages and sliced mushroom
Add all the other dumpling filling ingredients and stir to combines until fragrant
Turn off the heat, and add the egg yolk powder stir until combines, set aside to cool
Divide the dumpling filling into 8 parts (@10g) and keep the left over on the refrigerator for future usage (up to 3 days on refrigerator)
Assemble : using roller pin, flatten each dumpling dough into circle and put the filling balls on the center of each flattened dumpling dough
Wrap the dough and lightly assemble into half moon shape

KETO IRON CHEF - KETO-CHIFFON CAKE

4 – 6 serving size
Keto-Chiffon Cake Servings=4-6 Time=30mins
Ingredients
Dry Ingredients
40g Inulin Fiber (Chicory Root) – LC Foods
20g Micellar Casein

20g Isopure Whey Protein Isolate, Unflavored
10g Dried Egg Whites
10g Egg Yolk Powder
3g Xanthan Gum Powder
2g Salt
3g Baking Powder
2g Baking Soda
15g Sucralose
Wet Ingredient
150g Egg White
30g Egg Yolk
50g Heavy Whipping Cream
50g Coconut Milk
10g Cider Vinegar
50g Cream Cheese (softened)
50g Cheddar Cheese (grated)
100g Butter
Egg Wash
1 Egg yolk
1 tsp Coconut Milk
Topping
20g Cheddar Cheese (grated)
1 tsp Cinnamon Powder
Direction
Whisk all dry ingredients together on a medium bowl, set aside
On a medium glass stir heavy whipping cream, coconut milk and cider vinegar until combines, set aside (let it stay for 5 – 10 minutes before adding it onto the batter)
On a standing mixer with a paddle attachment, beat butter on speed 1 until white. Add egg yolk, cream cheese and cheddar cheese gradually by raising the speed into stage 2, until creamy and light

Add the heavy whipping cream and coconut milk mixture onto the batter, and raise the speed into stage 3, until creamy and thick
Lower the mixer speed back into stage 1, then add 1/3 of the whisked dry ingredients until combines. Turn off the mixer then pour the rest of the dry ingredients onto the mixer bowl and stir with a spatula until completely combined and the batter becomes thick

Remove the batter onto the medium bowl, set aside
Wash the mixer bowl and the paddle attachment until clean thoroughly without any greasy residues left on the mixer bowl and at the paddle attachment
Preheat the oven into 300F
Beat the egg white on the standing mixer with speed 1 about 10 minutes until stiff peak
Turn off the mixer and pour 1/3 of the batter into the meringues and fold with a spatula until just combines, then pour the rest of the batter and fold again until thoroughly combined

pour the batter onto 12 x 12 x 6 cm lightly greased baking pan
Bake for 30 minutes then remove the pan from the oven. Give an egg wash over the half done cake surface evenly using a soft brush
Sprinkle grated cheddar cheese and cinnamon powder evenly over the cake surface then bake again for another 20 minutes or until an inserted tooth pick comes out clean
Turn off the oven, and let the sponge cake cooled for 10 – 15 minutes before removing it onto a serving plate

Serve with black coffee or green tea

KETO IRON CHEF - KETO-GREEN TEA COOKIES

Keto-Green Tea Cookies
(4 – 6 serving size)
Ingredients
Dry Ingredients
40g Inulin Fiber (Chicory Root) – LC Foods
20g Micellar Casein
20gIsopure Whey Protein Isolate, Unflavored

10g Dried Egg Whites
10g Egg Yolk Powder
2g Xanthan Gum Powder
2g Salt
10g Sucralose
5g Japanese Matcha Green Tea Powder
1g Baking Soda
1g Bakers Ammonia
Wet Ingredients
30g Egg
50g Cheddar Cheese (grated)
80g Butter
Direction
Whisk all the dry ingredients together except for the Matcha Green Tea Powder on a medium bowl, set aside
On a standing mixer with a paddle attachment, beat butter until white with the speed set at stage 1
Add egg and grated cheddar cheese gradually, by raising the speed into stage 2 until light and creamy

Lower the mixer speed back into stage 1, then add the Matcha Green Tea Powder until combines.
Pour 1/3 of the whisked dry ingredient into the mixer bowl until combined and turn off the mixer, then pour the rest of the dry ingredients and fold with a spatula until thoroughly combines

Rest the cookie dough in the refrigerator for 10 minutes, and preheat the oven into 300F
Using roller pin, flatten the cookie dough into 1 cm thick on a silicone pad, then use a cookie cutter to shape the cookies and remove each cookies onto the baking pan

Bake for 10 – 15 minutes, until the cookies edge start to look brown
Cooled the cookies on the baking pan for 10 minutes before removing them onto a tight sealed jar

Serve with black coffee or green tea

THE KETO IRON CHEF'S KETO-SPONGE BROWNIES

The Keto iron Chef's Keto-Sponge Brownies Servings=1-2 Time=60mins
Ingredients
* For Batter
Dry Ingredients
15g Micellar Casein
10g Isopure Whey Protein Isolate, Unflavored
5g Dried Egg Whites
5g Egg Yolk Powder
15 Inulin Fiber (Chicory Root) – LC Foods
3g Xanthan Gum Powder
2g Salt
3g Baking Powder
2g Baking Soda
8g Sucralose
Wet Ingredient
30g Egg Yolk
80g Heavy Whipping Cream
3g Pandan Essence
* For Meringue
90g Dried Egg Whites
10g Inulin Fiber (Chicory Root) – LC Foods
10g Sucralose
* For Chocolate Frosting
30g Cocoa Powder
10g Egg Yolk Powder
40g Butter
10g Sucralose
Direction
Whisk all dry ingredients together on a medium bowl, set aside
On a standing mixer with a paddle attachment, beat heavy whipping cream on low speed until soft peak
Add egg yolk and pandan essence, then raise the speed into medium speed, until the batter become creamy and thick
Lower the mixer speed back into stage 1, then add 1/3 of the whisked dry ingredients until combines. Turn off the mixer then pour the rest of the dry ingredients onto the mixer bowl and stir with a spatula until completely combined and the batter becomes thick
Remove the batter onto the medium bowl, set aside
* For Meringue
Wash the mixer bowl and the paddle attachment until clean thoroughly without any greasy residues left on the mixer bowl and at the paddle attachment
Preheat the oven into 300F
Beat the egg white on the standing mixer with low speed about 5 minutes until soft peak
Add inulin powder and sucralose into the meringue then raise into medium speed until stiff peak
Turn off the mixer and pour 1/3 of egg white into the batter and fold with a spatula until just combines, then pour the rest of the egg white and fold again until thoroughly combined
pour the batter onto 12 x 12 x 6 cm greased baking pan
The height should be around 1 – 2 cm from the bottom of the pan.
Bake for 20 minutes, until the cake surface feels bouncy when slightly pressed
* For Chocolate Frosting
Mix all the Chocolate Frosting ingredients together on a medium bowll, until forming a thick chocolate paste, set aside
* Assemble

Turn off the oven, and let the sponge cake cooled for 10 – 15 minutes before removing it onto a serving plate
Divide the sponge cake into 4 squares, then spread the chocolate frosting evenly over the cake surface
Serve with black coffee or green tea

THE KETO IRON CHEF'S DESSERT PIZZA

Well it's another Keto-Dessert Pizza
But with a NEW CRUST formula
Hmmm.. so delicious & Crispy
Keto-Dessert Pizza (New Crust)

My Home made ketogenic pizza
Starch Free, Gluten Free, Sugar Free & Very Low Carbohydrate
Keto Pizza Servings=8 Time=30mins
Pizza Crust
Dry Ingredient :
30g Inulin Fiber (Chicory Root) – LC Foods
20g Almond Flour
20g Golden Flax Seeds
20g Isopure Whey Protein Isolate, Unflavored
20g Micellar Casein
5g Psyllium Husk
5g Gelatin Powder
2g Salt
1g Garlic Powder
1g Pepper
1g Nutmeg Powder
2g Baking Powder
1g Baking Soda

Wet Ingredient
30g Eggs
20g Cream Cheese
50g Coconut Milk
50g Warm Water
Cheese Sauce
30g Butter
30g Cream Cheese
30g Grated Cheddar Cheese
1 egg yolks
30g Stevia (concentrated – use 1tsp=1cup) * This one is good too. * I test with bulk using this, can be used with listed measurement
20g Inulin Fiber (Chicory Root) – LC Foods
5g Lemon Zest
20g Lemon Juice
2g Gelatin Powder
Topping
Grated Dark Chocolate 85%
Almond Slice
Grated Cheddar Cheese
Grated Mozarella
Stevia (concentrated – use 1tsp=1cup) * This one is good too. * I test with bulk using this, can be used with listed measurement
Sesame Seed
* Cream Cheese Frosting at the top
Direction
Preheat the oven at 300F
Mix all dry ingredients on a standing mixer and add the wet ingredient, mix for 5 minutes at speed 1 to 3 until forming a dough (a little tacky)
Form a round dough with roller pin (I use plastic wrap over the dough), aim as thin as possible, I use 32cm Pizza Pan or 20cm x 20cm cookies pan, which result 5mm to 8mm thick dough
bake for 15 minutes at 300F or until the edges has just starting to brown, set aside and let it cooling down for about 10 minutes
Mix all the cheese sauce ingredients with a mixer until thick and creamy (I start with creaming the butter, followed by gelatin powder, inulin powder and splenda until the mixtures thicken, then add the rest of the ingredients)
spread the sauce evenly over the half baked Pizza dough
Add your choice of Pizza topping and bake again for another 10 to15 minutes until the mozarella cheese has melt
Optional : you can give the dessert Pizza a cream cheese frosting (3tbsp cream cheese, 3tbsp coconut milk, 1tbsp butter, a pinch of salt and splenda to taste)
Serve with Black Coffee or Green Tea

THE KETO IRON CHEF'S KETO-SCHNEEBALLEN (GERMANS FRIED SNOWBALLS CAKE)

The Keto Iron Chef's Keto-Schneeballen (Germans Fried Snowballs Cake) Servings=4 Time=1:30hrs
Ingredient
10g Casein Protein Isolate Hardcore Micellar Casein
10g Isopure Whey Protein Isolate, Unflavored
5g Dried Egg Whites
10g Egg Yolk Powder
15g Inulin Fiber (Chicory Root) – LC Foods

1g Xanthan Gum
1g Baking Powder
0,5g Baking Soda
0,5g Salt
1g Rum Essence
5g Sucralose
* Note : The first 6 ingredients above are the Keto-Flour formula for this recipe
For crisper crust the Keto-Flour can be changed into this formula : 15g Wheat Protein Isolate 8000, 5g Casein Protein Isolate, 5g Whey Protein Isolate, 5g Egg White Powder, 10g Egg Yolk Powder, 10g Inulin Powder
Wet Ingredients
15g Egg White
20g Sour Cream
Topping
Cinnamon Powder
Sucralose
Direction
Whisk all the dry ingredients on a medium bowl
Add egg white then stir with a spatula, until combines and a rough dough formed
Add sour cream and switch using hand to combine and knead just until a the dough start to become elastic
Refrigerate the dough for 1 hour, then divide into 2 equal size
Flatten each dough using roller pin, into squares with 1/2 inch thickness
Cut each dough into stripes with 1/4 inch width, to get at least 12 – 15 stripes per dough
Arrange the stripes like a wood stack, by lining 4 – 5 stripes vertically, then lining second 4 – 5 stripes horizontally and finished with lining the last 4 – 5 stripes vertically again
Fold each dough stripes from one side to the other side, just like closing a book. Then wrap the stripes into a balls by pressing them using palms, but not to tight, just lightly squeeze them to collide and making a seam on the stripes end junction
Deep fry each dough balls, until golden brown on one side, then turn over and fry the other side until golden brown all over
Drain with paper towel, and dust them with cinnamon powder and sucralose
Serve with black coffee or green tea

The Keto Iron Chef's Keto-Schneeballen

(Germans Fried Snowballs Cake)

THE KETO IRON CHEF'S KETO-PAPADUMS INDIAN FRIED WAFER DOUGH

The Keto Iron Chef's Keto-Papadums Indian Fried Wafer Dough Servings=4 Time=4:30 hrs (including rest time)
Ingredients
Dry Ingredients
15g Casein Protein Isolate Hardcore Micellar Casein
10g Isopure Whey Protein Isolate, Unflavored
5g Dried Egg Whites
5g Egg Yolk Powder
15g Inulin Fiber (Chicory Root) – LC Foods
15g Psyllium Husk
1g Xanthan Gum
1g Salt
0,5g Garlic Powder
0,3g Cumin Powder
0,3g Pepper Powder
5g Golden Flax Seeds
* Note : The first 7 ingredients above are the Keto-Flour formula for this recipe
For crisper crust the Keto-Flour can be changed into this formula : 45g Wheat Protein Isolate 8000, 30g Casein Protein Isolate, 15g Whey Protein Isolate, 15g Egg White Powder, 15g Egg Yolk Powder, 30g Inulin Powder
Wet Ingredients
20g Water
6g Virgin Coconut Oil
Direction
Whisk all dry ingredients on a medium bowl. Add water and stir using spatula until a rough dough formed
Switch using hand to knead the dough until elastic.
Add the coconut oil and knead again until smooth
Divide the dough into 2 equal parts. Then roll each dough with a circular movement using rolling pin, until a very thin transparent dough are formed
Dry the rolled dough on a direct sunlight for 3 – 4 hours, until the dough became stiff. But watch and feel the dough as to not become too dry, because it tends to crack if it's too dry
* Frying Method (called Pappa Am)
Deep fry the flattened dough with high heat on a frying pan just for 5 – 10 seconds, just until the dough starts to brown
* Grilling Method (called Appal Am)
Using a slightly greased non stick frying pan, grill the dough with very low heat until the surface starts to become white, then flip to the other side to cook evenly
The original cooking method for grilling is by heating the dough directly over the stove with low heat, until the surface become white evenly on both side
Serve with curry dishes or as a snack

KETO-IRON CHEF'S KETO-LEMON CURD TARTLETS

Keto-Iron Chef's Keto-Lemon Curd Tartlets Servings=6-8 Time=60mins
Keto-Lemon Curd Tartlets
(Lemon Curd with Ketofied Pastry Dough)
(2 – 3 serving size)
Ingredients
* For Pastry Dough
Dry Ingredients
30g Casein Protein Isolate
20g Whey Protein Isolate
10g Egg White Powder
10g Egg Yolk Powder
30g Inulin Powder
3g Psyllium Husk
2g Xanthan Gum
2g Salt
2g Vanilla Extract
5g Sweetener
* Note : These ingredients are the Keto-Flour formula for this recipe
Wet Ingredients
15g Egg Yolk
25g Yogurt
20g Water
* For Pastry Batter
Dry Ingredients
50g Keto-Flour (half the quantity from the Keto-Flour formula listed above)
1g Salt
1g Vanilla Extract
3g Sweetener
Wet Ingredients
40g Butter
* For Lemon Curd
Dry Ingredients
50g Egg
15g Egg Yolk
2 tsp Sweetener
1 tsp Lemon Rind (Finely Grated)
2 tbsp Lemon Juice
50g Butter
Direction
* For Pastry Dough
Whisk all dry ingredients on a medium bowl. Add egg yolk and yogurt gradually, then stir using spatula until a rough dough formed, then switch using hand to knead the dough until elastic. Add water and knead again until smooth
Transfer the dough into a slicone pad, then divide the dough into 2 equal size,
Take one of the dough, flat the dough using roller pin, then fold each side to the center of the dough
Roll the back into rectangle, the fold the rough sides back into the center. Roll it again once more to make a smooth rectangle shape
Repeat these step to the other dough. See the attached pics for more details
Roll each dough up to stage 5 – 6 setting on the pasta machine, into a long sheet. Rest the rolled dough for 10 minutes

* For Pastry Batter
On a small bowl, combine Keto-Flour with butter using spatula, until a rough batter formed
Rest the batter for 5 minutes at the refrigerator
* For Lemon Curd
Place egg, egg yolk, sugar, lemon rind and lemon juice in a heavy-based saucepan
Whisk to combine. Add butter. Place over medium heat. Cook, whisking, for 7 to 8 minutes or until mixture coats the back of a spoon
Remove from heat. Stand for 5 minutes. Pour into a small bowl. Cover surface with plastic wrap. Set aside to cool completely.
* Assemble
Preheat the oven into 300F
On a silicone pad, spread the pastry batter evenly over each rolled dough
Fold the rolled dough from one side to the other side, making at least 4 – 5 fold into a square shape
Roll the folded dough to flatten it into 1/2 cm thick, by keep maintaining the square shape during rolling
Slice the dough into 4 with equal width, then arrange them into 6 – 8 holes muffin pan
(see the attached pics)
Bake the dough for 15 – 20 minutes, until light golden then cool in the pan for 10 minutes
Transfer to a wire rack to cool completely. Then spoon the lemon curd evenly onto each tartlets
Serve with black coffee or green tea

KETO IRON CHEF'S KETO-NEW YORK STYLE CHEESECAKE

Keto-Iron Chef's Keto-New York Style Cheesecake Servings=6-8 Time=60mins
(Rich & Creamy New York Style Cheesecake)
6 – 8 serving size
Ingredients
* Crust Base
1 cup Crushed Keto-Ritz Cracker
3 tbsp Melted Butter
Note : Refer to this link below for Keto-Ritz Cracker Recipe

Keto Ritz Crackers
* Filling
5 (8oz) packages cream cheese, softened
4oz Keto-Sugar (2oz Sweetener + 2oz Inulin Powder)
5 large eggs
1/2 cup Heavy Cream
3 tbsp Keto-Flour (1 tbsp Casein Protein Isolate + 1 tbsp Pea Protein Isolate + 1 tbsp Inulin Powder)
2 large egg yolks
1 tsp vanilla extract
Grated rind of one lemon
Direction
Make the base by mixing the crushed Keto-Ritz Cracker and butter and press into the bottom of an 8" or 9" springform pan
Place in preheated oven for 5 to 7 minutes until the edges are just beginning to color. Remove from oven and allow to cool
In the bowl of a large stand mixer, beat the cream cheese until smooth, then add the Keto-Sugar
Scrape down the sides of the bowl with a rubber spatula, then add the remaining ingredients: eggs, cream, Keto-Flour, yolks, vanilla and rind
Beat well for about 5 minutes, stopping occasionally to scrape down the sides of the bowl
Pour cheesecake batter into the the springform pan with the cooled base and bake for 12 minutes (see oven temp change above), then lower oven temperature to 300°F (150°C) and continue to bake for another 35 minutes
At the end of this cooking time, turn off the oven, but allow the cheesecake to remain in the oven for another 30 minutes
Remove cheesecake from the oven and cool in the pan on a wire rack. When completely cool, cover and refrigerate overnight or a minimum of 6 hours.
To Serve: Remove cheesecake from fridge and run a knife along the side of the tin, then remove the the springform side.
Place onto a serving plate and top with your choice of Keto Compatible toppings

THE KETO IRON CHEF MAKES KETO-CHINESE SWISS ROLL (CHINESE PANDAN SWISS ROLL)

Keto-Chinese Swiss Roll (Chinese Pandan Swiss Roll) Servings=8-10 Time=60mins

Ingredients
* For The Batter
Dry Ingredients
24g Isopure Whey Protein Isolate, Unflavored
16g Isopure Whey Protein Isolate, Unflavored
8g Dried Egg Whites
8g Egg Yolk Powder
24g Inulin Fiber (Chicory Root) – LC Foods
6g Sucralose
5g Vanilla Extract
* Note : For lighter crumb the Keto-Flour Mix can be changed into this formula : 24g Wheat Protein Isolate 8000, 16g Casein Protein Isolate, 8g Whey Protein Isolate, 8g Egg White Powder, 8g Egg Yolk Powder, 16g Inulin Powder, 5g Sucralose, 5g Vanilla Extract
Wet Ingredients
60g Egg Yolk
35g Coconut Milk
35g Virgin Coconut Oil
5g Pandan Leaves Extract
* For The Meringue
180g Egg White
18g Sucralose
* For The Filling
150g Heavy Whipping Cream
50g Cream Cheese
15g Sucralose
Direction
Preheat the oven into 300F
Whisk and sift all the dry ingredients together on medium bowl, set aside
Beat egg yolk on a standing mixer with low speed until creamy
Mix the pandan essence with coconut milk, then add into the egg yolk mixtures until combine
Add coconut oil then raise the mixer speed, until the batter become creamy and light
Lower the mixer speed, then spoon the dry ingredients into the batter gradually until thicken. Remove the batter into another bowl, set aside
* For The Meringue
Wash the used mixer bowl and the paddle attachment thoroughly, then wipe with a towel until completely dry
Beat the egg white with the cleaned mixer bowl and attachment, until stiff peak
Fold in 1/3 egg white mixture into the batter using rubber spatula to combine, then fold the rest of the egg white at once and stir until completely combined
Line the baking pan (25 x 25 x 10 cm) with a parchment paper, then cut the 4 corners of the paper to create a smooth overlap between the paper
Spread the batter evenly, with approximately 2 cm height, then knock the bottom of the pan several time to get rid any large bubbles on the cake surface
Bake for 15 minutes. When the cake surface feel bouncy when slightly pressed, then it's done
* For The Filling
Beat whipping cream, cream cheese and sucralose together on a standing mixer until creamy, then remove into another bowl, set aside
* Assemble & Shaping
Carefully remove the cake onto a work table, and let the cake cools for 5 minutes, but would still warm enough to be pliable
Cover the cake surface with another parchment paper, then carefully flip the cake to the other side
Peel the previous baked parchment paper then spread the filling mixtures evenly over the cake surface

To roll the cake up, taking out a rolling pin and place it underneath the parchment paper your cake is sitting on. Slowly roll the parchment paper onto the rolling pin one side as you roll up the cake on the other. Essentially, you're using the rolling pin to push the cake forward as you roll. At the same time, you're using the pin to roll up the loose parchment paper
Refrigerate for 1 hour, then slice the cake into 10 slice and serve with black coffee or green tea

THE KETO IRON CHEF'S KETO-CHURROS (SPANISH FRIED DOUGH)

The Keto Iron Chef's Keto-Churros (Spanish Fried Dough) Servings=2 Time=30mins
Starter & Fermented Batter Method
Ingredients
For Keto-Flour Mix
24gMicellar Casein
16g Isopure Whey Protein Isolate, Unflavored
8g Dried Egg Whites
8g Egg Yolk Powder
24g Inulin Fiber (Chicory Root) – LC Foods
2,4g Psyllium Husk
1,6g Xanthan Gum
1,5g Baking Powder
1g Salt
2,5g Cinnamon Powder
4g Sucralose
(Whisk & sift all these ingredients together)
* For Preferment Batter (Starter)
30g Keto-Flour Mix
30g Coconut Milk
1g Instant Dry Yeast
* For Churros Batter
50g Keto-Flour Mix
2g Instant Dry Yeast
90g Whipped Egg White (soft peak)
30g Egg Yolk
50g Butter
* For Dusting
Cinnamon Powder
Sucralose
Direction
* For Preferment Batter (Starter)
On a medium bowl, combine 30g Keto-Flour Mix, instant dry yeast and coconut milk together.
Stir using spatula until a thick batter formed
Rest the batter for 20 – 30 minutes until double in size
* For Churros Batter
On a food processor, mix butter and egg yolks until fluffy
Combine the egg yolk mixture with Keto-Flour Mix on a medium bowl, then stir with a spatula until a thick batter formed
Pour the batter onto the risen starter batter then stir using spatula to combine
Add in the whipped egg white to the batter, and stir again into a very thick batter
Rest the batter for another 20 minutes. The batter should rise again to almost double and will have many holes inside
Remove the batter into a piping bag
Deep fry the batter by squirting the batter over a hot frying oil, making 8 – 10cm line
Flip the Churros when the bottom has turn golden brown and cook until both side are done

Fry only 2 – 3 Churros at a time, so it will be easier to flip the batter during frying and also prevent the Churros batter from sticking to each other
Drain the fried Churros using a spider strainer, then use the paper towel the remove excess oil
Generously dust the fried Churros with cinnamon powder and sucralose, and serve right away while they're still warm

THE KETO IRON CHEF'S KETO-ROTI BOY AKA KETO-MEXICAN COFFEE BUN (SINGAPORE COFFEE COOKIE BUN)

Keto-Roti Boy aka Keto-Mexican Coffee Bun Servings=4 Time=60mins
Starter & Dough Method with Tang Zhong (Water Roux) Combination
Ingredients
* For Keto-Flour Mix
45g Micellar Casein
30g Isopure Whey Protein Isolate, Unflavored
15g Dried Egg Whites
15g Egg Yolk Powder
45g Inulin Fiber (Chicory Root) – LC Foods
8g Psyllium Husk
3g Xanthan Gum
3g Salt
1,5g Vanilla Extract
6g Sucralose
(Whisk & sift all these ingredients together)
* Note : For softer crumb the Keto-Flour Mix can be changed into this formula : 45g Wheat Protein Isolate 8000, 30g Casein Protein Isolate, 15g Whey Protein Isolate, 15g Egg White Powder, 15g Egg Yolk Powder, 30g Inulin Powder, 3g Salt, 1,5g Vanilla Extract, 6g Sucralose
* For Liquid Mix
30g Heavy Whipping Cream
5g Cider Vinegar
30g Water
(Stir & combine all these ingredients together)
* For Tang Zhong (Water Roux)
5g Keto-Flour Mix
25g Water
* For Preferment Batter (Starter)
50g Keto-Flour Mix
50g Liquid Mix
1,5g Instant Dry Yeast
* For Roti Boy Dough (Dough)
30g Egg
15g Liquid Mix
3g Instant Dry Yeast
15g Butter
The Rest of the Keto-Flour Mix
Tang Zhong
Preferment Dough
* For Cookies Batter Topping
Dry Ingredients
15g Inulin Fiber (Chicory Root) – LC Foods
15g Micellar Casein

10g Isopure Whey Protein Isolate, Unflavored

5g Dried Egg Whites

5g Egg Yolk Powder

1g Xanthan Gum

3g Instant Expresso Coffee Powder

1,5g Salt

1g Vanilla Extract

12g Sucralose

Wet Ingredients

10g Egg Yolk

50g Butter

* For Roti Boy Filling

50g Grated Cheddar Cheese

25g Butter

5g Sucralose

Direction

* For Tang Zhong

On a small sauce pan, combine 5g of Keto-Flour Mix with 25g of water, then stir using rubber spatula until there is no more lumps

Heat the mixture over a stove with a very low heat, and stir using rubber spatula until the mixture just starting to thicken and leaving a trail behind the rubber spatula

Turn off the heat and set aside. Let the Tang Zhong mixture cool on a room temperature spot for at least 10 minutes

* For Preferment Dough

On a medium bowl, combine 50g Keto-Flour Mix, 1,5g Instant Dry Yeast, and 50g Liquid Mix

Stir the batter using spatula to combines, until the batter become very thick

Rest the batter on a warm spot for 20 minutes, using plastic wrap to cover bowl so that the dough skin won't dry out

The batter should rise to double in size, and the surface will start to crack

* For Cookies Batter Topping

Whisk and sift all the dry ingredients together on a small bowl, set aside

On a standing mixer with low speed (stage 1), beat butter until white and creamy

Add egg yolk, then raise into medium speed (stage 2), until the batter become light and fluffy

Lower into low speed (stage 1) back, and spoon the dry ingredients into the batter, just until combine (do not over mix)

Remove the batter into piping bag with a round pastry tip, set aside

* For Roti Boy Filling

On a small bowl, combine grated cheddar cheese, sucralose and butter using fork

Divide the mixture into 5 equal size inside the bowl, then refrigerate until it's being used

* Assemble

Combine the rest of the Keto-Flour Mix with 3g Instant Dry Yeast, then pour over the risen Preferment dough on the mixer bowl

Using dough hook attachment (spiral hook), add in 30g egg and the cooled Tang Zhong mixture to the mixer bowl.

Mix at low speed (stage 1) until combines and a rough dough formed

Add in 15g Liquid Mix (the rest of the Liquid Mix) gradually, then raise the mixer speed into medium speed (stage 2) until combines and the dough start to look smooth but almost tack free if it's touched

Add 15g of softened butter, then raise the mixer speed into high speed (stage 3). Mix until the dough becomes very elastic and leaving no scrap on the mixer bowl (use spatula to scrap the mixer bowl side wall to adhere any sticking dough pieces into the main dough)

Turn off the mixer, and remove the dough onto a silicone pad

* Shaping the Buns

Knead the dough for a while until the surface becomes very smooth and dry, then shape into a round disc

Divide the dough into 5 equal parts, and shape them into balls

Roll out each dough into circles (1/2 inch thick) using roller pin, then arrange the refrigerated filling to the center of each circles

Shape each circles by wrapping the filling and seaming the dough back into balls

Arrange each buns on a cookies baking pan with the seam facing downward

Rest the buns for another 15 minutes on a warm spot, using plastic wrap to cover the buns

Preheat the oven into 300F

Check the buns readiness to bake, by finger pressing the risen buns. It should still bounce back quick but will leave a slight finger mark

Pipe the cookies batter onto the center of each risen buns, making a uniform spiral pattern

Bake for 20 minutes until the side of the buns starts to turn golden brown

Let the buns cools on the baking pan for 10 minutes before removing them into a wire rack

Serve the coffee buns while still warm with black coffee or green tea

THE KETO IRON CHEF'S KETO-MANTOU ROLLS (CHINESE STEAMED ROLLS)

The Keto Iron Chef's Keto-Mantou Rolls (Chinese Steamed Rolls) Servings=4 Time=60mins
Keto-Mantou Rolls
(Chinese Steamed Rolls)
Ingredients
* For Keto-Flour Mix

30g Micellar Casein
20g Isopure Whey Protein Isolate, Unflavored
10g Dried Egg Whites
10g Egg Yolk Powder
30g Inulin Fiber (Chicory Root) – LC Foods
5g Psyllium Husk
2g Xanthan Gum
2g Salt
1g Vanilla Extract
5g Sucralose
(Whisk & sift all these ingredients together)
* Note : For softer crumb the Keto-Flour Mix can be changed into this formula : 90g Wheat Protein Isolate 8000, 60g Casein Protein Isolate, 30g Whey Protein Isolate, 30g Egg White Powder, 30g Egg Yolk Powder, 60g Inulin Powder, 6g Salt, 3g Vanilla Extract, 15g Sucralose
* For Liquid Mix
20g Coconut Milk
5g Cider Vinegar
50g Water
(Stir & combine all these ingredients together)
* For Preferment Batter (Starter)
35g Keto-Flour Mix
30g Liquid Mix
1g Instant Dry Yeast
* For Mantou Dough
40g Liquid Mix
2g Instant Dry Yeast
The Rest of the Keto-Flour Mix
Preferment Dough
* For Chocolate Paste
10g Cocoa Powder
2g Sucralose
10g Butter
(Mix all these ingredients together into a paste)
Direction
* For Preferment Batter (Starter)
Combine 30g Keto-Flour Mix with 30g of Liquid Mix on a medium bowl. Stir using spatula until a thick batter formed (Starter)
Rest the Starter for 30 minutes until double in size and the surface starts to crack
* For Mantou Dough
Add the rest of the Keto-Flour Mix and instant dry yeast into the risen Starter bowl.
Add the Liquid Mix gradually by stirring to combine.
Switch using hand to mix and knead the dough, until it becomes elastic and smooth
Divide the dough into 2 equal size
Mix one of the divided dough with the chocolate paste mixture using spatula. Then switch using hand to knead it once more until the chocolate paste completely combines into the dough
Roll each dough into equal rectangles shape
Lay the chocolate dough over the Mantou dough, then roll once more until it reach 1/2 inch thick
Fold the Mantou dough into a log, from the longest side of the dough (just like folding a cinnamon rolls)
Pinch the edges to make a seam, then divide the log into 10 Mantou rolls
Rest the Mantou rolls for another 15 – 20 minutes until it double in size.
The dough surface should still bounce back a bit when pressed with a finger, and leave a slight marks on the surface

Steam the Mantou rolls for 10 – 15 minutes using low medium heat on a steamer pan, or you can use a rice cooker with steamer option features
Serve with black coffee or green tea

KETO-IRON CHEF'S KETO-GINGER SNAP COOKIES

Keto-Iron Chef's Keto-Ginger Snap Cookies Servings=1-2
Time=60mins
1 – 2 Serving Size
Ingredients
Dry Ingredients
20g Inulin Powder
20g Casein Protein Isolate
10g Whey Protein Isolate or Pea Protein Isolate
1g Xanthan Gum
1g Salt
2,5g Ground Ginger
2g Baking Soda
1g Cinnamon Powder
Wet Ingredient
10g Sour Cream
20g Sukrin Fiber Syrup Gold
40g Butter
* Keto-Sugar
5g Sweetener
5g Inulin Powder
* Keto-Cinnamon Sugar
5g Cinnamon Powder
5g Inulin Powder
10g Sweetener

Direction
Preheat oven to 350 degrees F (175 degrees C)
Sift all the dry ingredients into a mixing bowl. Stir the
mixture to blend evenly, and sift a second time into
another bowl
Place the butter and keto-sugar into a mixing bowl and
beat until creamy. Gradually beat in the sour cream, and
sukrin fiber syrup
Add 1/3 of the flour mixture into the butter mixture; stir to
thoroughly blend. Sift in the remaining Keto-Flour mixture,
and mix together until a soft dough forms
Pinch off small amounts of dough and roll into 1 inch
diameter balls between your hands. Roll each ball in Keto-
Cinnamon Sugar, and place 2 inches apart on an ungreased
baking sheet

Flat each cookies balls using your palm, into 1/4 inch thick
Bake in preheated oven until the tops are rounded and slightly cracked, about 15 minutes
Cool cookies on a wire rack. Store in an air tight container

KETO-IRON CHEF'S KETO-SHORTBREAD

Keto-Iron Chef's Keto-Shortbread Servings=1-2 Time=60mins

1 – 2 Serving Size

Ingredients

Dry Ingredients

20g Inulin Powder

20g Casein Protein Isolate

10g Whey Protein Isolate or Pea Protein Isolate

1g Xanthan Gum

1g Salt

2g Vanilla Extract

(Whisk and sift all these ingredients together as the Keto-Flour)

Wet Ingredient

35g Butter
* Keto-Sugar
5g Sweetener
5g Inulin Powder
Direction
Preheat oven to 350 degrees F (175 degrees C)
Sift all the dry ingredients into a mixing bowl. Stir the mixture to blend evenly, and sift a second time into another bowl
Place the butter and keto-sugar into a mixing bowl and beat until creamy
Stir in the Keto-Flour to get a smooth paste. Turn on to a work surface and gently roll out until the paste is 1cm thick
Cut into rounds or fingers and place onto a baking tray, then poke a hole using fork to each cookies dough
Sprinkle with sweetener and chill in the fridge for 20 minutes
Bake in the oven for 15-20 minutes, or until pale golden-brown. Set aside to cool on a wire rack

KETO-IRON CHEF'S KETO-FLAN

Keto-Iron Chef's Keto-Flan Servings=1-2 Time=60mins
(Spanish Baked Custard Caramel with Fiber Syrup – Isomaltooligosaccharide / IMO)
1 – 2 Serving Size

Ingredient
1 Large Egg
1 Egg Yolk
1/2 Cup Heavy Cream
1/3 Cup Coconut Milk
1 tsp Vanilla Extract
2 tbsp Sweetener
2 tbsp Inulin Powder
1/4 cup Sukrin Fiber Syrup Gold
Direction
Preheat oven to 350F
In a large bowl, beat eggs. Beat in heavy cream, coconut milk, vanilla extract and sweetener until smooth
In a small bowl, combine inulin powder and sukrin fiber syrup gold. Stir to dissolve into thick syrup consistency
pour the syrup into a 5 inch round glass baking dish, turning the dish to evenly coat the bottom and sides
Refrigerate the syrup for 15 minutes, then pour the egg mixture into the baking dish
Bake in preheated oven 60 minutes. Let cool completely
To serve, carefully invert on serving plate with edges when completely cool

KETO-IRON CHEF'S KETO-BANNOCK

Keto-Iron Chef's Keto-Bannock Servings=1-2 Time=60mins

(Yeasted Native American Quick Bread)

1 – 2 Serving Size

Ingredient

10g Casein Protein Isolate

10g Whey Protein Isolate

5g Egg White Powder

10g Egg Yolk Powder

15g Inulin Powder

1g Salt

5g Sweetener

2g Instant Dry Yeast

(Whisk & sift all these ingredients together)

Wet Ingredients

50g Butter Milk or Coconut Milk

Filling Ingredients

30g Grated Cheddar Cheese

30g Lemon Zest

30g Diced Roasted Almonds

Topping

Cinnamon Powder

Sweetener

Direction

Whisk all the dry ingredients on a medium bowl

Add the buttermilk gradually by keep stirring and folding with spatula until the batter become very thick

Fold in the filling ingredients into the mixture

Shape the dough into round and rest the dough in a warm spot for 30 minutes, using plastic wrap to cover the bowl

Use a pastry cutter or a knife to divide the rested dough into 6 squares, then deep fry them with low medium heat until the surface turns golden brown

Drain the fried Keto-Bannock with a spider strainer, then use paper towel to remove the excess oil

Generously dust them with cinnamon powder and sweetener

Serve with black coffee or green tea

KETO-IRON CHEF'S KETO-TRES LECHES

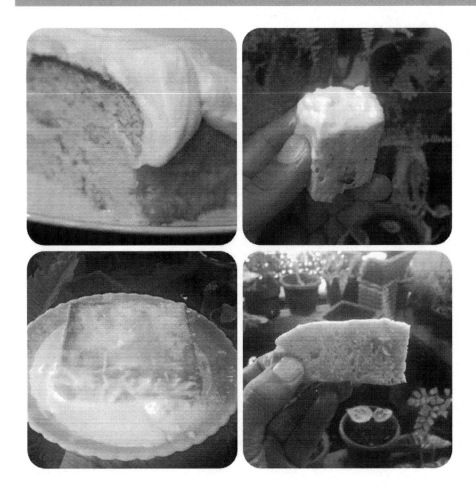

Keto-Iron Chef's Keto-Tres Leches Servings=4-6 Time=60mins
(Spanish Milk Cake)
4 – 6 Serving Size
Ingredients
Dry Ingredients
30g Inulin Powder
20g Casein Protein Isolate
20g Whey Protein Isolate
15g Egg White Powder
15g Egg Yolk Powder
1g Salt
5g Baking Powder
3g Vanilla Extract
(Whisk & sift all these ingredients together as a Keto-Flour Mix)
Wet Ingredient
3 Large Egg Yolk
3 Large Egg White
100g Butter
* For Keto-Sugar Mix
15g Inulin Powder

15g Sweetener
* For Meringue
3 Large Egg White
1/8 tsp Cream of Tartar
* For Filling
1 tsp Butter
1/2 cup Coconut Milk
1/2 cup Heavy Cream
1/4 cup Sukrin Fiber Syrup Gold
2 tbsp Sweetener
1 tsp Vanilla Extract
* For Topping
1 cup Heavy Whipping Cream
1 tbsp Sweetener
1 tsp Vanilla Extract
Direction
Whisk and sift all dry ingredients together on a medium bowl, set aside
On a standing mixer with a paddle attachment, beat butter and Keto-Sugar Mix on low speed until pale.
Add egg yolk gradually by raising the speed into medium speed, until creamy and light
Lower the mixer speed back into the lowest speed, then spoon in 1/3 of the dry ingredients
Turn off the mixer then spoon the rest of the dry ingredients onto the mixer bowl and stir with a spatula until completely combined and the batter becomes smooth without no lumps
Remove the batter into another bowl, set aside
Wash the mixer bowl and the paddle attachment until clean thoroughly without any greasy residues left on the mixer bowl and at the paddle attachment, then use to whip the egg white
Preheat the oven into 300F
Beat the egg white on the standing mixer on low speed about 2 – 3 minutes until soft peak
Sprinkle cream of tartar over the meringue, then raise the mixer into medium speed, until hard peak
Turn off the mixer, then scoop 1/3 of the meringue into the batter and fold with a spatula until just combines. then pour the rest of the batter and fold again until completely combines. The batter will become light and fluffy at this stage
Pour the batter onto a lightly greased baking pan (you can use any shape of pan mould that you like, but make sure that the batter will fill at least 1/3 of the pan mould volume)
Bake for 30 minutes. Insert a tooth pick to check the cake whether the cake has done or not. The tooth pick should comes out clean when the cake is done
Melt the butter on a small sauce pan then pour the coconut milk, heavy cream and sukrin fiber syrup. Stir to combine
When the mixture starts to bubbles, add in inulin powder, vanilla extract and sweetener. Stir until the mixture thickens
Turn off the oven, then remove the cake. Let the cake cools for 10 – 15 minutes before removing it onto a serving plate
Pour the milk mixture over the cake, and refrigerate for at least 2 hours
Whip the heavy whipping cream, sweetener and vanilla extract on a standing mixer until soft peak
Spread the whip cream over the cake evenly, then slice and serve as a Keto-Dessert

KETO IRON CHEF TAKES ON KETO-APPLE STRUDLE

Keto Iron Chef takes on Keto-Apple Strudle Servings=2-3 Time=45mins
(Viennese Apple Strudel using "Juicy" Mexican Yam Bean / Jicama / Xicama)
2 – 3 Serving Size
* Refer to this Link for Mexican Yam Bean
https://en.m.wikipedia.org/wiki/Pachyrhizus_erosus
Ingredients
* For Strudel Dough

Dry Ingredients

15g Micellar Casein

10g Isopure Whey Protein Isolate, Unflavored

5g Dried Egg Whites

5g Egg Yolk Powder

15g Inulin Fiber (Chicory Root) – LC Foods

2g Psyllium Husk

1g Xanthan Gum Powder

1g Salt

1g Vanilla Extract

3g Sweetener

* Note : The first 7 ingredients above are the Keto-Flour formula for this recipe

For more chewy noodles the Keto-Flour can be changed into this formula : 15g Wheat Protein Isolate 8000, 10g Casein Protein Isolate, 10g Whey Protein Isolate, 5g Egg White Powder, 5g Egg Yolk Powder, 5g Inulin Powder

Wet Ingredients

15g Egg

15g Water

3g Coconut Oil

* For Strudel Filling

80g Sliced Mexican Yam Bean (Jicama / Xicama)

Nutrition Fact for 80g Yam Bean

(3g Net Carb : 0,6g Protein : 0g Fat : 30 Cal)

http://nutritiondata.self.com/.../vegetables-and-veget.../2727/2

15g Butter

30g Roasted Almond Flour

(fry the almond flour without oil on a skillet with low heat until brown)

2g Cinnamon Powder

2g Sweetener

Direction

* For Strudel Dough

Whisk all dry ingredients on a medium bowl. Add egg and stir using spatula until a rough dough formed

Add water gradually then switch using hand to knead the dough until elastic

Add coconut oil and knead the dough until the surface become smooth

Shape the dough into round, then rest for 15 minutes

Roll the dough into an oval shape using roller pin, then fold each side into the center

Roll again into a large rectangle shape, and the dough becomes very thin and transparent

Rest the rolled dough for 1 hour, until almost dry to the touch

* For Strudel Filling

Peel the yam bean, quarter and core it. Chop every quarter into 1/8 to 1/4 inch thick slices

Mix butter and roasted almond flour on a small bowl into paste

Add cinnamon powder and sweetener into the almond paste, stir to combine

* Assemble

Preheat the oven into 300F

Brush one half of the rolled dough with melted butter, spread the almond paste on the other side

Spread the chopped yam beans over the almond paste, leaving 1 to 1,5 inch to the edge

Fold in the sides so the filling won't get lost during rolling

Roll the dough over the filling, starting at the yam bean top end, lifting the filling's weight with your hand carefully

Roll the dough carefully into a log, then transfer the dough onto a greased baking pan, seam-side down

Brush the dough surface with melted butter, and bake for 15 – 20 minutes until the crust turns golden brown

Let cool slightly then cut the Keto-Apple Strudel into 6 slices

Serve with generous dust of sweetener

KETO-IRON CHEF'S PERFECT POUND CAKE

Keto-Iron Chef's Perfect Pound Cake Servings=4-6 Time=60mins
(Keto-Iron Chef Basic Buttery, Fluffy & Moist Pound Cake Recipe)
4 – 6 Serving Size
* This basic pound cake can be use for many variety of fluffy Keto-Cake with different filling and topping
Ingredients
* For Basic Pound Cake Batter
Dry Ingredients
30g Inulin Fiber (Chicory Root) – LC Foods
30g Micellar Casein
10g Isopure Whey Protein Isolate, Unflavored
10g Dried Egg Whites
10g Egg Yolk Powder
3g Xanthan Gum Powder
1g Salt
4g Baking Powder
#Optional Dry Ingredients#
3g – 5g Essence (Vanilla, Pandan, Chocolate, Green Tea, etc)
5g – 10g Dry Powder (Cocoa Powder, Buttermilk Powder, Green Tea Powder, etc)
Wet Ingredient
50g Egg Yolks
100g Butter
50g – 100g Liquid (Coconut Milk, Heavy Cream, Buttermilk, Creme Fraiche, Yogurt, Sour Cream, etc) ; The higher the liquids, the lighter the cake
#Optional Wet Ingredients#
50g – 100g Soft Cheese (Cream Cheese, Ricotta, Mascarpone, etc)
3g – 5g Liquid Essence or Food Grade Colorant
* For Keto-Sugar Mix
20g Inulin Fiber (Chicory Root) – LC Foods
10g – 20g Sweetener (Sucralose, Erythritol, Xylitol, Stevia (concentrated – use 1tsp=1cup) * This one is good too. * I test with bulk using this, can be used with listed measurement, Inulin, Monk Fruit/Luo Han Guo, etc)
* For Meringue
200g Egg White
2,5g Cream of Tartar
* Optional Filling
20g – 30g Dry Filling
Nuts (Almond/Pecan/Hazelnut/Walnut, etc), Hard Cheese (grated Cheddar, Parmesan, etc), Dessicated Coconut, Unsweetened Dried Berries, Low Carb Chocolate Chips, etc
* Optional Topping
Cream Cheese Frosting
150g Cream Cheese
50g Butter
10g Vanilla Extract
20g Sweetener
2g – 3g Food Colorant (Optional)
(Beat all these ingredients together then transfer into a piping bag with preferred nozzle pattern)
Direction
* For Basic Pound Cake Batter
Whisk and sift all dry ingredients together on a medium bowl, set aside. At this stage, you can add any essences or dry powder ingredients, such as cocoa powder

On a standing mixer with a paddle attachment, beat butter and Keto-Sugar Mix on low speed until pale.

Add egg yolk and soft cheese (optional) gradually by raising the speed into medium speed, until creamy and light

Add the liquid mixture onto the batter, and raise the mixer into high speed, until creamy and thick

Lower the mixer speed back into the lowest speed, then spoon in 1/3 of the dry ingredients. The batter will be thick and lumpy at this stage

Turn off the mixer then spoon the rest of the dry ingredients onto the mixer bowl and stir with a spatula until completely combined and the batter becomes smooth without no lumps

Optional – add liquid essences or food grade colorant at this stage to create many variety of cakes such as Red Velvet Cake

Remove the batter into another bowl, set aside

Wash the mixer bowl and the paddle attachment until clean thoroughly without any greasy residues left on the mixer bowl and at the paddle attachment, then use to whip the egg white

Preheat the oven into 300F

* For The Meringue

Beat the egg white on the standing mixer on low speed about 2 – 3 minutes until soft peak

Sprinkle cream of tartar over the meringue, then raise the mixer into medium speed, until hard peak

Turn off the mixer, then scoop 1/3 of the meringue into the batter and fold with a spatula until just combines. then pour the rest of the batter and fold again until completely combines. The batter will become light and fluffy at this stage

Fold in the dry filling of your choice into the batter, and stir until evenly distributed

pour the batter onto a lightly greased baking pan (you can use any shape of pan mould that you like, but make sure that the batter will fill at least 1/3 of the pan mould volume)

Bake for 45 – 50 minutes. Insert a tooth pick to check the cake whether the cake has done or not. The tooth pick should comes out clean when the cake is done

Turn off the oven, then remove the cake. Let the pound cake cools for 10 – 15 minutes before removing it onto a serving plate

At this stage you can top the cake with anything that you want, such as with cream cheese frosting

THE KETO IRON CHEF SHARES HIS KETO-BATAGOR (INDONESIAN FRIED DUMPLING)

Keto-Batagor (Indonesian Fried Dumpling) Servings=2-3 Time=30mins

Ingredients

* For Batagor Dough

Dry Ingredients

15g Micellar Casein

10g Isopure Whey Protein Isolate, Unflavored

5g Dried Egg Whites

5g Egg Yolk Powder

15g Inulin Fiber (Chicory Root) – LC Foods

1,5g Psyllium Husk

1g Xanthan Gum Powder

1,5g Salt

1g Garlic Powder

* Note : The first 7 ingredients above are the Keto-Flour formula for this recipe

Wet Ingredients

10g Egg

20g Sour Cream

3g Butter

* For Batagor Filling

50g Keto-Flour (refer to the Keto-Flour formula listed above)

120g Mackerel (softened on a food processor)

30g Egg Yolk

2,5g Salt
1g Garlic Powder
1g Pepper
Optional – Sliced Scallion & Diced Onion
* For Batagor Dipping Batter
25g Keto-Flour (half the quantity of the Keto-Flour Formula listed above)
30g Egg
50g Water
* For Batagor Peanut Butter Sauce
100g Natural Peanut Butter
80g Water
2 cloves Garlic (grounded)
3 pcs Red Chillies (diced)
2g Salt
5g Sucralose
(Mix all these ingredients on a food processor)
Direction
* For Batagor Dough
Whisk all dry ingredients on a medium bowl. Add egg and sour cream gradually, then stir using spatula until a rough dough formed, then switch using hand to knead the dough until elastic. Add the softened butter and knead again until smooth
Shape the dough into a balls, then flaten the dough using rolling pin on a silicone pad. Fold the vertical edges to the center, turn 90 degree then roll it again. Repeat the steps one more time until forming a rectangle with a smooth edges
Then using a pasta machine, roll the dough into stage 5 – 6 setting on the pasta machine
Rest the rolled dough for 10 minutes, before cutting
* For Batagor Filling
On a medium bowl, whisk 50g of Keto-Flour with the seasoning.
Combine the softened mackerel with the flour using spatula, until a rough dough formed
Add the egg yolk and stir again to combine, until a tacky thick batter formed, set aside
Optional – Add sliced scallion & diced onion into the batter
* For Batagor Dipping Batter
On a medium bowl, combine 25g of Keto-Flour, egg and water
Stir to combine into a slurry batter
* Assemble & Cooking
On a silicone pad, cut the rolled dough with pastry cutter or a knife into squares
Spoon some Batagor filling into the center of the squares, then fold each 4 corners of the squares making an exposed smaller squares filling. Press to seal the edges (refer to the attached pics for details)
Dip all shaped Batagor dough into the dipping batter, until thoroughly wet
Deep fry the dipped Batagor on a low medium heat with coconut oil, until golden brown
Drain the fried Batagor with a spider strainer, then use paper towels to remove excess oil
Serve the Keto-Batagor with the mixed Peanut Butter Sauce

THE KETO IRON CHEF WHIPS UP SOME ZERO CARB KETO-OLIEBOLLEN (DUTCH FRIED DOUGHNUT)

Zero Carb Keto-Oliebollen (Dutch Fried Doughnut) Servings=1-2 Time=30mins
Ingredient
* For Batter
Dry Ingredients
10g Micellar Casein
10g Whey Protein Isolate, Unflavored
5g Dried Egg Whites
10g Egg Yolk Powder
15g Inulin Fiber (Chicory Root) – LC Foods
1g Xanthan Gum Powder
1g Salt
1g Vanilla Extract
1,5g Instant Dry Yeast
Wet Ingredients
30g Egg Yolk
50g Heavy Whipping Cream

40g Butter
* For Meringue
70g Egg White
5g Inulin Fiber (Chicory Root) – LC Foods
15g Sucralose
* For Filling
50g Grated Cheddar Cheese
(Optional : Zucchini or Low Carb Chocolate Chips)
* For Dusting
Cinnamon Powder
Sucralose
Direction
* For Batter
Whisk all the dry ingredients on a medium bowl,set aside
On a standing mixer, cream butter until light with low speed stage. Then add egg yolk until combined. Gradually add heavy whipping cream while raising the speed into medium stage, until the batter thicken and fluffy
Lower the mixer speed into low stage and gradually add the dry ingredients using a spoon until completely combines and a very thick batter formed
Rest the batter for 1 hour for bulk fermentation, until slightly expanded by the yeast leavening action and the batter become lighter when stirred using spatula
* For Meringue
Using another mixer bowl, or removing the batter first into another bowl then completely clean the mixer bowl so there's grease residue on the bowl.
Whip the egg white into foam with low peak on the standing mixer using low speed (about 5 – 10 minutes)
Sprinkle inulin powder and sucralose into the egg white by raising the speed into medium speed, until the egg white foam has a stiff peak
* Combining & Frying
Mix the fermented batter with grated cheddar cheese until combines
On the standing mixer, add the fermented batter mixture into the egg white mixture using low speed until completely combined and a fluffy thick batter is formed
Heat at least 2 inch of coconut oil in a frying pan over low medium heat
Use a small ice cream scoop or a spoon to drop about 1 tbsp of the batter into the oil. They will puff up considerably. Fry in batches
Turn the Keto-Oliebollen after several minutes, and continue to cook until each side is golden, the oliebollen is puffed, and it is started to create a seam. This will take about 3 to 5 minutes of frying
Drain the cooked Keto-Oliebollen with a spider strainer from the hot oil, then use paper towels afterward to remove any excess oil
Serve immediately with sprinkle of cinnamon powder and sucralose
Note : The fermentation over the batter for 1 hour on a high hydration batter environment, will make the yeast to work fast to consume all the carbs within this recipes ingredients.

THE KETO IRON CHEF DOES ZERO CARB KETO-ZEPPOLE (ITALIAN FRIED DOUGHNUT)

Zero Carb Keto-Zeppole(Italian Fried Doughnut) Servings=1-2 Time=30mins
Ingredient
Dry Ingredients
10g Micellar Casein
10g Whey Protein Isolate
5g Dried Egg Whites
10g Egg Yolk Powder
15g Inulin Fiber (Chicory Root) – LC Foods
1g Xanthan Gum Powder
1g Salt
1g Vanilla Extract
10g Sucralose
2g Instant Dry Yeast
* Note : The first 6 ingredients above are the Keto-Flour formula for this recipe
For crisper crust the Keto-Flour can be changed into this formula : 15g Wheat Protein Isolate 8000, 5g Casein Protein Isolate,
5g Whey Protein Isolate, 5g Egg White Powder, 10g Egg Yolk Powder, 10g Inulin Powder
Wet Ingredients
30g Egg Yolk
20g Egg White
50g Ricotta Cheese
50g Heavy Whipping Cream
40g Butter
* For Dusting
Sucralose

Direction

Whisk all the dry ingredients on a medium bowl except for sucralose, set aside

On a standing mixer, cream butter and sucralose until light with low speed stage. Then add egg yolk and egg white until combines and creamy

Add ricotta cheese and heavy whipping cream gradually, while raising the speed into medium stage, until the batter thicken and fluffy

Lower the mixer speed into low stage and gradually add the dry ingredients using a spoon until completely combines and a very thick batter formed

Rest the batter for 1 hour to ferment, until slightly expanded by the yeast leavening action and become lighter when stirred using spatula

Heat at least 2 inch of coconut oil in a frying pan over low medium heat

Use a small ice cream scoop or a spoon to drop about 1 tbsp of the batter into the oil. They will puff up considerably. Fry in batches

Turn the Keto-Zeppole after its starting to puff and continue to cook until each side is golden brown

Drain the cooked Keto-Zeppole with a spider strainer from the hot oil, then use paper towels afterwards to remove any excess oil

Serve immediately with sprinkle of sucralose

Note : The fermentation over the batter for 1 hours on high hydration batter environment makes the yeast work fast to consume all the carbs within the recipes ingredients.

KETO IRON CHEF'S RED VELVET CAKE & CUP CAKE

Keto Iron Chef's Red Velvet Cake & Cup Cake Servings=4 Time=30mins
(Red Velvet Cake & Cup Cake Using Keto-Iron Basic Pound Cake Recipe)
4 – 6 Serving Size
Ingredients
* For Red Velvet Cake Batter
Dry Ingredients
90g Inulin Fiber (Chicory Root) – LC Foods
90g Micellar Casein
30g Isopure Whey Protein Isolate, Unflavored
30g Dried Egg Whites
30g Egg Yolk Powder
9g Xanthan Gum Powder
3g Salt
12g Baking Powder
6g Baking Soda
5g Vanilla Extract
20g 100% Dark Cocoa Powder
Wet Ingredient
150g Egg Yolks
300g Butter
200g Buttermilk
150g Cream Cheese
15g Liquid or Gel Red Food Coloring
* For Keto-Sugar Mix
60g Inulin Fiber (Chicory Root) – LC Foods
60g Sweetener
* For Meringue
600g Egg White
8g Cream of Tartar
* For Cream Cheese Frosting
150g Cream Cheese
50g Butter
10g Vanilla Extract
20g Sweetener
(Beat all these ingredients together using a handheld mixer until creamy, set aside)
Direction
* For Red Velvet Cake Batter
Whisk and sift all dry ingredients together on a medium bowl, set aside
On a standing mixer with a paddle attachment, beat butter and Keto-Sugar Mix on low speed until pale.
Add egg yolk and cream cheese gradually by raising the speed into medium speed, until creamy and light
Add buttermilk onto the batter, and raise the mixer into high speed, until creamy and thick
Lower the mixer speed back into the lowest speed, then spoon in 1/3 of the dry ingredients. The batter will be thick and lumpy at this stage
Turn off the mixer then spoon the rest of the dry ingredients onto the mixer bowl and stir with a spatula until completely combined and the batter becomes smooth without no lumps
Add the liquid or gel red food coloring, then stir again until completely dissolve to the batter
Remove the batter into another bowl, set aside
Wash the mixer bowl and the paddle attachment until clean thoroughly without any greasy residues left on the mixer bowl and at the paddle attachment, then use to whip the egg white

Preheat the oven into 300F

* For The Meringue

Beat the egg white on the standing mixer on low speed about 2 – 3 minutes until soft peak

Sprinkle cream of tartar over the meringue, then raise the mixer into medium speed, until hard peak

Turn off the mixer, then scoop 1/3 of the meringue into the batter and fold with a spatula until just combines. then pour the rest of the batter and fold again until completely combines

pour 1/4 of the batter onto a lightly greased square baking pan and covered with a parchment paper (use small square pan that will fill 1/2 the pan height, from using 1/4 – 1/3 of the batter)

Bake for 30 minutes. Insert a tooth pick to check the cake whether the cake has done or not. The tooth pick should comes out clean when the cake is done

Repeat with another 1/4 batter two more times, to make 3 layer Red Velvet Cake

Use the last 1/4 of the batter for cupcakes, by using muffin pan and paper cups

Spoon the batter left over to the paper cup, fills only 1/3 volume of the muffin cones mould

After the last cake cools for 10 minutes, spread the cream cheese frosting evenly on one of the cake, then gently put another cake over the frosting

Repeat until 3 layer cake is formed, then spread the cream cheese frosting evenly over the outer cake surface

Transfer the cream cheese frosting left over to a piping bag with star nozzle, to decorate the baked cupcake

Refrigerate the cake and cupcake for 1 hour before cutting and serving

THE KETO IRON CHEF DOES AN AMERICAN CLASSIC - ZERO CARB KETO-FUNNEL CAKE

Zero Carb Keto-Funnel Cake Servings=1-2 Time=30mins

(American Carnival Funnel Cake)

1 – 2 Serving size

Ingredients

* For Batter

Dry Ingredients

10g Isopure Whey Protein Isolate, Unflavored

5g Dried Egg Whites

5g Egg Yolk Powder

5g Inulin Fiber (Chicory Root) – LC Foods

0,5g Xanthan Gum Powder

0,5g Salt

1g Baking Powder

1g Vanilla Extract

3g Sweetener

1g Instant Dry Yeast

Wet Ingredient

60g Egg White

30g Egg Yolk

15g Heavy Whipping Cream

15g Cream Cheese (softened)

50g Butter

* For Frying

Virgin Coconut Oil

* For Dusting

Zero Calories Sweetener

Direction

Whisk all dry ingredients together on a medium bowl, set aside. Using a food processor or a blender, pulse the egg egg white into foam with medium peak. Transfer into another bowl, set aside

Continue to beat butter and egg yolks on the food processor, until light and creamy, then pour the mixture onto a mixing bowl. Still using a food processor, combine cream cheese and heavy whipping cream then beat into thick mixture. Combine the cream cheese and egg yolk mixture using spatula, then gradually add the dry ingredients. Keep stirring until the batter becomes very thick. Fold in the egg white into the batter, by scooping the bottom of the batter over the meringue, forming a fluffy batter mixture. Cover the mixing bowl with a towel, then rest the batter for 30 – 45 minutes, to let the yeast ferment. On a medium frying pan, pour coconut oil until reaching half the pan height. Use low medium heat to slowly raise the oil temperature into 300F. Put your finger over the bottom opening of a regular cooking funnel, and fill the funnel with the batter. Hold the funnel close to the surface of the oil, and release the batter into the oil while making a circular motion Fry until golden brown. Use tongs and wide spatula to turn the cake over carefully. Fry the second side one minute. Drain on paper towels, and serve with sprinkle of your chosen zero calories sweetener.

KETO-ROTI JALA (MALAYSIAN NET PANCAKE)

Keto-Roti Jala (Malaysian Net Pancake) Servings=4 Time=30mins
1 – 2 Serving Size
Ingredient
Dry Ingredients
10g Micellar Casein
10g Isopure Whey Protein Isolate, Unflavored
5g Dried Egg Whites
10g Egg Yolk Powder
15g Inulin Fiber (Chicory Root) – LC Foods
1g Xanthan Gum Powder
1g Salt
0,5g Garlic Powder
1g Curry Powder
Wet Ingredients
50g Egg
50g Coconut Milk
5g Coconut Milk
Direction
Whisk all the dry ingredients on a medium bowl
Add egg and coconut milk, then stir with a spatula forming a thick batter
Add the coconut oil and stir until the batter consistency become slurry and smooth
Transfer the batter into a plastic bottle with the holes on the bottle cap (you can make this yourself by making multiple hole over a cap from mineral water bottle)
Heat 1 tsp oil in a non-stick frying pan. Squeeze the bottle and scribble a net of the batter into the pan making a circle net shape, working as quickly as you can
When the pancake has set (after about 30 secs), fold the cake into a half circle using cookie spatula, then fold once again into a quarter circle.
Transfer into a plate, then repeat with the remaining batter, adding more oil as needed.
Layer the pancakes between sheets of baking parchment and keep warm in the oven while you cook the rest.
Serve Roti Jala with chicken curry or lamb curry
* Note : Roti Jala can be served as a dessert by omitting the curry powder from the dry ingredients and replace it with vanilla extract and sweetener, then generously dust with cinnamon powder and sweetener

KETO-IRON PÂTE À CHOUX (KETO-IRON CHEF CREAM PUFFS & ICE CREAM PUFFS RECIPE)

Keto-Iron Pâte à Choux (Keto-Iron Chef Cream Puffs & Ice Cream Puffs Recipe) Servings=4 Time=30mins
4 – 6 Serving Size
* Dedicated to all children on Therapeutic Ketogenic Diet
Ingredients
For Keto-Pâte à Choux Batter :
Dry Ingredients
15g Micellar Casein
10g Isopure Whey Protein Isolate, Unflavored
10g Dried Egg Whites
10g Egg Yolk Powder
5g Inulin Fiber (Chicory Root) – LC Foods
1,5g Xanthan Gum Powder
1g Salt
2g Baking Powder
1g Vanilla Extract
Wet Ingredients
50g Egg Yolk
50g Crème Fraîche
50g Butter
* For Keto-Sugar
20g Inulin Fiber (Chicory Root) – LC Foods
10g Sweetener
(Whisk these ingredients together)
* For Meringue
100g Egg White
1/2 tsp Cream of Tartar Powder
* For Cream Puffs Filling
120g Heavy Whipping Cream
10g Butter
15g Egg Yolk
10g Micellar Casein
10g Egg White Powder
10g Inulin Fiber (Chicory Root) – LC Foods
20g Sweetener
5g Vanilla Extract
* For Ice Cream Puffs Filling
Scoops of Keto-Iron Chocolate Ice Cream
Direction
* For Pâte à Choux Batter
Whisk and sift all the dry ingredients on a medium bowl, set aside
On a standing mixer, beat butter and Keto-Sugar until pale
Add egg yolk and crème fraîche one at a time, continue to beat until the batter become light and fluffy
Spoon the dry ingredients into the batter gradually. When the mixture start to thicken, turn off the mixer and switch using spatula to fold the batter until completely combines (do not over mix)
Remove the batter onto a medium bowl, set aside. Wash the paddle attachment and mixer bowl until thoroughly clean, then dry them with a towel
Beat the egg white with low speed on the standing mixer, until low peak. Sprinkle cream of tartar powder over the meringue and continue to beat until stiff peak
Fold 1/3 of the meringue into the batter by scooping the batter from the bottom and folding it into the meringue. Fold quickly

to combine

Continue with the rest of the meringue, 1/3 at a time, until completely combine and the batter become thick and fluffy

Scoop the batter onto a baking sheet, using an ice cream scoop. You can also transfer the batter to a piping bag to pipe specific shape. Space the pastries slightly apart on the baking sheet

Bake For 15 minutes until the pastry puff and golden brown in color

* For Cream Puffs Filling

On a small sauce pan, melt butter then pour in heavy whipping cream. Continue to stir with a rubber spatula until the mixture start thicken

Add in egg yolk, stir to combine. Then pour the whisked casein protein isolate, egg white powder and inulin powder into the mixture all at once

Quickly stir and fold, until the mixture become very thick and no more lumps

Let the cream filling cools for 15 minutes on a room temperature, then transfer into a piping bag with the preferred nozzle

* Assemble

Cut off the pastry top with circling pattern using a small scissor. Reserve an inch space un cut to keep the puffs hold together

Generously pipe in the bottom halves with the cream filling, until almost flooding the edges

For Ice Cream Puffs, scoop in the bottom halves with Keto-Iron Chocolate Ice Cream using an ice cream scoop, then gently press the top until the ice cream flood the edges

Serve the cream puffs and ice cream puffs with sprinkle of sweetener and cinnamon powder over the top

KETO-IRON CHEF'S KETO-GULAB JAMUN

Keto-Iron Chef's Keto-Gulab Jamun Servings=1-2 Time=60mins

(Indian Fried Dumpling with Keto-Sugar Syrup)

1 – 2 Serving Size

Ingredients

* For Keto-Gulab Jamun Dough

50g Whey Protein Isolate

5g Casein Protein Isolate

5g Inulin Powder

1/8 tsp Salt

1/8 tsp Baking Soda

2 – 3 tbsp Yogurt

* For Keto-Sugar Syrup

200ml Water

2 tbsp Rose Scented Water

50g Sukrin Fiber Syrup Gold

20g Inulin Powder

20g Sweetener

1/4 tsp Ground Cardamom

1/4 tsp Turmeric Powder

* For Garnish

Dessicated Coconut

Direction

* For Keto-Sugar Syrup

Heat the water, rose scented water, and sukrin fiber syrup gold in a small sauce pan. Bring it to a boil

Add inulin powder and sweetener, stir to dissolve

Add turmeric powder and ground cardamom, then lower the heat and cook until the mixture reduced and thicken

Turn off the heat and transfer to a bowl. Let cool for 10 minutes. Set aside

* For Keto-Gulab Jamun Dough

Mix whey protein isolate, casein protein isolate, inulin powder, xanthan gum, salt and baking soda in a medium bowl

mix and keep on adding little of the yogurt to get a soft sticky mixture

the dough should not be crumbly or dry. if it is then add some yogurt

make smooth small balls from the dough

heat the coconut oil and then reduce the flame to low

add the balls and fry them stirring often to get even color

when they become golden, remove from a slotted spoon and add them to the sugar syrup

let them soak in the Keto-Sugar Syrup for at least 1-2 hours

Serve with dessicated coconut as the garnish

KETO-IRON CHEF'S KETO-TRIPLE CHOCOLATE BANANA BREAD

Keto-Iron Chef's Keto-Triple Chocolate Banana Bread Servings=4 Time=60mins
(Triple Chocolate Banana Bread using Egg Yolk Powder)
4 – 6 Serving Size
Ingredients
Dry Ingredients
30g Inulin Powder
20g Casein Protein Isolate
20g Whey Protein Isolate
15g Egg White Powder
15g Egg Yolk Powder
1g Salt
2g Baking Powder
3g Baking Soda
(Whisk & sift all these ingredients together as a Keto-Flour Mix)
Additional Ingredients
30g 100% Dark Cocoa Powder
50g Egg Yolk Powder
50g Low Carb Chocolate Chips
Wet Ingredient
50g Egg Yolks
50g Butter
150g Butter Milk

3g Banana Essence

* For Keto-Sugar Mix

20g Inulin Powder

20g Sweetener

* For Meringue

180g Egg White

2g Cream of Tartar

* Glazing

20g Low Carb Chocolate Chips

5g Butter

20g Butter Milk

5g Sweetener

2g Vanilla Extract

Direction

Whisk and sift all dry ingredients together on a medium bowl, set aside

On a standing mixer with a paddle attachment, beat butter and Keto-Sugar Mix on low speed until pale.

Add egg yolk gradually by raising the speed into medium speed, until creamy and light

Add butter milk, banana essence, egg yolk powder and dark chocolate powder one at a time onto the batter, and raise the mixer into high speed, until creamy and thick

Lower the mixer speed back into the lowest speed, then spoon in 1/3 of the dry ingredients

Turn off the mixer then spoon the rest of the dry ingredients onto the mixer bowl and stir with a spatula until completely combined and the batter becomes smooth without no lumps

Fold in the low carb chocolate chips into the batter, and stir until evenly distributed

Remove the batter into another bowl, set aside

Wash the mixer bowl and the paddle attachment until clean thoroughly without any greasy residues left on the mixer bowl and at the paddle attachment, then use to whip the egg white

Preheat the oven into 300F

Beat the egg white on the standing mixer on low speed about 2 – 3 minutes until soft peak

Sprinkle cream of tartar over the meringue, then raise the mixer into medium speed, until hard peak

Turn off the mixer, then scoop 1/3 of the meringue into the batter and fold with a spatula until just combines. then pour the rest of the batter and fold again until completely combines. The batter will become light and fluffy at this stage

Pour the batter onto a lightly greased loaf pan (you can use any shape of pan mould that you like, but make sure that the batter will fill at least 1/3 of the pan mould volume)

Bake for 45 – 50 minutes. Insert a tooth pick to check the cake whether the cake has done or not. The tooth pick should comes out clean when the cake is done

Melt the butter on a small sauce pan then pour the butter milk. Stir to combine

When the mixture starts to bubbles, add in vanilla extract and sweetener. Stir to dissolve

Turn off the heat and stir in the low carb chocolate chips. Keep stirring until the chocolate chips melt and the glaze thickens

Transfer the glaze into a plastic piping bag with round tip

Turn off the oven, then remove the cake. Let the cake cools for 10 – 15 minutes before removing it onto a serving plate

Drizzle the cake with the chocolate glaze, then slice and serve as a Keto-Dessert

KETO-IRON CHEF'S KETO-BOLO BAO

Keto-Iron Chef's Keto-Bolo Bao Servings=4 Time=60mins
(Hongkong Pineapple Buns using Tang Zhong Method)
4 Serving Size
Ingredients
* For Keto-Flour Mix
45g Casein Protein Isolate
30g Whey Protein Isolate
15g Egg White Powder
15g Egg Yolk Powder
45g Inulin Powder
8g Psyllium Husk
3g Xanthan Gum
3g Salt
8g Custard Powder
6g Sweetener
(Whisk & sift all these ingredients together as a Keto-Flour Mix)
* For Tang Zhong (Water Roux)
10g Keto-Flour Mix

40g Water
* For The Buns
30g Egg
50g Coconut Milk
5g Instant Dry Yeast
15g Butter
The Rest of the Keto-Flour Mix
Tang Zhong
* For The Cookie Dough
15g Inulin Powder
15g Casein Protein Isolate
10g Whey Protein Isolate
5g Egg White Powder
5g Egg Yolk Powder
5g Custard Powder
(Whisk & sift all the ingredients above together)
10g Sweetener
10g Egg Yolk
50g Butter
Direction
* For Tang Zhong
On a small sauce pan, combine 10g of Keto-Flour Mix with 40g of water, then stir using rubber spatula until there is no more lumps
Heat the mixture over a stove with a very low heat, and stir using rubber spatula until the mixture just starting to thicken and leaving a trail behind the rubber spatula
Turn off the heat and set aside. Let the Tang Zhong mixture cool on a room temperature spot for at least 10 minutes
* For Cookie Dough
Whisk and sift all the dry ingredients together except for the sweetener, in a small bowl. Set aside
On a standing mixer with low speed (stage 1), beat butter and sweetener until white and creamy
Add egg yolk, then raise into medium speed (stage 2), until the batter become light and fluffy
Lower into low speed (stage 1) back, and spoon the dry ingredients into the batter, just until combine (do not over mix)
Rest the cookie dough in the refrigerator for 10 – 15 minutes
* For The Buns
Combine the rest of the Keto-Flour Mix with 5g Instant Dry Yeast on a mixer bowl
Using dough hook attachment (spiral hook), add in 30g egg and the cooled Tang Zhong mixture to the mixer bowl.
Mix at low speed (stage 1) until combines and a rough dough formed
Add in 50g coconut milk gradually, then raise the mixer speed into medium speed (stage 2) until combines and the dough start to look smooth but almost tack free if it's touched
Add 15g of softened butter, then raise the mixer speed into high speed (stage 3). Mix until the dough becomes very elastic and leaving no scrap on the mixer bowl (use spatula to scrap the mixer bowl side wall to adhere any sticking dough pieces into the main dough)
Turn off the mixer, and shape the dough into round
Rest the dough for 20 minutes, until it is double in size
Divide the rested dough into 4 equal parts, and shape them into smooth round balls
Transfer the buns onto baking pan with the seam facing downward
Rest the buns for another 20 minutes on a warm spot, using plastic wrap to cover the buns until they are double in size
Preheat the oven into 300F
Check the buns readiness to bake, by finger pressing the risen buns. It should still bounce back quick but will leave a slight finger mark
Divide the refrigerated cookie dough into 4 equal size. Flatten each piece into a round circle shape
Place a piece of the flattened cookie pieces on top of each risen buns

Bake for 20 minutes until the side of the buns starts to turn golden brown
Let the buns cools on the baking pan for 10 minutes before removing them into a wire rack
Serve the Keto-Bolo Bao while still warm with black coffee or green tea

KETO-IRON CHEF'S KETO-KHANOM BA BIN (THAILAND STREET FOOD - COCONUT CAKE)

Keto-Iron Chef's Keto-Khanom Ba Bin (Thailand Street Food – Coconut Cake) Servings=2-3 Time=60mins
2 – 3 Serving Size
Ingredients
2 cup Dessicated Coconut
2 tsp Egg White Powder
2 tsp Egg Yolk Powder
2 tsp Inulin Powder
1 cup Coconut Milk
1 tsp Sweetener
1/4 tsp Salt
1 tbsp Coconut Oil
Direction
Mix egg white powder, egg yolk powder, inulin powder, salt and sweetener in a small bowl, set aside
Whisk the dessicated coconut and dry ingredients mix in a medium bowl
Add in coconut milk and stir until thoroughly combined
Oil the inside of a baking pan with coconut oil. Then pour the coconut mixture into this pan and spread evenly
Bake in an oven for 30 minutes until the cake is cooked and browned on top
Take cake out of the oven and let cool. Once cool, cut into squares and serve

KETO-IRON CHEF'S KETO-FLOATING ISLANDS / KETO-ÎLES FLOTTANTES

Keto-Iron Chef's Keto-Floating Islands / Keto-îles flottantes Servings=1-2 Time=60mins
(French Meringues Dessert with Custard)
1 – 2 Serving Size
Ingredients
* For Crème Anglaise
1 cup Heavy Cream or Coconut Milk
2 Large Egg Yolks
2 teaspoon Sweetener
1/8 teaspoon Vanilla Essence
* For The Poaching Liquor
1/2 cup Heavy Cream or Coconut Milk
1/2 cup Water
1 teaspoon Sweetener
* For The Meringue
2 Large Egg Whites
2 teaspoon Inulin Powder
2 teaspoon Sweetener
1/8 teaspoon Cream of Tartar
Pinch of salt
Direction
For the crème anglaise, heat the heavy cream in a saucepan over a medium heat. Simmer for 4-5 minutes
Mix sweetener and vanilla extract, stir into the heavy cream until dissolve

Turn off the heat, and add the egg yolks, whisking continuously until smooth and creamy

Turn on the heat back with low-medium heat, and stir for 4 – 5 minutes, or until the mixture has thickened enough to coat the back of a spoon

Strain the through a sieve into a bowl, leave to cool then refrigerate

For the poaching liquor, combine the heavy cream and half cup of water with the sweetener in a saucepan, stirring to dissolve the sweetener

* For The Meringue

Mix inulin powder and sweetener as a Keto-Sugar

Using a standing mixer, beat the whites in the mixer bowl until stiff peaks form when the paddle attachment is removed, but the mixture should not look too dry. Add the Keto-Sugar to the egg whites, and continue to beat until the mixture comes back to stiff peaks

Sprinkle cream of tartar and salt over the meringue, then raise the mixer speed until the meringue is thick and glossy

Using a serving spoon dipped in cold water, shape big quenelles of the meringue and gently poach in the heavy cream and water solution, turning after 4-5 minutes to ensure they are cooked on both sides. Make sure the liquid doesn't boil or the meringues will puff then collapse. When fully cooked, gently place on a wire rack to drain

When set, take the meringues off the tray and serve in a generous pool of the crème anglaise

KETO-IRON CHEF'S KETO-EGG LESS CAKE

Keto-Iron Chef's Keto-Egg Less Cake Servings=2-3 Time=60mins

(Keto-Iron Chef Basic Fluffy & Moist Egg Less Cake Recipe)

2 – 3 Serving Size

* This basic egg less cake can be use for many variety of egg less layer Keto-Cake

Ingredients

* For Egg Less Cake Batter

Dry Ingredients

20g Inulin Powder

20g Casein Protein Isolate

10g Whey Protein Isolate or Pea Protein Isolate

1g Xanthan Gum

1g Salt

2g Baking Powder

1g Baking Soda

1g Vanilla Extract

15g 100% Dark Cocoa Powder (Optional)

Wet Ingredient

50g Cream Cheese

30g Sour Cream

50g Butter

150g Heavy Whipping Cream

1/4 tsp Cream of Tartar

* For Keto-Sugar Mix

10g Inulin Powder

10g Sweetener

Direction

* For Egg Less Cake Batter

Whisk and sift all dry ingredients together on a medium bowl except for the dark cocoa powder, set aside

On a standing mixer with a paddle attachment, beat butter and Keto-Sugar Mix on low speed until pale.

Add sour cream and cream cheese gradually by raising the speed into medium speed, until creamy and light

Add the dark cocoa powder onto the batter, and scrap the bowl sides with spatula

Lower the mixer speed back into the lowest speed, then spoon in 1/3 of the dry ingredients. The batter will be thick and lumpy at this stage

Turn off the mixer then spoon the rest of the dry ingredients onto the mixer bowl and stir with a spatula until completely combined and the batter becomes smooth without no lumps

Remove the batter into another bowl, set aside

Wash the mixer bowl and the paddle attachment until clean thoroughly without any greasy residues left on the mixer bowl and at the paddle attachment

Preheat the oven into 300F

Beat the heavy whipping cream on the standing mixer on low speed about 2 – 3 minutes until soft peak

Sprinkle cream of tartar over, then raise the mixer into medium speed, until stiff peak

Turn off the mixer, then scoop 1/3 of the whipped cream into the cake batter and fold with a spatula until just combines. then pour the rest of the whipped cream and fold again until completely combines. The batter will become light and fluffy at this stage

Pour the batter onto a lightly greased square baking pan and covered with a parchment paper (use small square pan that will fill 1/2 the pan height), then level out the surface with a rubber spatula

Bake for 45 – 50 minutes. Insert a tooth pick to check the cake whether the cake has done or not. The tooth pick should comes out clean when the cake is done

Turn off the oven, then remove the cake. Let the cake cools for 10 – 15 minutes before removing it onto a serving plate

At this stage you can top the cake with anything that you want, such as with cream cheese frosting

THE KETO IRON CHEF'S KETO-KING CAKE

Keto-Iron Chef's Keto-King Cake Servings=6-8 Time=60mins
(New Orleans Mardi Gras King Cake)
Poolish Method
Ingredients
* For Keto-Flour Mix
90g
Casein Protein Isolate
60g Isopure Whey Protein Isolate, Unflavored
30g Dried Egg Whites
30g Egg Yolk Powder
90g
Inulin Powder
15g Psyllium Husk
6g Xanthan Gum Powder
6g Salt
5g Cinnamon Powder
5g Cardamom (grounded)
3g Nutmeg Powder
5g Lemon Zest
15g Sweetener
12g Instant Dry Yeast
(Whisk & sift all these ingredients together as the Keto-Flour Mix)
* For Poolish Batter (Preferment / Starter)
100g Keto-Flour Mix
100g Heavy Cream
15g Egg Yolk
* For Bread Dough (Main Dough)
70g Egg

30g Sour Cream
25g Butter
The Rest of the Keto-Flour Mix
Preferment Batter (Poolish)
* For Cream Cheese Filling
10g Cinnamon Powder
20g Sweetener
10g Inulin Fiber (Chicory Root) – LC Foods
1g Salt
100g Cream Cheese
50g Butter
10g Egg Yolk
* For Cream Cheese Frosting
50g Cream Cheese
30g Butter
10g Sweetener
10g Inulin Fiber (Chicory Root) – LC Foods
2 drops Yellow Food Coloring
2 drops Green Food Coloring
2 drops Purple Food Coloring
* For Egg Wash
1 Egg Yolk
1 tbsp Water
Direction
* For Poolish Batter (Preferment / Starter)
On a medium bowl, combine 100g Keto-Flour with 15g egg yolk and 100g heavy cream. Stir until forming a thick smooth batter without lumps
Rest the batter on a warm spot for 20 minutes, using plastic wrap to cover the bowl so that the batter surface won't dry out
The batter should rise to almost double in size, and will have many holes inside the mixture
* For The Filling
Whisk cinnamon powder, inulin powder, salt and sweetener on a bowl
Beat butter and the whisked ingredients with low speed on standing mixer, until white
Add the egg yolk and cream cheese. Beat until light and creamy
* For Cream Cheese Frosting
Beat butter, inulin powder and sweetener until white
Add cream cheese and keep beating until creamy
Divide the frosting mixture into 3 parts. Give each part 2 drops of yellow, green and purple food coloring. Stir well
* Assemble
Combine the rest of the Keto-Flour Mix and Poolish batter on the mixer bowl
Using spiral hook attachment, mix at low speed (stage 1) until combines and a rough dough formed
Add in 70g egg white and 30g sour cream gradually, then raise the mixer speed into medium speed (stage 2) until combines and the dough start to look smooth but almost tack free if it's touched
Spread 25g softened butter over the dough, by raising the mixer speed into high speed (stage 3). Mix until the dough becomes very elastic and leaving no scrap on the mixer bowl (use spatula to scrap the mixer bowl side wall to adhere any sticking dough pieces into the main dough)
Turn off the mixer, and remove the dough onto a silicone pad
Knead the dough for a while until the surface becomes very smooth and dry, then shape into a round disc
Roll the dough into large rectangle (1/2 inch thick) using roller pin, then spread the filling evenly over the dough
Fold the dough into a log (just like shaping a cinnamon roll dough) and combine the edges into a round donut shape. Pinch the tip ends to create a seam
Transfer the dough into a greased baking sheet, with the seam facing downward

Rest the dough for 15 – 20 minutes on a warm spot, using plastic wrap to cover the dough

Preheat the oven into 300F

Check the dough readiness to bake, by finger pressing the risen dough. It should still bounce back quick but will leave a slight finger mark

Give an even egg wash over the dough surface, then bake for 30 minutes until the crust look golden brown

Remove the cake from the oven, then decorate with the prepared cream cheese frosting

KETO-IRON CHEF'S KETO-COCONUT MILK BREAD PUDDING

Keto-Iron Chef's Keto-Coconut Milk Bread Pudding Servings=2-3 Time=60mins

(Singapore Coconut Milk Bread Pudding)

Using Chinese Keto-Coconut Milk Bread

For Chinese Keto-Coconut Milk Bread Recipe, refer to this link here

Ingredients

10 slices of Keto-Coconut Milk Bread

200g Coconut Milk

50g Egg (1 medium egg)

15g Egg Yolk (1 egg yolk)

15g Butter

10g Inulin Powder

10g Sweetener

5g Rum Essence

5g Cinnamon Powder (for dusting)

Direction

Preheat the oven into 300F

Combine Inulin Powder and Sweetener on a small bowl as Keto-Sugar. Set aside

Stir Coconut milk and Rum Essence until dissolve. Set aside

Cut 10 slices of Keto-Coconut Milk Bread, then cut each slice diagonally into triangle. Set aside

On a medium sauce pan, melt butter with low-medium heat, then pour coconut milk. Stir to combine

When the mixture start to bubbles, add in the Keto-Sugar and stir to combine

Turn off the heat and pour in the eggs all at once. Stir until completely combine and forming a thick batter

Arrange the bread slices on a Pyrex casserole dish, covering the bottom of the plate

Spread the batter evenly over the bread, then cover again with the bread slices

Spread the batter once more until all the batter use, then dust with cinnamon powder

Bake for 40 minutes until the surface turns golden and the edges are browning

Cool the Keto-Bread Pudding for 15 minutes, then cut into 8 slices

Serve with black coffee or green tea

BREADS AND PASTA

KETO-IRON CHEF'S KETO-BOLILLO

Keto-Iron Chef's Keto-Bolillo Servings=4 Time=60mins
(Mexican Crusty Rolls)
Starter Method
Ingredients
* For Keto-Flour Mix
30g Casein Protein Isolate
20g Whey Protein Isolate
10g Egg White Powder
10g Egg Yolk Powder
30g Inulin Powder
5g Psyllium Husk
2g Xanthan Gum
2g Salt
(Whisk & sift all these ingredients together)
* Note : For softer crumb the Keto-Flour Mix can be changed into this formula : 30g Wheat Protein Isolate 8000, 10g Casein

Protein Isolate, 10g Whey Protein Isolate, 10g Egg White Powder, 10g Egg Yolk Powder, 30g Inulin Powder, 2g Salt
* For Starter
30g Keto-Flour Mix
60g Water
1g Instant Dry Yeast
* For Keto-Bolillo (Main Dough)
30g Water
3g Instant Dry Yeast
10g Butter (melted)
The Rest of the Keto-Flour Mix
Starter Dough
* For Egg Wash
1 Egg Yolk
1 tbsp Water
Direction
* For Starter
On a medium bowl, combine 30g Keto-Flour Mix with 30g water. Stir until forming a thick smooth batter without lumps
Rest the batter on a warm spot for 20 minutes, using plastic wrap to cover the bowl so that the batter surface won't dry out
The batter should rise to almost double in size, and will have many holes inside the mixture
* For Keto-Bolillo
Combine the rest of the Keto-Flour Mix with 3g Instant Dry Yeast in a mixing bowl, then add the risen starter dough onto the bowl
Mix using spatula, until combines and a rough dough formed
Add in 30g water gradually, and fold using spatula until combines and the dough start to look smooth but almost tack free if it's touched
Add 10g melted butter over the dough, then knead the dough using your hand, until the dough becomes very elastic and just a bit tacky to the touch
* Shaping Keto-Bolillo
To form the bolillos-rolls, transfer the dough onto a silicone pad and divide into 2 equal dough
Flatten one piece of dough with the palm of your hand and fold 1/3 of the dough towards you and press down with your fingers, sealing it very well
Fold the dough again, repeating the sealing process until you form a roll, pinching the dough tightly. Make sure all the the ends are sealed
To shape the rolls, place your hands over the dough and press gently but firmly, cupping your fingers, rolling back and forth
While doing this, press the heel of your hands to leave some dough uncovered to form the traditional bolillo ears
Place each bolillo/roll seam side down on the greased baking sheet and cover with a plastic wrap
Allow them to rise until they've doubled in volume. About 30 minutes
Preheat the oven into 300F
Check the rolls readiness to bake, by finger pressing the risen dough. It should still bounce back quick but will leave a slight finger mark
Once the rolls have doubled in volume, make a deep cut using a sharp serrated knife or a razor blade, holding your hand at a 45 degree angle
Give an even egg wash over each rolls surface, then bake for 20 minutes until the crust look golden brown
Let the baked rolls cools on the baking sheet for 10 minutes before removing it to a wire rack

KETO-IRON CHEF'S KETO-BAGELEN

Keto-Iron Chef's Keto-Bagelen Servings=12 Time=60mins
Keto-Bagelen
(Indonesian Style Biscotti Using Dried Keto-Dinner Rolls)

For Keto-Dinner Rolls Recipe, refer to this link
Ingredients
12 pcs Dinner Rolls
50g Butter
50g Grated Cheddar Cheese
20g Cream Cheese
20g Sweetener
10g Inulin Powder
Direction
Slice each dinner rolls into halves, making 24 pcs ready to use bread
Arrange the sliced bread on a tray, then dry them over the sun for at least 5 hours or leave them overnight in a room temperature
* For Butter Icing
On a standing mixer, beat butter with sweetener and inulin powder until white
Add the softened cream cheese then mix until light and creamy
Pour grated cheddar cheese and mix just until combines (do not over mix)
Using pastry brush, spread the butter icing over each dried bread evenly
Bake for 30 – 40 minutes until the bread turns brown and crispy
Serve with black coffee or green tea

KETO-IRON CHEF'S KETO-DINNER ROLLS / KETO-HAMBURGER BUNS

Keto-Iron Chef's Keto-Dinner Rolls / Keto-Hamburger Buns Servings=12 Time=60mins
(Soft & Fluffy Ketofied Dinner Rolls or Hamburger Buns)
Poolish Method
Ingredients
* For Keto-Flour Mix
60g Micellar Casein
40g Isopure Whey Protein Isolate, Unflavored
20g Dried Egg Whites
20g Egg Yolk Powder
60g Inulin Fiber (Chicory Root) – LC Foods
10g Psyllium Husk
4g Xanthan Gum Powder
4g Salt
2g Vanilla Extract
5g Sweetener
(Whisk & sift all these ingredients together)
* Note : For softer crumb the Keto-Flour Mix can be changed into this formula : 60g Wheat Protein Isolate 8000, 40g Casein Protein Isolate, 20g Whey Protein Isolate, 20g Egg White Powder, 20g Egg Yolk Powder, 40g Inulin Powder, 4g Salt, 2g Vanilla Extract, 5g Sweetener
* For Poolish Batter (Preferment / Starter)
60g Keto-Flour Mix
60g Coconut Milk
2g Instant Dry Yeast
* For Dinner Rolls (Main Dough)
100g Egg
6g Instant Dry Yeast
15g Butter
The Rest of the Keto-Flour Mix

Poolish Batter
* For Egg Wash
1 Egg Yolk
1 tbsp Water
Direction
* For Poolish Batter (Preferment / Starter)
On a medium bowl, combine 60g Keto-Flour Mix with 60g coconut milk. Stir until forming a thick smooth batter without lumps
Rest the batter on a warm spot for 20 minutes, using plastic wrap to cover the bowl so that the batter surface won't dry out
The batter should rise to almost double in size, and will have many holes inside the mixture
* For Dinner Rolls
Combine the rest of the Keto-Flour Mix with 6g Instant Dry Yeast, then pour over the risen Poolish batter on the mixer bowl
Using the dough hook attachment, mix at low speed (stage 1) until combines and a rough dough formed
Add in 100g egg gradually, then raise the mixer speed into medium speed (stage 2) until combines and the dough start to look smooth but almost tack free if it's touched
Spread 15g softened butter over the dough, then raise the mixer speed into high speed (stage 3). Mix until the dough becomes very elastic and leaving no scrap on the mixer bowl (use spatula to scrap the mixer bowl side wall to adhere any sticking dough pieces into the main dough)
Turn off the mixer, and remove the dough onto a silicone pad
* Shaping Dinner Rolls
Knead the dough for a while until the surface becomes very smooth and dry, then shape into a round disc
Divide the dough into 12 equal parts using weight scale to be accurate
Shape the dough into rolls by duplicating a bowl with your palm and gently roll the dough in circular pattern against the silicone pad. The dough should turn into a smooth ball shape with a seam forming underneath the dough
Transfer each shaped dough balls into a greased baking pan
Rest the dough for another 15 – 20 minutes on a warm spot, using plastic wrap to cover the baking sheet
Preheat the oven into 300F
Check the rolls readiness to bake, by finger pressing the risen dough. It should still bounce back quick but will leave a slight finger mark
Give an even egg wash over each rolls surface, then bake for 20 minutes until the crust look golden brown
Let the baked rolls cools on the baking sheet for 10 minutes before removing it to a wire rack

KETO-IRON CHEF'S KETO-COCONUT MILK BREAD

Keto-Iron Chef's Keto-Coconut Milk Bread Servings=2-3 Time=60mins
(Chinese Coconut Milk Bread)
Tangzhong & Poolish Method
Ingredients
* For Keto-Flour Mix

90g Micellar Casein
60g Isopure Whey Protein Isolate, Unflavored
30g Dried Egg Whites
30g Egg Yolk Powder
90g Inulin Fiber (Chicory Root) – LC Foods
15g Psyllium Husk
6g Xanthan Gum Powder
6g Salt
3g Vanilla Extract
15g Sweetener

12g Instant Dry Yeast
(Whisk & sift all these ingredients together)
* Note : For softer crumb the Keto-Flour Mix can be changed into this formula : 90g Wheat Protein Isolate 8000, 60g Casein Protein Isolate, 30g Whey Protein Isolate, 30g Egg White Powder, 30g Egg Yolk Powder, 60g Inulin Powder, 6g Salt, 3g Vanilla Extract, 15g Sweetener
* For Tang Zhong (Water Roux)
15g Keto-Flour Mix
75g Coconut Milk
* For Poolish Batter (Preferment / Starter)
100g Keto-Flour Mix
100g Coconut Milk
15g Egg Yolk
* For Bread Dough (Main Dough)
60g Egg
25g Butter
The Rest of the Keto-Flour Mix
Tang Zhong (Water Roux)
Preferment Batter (Poolish)
* For Egg Wash
1 Egg Yolk
1 tsp Coconut Milk
Direction
* For Tang Zhong (Water Roux)
On a small sauce pan, combine 15g of Keto-Flour Mix with 75g of Liquid Mix then stir using rubber spatula until there is no more lumps
Heat the mixture over a stove with a very low heat, and stir using rubber spatula until the mixture just starting to thicken and leaving a trail behind the rubber spatula
Turn off the heat and set aside. Let the Tang Zhong mixture cool on a room temperature spot for at least 10 minutes
* For Poolish Batter (Preferment / Starter)
On a medium bowl, combine 100g Keto-Flour with 15g egg yolk and 100g coconut milk. Stir until forming a thick smooth batter without lumps
Rest the batter on a warm spot for 20 minutes, using plastic wrap to cover the bowl so that the batter surface won't dry out
The batter should rise to almost double in size, and will have many holes inside the mixture
* Assemble
Combine the rest of the Keto-Flour Mix with the cooled Tang Zhong mixture and Poolish batter on the mixer bowl
Using spiral hook attachment, mix at low speed (stage 1) until combines and a rough dough formed
Add in 60g Egg, then raise the mixer speed into medium speed (stage 2) until combines and the dough start to look smooth but almost tack free if it's touched
Spread 25g softened butter over the dough, by raising the mixer speed into high speed (stage 3). Mix until the dough becomes very elastic and leaving no scrap on the mixer bowl (use spatula to scrap the mixer bowl side wall to adhere any sticking dough pieces into the main dough)
Turn off the mixer, and remove the dough onto a silicone pad
* Shaping the Loaf
Knead the dough for a while until the surface becomes very smooth and dry, then shape into a round disc
Divide the dough into 3 equal parts, and shape them into balls
Roll out each dough into long oval shape (1/2 inch thick) using roller pin, then fold the each side of the longest part into the center of the dough
Fold each dough into a log and pinch the tip ends to create a seam
Arrange each dough on a loaf pan (22cm x 10cm x 7cm) with the seam facing downward
Rest the dough for 15 – 20 minutes on a warm spot, using plastic wrap to cover the loaf pan
Preheat the oven into 300F

Check the loaf readiness to bake, by finger pressing the risen dough. It should still bounce back quick but will leave a slight finger mark

Give an even egg wash over the loaf surface, then bake for 30 – 40 minutes until the crust look golden brown

Remove the loaf pan from the oven, then brush the crust with softened butter that will melt upon contact with the hot crust

Let the baked loaf cools on the loaf pan for 10 minutes before removing it to a wire rack

KETO IRON CHEF'S KETO CORN TORTILLA

Keto Iron Chef's Keto Corn Tortilla Servings=4 Time=60mins

(Mexican Corn Tortilla using Bean Sprouts)

1 – 2 Serving Size

* Refer to this Link for Asian Bean Sprout

https://en.m.wikipedia.org/wiki/Bean_sprout

Ingredients

* For Tortilla Dough

Dry Ingredients

15g Micellar Casein

10g Isopure Whey Protein Isolate, Unflavored

5g Dried Egg Whites

5g Egg Yolk Powder

15g Inulin Fiber (Chicory Root) – LC Foods

2g Psyllium Husk

1g Xanthan Gum Powder

1g Salt

* Note : The first 7 ingredients above are the Keto-Flour formula for this recipe

For more crisper pastry, the Keto-Flour can be changed into this formula : 15g Wheat Protein Isolate 8000, 10g Casein Protein Isolate, 10g Whey Protein Isolate, 5g Egg White Powder, 5g Egg Yolk Powder, 5g Inulin Powder

Wet Ingredients

15g Egg

20g Water

3g Virgin Coconut Oil

* For Corn Mixture

30g Bean Sprout

Nutrition Fact for 30g Asian Bean Sprouts

(1,2g Net Carb : 0,9g Protein : 0g Fat : 9 Cal)

http://nutritiondata.self.com/facts/custom/509870/2

10g Egg Yolk Powder

Direction

Whisk all dry ingredients on a medium bowl. Add egg and stir using spatula until a rough dough formed

Add water gradually then switch using hand to knead the dough until elastic

Add coconut oil and knead the dough until the surface become smooth, but still a little tacky. Set aside

Grind the bean sprouts with a blender or a food processor into coarse paste

Mix the egg yolk powder with the bean sprout paste using spatula, then combine it with the tortilla dough and knead with hand until the dough become smooth and dry to the touch

Divide the dough into 2 equal dough balls, then roll each dough into a thin tortilla shape

Warm a large, flat cast iron griddle or skillet over medium-high heat. When ready, a few drops of water flicked onto the surface should sizzle immediately

Cook for 1 to 2 minutes, until the edges are starting to curl up and the bottoms look dry and pebbly

Flip and cook another 1 to 2 minutes on the other side. When done, both sides should be dry to the touch and beginning to show some brown, toasted spots

Serve the Keto-Corn Tortillas for Tacos, Tostadas, Enchiladas, Flautas / Taquitos, Quesadillas, Chilaquiles, and Tortilla Soups
* Note : Any leftover tortillas that become too stale or dry to eat as tacos or other mexican dishes can be fried or baked into tortilla chips

KETO IRON CHEF'S KETOFIED RITZ CRACKERS

Keto Iron Chef's Ketofied Ritz Crackers Servings=1-2 Time=60mins
Keto-Crackers
(Ketofied Ritz Crackers)
1 – 2 Serving Size
Ingredients
* For Crackers Dough
Dry Ingredients
20g Inulin Fiber (Chicory Root) – LC Foods
10g Micellar Casein
10g Isopure Whey Protein Isolate, Unflavored
5g Dried Egg Whites
5g Egg Yolk Powder
2g Xanthan Gum Powder
2g Salt
2g Baking Powder
5g Sweetener
Wet Ingredients
30g Cold Butter
10g Virgin Coconut Oil
50g Cold Water
* For Brushing
Butter (melted)
Salt (to taste)
Direction
Preheat oven to 300 F
Put the whisked dry ingredients in the food processor. Pulse to combine
Add cold butter a few small pats at a time, and pulse to combine
Add coconut oil. Pulse to combine
Add cold water a little bit at a time. Pulse to combine after each addition. The dough should start to form a ball
Roll dough out as thin as you can.
Use cookie cutters to cut the dough out. You can make them "Ritz Shaped" or any shape that you like
Poke holes in the dough in the Ritz pattern or any pattern you like. Keep in mind that the holes are not just decorative, they help the crackers to bake correctly
While the crackers are baking, melt the remaining butter and mix in the salt
As soon as you remove the crackers from the oven, brush them with the salty butter
Serve with black coffee or green tea

KETO IRON CHEF'S KETO-CHINESE NOODLES & KETO-SHANGHAI FRIED NOODLES

Keto-Chinese Noodles & Keto-Shanghai Fried Noodles Servings=2-3 Time=45mins
(Shanghai Fried Noodles Using Keto-Chinese Noodles)
2 – 3 Serving Size
Ingredients

* For Keto-Chinese Noodles
Dry Ingredients
30g Micellar Casein
20g Isopure Whey Protein Isolate, Unflavored
10g Dried Egg Whites
10g Egg Yolk Powder
30g Inulin Fiber (Chicory Root) – LC Foods
3g Psyllium Husk
2g Xanthan Gum Powder
1g Baking Soda
2g Salt
1g Garlic Powder
0,5g Pepper Powder
* Note : The first 7 ingredients above are the Keto-Flour formula for this recipe
Wet Ingredients
15g Sour Cream
35g Water
* For Keto-Shanghai Fried Noodles
100g Chicken Breast (shredded)
10 pcs Shrimp (skin peeled)
8 pcs Shitakee Mushroom
1 Scallion (sliced)
3 pcs Cabbage leaves (sliced)
1 small Bok Choy / Chinese Cabbage (sliced)
2 Large Red Chilli (sliced)
* For Marinade
3/4 tsp Keto-Flour
1 tsp Coconut Aminos
1 tsp Shaoxing Wine
1/4 tsp Sweetener
* For Seasoning
3 tbsp Coconut Oil
2 Cloves Garlic (diced)
1 tbsp Natural Peanut Butter
3 tbsp Coconut Aminos
1/2 tsp Ground Pepper
1/4 tsp Sweetener
Direction
* For Keto-Chinese Noodles
Whisk all dry ingredients on a medium bowl. Add sour cream and stir using spatula until a rough dough formed
Add water gradually then switch using hand to knead the dough until elastic and smooth
Divide the dough into 2 equal parts. Flatten each balls using rolling pin on a silicone pad. Fold the vertical edges to the center, turn 90 degree then roll it again. Repeat the steps one more time until forming a rectangle with a smooth edges
Then using a pasta machine, roll each dough up to stage 7 – 8 setting on the pasta machine
Rest the rolled dough for 1 hour, then continue to cut each dough using the Fettucine cutter on the pasta machine
Cook the noodles on a salted boiling water, strain when the noodles are already floating. Sprinkle some coconut oil over the drained noodles to keep them from sticking, set aside
* Cooking Keto-Shanghai Fried Noodles
Mix together chicken breast, shrimps and marinade ingredients and set aside for 5-10 minutes while you prepare the other ingredients.
Heat a tablespoon of coconut oil in a wok over high heat. Add the chicken breast and shrimps stir-fry until browned

Turn down the heat, remove the chicken breast and shrimps from the wok, set aside. Add a couple more tablespoons of coconut oil to the wok and sautee the shiitake mushrooms and garlic for about 2 minutes using medium heat

Break up the boiled noodles gently with your hands and add them to the wok

Add the coconut aminos, peanut butter, ground pepper and sweetener. Stir-fry everything together until the noodles get an even brown color

Add the cabbage, bok choy, scallions and mix in with the noodles until wilted

Serve with a hot chilli sauce

KETO-IRON CHEF HAMMERS OUT KETO-BRIOCHE LOAF / KETO-FRENCH TOAST / KETO-BRUSCHETTA / KETO-ROTI BAKAR. YES. ALL THAT!!!

Keto-Brioche Loaf / Keto-French Toast / Keto-Bruschetta / Keto-Roti Bakar" time="60mins

Keto-Brioche Loaf / Keto-French Toast / Keto-Bruschetta / Keto-Roti Bakar

(4 in 1 Keto-Recipes)

Keto-Brioche Loaf

(Sponge & Dough Method)

Ingredients

* For Keto-Flour Mix

90g Micellar Casein

60g Isopure Whey Protein Isolate, Unflavored

30g Dried Egg Whites

30g Egg Yolk Powder

90g Inulin Fiber (Chicory Root) – LC Foods

15g Psyllium Husk

6g Xanthan Gum Powder

6g Salt

3g Vanilla Extract

15g Sucralose

(Whisk & sift all these ingredients together)

* Note : For softer crumb the Keto-Flour Mix can be changed into this formula : 90g Wheat Protein Isolate 8000, 60g Casein Protein Isolate, 30g Whey Protein Isolate, 30g Egg White Powder, 30g Egg Yolk Powder, 60g Inulin Powder, 6g Salt, 3g Vanilla Extract, 15g Sucralose

* For Preferment Dough (Sponge)

100g Keto-Flour Mix

100g Coconut Milk

3g Instant Dry Yeast

* For Brioche Dough (Dough)

150g Egg (around 3 medium eggs)

6g Instant Dry Yeast

60g Butter

The Rest of the Keto-Flour Mix

Preferment Dough

* For Egg Wash

1 Egg Yolk

1 tsp Heavy Cream

* For Topping

Grated Cheddar Cheese

Diced Almonds

Direction

* For Preferment Dough (Sponge)

On a standing mixer bowl with a pair of dough hooks (spiral hooks) attached, combine 100g Keto-Flour Mix, 3g Instant Dry Yeast, and 100g Coconut Milk

Mix on low speed (stage 1) until a rough wet dough is formed then switch to medium speed (stage 2) until it becomes elastic

Turn off the mixer, then knead the dough using hands, until the surface become smooth and a little bit tacky

Rest the dough in a small bowl on a warm spot for 15 minutes, using plastic wrap to cover the mixer bowl so that the dough skin won't dry out

The dough should rise to almost double in size, leaving a slight mark when it is pressed but still bounce back slowly

* For Brioche Dough (Dough)

Combine the rest of the Keto-Flour Mix with 6g Instant Dry Yeast, then pour over the risen Preferment dough on the mixer bowl

Still using the dough hook attachment, add in 150g egg gradually to the mixer bowl.

Mix at low speed (stage 1) until combines and a rough dough formed, then raise the mixer speed into medium speed (stage 2) until the dough start to look smooth but almost tack free if it's touched

Add 60g softened butter over the dough, by raising the mixer speed into high speed (stage 3). Mix until the dough becomes very elastic and leaving no scrap on the mixer bowl (use spatula to scrap the mixer bowl side wall to adhere any sticking dough pieces into the main dough)

Turn off the mixer, and remove the dough onto a silicone pad

Knead the dough for a while until the surface becomes very smooth and dry, then shape into a round disc

Let the dough rest for 10 minutes

Fit the dough on a loaf pan (22cm x 10cm x 7cm) with the seam facing downward

Rest the dough for another 20 minutes on a warm spot, using plastic wrap to cover the loaf pan

Preheat the oven into 300F

Check the loaf readiness to bake, by finger pressing the risen dough. It should still bounce back quick but will leave a slight finger mark

Give an even egg wash over the loaf surface, then spread the topping evenly

Bake for 30 – 40 minutes until the crust look golden brown

Keto-French Toast

(Paris Style French Toast)

Ingredients

100g Egg (around 2 medium eggs)

200ml Heavy Cream

3 tbsp Cognac (Optional)

6 – 8 slices of Keto-Brioche Loaf

2 tbsp Butter

Sweetener for dusting

Direction

In a mixing bowl combine the eggs, heavy cream, and the cognac (optional). Whisk until combined

In a medium size frying pan melt 1/2 tablespoon butter

Dip the brioche slices into the eggs mixture and then gently transfer them to the evenly coated pan

Lightly cook each side for two minutes, or until gets golden-brown finish

Repeat with the rest of the pieces, and coat the frying pan for every batch

Serve immediately, dusted with zero calorie sweetener and a side of cream cheese, peanut butter and low carb berries jam

Keto-Bruschetta

(Italian Red Pepper Bruschetta)

Ingredients

6 – 8 slices of Keto-Brioche Loaf

1 clove garlic (minced)

1 tbsp olive oil

1 large red peppers (chopped)

1/2 medium onion (chopped)

1 tsp Italian seasoning

1/4 cup coarsely chopped fresh basil, divided
1 tbsp minced fresh parsley
1/2 tbsp minced fresh oregano
4 plum tomatoes (sliced)
1/4 cup shredded part-skim mozzarella cheese
2 slices reduced-fat provolone cheese
1/4 cup shredded Parmesan cheese

Direction

In a nonstick skillet, saute 1/2 garlic clove in 1/2 tablespoons olive oil until tender. Brush over one side of each brioche

In the same skillet, sautee the red peppers, onion, Italian seasoning and remaining garlic in remaining olive oil until vegetables are tender, remove from the heat

Add 1 tablespoons basil, parsley and oregano; cool slightly. Place in a blender or food processor, cover and process until pureed. Spread over brioche

Top with tomato slices and cheese. Sprinkle with remaining basil

Bake at 400° for 10-13 minutes or until cheese is melted and edges are golden brown

Keto-Roti Bakar
(Indonesian Grilled Bread)
Ingredients
3 tbsp Butter
100g 100% Dark Cocoa Powder
100g Grated Cheddar Cheese
20g Sweetener for dusting
50ml Heavy Cream

Direction

In a non stick skillet, melt 1 tablespoon butter

Coat each side of brioche slices with butter, using pastry brush

Grill each side of brioche slices until golden brown. Coat the skillet with butter for every batch

Brush one side of grilled brioche with butter, then sprinkle with cocoa powder and sweetener. Cover with another slice then brush once again with butter

Repeat until all brioche slices are used

Spread grated cheddar cheese over the prepared slices, then pour heavy cream over the cheese

Dust generously with sweetener, and serve will still warm

KETO-IRON CHEF THIN CRISPY CREPES & CONDENSED MILK RECIPE

Keto-Iron Crepes & Keto-Iron Condensed Milk Servings=4 Time=30mins
(Keto-Iron Chef Thin Crispy Crepes & Condensed Milk Recipe)
1 – 2 Serving Size
Ingredient
* For Crepes Batter
Dry Ingredients
10g Micellar Casein
10g Isopure Whey Protein Isolate, Unflavored
5g Dried Egg Whites
10g Egg Yolk Powder
15g Inulin Fiber (Chicory Root) – LC Foods
1g Baking Soda
1g Salt
1g Vanilla Extract
5g Sweetener

1g Instant Dry Yeast
Wet Ingredients
15g Egg
20g Coconut Milk
30g Water
* For Topping
90% Dark Chocolate (grated)
Diced Peanut or Almond (roasted)
Sesame Seeds
Cheddar Cheese (grated)
Heavy Whipping Cream
Sweetener (for dusting)
* For Keto-Iron Condensed Milk
Ingredients
Dry Ingredients
15g Inulin Fiber (Chicory Root) – LC Foods
5g Micellar Casein
10g Sweetener
Wet Ingredients
30g Heavy Cream
20g Coconut Milk
Direction
* For Crepes Batter
Whisk all the dry ingredients on a medium bowl
Add egg and coconut milk one at a time, while stirring with a spatula forming a thick batter
Add water and stir until the batter consistency become slurry and smooth
Rest the batter for 30 minutes, to let the yeast ferment. The mixture should show many tiny bubbles when it's ready to be cooked
* For Keto-Iron Condensed Milk
Whisk all the dry ingredients on a small bowl
Mix heavy cream and coconut milk on a cup
Combine the dry ingredients with the wet ingredients together on a sauce pan, stir until no more lumps appear
Heat the mixture over low heat, just until it starts to thicken
Turn off the heat, then transfer the condensed milk mixture into a small bottle or a jar, set aside
* Cooking Keto-Iron Crepes
Heat a flat iron griddle or a non stick pan using a VERY LOW HEAT
Apply 1 tsp coconut oil on the griddle. If using non stick pan than no need to use the oil on the griddle
Take a a big spoonful of the fermented batter. Pour it on the griddle. As soon as you pour it, quickly spread the batter in a circular manner with the spoon bottom, to get a thin and round crepe
Let the batter cook for 1 – 2 minutes, until the thick part of the batter start to look dry
Gently scrap every batter lump that has dry out using spatula, but be careful to not scraping the crepe surface too deep that will tear the thin crepe skins
Cover the griddle with a lid for a moment, and check the batter every 10 – 20 second.
The crepe will start too look golden brown when it's cooked
Brush the cooked crepe with butter evenly, then generously dust the sweetener followed with grated dark chocolate, diced peanut, sesame seeds and grated cheese.
Scribble Keto-Condensed Milk with a spoon in a circular manner over the filling, then fold the crepe into half circle
Turn off the heat, then transfer the crepes onto a working table. Lightly brush the surface with some more butter, then divide into 6 pizza shape slices
Repeat the cooking steps for the rest of the batter and Serve Keto-Iron Crepes with a black coffee or green tea

KETO-IRON CHEF'S ZUPPA SOUP PASTRY

Keto-Iron Chef's Zuppa Soup Pastry Servings=4 Time=30mins
(Italian Zuppa Toscana Soup with Croissant Pastry)
2 – 4 Serving Size
Ingredients
* For Pastry Dough
Dry Ingredients
15g Micellar Casein
10g Isopure Whey Protein Isolate, Unflavored
5g Dried Egg Whites
5g Egg Yolk Powder
15g Inulin Fiber (Chicory Root) – LC Foods
1,5g Psyllium Husk
1g Xanthan Gum Powder
1,5g Salt
1g Garlic Powder
1g Instant Dry Yeast
* Note : The first 7 ingredients above are the Keto-Flour formula for this recipe
For more crisper puff pastry the Keto-Flour can be changed into this formula : 15g Wheat Protein Isolate 8000, 10g Casein Protein Isolate, 10g Whey Protein Isolate, 5g Egg White Powder, 5g Egg Yolk Powder, 5g Inulin Powder
Wet Ingredients
10g Cold Sour Cream or Egg
20g Cold Water (to suspend the yeast leavening action during shaping)
3g Butter
* For Pastry Batter
20g Keto-Flour (Refer to the Keto-Flour formula above)
25g Butter
* For Soup Filling
50g Sliced Salami or Bacon
5g Onion (diced)
2,5g Garlic (diced)
1 tbsp Butter (for stir frying)
* For Cream Soup
20g Keto-Flour (half the quantity of the Keto-Flour Formula listed above)
20g Butter
100g Heavy Cream
30g Cheddar Cheese (grated)
1/4 tsp Chicken Broth Powder
Salt & Pepper to taste
* For Topping
Egg Wash (1 Egg Yolk + 1 tsp Heavy Cream)
Italian Seasoning (diced dry oregano, thyme & basil leaves)
Direction
* For Pastry Dough
Whisk all dry ingredients on a medium bowl. Add sour cream and watergradually, then stir using spatula until a rough dough formed, then switch using hand to knead the dough until elastic. Add the softened butter and knead again until smooth
Shape the dough into a balls, then flaten the dough using rolling pin on a silicone pad. Fold the vertical edges to the center, turn 90 degree then roll it again. Repeat the steps one more time until forming a rectangle with a smooth edges
Divide the rolled dough into 2 equal rectangles
Then using a pasta machine, roll each dough up to stage 5 – 6 setting on the pasta machine

Rest the rolled dough for 10 minutes in the refrigerator
* For Pastry Batter
On a small bowl, combine Keto-Flour with butter using spatula, until a rough batter formed. Add the coconut oil and mix again until completely combines
Rest the batter for 10 minutes at the refrigerator
* For Soup Filling
Bring a skillet over medium heat and melt the butter
Sautee the onion and garlic until fragrant, then add the diced salami or bacon.
Cook the salami or bacon until it starts to sizzle and then stir occasionally, continuing to cook it until the pieces are crisp and red/browned
Remove to a paper towel, set aside
* For Cream Soup
On a medium sauce pan with low heat, melt the butter and pour the heavy cream, stir to combine
When the mixture start to bubbles, stir in grated cheddar cheese until dissolve
Add the Keto-Flour all at once, and stir quickly to combine, until there is no more lump and the mixture thicken
Add chicken broth, salt and pepper into the mixture, stir to dissolve
Turn off the heat, then add the cooked salami or bacon to combine. Taste for perfection, add more salt and pepper if needed
Spoon the Zuppa Soup to 4 tin cup evenly, set aside
* Assemble
On a silicone pad, spread the pastry batter evenly over the rolled dough
Fold each rolled dough from one side to the other side, making at least 4 – 5 fold into a square shape
Divide each folded dough into halves, making 4 square shape, then roll them again into rectangles to make the size larger than Zuppa soup tin mould
Cover each Zuppa Soup cup with the rolled dough, by gently pressing the dough over the cup edges
Rest for 15 – 20 minutes, until the dough feel soft when touched, and leave a slight finger mark when pressed
Preheat the oven into 300F
Brush each rested dough with an egg wash, then sprinkle Italian seasoning over the dough
Bake for 15 minutes, until golden brown
Serve immediately while still warm or refrigerate the Zuppa Soup and microwave for 2 minutes for ser

KETO-IRON CHEF'S KETO-HOT CROSS BUNS

Keto-Iron Chef's Keto-Hot Cross Buns Servings=3-5 Time=60mins
(British Spiced Sweet Buns)
3 – 5 Serving Size

Ingredients
* For Keto-Flour Mix
45g Casein Protein Isolate
30g Whey Protein Isolate
15g Egg White Powder
15g Egg Yolk Powder
45g Inulin Powder
8g Psyllium Husk
3g Xanthan Gum
3g Salt
3g Cinnamon Powder
2g Mixed Spice
2g Nut Meg Powder
5g Sweetener
5g Instant Dry Yeast
(Whisk & sift all these ingredients together)
* Note : For softer crumb the Keto-Flour Mix can be changed into this formula : 45g Wheat Protein Isolate 8000, 20g Casein Protein Isolate, 20g Whey Protein Isolate, 15g Egg White Powder, 15g Egg Yolk Powder, 35g Inulin Powder, 3g Salt, 3g Cinnamon Powder, 2g Mixed Spice, 2g Nutmeg Powder, 5g Sweetener, 5g Instant Dry Yeast
Wet Ingredients
1 Large Egg Yolk
100ml Coconut Milk
1 tbsp Butter (softened)
* For Filling
20g Chopped Chayotes (apple substitute)
20g Diced Cheddar Cheese
1 tbsp Lemon or Orange Zest
Optional : mixed nuts
* For The Cross
1 tsp Micellar Casein
1 tsp Whey Protein Isolate
1 tsp Inulin Powder
1 tbsp Water
(Mix all these ingredients into a thick paste)
* For Glazing
1 tbsp Sukrin Fiber Syrup Gold
1/4 tsp Apricot or Apple Essence
Direction
Whisk and sift all the Keto-Flour Mix Ingredients together in a mixer bowl
Using the dough hook attachment, pour the coconut milk gradually while mixing at low speed (stage 1) until combines and a rough dough formed
Add in the egg yolk, then raise the mixer speed into medium speed (stage 2) until combines and the dough start to look smooth but almost tack free if it's touched
Spread 1 tablespoon of softened butter over the dough, then raise the mixer speed into high speed (stage 3). Mix until the dough becomes very elastic and leaving no scrap on the mixer bowl (use spatula to scrap the mixer bowl side wall to adhere any sticking dough pieces into the main dough)
Turn off the mixer and shape the dough into round. Rest the dough for 20 minutes, until it's almost double in size
Add in all the filling ingredients into the risen dough, and mix with your hand until distributed evenly
Divide the dough into 5 equal parts using weight scale to be accurate
Shape the dough into rolls by duplicating a bowl with your palm and gently roll the dough in circular pattern against the silicone pad. The dough should turn into a smooth ball shape with a seam forming underneath the dough

Transfer each shaped dough balls into a greased baking pan

Rest the dough for another 20 – 30 minutes on a warm spot, using plastic wrap to cover the baking sheet

Preheat the oven into 300F

Check the rolls readiness to bake, by finger pressing the risen dough. It should still bounce back quick but will leave a slight finger mark

Mix all the cross ingredients in a small bowl and stir just until forming a thick paste

Transfer the mixture into piping bag, and make a cross pattern over each risen buns

Bake the buns for 20 minutes until the crust look golden brown

Turn off the oven and remove the baking pan into a working table. Immediately brush the buns with the glaze ingredients while they're still hot

Transfer the glazed buns onto a wire rack and let them cool for 10 minutes before serving

THE KETO IRON CHEF CRANKS OUT SOME KETO-BAGEL NYC STYLE CHEWY BAGEL

The Keto Iron Chef cranks out some Keto-Bagel NYC Style Chewy Bagel Servings=1 Time=45mins

ngredient

* Keto-Bread Flour Mix

25g Inulin Fiber (Chicory Root) – LC Foods

10g Micellar Casein

5g Isopure Whey Protein Isolate, Unflavored

10g Dried Egg Whites

5g Egg Yolk Powder

2,5g Psyllium Husk

1g Xanthan Gum Powder or Guar Gum Powder

2g Instant Dry Yeast

1,5g Salt

1g Garlic Powder

0,5g Nutmeg Powder

2,5g Splenda (Optional)

* Egg Mixture

25g Egg

1g Honey (consumed by the yeast on proofing)

* Liquid Mixtures

10g Coconut Milk or Heavy Cream

15g Warm Water

* Oil Mixture

4g Virgin Coconut Oil

* Topping

10g Dessicated Coconut

* Other

2 quart of water to be boiled

1 tsp Baking Soda

1 tbsp Virgin Coconut Oil

Direction

Sift all the Keto-Flour ingredients together on a big bowl or mixer bowl

Combine all the egg mixtures on a medium bowl, stir until dissolve, set aside

Combine all the liquid mixtures on a medium bowl, stir until combines, set aside

Scale and prepare the coconut oil on a small bowl

On the Keto-Flour bowl, pour the egg mixtures then stir with a spatula until a crumble dough formed

Add the liquid mixtures gradually until a thick batter formed, and keep stirring with the spatula until the dough getting elastic

Add the coconut oil and keep kneading using spatula until the dough become smooth, then start using your hand to knead the dough using egg yolk powder as the bench flour.

After a smooth elastic dough has formed, use your finger to create a hole in the center of the dough, making a doughnut shape, then proof (ferment) the dough on a warm spot for 30 minutes until 1,5x its original size.

Preheat oven into 300F

Boil 2 quart of water with 1 teaspoon of baking soda and 1 tablespoon of coconut oil

Pouch the risen dough for 30 seconds and flip to the other side for another 30 seconds

Place the dough on a greased baking pan, and sprinkle with dessicated coconut while it still wet.

Bake for 20 minutes until golden brown

Serve with Cream Cheese or anything you like

THE KETO IRON CHEF'S KETO-HOKKAIDO MILKY LOAF

The Keto Iron Chef's Keto-Hokkaido Milky Loaf" time="120mins
Ingredients
* For Keto-Flour Mix
90g Casein Protein Isolate Hardcore Micellar Casein
60g Whey Protein Isolate Isopure Whey Protein Isolate, Unflavored
30g Egg White Powder Egg White Powder
30g Egg Yolk Powder
90g Inulin Powder Inulin Fiber (Chicory Root) – LC Foods
15g Psyllium Husk Psyllium Husk
6g Xanthan Gum Xanthan Gum
6g Salt
3g Vanilla Extract
15g Sucralose
(Whisk & sift all these ingredients together)
* Note : For softer crumb the Keto-Flour Mix can be changed into this formula : 90g Wheat Protein Isolate 8000, 60g Casein Protein Isolate, 30g Whey Protein Isolate, 30g Egg White Powder, 30g Egg Yolk Powder, 60g Inulin Powder, 6g Salt, 3g Vanilla Extract, 15g Sucralose
* For Liquid Mix
30g Heavy Whipping Cream
30g Coconut Milk
10g Cider Vinegar

110g Water
(Stir & combine all these ingredients together)
* For Tang Zhong (Water Roux)
10g Keto-Flour Mix
50g Liquid Mix
* For Preferment Dough (Sponge)
100g Keto-Flour Mix
100g Liquid Mix
3g Instant Dry Yeast
* For Hokkaido Dough (Dough)
30g Egg
30g Liquid Mix
6g Instant Dry Yeast
25g Coconut Oil Virgin Coconut Oil
The Rest of the Keto-Flour Mix
Tang Zhong
Preferment Dough
* For Egg Wash
1 Egg Yolk
1 tsp Coconut Milk
Direction
* For Tang Zhong
On a small sauce pan, combine 10g of Keto-Flour Mix with 50g of Liquid Mix then stir using rubber spatula until there is no more lumps
Heat the mixture over a stove with a very low heat, and stir using rubber spatula until the mixture just starting to thicken and leaving a trail behind the rubber spatula
Turn off the heat and set aside. Let the Tang Zhong mixture cool on a room temperature spot for at least 10 minutes
* For Preferment Dough
On a standing mixer bowl with a pair of dough hooks (spiral hooks) attached, combine 100g Keto-Flour Mix, 3g Instant Dry Yeast, and 100g Liquid Mix
Mix on low speed (stage 1) until a rough wet dough is formed then switch to medium speed (stage 2) until it becomes elastic
Turn off the mixer, then knead the dough using hands, until the surface smoother but still a little bit tacky
Rest the dough at the mixer bowl on a warm spot for 15 minutes, using plastic wrap to cover the mixer bowl so that the dough skin won't dry out
The dough should rise to almost double in size, leaving a slight mark when it is pressed but still bounce back slowly
* Assemble
Combine the rest of the Keto-Flour Mix with 6g Instant Dry Yeast, then pour over the risen Preferment dough on the mixer bowl
Still using the dough hook attachment, add in 30g egg and the cooled Tang Zhong mixture to the mixer bowl.
Mix at low speed (stage 1) until combines and a rough dough formed
Add in 30g Liquid Mix (the rest of the Liquid Mix) gradually, then raise the mixer speed into medium speed (stage 2) until combines and the dough start to look smooth but almost tack free if it's touched
Pour 25g Coconut milk over the dough, by raising the mixer speed into high speed (stage 3). Mix until the dough becomes very elastic and leaving no scrap on the mixer bowl (use spatula to scrap the mixer bowl side wall to adhere any sticking dough pieces into the main dough)
Turn off the mixer, and remove the dough onto a silicone pad
* Shaping the Loaf
Knead the dough for a while until the surface becomes very smooth and dry, then shape into a round disc
Divide the dough into 3 equal parts, and shape them into balls
Roll out each dough into long oval shape (1/2 inch thick) using roller pin, then fold the each side of the longest part into the center of the dough

Fold each dough into a log and pinch the tip ends to create a seam

Arrange each dough on a loaf pan (22cm x 10cm x 7cm) with the seam facing downward

Rest the dough for another 15 minutes on a warm spot, using plastic wrap to cover the loaf pan

Preheat the oven into 300F

Check the loaf readiness to bake, by finger pressing the risen dough. It should still bounce back quick but will leave a slight finger mark

Give an even egg wash over the loaf surface, then bake for 30 – 40 minutes until the crust look golden brown

Remove the loaf pan from the oven, then brush the crust with softened butter that will melt upon contact with the hot crust

Let the baked loaf cools on the loaf pan for 10 minutes before removing it to a wire rack

Slice the loaf at 1cm width and serve with "High Fat" toppings or fillings, since this loaf has a very high protein macro profile although the net carb is very low, and needs to be eaten with proper fat to protein keto macros ratio

THE KETO IRON CHEF'S KETO-BAKLAVA (TURKISH PHYLLO PASTRY - ROLLED BAKLAVA)

The Keto Iron Chef's Keto-Baklava (Turkish Phyllo Pastry – Rolled Baklava) Servings=2 Time=60mins

Ingredients

* For Baklava Phyllo Dough

Dry Ingredients

15g Casein Protein Isolate Hardcore Micellar Casein

10g Isopure Whey Protein Isolate, Unflavored

5g Dried Egg Whites

5g Egg Yolk Powder

15g Inulin Fiber (Chicory Root) – LC Foods

1,5g Psyllium Husk

1g Xanthan Gum

1g Salt

1g Sucralose

* Note : The first 7 ingredients above are the Keto-Flour formula for this recipe

For crisper crust the Keto-Flour can be changed into this formula : 15g Wheat Protein Isolate 8000, 10g Casein Protein Isolate, 10g Whey Protein Isolate, 5g Egg White Powder, 5g Egg Yolk Powder, 5g Inulin Powder

Wet Ingredients

30g Water

3g Coconut Oil Virgin Coconut Oil

* For Brushing Phyllo Dough

5g Melted Butter

* For Baklava Filling

40g Diced Almonds

20g Sesame Seeds

20g Grated Parmesan Cheese

10g Egg Yolk Powder

10g Ricotta Cheese

1g Salt

1g Nut Meg Powder

3g Cinnamon Powder

15g Sucralose

20g Butter

* For Baklava Sauce

30g Cream Cheese

60g Heavy Cream

5g Inulin Powder Inulin Fiber (Chicory Root) – LC Foods

5g Sucralose
1g Salt
5g Butter
Direction
* For Baklava Phyllo Dough
Whisk all dry ingredients on a medium bowl. Add water gradually, then stir using spatula until a rough dough formed, then switch using hand to knead the dough until elastic. Add the coconut oil and knead again until smooth
Rest the dough for 10 minutes
Divide the rested dough into 2 equal parts. Using roller pin, flaten each dough into rectangle, then fold the vertical edges into the center of the dough. Roll again to flaten, then repeat the folding from the horizontal edges into the center of the dough and flaten to make smooth edges of rectangles.
Rest the rolled dough back for another 10 minutes
Continue rolling each dough using a pasta machine up to the thinnest setting, so that the sheet would be very thin and transparent (stage 7 – 8 setting on the pasta machine)
* For Baklava Filling
Combine all the Baklava filling ingredients onto a food processor, then pulse several time until a coarse paste is formed
Shape the paste into a log, with the length being measured to fit the rolled Phyllo dough width. Divide the log into 2 equal parts, set aside
* For Baklava Sauce
Melt butter on a small sauce pan, with low heat.
Add heavy cream and cream cheese, then stir to combines
When the mixture has bubbles, add in inulin powder, sucralose and salt into the mixture, then turn off the heat and stir until the mixture thicken
Remove the sauce onto a small sauce bowl, set aside
* Assemble
Preheat the oven into 300F
On a silicone pad, spread the melted butter thinly using brush, over each phyllo sheet
Put one filling paste log on one side of the phyllo sheet (leaving 1/3 space of the sheet width), then wrap the paste and fold by keeping the sheet tightly wrapping the filling up to the other edge of the phyllo sheet
Make a seam by brushing an egg white on the last edge of phyllo sheet as the glue
Cut the bottom edges of phyllo sheet on 4 side using scissor, then fold into the center creating a seam (use egg white for the glue)
Repeat the steps for the other phyllo sheet and filling paste log
Arrange them onto a greased muffin or cup cake mould, with the seam facing the bottom
Bake for 10 – 15 minutes, until the top edges starts to darken
Serve the Keto-Baklava by pouring the sauce over the dome until it's flowing over the edge like a lava from a mountain..LOL

THE KETO IRON CHEF'S KETO-BINANGKAL (PHILIPPINES SESAME BALLS)

The Keto Iron Chef's Keto-Binangkal (Philippines Sesame Balls) Servings=1 Time=30mins
Ingredient
10g Hardcore Micellar Casein
10g Isopure Whey Protein Isolate, Unflavored
5g Dried Egg Whites
10g Egg Yolk Powder
15g Inulin Fiber (Chicory Root) – LC Foods
1g Xanthan Gum
1g Baking Powder
0,5g Baking Soda
1g Salt

1,5g Cinnamon Powder

1g Vanilla Extract

3g Sucralose

* Note : The first 6 ingredients above are the Keto-Flour formula for this recipe

For crisper crust the Keto-Flour can be changed into this formula : 10g Wheat Protein Isolate 8000, 10g Casein Protein Isolate, 5g Whey Protein Isolate, 5g Egg White Powder, 10g Egg Yolk Powder, 10g Inulin Powder

Wet Ingredients

10g Egg

20g Coconut Milk

5g Butter

Coatings

25g Sesame Seed

Direction

Whisk all the dry ingredients on a medium bowl

Add egg and coconut milk gradually by stirring with spatula until a rough dough forms

Add butter then knead just until combine (do not over knead)

Take a teaspoon of the batter and roll between palms to form a ball shape. Repeat until all batter is used

Drop the balls into a plate of sesame seeds and roll the balls until the surfaces are evenly coated with sesame seeds

Deep fry the coated balls with low medium heat until slightly dark brown. This is crispy outside but soft inside

Drain the fried Keto-Binangkal with a spider strainer then use paper towel to remove the excess oil

Serve with black coffee or green tea

THE KETO IRON CHEF'S KETO-HYBRID OF CROISSANT AND CANNOLI

The Keto Iron Chef's Keto-hybrid of Croissant and Cannoli Servings=3 Time=60mins

A hybrid of Croissant and Cannoli in a Ketofied Way

Ingredients

* For hybrid of Croissant and Cannoli Dough

Dry Ingredients

15g Casein Protein Isolate Hardcore Micellar Casein

10g Isopure Whey Protein Isolate, Unflavored

5g Dried Egg Whites

5g Egg Yolk Powder

15g Inulin Fiber (Chicory Root) – LC Foods

1,5g Psyllium Husk

1g Xanthan Gum

1g Salt

1,5g Cinnamon Powder

5g Sucralose

* Note : The first 7 ingredients above are the Keto-Flour formula for this recipe

For crisper crust the Keto-Flour can be changed into this formula : 15g Wheat Protein Isolate 8000, 10g Casein Protein Isolate, 10g Whey Protein Isolate, 5g Egg White Powder, 5g Egg Yolk Powder, 5g Inulin Powder

Wet Ingredients

10g Egg White

15g Water (Marsala Wine)

5g Butter

* Note : The original recipe is using "Marsala Wine", but since I'm a moslem and can't consume wine (alcohol) I use water to substitute the wine

* For Pastry Batter

Dry Ingredients

25g Keto-Flour (half the quantity from the Keto-Flour formula listed above)
0,5g Salt
0,5g Cinnamon Powder
2,5g Sucralose
Wet Ingredients
5g Virgin Coconut Oil
20g Butter
* For hybrid of Croissant and Cannoli Filling
120g Mascarpone Cheese
0,5g Salt
1g Vanilla Extract
10g Sucralose
10g Egg Yolk Powder Egg Yolk Powder
Direction
* For hybrid of Croissant and Cannoli Dough
Whisk all dry ingredients on a medium bowl. Add egg white and water gradually, then stir using spatula until a rough dough formed, then switch using hand to knead the dough until elastic. Add the softened butter and knead again until smooth
Rest the dough for 10 minutes
Divide the rested dough into 2 equal parts. Then using a pasta machine, roll each dough into stage 5 – 6 setting on the pasta machine
Rest the rolled dough back for another 10 minutes
* For Pastry Batter
On a small bowl, combine Keto-Flour with butter using spatula, until a rough batter formed. Add the coconut oil and mix again until completely combines
Rest the batter for 10 minutes at the refrigerator
* For hybrid of Croissant and Cannoli Filling
Add all the filling ingredients on a medium bowl, and stir using rubber spatula until completely combines
Remove the filling into a piping tube, set aside
* Assemble
On a silicone pad, spread the pastry batter evenly over each rolled dough
Fold each rolled dough from one side to the other side, making at least 4 – 5 fold into a square shape
Roll each folded dough to flatten it into 1/2 cm thick, by rolling it vertically and horizontally on both side of the dough
Cut each dough into a circle shape using round cookies cutter
Fold each dough on a roller pin or other pipe shape object, by pressing the surface contact of each dough edges using finger to create a seam
Refrigerate for 10 minutes, to make the pipe shape harden
Deep fry the dough using low to medium heat, until golden brown
Fill each hybrid of Croissant and Cannoli with the filling and serve with black coffee or green tea

KETO IRON CHEF'S KETO-CROFFINS

Keto-Croffins Servings=2 Time=60mins" difficulty="moderate"]
A hybrid of Croissant and Muffins in a Ketofied Way
Ingredients
* For Croffins Dough
Dry Ingredients
15g Hardcore Micellar Casein
10g Isopure Whey Protein Isolate, Unflavored
5g Dried Egg Whites
5g Egg Yolk Powder

15g Inulin Fiber (Chicory Root) – LC Foods
1,5g Psyllium Husk
1g Xanthan Gum
1g Salt
1g Vanilla Extract
3g Sucralose
1g Instant Dry Yeast
* Note : The first 7 ingredients above are the Keto-Flour formula for this recipe
For crisper crust the Keto-Flour can be changed into this formula : 15g Wheat Protein Isolate 8000, 10g Casein Protein Isolate, 10g Whey Protein Isolate, 5g Egg White Powder, 5g Egg Yolk Powder, 5g Inulin Powder
Wet Ingredients
20g VERY COLD WATER (to suspend the yeast leavening action over the dough, during the rolling & folding process)
10g Yogurt
4g Butter
* For Pastry Batter
Dry Ingredients
25g Keto-Flour (half the quantity from the Keto-Flour formula listed above)
0,5g Salt
0,5g Vanilla Extract
2g Sucralose
Wet Ingredients
5g Coconut Oil Virgin Coconut Oil
20g Butter
* For Muffin Batter
Dry Ingredients
25g Keto-Flour
0,5g Salt
0,5g Vanilla Extract
5g Sucralose
1g Baking Powder
Wet Ingredients
10g Egg White (beat to a stiff peak)
5g Egg Yolk
10g Ricotta Cheese
30g Coconut Milk
10g Butter
Direction
* For Croffins Dough
Whisk all dry ingredients on a medium bowl. Add water and yogurt gradually, then stir using spatula until a rough dough formed, then switch using hand to knead the dough until elastic. Add the softened butter and knead again until smooth
Rest the dough for 10 minutes at the refrigerator
Roll the dough up to stage 5 – 6 setting on the pasta machine, into a long sheet

Rest the rolled dough back in the refrigerator for another 10 minutes
* For Pastry Batter
On a small bowl, combine Keto-Flour with butter using spatula, until a rough batter formed. Add the coconut oil and mix again until completely combines

Rest the batter for 10 minutes at the refrigerator

* For Muffins Batter
On a standing mixer, beat butter until white then add egg yolk and ricotta cheese. Raise the speed into medium stage until the batter becomes light and creamy
Lower the mixer speed, then add the Keto-Flour mix gradually until the batter becomes thick
Add the whipped egg white into the batter and mix for 10 – 15 second, just until combined. Do not over mix

* Assemble
On a silicone pad, spread the pastry batter evenly over the rolled dough
Fold the rolled dough from one side to the other side, making at least 4 – 5 fold into a square shape
Roll the folded dough to flatten it into 1/2 cm thick, by keep maintaining the square shape during rolling
Slice the dough into 16 long rectangles with equal width, then arrange them into 2 muffins cup
(see the attached pics)
Rest the arranged dough for 15 minutes, until the skin become softer (risen)

Preheat the oven into 300F
Bake the risen dough for 10 minutes, then scoop the muffins batter into each cups equally reaching 3/4 height of the cups
Bake again for another 15 – 20 minutes until the batter set, and an inserted tooth pick comes out clean
Serve with black coffee or green tea

THE KETO IRON CHEF'S KETO-BHATOORA

The Keto Iron Chef's Keto-Bhatoora Servings=2 Time=30mins" difficulty="moderate"]
Keto-Bhatoora
(2 serving size)
Ingredients
Dry Ingredients
30g Casein Protein Isolate Hardcore Micellar Casein
20g Isopure Whey Protein Isolate, Unflavored
10g Dried Egg Whites
10g Egg Yolk Powder
30g Inulin Fiber (Chicory Root) – LC Foods
3g Psyllium Husk
2g Xanthan Gum
2g Salt
2g Vanilla Extract
5g Sucralose
1,5g Baking Powder
1g Baking Soda
* Note : The first 7 ingredients above are the Keto-Flour formula for this recipe
For crisper crust the Keto-Flour can be changed into this formula : 45g Wheat Protein Isolate 8000, 30g Casein Protein Isolate, 15g Whey Protein Isolate, 15g Egg White Powder, 15g Egg Yolk Powder, 30g Inulin Powder
Wet Ingredients
25g Yogurt
15g Water
5g Virgin Coconut Oil
Direction
Whisk all dry ingredients on a medium bowl. Add yogurt and stir using spatula until a rough dough formed
Add the water, then switch using hand to knead the dough until elastic.

Add the coconut oil and knead again until smooth

Divide the dough into 2 equal parts. Then roll each dough into round shape with 1/2 inch thickness, using roller pin

Deep fry the flattened dough with medium high heat on a frying pan and splash the hot oil over the dough surface to create steams inside the dough that will make it puffing
(the oil used for frying must be very hot around 200C – 250C, in order to make the dough puff and doesn't absorb too many oil afterwards)
Flip the dough to the other side when the first upward surface has puff and turn golden brown
Drain the Keto-Bhatoora with spider strainer then use paper towel remove the excess oil

Serve with curry dishes or India chicken massala dishes

THE KETO IRON CHEF'S KETO-BUNUELOS

Keto-Bunuelos Servings=1-2" difficulty="medium"]
Keto-Bunuelos
(1 – 2 Serving Size)
Ingredient
10g Casein Protein Isolate Hardcore Micellar Casein
10g Isopure Whey Protein Isolate, Unflavored
5g Dried Egg Whites
10g Egg Yolk Powder
15g Inulin Fiber (Chicory Root) – LC Foods
1g Xanthan Gum
1g Salt
1g Vanilla Extract
2g Sucralose
* Note : The first 6 ingredients above are the Keto-Flour formula for this recipe
For crisper crust the Keto-Flour can be changed into this formula : 15g Wheat Protein Isolate 8000, 5g Casein Protein Isolate, 5g Whey Protein Isolate, 5g Egg White Powder, 10g Egg Yolk Powder, 10g Inulin Powder
Wet Ingredients
50g Egg White
25g Egg Yolk
60g Coconut Milk
40g Butter
Topping
Cinnamon Powder
Sucralose
Direction
Whisk all the dry ingredients on a medium bowl,set aside
Melt butter then add coconut milk on a sauce pan using very low heat
Stir the mixture using spatula until it start to bubbles, then add the whisked dry ingredients all at once by keep stirring fast until a very sticky batter formed

Turn off the heat and add the egg yolk to the batter, by keep stirring until the batter thicken
Add egg white gradually by keep stirring and folding with spatula until the batter become very thick and can be shaped
Use a spoon to divide the thick batter into small balls, then deep fry them with low medium heat until the surface turns golden brown

Drain the fried Keto-Bunuelos with a spider strainer, then use paper towel to remove the excess oil
Generously dust them with cinnamon powder and sucralose. Serve with black coffee or green tea

THE KETO IRON CHEF'S KETO-CROZELS

The Keto Iron Chef's Keto-Crozels Servings=3" difficulty="moderate"]
Keto-Crozels
(3 serving size)
A hybrid of Croissant and Pretzels in a Ketofied Way
Ingredients
* For Crozza Dough
Dry Ingredients
30g Micellar Casein
20g Isopure Whey Protein Isolate, Unflavored
10g Dried Egg Whites
10g Egg Yolk Powder
30g Inulin Fiber (Chicory Root) – LC Foods
3g Psyllium Husk
2g Xanthan Gum
2g Salt
2g Vanilla Extract
5g Sucralose
2g Instant Dry Yeast
* Note : The first 7 ingredients above are the Keto-Flour formula for this recipe
For crisper crust the Keto-Flour can be changed into this formula : 45g Wheat Protein Isolate 8000, 30g Casein Protein Isolate, 15g Whey Protein Isolate, 15g Egg White Powder, 15g Egg Yolk Powder, 30g Inulin Powder
Wet Ingredients
40g VERY COLD WATER (to suspend the yeast leavening action over the dough, during the rolling & folding process)
20g Coconut Milk
8g Butter
* For Pastry Batter
Dry Ingredients
50g Keto-Flour (half the quantity from the Keto-Flour formula listed above)
1g Salt
1g Vanilla Extract
3g Sucralose
Wet Ingredients
10g Virgin Coconut Oil
40g Butter
* For Crozels Topping
Sesame seeds
Grated Cheddar Cheese
Cinnamon Powder
* Egg Wash
1 Egg Yolk
1 tsp Coconut Milk
Direction
* For Crozels Dough
Whisk all dry ingredients on a medium bowl. Add water and coconut milk mixture gradually and stir using spatula until a rough dough formed, then switch using hand to knead the dough until elastic. Add the softened butter and knead again until smooth
Rest the dough for 10 minutes at the refrigerator

Divide the rested dough into 3 equal parts. Then using a pasta machine, roll each dough into stage 5 – 6 setting on the pasta machine

Rest the rolled dough back in the refrigerator for another 10 minutes
* For Pastry Batter
On a small bowl, combine Keto-Flour with butter using spatula, until a rough batter formed. Add the coconut oil and mix again until completely combines
Rest the batter for 10 minutes at the refrigerator

* Assemble
On a silicone pad, spread the pastry batter evenly over the rolled dough
Fold the dough from the longest side forming a rope and press each end using finger to seam. Shape into a pretzels and rest the dough in a warm spot for 20 – 30 minutes until it rise
Preheat the oven into 300F

Give an egg wash over risen Crozels dough, then sprinkle each Crozels with 3 different topping, such as sesame seeds, grated cheddar cheese and cinnamon powder
Bake for 20 minutes, until golden brown
Serve with black coffee or green tea

THE KETO IRON CHEF'S KETO-CROKIES (GREEN TEA CROKIES)

Keto-Crokies
(Green Tea Crokies)
A Hybrid of Croissant Dough & Cookies Batter in a Ketofied Way

Green Tea Crokies Servings=20 Time=60mins" difficulty="moderate"]
Ingredients
Dry Ingredients
60g Micellar Casein
40g Isopure Whey Protein Isolate, Unflavored
20g Dried Egg Whites
20g Egg Yolk Powder
60g Inulin Fiber (Chicory Root) – LC Foods

6g Psyllium Husk
4g Xanthan Gum
4g Salt
20g Sucralose
5g Baking Powder
8g Green Tea Powder
* Note : The first 7 ingredients above are the Keto-Flour formula for this recipe
For crisper crust the Keto-Flour can be changed into this formula : 60g Wheat Protein Isolate 8000, 40g Casein Protein Isolate, 20g Whey Protein Isolate, 20g Egg White Powder, 20g Egg Yolk Powder, 40g Inulin Powder
Wet Ingredients
40g Egg White
30g Heavy Whipping Cream
30g Water
10g Butter
* For Green Tea Cookies Batter
Dry Ingredients
100g Keto-Flour (half the quantity from the Keto-Flour formula listed above)
2g Salt
4g Green Tea Powder
10g Sucralose
2g Baker's Ammonia
2g Baking Soda
(Whisk all these ingredients together)
Wet Ingredients
20g Egg Yolk
100g Butter
Direction
* For Green Tea Crokies Dough
Whisk all dry ingredients on a mixer bowl. Using low speed stage, mix in egg white until crumbly dough formed, then add water gradually while raising the mixer speed into medium stage until a dough completely formed

Rest the dough for 10 minutes

Divide the rested dough into 6 equal parts. Then using a pasta machine, roll each dough into stage 7 – 8 setting on the pasta machine

Rest the rolled dough back for another 10 minutes
* For Green Tea Cookies Batter
On a standing mixer, cream butter until light with low speed. Then add egg yolk until combined and gradually add the Keto-Flour mix using spoon until the batter thicken

Rest the batter for 10 minutes at the refrigerator, then divide the rested batter into 6 equal parts.
Preheat the oven into 300F
* Assemble
On a silicone pad, spread the rolled dough with the batter evenly
Make 4 – 5 fold from one side to the other end of the rolled dough
Roll the dough at one direction to flatten and seaming the batter within.
Cut the dough using knife or pastry cutter into multiple equal squares, then remove the Crokies squares onto a baking pan with 1 – 2 cm space apart

Preheat the oven into 300F

Bake for 10 – 15 minutes, until the Crokies edges has just started to browns

Let the baked Crokies cools on the baking pan for at least 10 minutes, before removing them into a cookies jar

Served with black coffee or green tea

THE KETO IRON CHEF'S KETO BREAD

Good Morning (in my time)

As I have promised before, this monday I will post the recipe for Keto-Bread that doesn't taste suck, and also have a texture and the properties almost exactly like a real bread.

I've been making several batch during my experiment and found the secret to soft & fluffy Keto-Bread was on the hydration level (120%) and the assembling methods. I'm using a "sponge & dough" method to get twice fermentation as in the "straight dough" method on regular white bread. Since Keto-Bread cannot rise twice if it use "straight dough" method which has bulk ferment & final proofing for rising the regular bread dough.

And I also use a "water roux" method (originally it's Thangzhong Method for Asian Soft Breads) to keep the bread crumbs fluffy and hold the moisture better, so it won't stall quickly and keep the crumbs soft.

This recipe will looks too technical but it is the best way that I've found after several trial & error that I'd encountered.

Proofing time is crucial for this Keto-Bread recipe, as over-proofing can lead to a collapsing bread after it bakes and result in a dense small bread.

Baking time is also crucial to make sure the crumbs are well baked. Using a thermometer to measure the crumbs temperature would be a good idea (it's done when the center of the crumbs reach 200F)

Well here it goes

Keto-Bread Loaf Servings=12 Time=1:30mins" difficulty="moderate"]

(8,4g Net Carb / 87g Protein / 42g Fat) – 455g (whole)

(0,5g Net Carb / 5,4g Protein / 2,6g Fat) – 28g (perSlice)

(Gluten Free, Nuts Free, Seeds Free)

Ingredient

* Keto-Bread Flour Mix

100g Inulin Fiber (Chicory Root) – LC Foods

40g Micellar Casein

20g Isopure Whey Protein Isolate, Unflavored

20g Dried Egg Whites

10g Egg Yolk Powder

10g Psyllium Husk

4g Xanthan Gum or Guar Gum Powder

1g Cream of Tartar

4g Salt

Wet Ingredient

* Liquid Mix

20g Whip Cream

20g Coconut Milk

110g Warm Water

Total Liquid Mix = 150g

* Egg Mix

60g Eggs (one large eggs)

10g Cider Vinegar

4g Stevia (concentrated – use 1tsp=1cup) * This one is good too. * I test with bulk using this, can be used with listed measurement

4g Vanilla Essence

2g Honey (consumed by the yeast on main dough proofing)

* Oil Mix
8g Virgin Coconut Oil
8g Melted Butter
Assemble the ingredients above into :
* Water Roux
10g Keto-Flour
50g Liquid Mix
* Sponge Mix
100g Keto-Flour
100g Liquid Mix
3g Instant Dry Yeast
2g Honey (consumed by the yeast on sponge dough proofing)
Main Dough Mix (30 minutes final proofing)
90g Keto-Flour
Water Roux Mixture
Egg Mixture
6g Instant Dry Yeast
2g Honey
Risen Sponge Dough (divide into 4 – 6 slices)
6g Baking Powder
3g Baking Soda
Oil Mixtures
Direction
Sift all the Keto-Flour ingredients together then divide and scale them evenly into 2 medium bowl, set aside
Combine coconut milk and warm water on a medium bowl, stir until dissolve, set aside
Combine one large egg, apple cider vinegar, splenda, honey and vanilla essence on a medium bowl, mix thoroughly until all the ingredients dissolve
Prepare the oil mix by combining coconut oil & melted butter on a small bowl, stir until combine
Scale the sponge dough yeast and the main dough yeast on separate container
Scale the baking powder and baking soda on a small container
Assembling
For the Water Roux : on a small sauce pan, stir & combine the water roux ingredients. Using a low heat stir the mixture with spatula until it form a thick pudding consistency (if you use thermometer stop cooking when the batter reach 65C).
For the Sponge Dough : on a standing mixer, pour the liquid mix, add the honey and the instant dry yeast then stir until combine. Wait for 5 minutes until it start to bubbles, then add the Sponge Dough Keto-Flour and mix with speed 1 to 3 until a tacky dough formed.
Kneading & Bulk Ferment : Move the dough on a sill plate and knead the dough using egg yolk powder as the bench flour. The final sponge dough should be dry but a little tacky if you press deep with your finger.
Ferment the sponge dough until 1,5x the original size (not 2x like regular white flour dough). It takes around 20 minutes to 30 minutes to proof the dough on a warm spot.
For the Main Dough : on a standing mixer, pour the egg mix, add the honey and the instant dry yeast then stir until combine. Wait for 5 minutes until it start to bubbles, then add the Water Roux mixture, and the Main Dough Keto-Flour and mix with speed 1 until they form a thick batter.
Sprinkle the baking powder and baking soda, then continue to mix until dissolves.
Cut the risen sponge dough into 4 – 6 pieces and combine with the mixed batter one at a time by also increasing the mixer speed to level 2.
After a tacky dough start to forms, add oil mixtures into the dough and raise the speed to level 3 until a slightly tacky dough forms.
Shaping The Loaf : Move the final dough to sill plate and knead the dough using egg yolk powder as the bench flour until a smooth dough formed.

Roll the dough into rectangles using roller pin (1/2 inch thick dough), then fold each side of the rectangles into the middle, rotate 90 degree then roll again into rectangle.

Fold the dough forward into a log, and seam each side of the log.

Final Proofing & Baking The Loaf : Move the dough into a greased loaf pan, and press the dough until flat and fill the loaf pan evenly.

Preheat the oven into 300F

Proof the dough using plastic wrap to cover the loaf pan on a warm spot. Proof only until the dough has risen to 1,5x time it's size (around 20 minutes – 30 minutes), then brush some egg wash before baking the risen dough for 30 minutes to 45 minutes.

Turn off the oven then immediately brush the baked loaf with some butter and wait for 10 minutes before removing the loaf to the wire rack.

* I made sweet cheese filled buns too with some left over, and turns out amazing.. Yumms

THE KETO IRON CHEF'S PASTA & NOODLES

My Keto-Asian Meals

Good Morning (my time)

Today I'm going to fulfil my promises to some of the group member for their request on ketofying their past beloved high carb Pasta & Noodles, and turn them into the "protein source foods" to be tailored by anyone (Fellow Ketoers) for their Keto macros plan by combining them with other fatty ingredients in any recipes.

Now I'm going to show you my experiment for the pasta and noodles recipes. I hope u guys like this recipes, so it is worth the waiting until now at Monday on

Here it goes

Keto pasta Servings=varies" time="1:30mins

100g Keto-Flour Formula (The Basic Keto-Flour)

70g Inulin Fiber (Chicory Root) – LC Foods

20g Micellar Casein

10g Isopure Whey Protein Isolate, Unflavored

(Net Carb : 2,4g / Protein : 26g / Fat : 0,4g)

1) Keto-Pasta / Spaghetti / Fettucine

For 2 serving size

Ingredient :

100g Keto-Flour

10g Psyllium Husk

2g Salt

50g Whole Egg (one medium egg)

30g Egg Yolk (2 egg yolks)

(Net Carb : 4,8g / Protein : 38g / Fat : 19,2g)

* Net Carb per serving size = 2,4g

Direction

Combine all the ingredients in the bowl of a food processor. Pulse until combined, then run the processor until a rough crumble is formed.

Remove the dough from the food processor and press them into a dough. Rest the dough for 30 minutes on a ziplock bag, then proceed with kneading the dough over a sill plate so you won't need bench flour (but if you do need one, use the inulin powder or egg yolk powder as the bench flour)

Divide the dough into two equal portion, then shape them into 2 inch wide rectangles before proceeding to Pasta Machine

Follow the Pasta Machine instruction for rolling the pasta dough or see the picture above. (I use the 5th setting as the maximum setting for pasta thickness)
Rest the rolled dough for another 15 to 30 minutes to make them dryer.

Continue with shredding the pasta with the shape that you choose such as Fettucine setting or Spaghetti setting. For Lasagna leave the pasta in long sheets and for Ravioli, cut the rolled out pasta into 2 inch square pieces. Dollop the filling in the middle of a square of pasta. Brush the edges of pasta with an egg wash. Place another pasta square on top and press down, crimping the edges.
Dehydrate the shaped pasta on a baking tray in your backyard for 2 to 3 hours to evaporate the moisture within, it will also slightly cook them and prevent them from sticking to each other if you decide to store them in the refrigerator with ziplock bags, otherwise cook them right away.
To cook the pasta, bring a large pot of salted water to boil. Put pasta shape of your choice into the boiling water. When pasta rises to the surface, take a little piece and taste it. You should be able to bite into it without falling apart, it's a fine line. One moment it's al dente, and the next it's one big ball of mush, so watch the pot. Cooking times will vary for the different shape. The rule of thumb is the thinner the shape the faster it cooks.

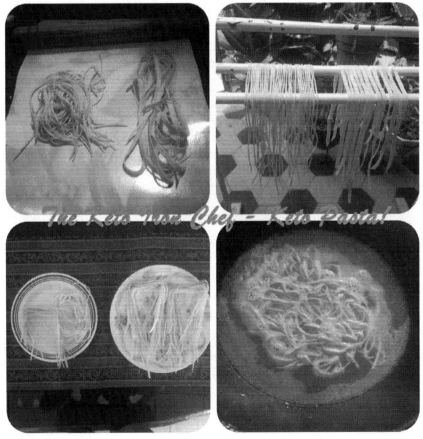

Scoop up the cooked pasta with spider strainer into a colander. Rub coconut oil into the warm pasta, and place pasta into baking tray to cool before use.
Use the cooked pasta for your favourite pasta dishes
2) Keto-Noodles / Hokkien Mee / Mee Goreng
For 2 serving size
Ingredients
100g Keto-Flour
10g Psyllium husk
2g Salt

2g Sodium Bicarbonate & Potassium Bicarbonate – Kansui (or just Baking Soda but heated first on the oven at 300F for 10 minutes)
50g Warm Water
(Net Carb : 3,4g / Protein : 26g / Fat : 0,4g)
*Net Carb per serving size = 1,7g
Direction
Follow the instruction as The Keto-Pasta procedures, but use the Pasta Machine setting up to stage 3 for Hokkien Noodles and stage 5 for Mee Goreng.
Use the spaghetti setting on the Pasta Machine to shred the rolled dough
Cook the noodles with the same method as Keto-Pasta, then use it right away for making the Hokkien Mee or Mee Goreng recipes.
3) Keto-Pho Noodles / Kwetiauw
For 2 serving size
Ingredients
80g Inulin Powder
20g Casein Protein Powder
2g Salt
120g Water
(Net Carb : 2,3g / Protein : 17,2g / Fat : 0,3g)
* Net Carb per serving size = 1,2g
Direction
Combine the dry ingredients with a whisk on a big bowl. Add the water all at once and mix well
Microwave the dough at 500W for 30 seconds, and then mix well with a spatula. Microwave for another 30 seconds. When the dough comes together, take it out of the bowl by scooping it out from the bottom with spatula. Microwave in additional 30 second increments if needed
The dough will be very hot, so press and roll it out with spatula, being careful not to burn yourself. When it cools down enough, knead the dough with your hands.
Use a rolling pin and roll the dough out. It's pretty hard to roll out, but give it your best shot
It's hard to roll this dough out very thin, so slice it about 1 to 2 mm thick (I use a transparent Tupperware lid as my cutting guide)
Loosen the noodles and they are done. Bring a generous amount of water to boil with 1 teaspoon of salt, and boil the noodles for 30 seconds to 1 minutes. When they float to the surface, drain with a spider strainer and rinse in plenty of cold running water to stop the cooking process.
Give some coconut oil to keep the noodles separated and use it right away for making the Keto-Pho Noodles or Kwetiau recipes

KETO IRON CHEF - KETO-CRACKERS (FISH / PRAWN CRACKERS)

An Asian cuisine
It's a Keto-Crackers, that can be made with many protein source options like fish, prawns, crabs, chickens etc
This crackers is so much better and tasty than an ordinary Keto-Tortilla chips which only use seasoning for it taste. And also this crackers will give more nutrients profile than any crackers recipes for its versatility in protein source addition
I don't think I can make it to write down the recipes for Keto-Cronut & Keto-Eclairs that I've promised to some member of the keto-group, since monday is almost over in US.
Well the recipes had just to wait for the next Monday then, I hope not to disappoint anyone that have request them
This one for you @Kay Wong
Keto-Crackers (Fish / Prawn Crackers) Servings=1 Time=30mins
Nutrition Fact (without counting the absorbed fat from deep frying with the coconut oil)
* 1 serving 126g (3,3g Net Carb : 22,6g Protein : 12,4g Fat)

Ingredients
Dry Ingredients
35g Inulin Fiber (Chicory Root) – LC Foods
10g Micellar Casein
5g Dried Egg Whites
1,5g Psyllium Husk
1g Xanthan Gum
1g Baking Soda
1,5g Baking Powder
2g Salt
2g Garlic Powder
1g Pepper
2g Beef Broth Powder
Wet Ingredients
50g Mackerel Fish
5g Virgin Coconut Oil
10ml Warm Water (only to adjust the hydration to get the pasta dough consistency)
Other
Coconut oil for deep frying
Direction
Sift all dry ingredients together until well combines on a mixer bowl
Using food processor or a blender, turn the mackerel into a smooth batter consistency, using some water to help the process
Combine the mackerel into the mixer bowl and mix a pasta dough consistency is reached, by adjusting with warm water to get the hydration right (I use only 10ml of water to adjust, since the mackerel have already hydrated on the blender)

Knead the crackers dough with hand for several minutes then proceed with roller pin to shape the dough into thin rectangles (1/2 inch thick)

Proceed the dough to be rolled on the pasta machine until the thinnest setting you can reach without torning the dough sheet. (I made it into stage 7 from the 9 stage available on the pasta machine)
Slice the rolled dough into squares (5 x 5 inch) and followed by deep frying them until golden brown

Serve with curry dishes or with Keto-Fried Rice from the previous post
Keep the left over in a sealed jar to keep them crisp

* Note : be creative with the crackers combination by using chickens, meats or prawns

Make a seam on the outer circle of the dough by folding from one edge to another edge in dumpling folding pattern (see pictures)
Steam the dumplings for 30 minutes on low heat or deep fry them until golden brown for crisper textures
Serve with chilli sauce, peanut butter chilli sauce or coconut aminos as the soy sauce substitute

* Note : be creative with the filling by using chickens, meats or white fish

KETO IRON CHEF'S KETO-BAGUETTE

Keto-Baguette
(4 serving size)
Sponge & Dough Method
Keto-Baguette Servings=4 Time=60mins
Ingredients
Dry Ingredients
20g Micellar Casein
20g Isopure Whey Protein Isolate, Unflavored
10gDried Egg Whites
10gEgg Yolk Powder
40g Inulin Fiber (Chicory Root) – LC Foods
5gPsyllium Husk
2g Xanthan Gum
2g Salt
1g Garlic Powder
1g Ginger Powder
1g Nut Meg Powder
3g Instant Dry Yeast

* Note : The first 7 ingredients above are the Keto-Flour formula for this recipe
For fluffier bread, the Keto-Flour can be changed into this formula : 30g Wheat Protein Isolate 8000, 20g Casein Protein Isolate, 10g Whey Protein Isolate, 10g Egg White Powder, 10g Egg Yolk Powder, 20g Inulin Powder
Wet Ingredients
80g Water
5g Virgin Coconut Oil
Direction
Whisk all the dry ingredients together except for the instant dry yeast, on a medium bowl
Divide and sclae the whisked dry ingredients into different bowl, which are 40g for the sponge and 60g for the dough
* For the Sponge
Add 1g of instant dry yeast into the bowl and whisk to combine. Then add 40g of water gradually while keep folding using spatula until the mixture become elastic but still quite tacky

Rest the sponge for 20 minutes until it double in size

* For the Dough
Combine the fermented sponge with the rest of the dry ingredients and instant dry yeast. Then add 40g of water gradually while keep folding using spatula until the mixture combines and become elastic

Switch using hands to knead the dough until the dough become very elastic. Then add the coconut oil by also keep kneading until the dough is smooth (use egg yolk powder as the bench flour to get the dough surface smooth faster)

Shape the dough into a log, then rest the dough for 20 minutes until almost double in size, on a greased baking pan

Preheat the oven into 300F
Score an arrow marks over the risen dough, then bake for 25 – 30 minutes until the crust is brown

Serve with cream cheese sauce or it can be use to make Keto-Bruschetta with butter and sprinkles of Italian seasoning

KETO IRON CHEF'S KETO-FRIED MOLLEN

Keto-Fried Mollen Servings=1 Time=50mins
Ingredients
* For Mollen Dough
Dry Ingredients
15g Micellar Casein
10g Isopure Whey Protein Isolate, Unflavored
5g Dried Egg Whites
5g Egg Yolk Powder
15g Inulin Fiber (Chicory Root) – LC Foods
2g Psyllium Husk
1g Xanthan Gum
1g Salt
0,5g Vanilla Extract
3g Sucralose
* Note : The first 7 ingredients above are the Keto-Flour formula for this recipe
For crisper crust the Keto-Flour can be changed into this formula : 15g Wheat Protein Isolate 8000, 10g Casein Protein Isolate, 5g Whey Protein Isolate, 5g Egg White Powder, 5g Egg Yolk Powder, 10g Inulin Powder

Wet Ingredients
25g Water
10g Butter
* For Cheese Filling
25g Cheddar Cheese (grated)
15g Egg Yolk Powder
3g Sucralose
15g Butter
3g Lemon Juice
* For Chocolate Filling
25g 100% Cocoa Powder (or 30g 90% Dark Chocolate + 20g 100% Cocoa Powder)
5g Egg Yolk Powder
5g Sucralose
25g Butter
* Other
1 Egg White for brushing the dough (as a glue)
* The original recipe is using banana as the fried mollen filling
Direction
* For Mollen Dough
Whisk all the dry ingredients together on a mixer bowl
Then using low speed, add water gradually while scraping the side of the bowl with a spatula to combines. When a rough dough has formed, switch using your hand to knead until almost elastic then add the softened butter to make the dough smoother. Rest the dough for 10 minutes

Submerged the dough in coconut oil using a small bowl for at least 1 hour, so the dough will be very elastic to be rolled into a very thin round shape
* For Cheese Filling
Mix all the cheese filling ingredients until completely incorporated
* For Chocolate Filling
Mix all the chocolate filling ingredients until completely incorporated
* Assemble
Drain the dough on a spider strainer, then divide and shape the dough into 2 equal balls. Roll each dough into a very thin round shape with a roller pin

Spread the cheese and chocolate filling evenly over the rolled mollen dough, leaving 1/2 inch space from the edge.
Brush the edge thinly with an egg white, then fold each dough into a log shape and seam each end of with your finger

Deep fry each dough with a very low heat on griddle or frying pan for 2 minutes, until the skin are golden
Serve while they're still warm

KETO IRON CHEF - KETO-PANETTONE

Keto-Panettone Servings=4 Time=30mins
Water Roux + Sponge & Dough Method
Ingredients
Dry Ingredients
20g Micellar Casein
20g Isopure Whey Protein Isolate, Unflavored
10g Dried Egg Whites
10g Egg Yolk Powder

40g Inulin Fiber (Chicory Root) – LC Foods
5g Psyllium Husk
2g Xanthan Gum
2g Salt
2g Vanilla Extract
5g Sucralose
3g Instant Dry Yeast
* Note : The first 7 ingredients above are the Keto-Flour formula for this recipe
For fluffier bread, the Keto-Flour can be changed into this formula : 30g Wheat Protein Isolate 8000, 20g Casein Protein Isolate, 10g Whey Protein Isolate, 10g Egg White Powder, 10g Egg Yolk Powder, 20g Inulin Powder
Wet Ingredients
25g Eggs
15g Egg Yolk
20g Coconut Milk
30g Water
20g Butter
Filling
30g Roasted Almond (diced)
Egg Wash
1 Egg Yolk
1 tsp Coconut Milk
Topping
20g Cheddar Cheese (grated)
Direction
Whisk all the dry ingredients together except for the instant dry yeast, on a medium bowl
Scale 10g of the whisked dry ingredients, then mix with 30g of water on a sauce pan and stir to combine until there are no lumps

Heat the mixture using a low to medium heat, while keep stirring the mixture until it just begin to thicken.
Cooled the mixture for 10 minutes, then add 1g of instant dry yeast and stir to combine. Fold the tacky batter using spatula until it's becoming elastic but still quite tacky.
Rest the batter for 15 minutes until the surface are full of holes

Combine the fermented batter with the rest of the dry ingredients and instant dry yeast on a large bowl
Add egg, egg yolk and coconut milk to the bowl and combine using spatula until it become a runny dough
Switch using hands to knead the dough until it become elastic but still quite tacky. Then add the softened butter by also keep kneading until the dough become smooth and elastic
Flatten the dough into rectangle shape on a silicone pad, then sprinkle the diced almond evenly. Fold the dough to combine the diced almond until there are no almond left over

Divide the dough into 4 balls and fit each into the greased cylinder mould (I'm using cup cakes mould, since I don't have the panettone cylinder mould)

Let the dough rest for another 20 minutes until double in size, then score an "X" mark using knife on each dough surface
Preheat the oven to 300F
Give an egg wash over each dough and sprinkle some grated cheddar cheese evenly
Bake for 20 minutes, until golden brown
Serve with butter while the Keto-Panettone still warm

KETO IRON CHEF - KETO-COTTON PANCAKE

Keto-Cotton Pancake Servings=4 Time=30mins
Ingredients
Dry Ingredients
40g Inulin Fiber (Chicory Root) – LC Foods
20g Micellar Casein
20g Isopure Whey Protein Isolate, Unflavored
10g Dried Egg Whites
10g Egg Yolk Powder
2g Xanthan Gum
2g Salt
5g Sucralose
2g Vanilla Extract
3g Baking Powder
Wet Ingredients
15g Egg Yolk
45g Egg White (Whipped into Soft Peak)
50g Cream Cheese
100g Coconut Milk
10g Cider Vinegar
30g Butter
* For Pancake Cheese Sauce
60g Coconut Milk
40g Cream Cheese
10g Sucralose
10g Inulin Fiber (Chicory Root) – LC Foods
2g Vanilla Extract
10g Butter
Direction
* For Fluffy Pancake
Whisk all the dry ingredients together on a medium bowl, set aside
Mix coconut milk and cider vinegar, set aside and let it stay for at least 10 minutes

On a standing mixer, beat butter until white with mixer speed set at stage 1
Raise the speed into stage 2, then add egg yolk and cream cheese until creamy and light
Pour the coconut milk mixture and raise the speed into stage 3 until combines then lower the speed back into stage 1 and pour the dry ingredients until the batter become thick
Turn off the mixer, then add the soft peak meringues onto the batter and fold with a spatula until completely combines

On a griddle or frying pan with a very low heat, pour 1/4 cup of the batter over a pancake ring until half the height of the ring (I'm using 4 inch square cookies cutter as a pancake ring)
Wait until the batter bubbles then flip into the other side. Cook each side until golden brown.

* For Pancake Cheese Sauce
On a sauce pan with a low to medium heat, melt butter and add coconut milk by continuously stirring with a spatula until the mixtures bubbles
Add cream cheese and stir until combines
Turn off the heat, then add inulin powder and sucralose until the sauce thicken

Serve the pancake with butter and cheese sauce

Made in the USA
San Bernardino, CA
05 December 2016